THE SUM OF
THE PEOPLE

THE SUM OF THE PEOPLE

HOW THE CENSUS HAS SHAPED NATIONS, FROM THE ANCIENT WORLD TO THE MODERN AGE

ANDREW WHITBY

BASIC BOOKS

New York

Basic Books
Hachette Book Group
1290 Avenue of the Americas, New York, NY 10104
www.basicbooks.com

Printed in the United States of America

First Edition: March 2020

Published by Basic Books, an imprint of Perseus Books, LLC, a subsidiary of Hachette Book Group, Inc. The Basic Books name and logo is a trademark of the Hachette Book Group.

The Hachette Speakers Bureau provides a wide range of authors for speaking events. To find out more, go to www.hachettespeakersbureau.com or call (866) 376-6591.

The publisher is not responsible for websites (or their content) that are not owned by the publisher.

Library of Congress Control Number: 2019956629

ISBNs: 978-1-5416-1934-0 (hardcover), 978-1-5416-1933-3 (ebook)

LSC-C

10 9 8 7 6 5 4 3 2 1

To Anna—
Some things are beyond quantification.

And Moses and Eleazar the priest spake with them in the plains of Moab by Jordan near Jericho, saying, Take the sum of the people, from twenty years old and upward; as the Lord commanded Moses and the children of Israel, which went forth out of the land of Egypt.

—Numbers 26:3–4, King James Version

CONTENTS

WHERE COUNTING REALLY COUNTS

IN THE FAR NORTH of the West Bank, just outside the village of Faqqu'a, Mohammed Atari stands in the generous shade of an olive grove. These trees, he tells me, are Roman—an extraordinary claim, but one corroborated by their gnarled trunks, two or three arm-spans in circumference. Mohammed is dressed in a black shirt, zip-off trousers, a wide-brimmed cloth hat, and a black-and-brown keffiyeh. He watches the trailing members of our group descend the hill toward us, counting them wordlessly as they approach. He does this with his right hand, middle and index fingers extended, marking out each pair as they settle amid the trees. In total we are eighteen: fourteen Swiss tourists and their Swiss guide; me, the Australian interloper; Mohammed, Palestinian; and his colleague, Ahmed, also Palestinian, who leads a donkey named Casimiro.

One day's walking ahead of us is another, larger party, of thirty Norwegians. Their guide, Nedal, does not count them directly. Instead, he has divided them into six groups of five; when they stop, each group quickly enumerates itself to check that nobody is missing. This efficient procedure is necessary because unlike us they stop often, to sing a hymn or read from the Bible. The Norwegians are pilgrims, whereas the Swiss, for the most part, are just regular tourists—albeit intrepid ones—here to enjoy the landscape, the culture and the history, as well as the physicality of traveling by foot.

Both Mohammed and Nedal watch carefully, each in his own way, over their respective flocks. We're all following the Nativity Trail, a long-distance walking route from Nazareth in Israel to Bethlehem in the West Bank, and our guides don't want us wandering off. This ancient landscape is shot through with modern lines, not all of them visible: the unhealed wounds of an unsolved conflict.

But today, under the olive trees, all is peaceful. The sun is shining, the path is relatively smooth, and the walking is easy. Mohammed's group is happy and relaxed. This is what they came for. My interest in this place is different. Though these adventurous Swiss retirees have kindly adopted me, I relate more strongly to the pious Norwegian group. Though religion is not my motivation, I too am embarking on a pilgrimage.

• • •

In fifth grade—1991—my parents transferred me to a well-regarded Anglican school. We weren't particularly religious, but it was a good school, and I soon got used to the weekly rhythm of chapel services. One day, in the final school week of that first year, I sat on a wooden pew, stewing in the heavy, listless air of a Brisbane summer. A boy stood and took his place at the eagle-winged lectern. "A reading from the book of Luke," he began, "chapter two, verses one to seven" (New International Version).

> In those days Caesar Augustus issued a decree that a census should be taken of the entire Roman world. (This was the first census that took place while Quirinius was governor of Syria.) And everyone went to their own town to register. So Joseph also went up from the town of Nazareth in Galilee to Judea, to Bethlehem the town of David, because he belonged to the house and line of David. He went there to register with Mary, who was pledged to be married to him and was expecting a child. While they were there, the time came for the baby

to be born, and she gave birth to her firstborn, a son. She wrapped him in cloths and placed him in a manger, because there was no guest room available for them.

He stumbled over *Quirinius*. I marveled at the exotic sound of *Galilee* and *Judea*. And of *census*, a word new to me.

Had I been a more attentive child, it wouldn't have been, for Australia had conducted its own census just a few months earlier, on August 6, 1991. Though I evidently took no note of it, it duly noted me among nearly seventeen million others. I imagine that my mother filled out the orange-tinted form on our kitchen bench, amid the usual pile of half-opened mail. (I was probably watching television in another room.)

Years later, now living in the United States, I found an archived blank of the 1991 Australian census form online. "The Census is like a stocktake of our nation," it begins. That's a favorite description of census takers, one that goes back more than century. I think I understand why they keep using it: whereas the suspiciously sibilant *census* comes from Latin, *stocktaking* is reassuringly Anglo-Saxon. Stocktaking suggests counting boxes on the shelves of a warehouse: this many of product A, that many of product B. A stocktaking is routine: nothing to worry, or even think particularly hard, about.[1]

But counting people is quite different from counting boxes. People do not sit still, waiting inertly to be tallied, as boxes do. People do not come in simple varieties—"zero percent fat" and "low carb"—although statisticians sometimes like to pretend they do. There is a method to counting people, a science even, but it's not accounting. Boxes are unaffected by being counted, whereas the act of counting people can oppress or empower them, or even change their self-identities. People may embrace, or resist, being counted.

Today, the vast majority of the world's nations conduct a count of their populations at least once every decade: a *decennial* census, the adjective another Latin import. Between the words we use to describe it and Luke's account of the nativity, quoted above, you could be forgiven for supposing the Romans started all this, but they did not. As with laws, taxes, and religion, counting people is an institution of community that goes back as far as community itself, in ancient China, the Fertile Crescent, and probably everywhere else that people began to live together in large numbers.

Nor does the modern census look much like the Roman one. Like any long-lived institution, the census has had many different, conflicting functions over its history. It arose to satisfy the administrative needs of despots yet eventually developed a crucial role in supporting democracy. It drew the attention of statisticians before they called themselves that, and then flourished, as an instrument of scientific inquiry, once they did. As nations and empires coalesced, it served to define and support them. More than once, it was coopted for protest and dissent against those empires.

The idea of a census is not limited to nations and empires: smaller communities, cities, and provinces, hold them too. Even Black Rock City, a temporary town in the Nevada desert, rebuilt from scratch every year for the anarchist-inspired Burning Man festival, has a census (2018 population: around seventy thousand). But the census of nations is the focus of this book. That procedure is heavy with symbolism. It delineates boundaries no less than a map or border wall does. It is a moment of communal self-reflection: a stocktaking only if you imagine that cans of beans could decide to count themselves.[2]

· · ·

I've come to the Holy Land, and specifically to the West Bank, to try to understand this ancient institution more deeply. I want to retrace the steps of that famous biblical account of the institution's Roman ancestor; that is my pilgrimage. But this is also a revealing part of the world in which to examine the modern census. Palestine is an unfinished state. Like the jumble of pipes, wires, and elevator shafts visible in a building under construction, the infrastructure of a modern state—which includes the census—lies exposed in Palestine.

There's a further reason I've come here in particular: in the narrow strip of land between the Mediterranean Sea and the Jordan River,

PROLOGUE

demography is a battlefield. According to its latest count, Israel has around nine million inhabitants, of whom seven million are Jewish and the remainder mostly Arab Israeli or—equivalently but not identically, in a region where terms are never neutral—Palestinian Israeli. Adjacent to Israel lie the Palestinian territories: the West Bank, sandwiched between coastal Israel and Jordan, and Gaza, a tiny sliver of land adjacent to Egypt, in-cut to Israel's coast. They are home to around five million people, who by ethnicity if not citizenship are the siblings of those two million Arab Israelis. Here, seven million Jews and seven million Arabs lie on either side of an arithmetic knife-edge.

The land comprising Israel and Palestine, around the size of Belgium, is the subject of two incompatible claims to sovereignty. That conflict has simmered for decades, exploding into violence with deadly regularity. It looms disproportionately large on the global stage, a byword for complex, intractable problems. The history of the region is vigorously contested. Even present facts rarely escape dispute—including the populations I quoted above. There is, however, one thing that people generally agree upon. The conflict, if it is resolved, will be resolved in one of two ways: a "two-state solution" or a "one-state solution."

The two-state solution was formalized in the 1947 United Nations partition plan for what was then the British Mandate of Palestine. This proposal, a state of Israel alongside a fully realized state of Palestine, has long been favored by the international community. It has been consistently popular among ordinary Israelis and Palestinians. Its high-water mark came with the mid-1990s Oslo accords, a series of agreements that established a working relationship between Israel and the Palestinians and gave form to Palestine's embryonic government. Not long afterward, the Israeli prime minister, Yitzhak Rabin, was assassinated at a peace rally by one of his own citizens. Prospects for a two-state solution have been receding ever since.

The alternative one-state solution imagines the two groups, Jewish and Palestinian, living harmoniously within a single set of borders, sharing sovereignty and power in government. Israel today is already de facto a binational state by virtue of its substantial Arabic-speaking non-Jewish

5

minority. But if the West Bank and Gaza were formally incorporated, this minority would be much larger, a numerically coequal nation within the shared state. This makes the one-state solution unimaginable to many Jewish Israelis, who hold foundational the principle that Israel should be a refuge for the Jews.

• • •

Challenging demography is nothing new to Israel. The 1947 UN partition plan was based on population data drawn from the British censuses of 1922 and 1931. Muslims, Jews, Christians, and others were cleanly separated in the columns of the census report, but on the ground they were mixed. Under the UN plan—under any possible plan—a substantial minority of Arabs would be included in the proposed Jewish state. "That is the demerit of the scheme," the official report noted drily. The Jewish majority, in fact, would be barely 50 percent: hardly a comfortable margin to maintain a purportedly Jewish state. For Israel's founders, this was not merely a demerit but an existential threat.[3]

Conflict broke out sporadically starting in late 1947 and in earnest after Israel's declaration of independence in 1948. The demographic situation changed rapidly. As many as three-quarters of a million Arabs fled their homes in the territory designated for the Jewish state (the figures, again, are contested). It was, at least in part, an intentional campaign of expulsion. Palestinians call it the *Nakba,* the catastrophe. Today it is the defining event in their national story, their own Exodus.

On the demographic battlefield, the census was quickly weaponized. The first enumeration of the state of Israel occurred quickly, on November 8, 1948, at the height of the war. From a statistical perspective, this was absurd: for accuracy, censuses should be timed with periods of stability. Current international recommendations state that "a time should be chosen when most people are staying at their place of usual residence.... Traditional festivals, pilgrimages and fasting periods are...unsuitable times for census work." The midst of war is so obviously unsuitable that it doesn't even make the list. Nevertheless, a seven-hour curfew was imposed to ensure residents remained at home, enumerators were given military escorts, and it was done.[4]

At the time, the *Palestine Post* opined disapprovingly that the government was exploiting "a time of emergency to saddle on the people a permanent system of surveillance." The *Post* was half right. Though Israel's government was exploiting a time of emergency, it was not building a system of surveillance but defining something far more foundational: the citizenry of the new state. Each resident of a household was issued a registration number as they were enumerated, and this became his or her record of citizenship. People absent from their homes—not least, several hundred thousand displaced Arabs—were not counted, did not receive a registration number, and did not become Israeli. Literally overnight they lost the chance to become citizens in the state that now claimed their homes. This was no stocktaking. The first Israeli census did not so much count a population as create one, making permanent a favorable demographic balance.[5]

It worked. By the time 1948 was over, the Jewish population of Israel exceeded 80 percent, a far more convincing guarantee of the Jewishness of the state. For hundreds of thousands of Palestinian refugees, the census turned short-term displacement into long-term exclusion, creating a humanitarian calamity, a permanent refugee problem, and a major obstacle to peace.[6]

• • •

International recommendations for census taking specify far more than just timing. The UN Statistics Division, custodian of such things, defines a population census as:

> the total process of planning, collecting, compiling, evaluating, disseminating and analysing demographic, economic and social data at the smallest geographic level pertaining, at a specified time, to all persons in a country or in a well-delimited part of a country.[7]

These words come from the bible of enumeration, *Principles and Recommendations for Population and Housing Censuses.* For a long, technical document written by committee, *Principles and Recommendations* is a model of clarity. At least I thought so, when I first paged through it near the UN's headquarters in midtown Manhattan. Now, in the West Bank, it seems riddled with ambiguity, full of terms that are suddenly ill-defined: citizen, resident, territory, legal authority, country.

Palestine in 2019 is not quite a country. In 1988, the Palestinian leader Yasser Arafat declared, from exile, an independent Palestinian state. As I write this, Palestine is recognized as such by 137 out of 193 UN member states. Israel is not among them, but it does recognize and deal with Palestine's government, the Palestinian Authority. Palestine claims all of the West Bank, although in practice the Authority governs only an archipelago of enclaves amid areas controlled by Israel. It also claims the Gaza Strip, although that has been ruled by a competing Palestinian faction, Hamas, since 2007. Palestine claims Jerusalem as its capital, and some of the city's residents as citizens, but the Palestinian Authority is forbidden from operating there.[8]

Within the West Bank, two communities live in superposition. The Palestinian state exists, practically speaking, in regions designated Areas A and B. These are the areas that, when the Oslo accords were being negotiated in the 1990s, had substantial Palestinian populations—people who are now effectively citizens of Palestine. The rest of the West Bank, designated Area C, is under Israeli control, beyond the jurisdiction of the Palestinian Authority. It contains some six hundred thousand Israeli citizens living in more than one hundred settlements, built progressively since Israeli occupation began in 1967. The UN Security Council considers these settlements a violation of international law.[9]

As my Swiss companions and I walk each day, we encounter scattered physical signs of this complex geopolitical landscape. The most prominent is the so-called Separation Barrier, which the government of Israel has built to control movement between its territory and the West Bank. The barrier (at its most imposing, a twenty-six-foot-tall wall) generally follows the 1949 armistice line, but in places it detours deep inside the

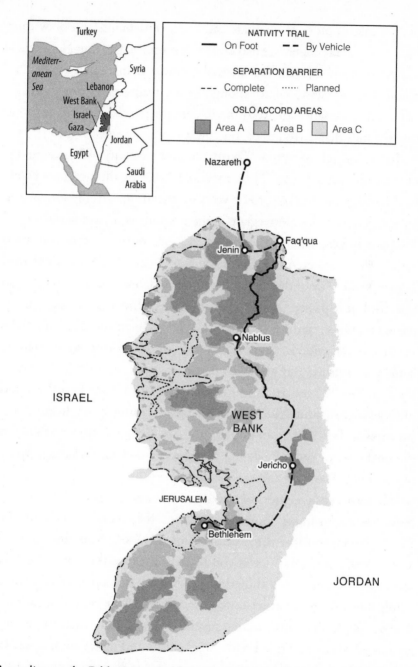

According to the Bible, Mary and Joseph traveled from Nazareth to Bethlehem to register for a Roman census. The Nativity Trail, a modern tourist route, loosely retraces the biblical journey across a complex political landscape. (Map data credit: Natural Earth, UN OCHA oPT, Imbach Reisen.)

West Bank, in order to wrap around larger settlements and draw them back in to Israel proper. We had crossed it soon after leaving Nazareth, at a checkpoint near Jenin. The internal boundaries that separate the Oslo accord areas are less obvious, though I soon realize that's partly because our route is designed to avoid them. Settlements are ever-present, dotting the hills that surround us, but always some distance away.

In the central part of the West Bank, in the vicinity of Jerusalem, the official frontiers are especially convoluted. Walking through here would be difficult, so instead our route veers southeast, toward the Jordan Valley and Jericho. The Norwegians' guide, Nedal, explains that Mary and Joseph may have taken a similarly circuitous route two thousand years ago, as they answered the call of the Roman census. An ancient road known as the Way of the Patriarchs connected Nazareth and Bethlehem directly, but it passed through the territory of the Samaritans, a group related to, but sometimes hostile to, the Jews. There's no clear consensus on this; other evidence suggests that Jewish travel through Samaritan lands was routine. But even this best case meant a journey of around eighty miles. The terrain in this region is beautiful but often stony and unforgiving. At times Ahmed has to cajole Casimiro, the donkey, into continuing. It would be an unpleasant trip, I imagine, for somebody in the final days of pregnancy—infuriating, even, given that the purpose of the census was Roman tax collection.[10]

Modern censuses are not used for collecting taxes. Nor do they require such arduous journeys of those they count. Each of the Palestinian Authority's three censuses of the West Bank and Gaza—1997, 2007, and 2017—was conducted in accordance with the UN recommendations. Two thousand years ago, Roman census records would have been recorded onto papyrus scrolls at central locations. Today, Palestinian enumerators travel to the homes of the people they are tasked to count, armed with paper forms and tablet computers. In richer countries, people often enumerate themselves, receiving and returning a census form by mail or completing it online. In a handful of countries, censuses are now virtual, compiled from a register of the entire population that is kept continuously up to date.

Palestine is not there yet. Even in 2017, its tablet-toting census takers followed a fairly traditional process, first mapping out the areas where people were thought to live and then traveling door-to-door, collecting information about each person in every household they encountered. It was the enumerators, and not those being enumerated, who had to contend with the complex topology of the Palestinian proto-state: the manned and unmanned checkpoints, the walls, gates, ditches, and barbed wire. Census taking everywhere involves more logistics than statistics, but in Palestine it involves diplomacy as well.

• • •

I meet the census team from the Palestinian Central Bureau of Statistics (PCBS) at their office in Ramallah, the administrative capital of the Palestinian Authority. Ramallah is located to the north of Jerusalem, just off Highway 60, the modern-day equivalent of the Way of the Patriarchs. Mary and Joseph might have passed here on the way to Bethlehem, which is only sixteen miles further south. Today that distance seems much greater, stretched by the tangled frontiers that surround Jerusalem. Since our nativity route took us west to avoid all that, I have circled back afterward, on my own.

Once I find the right building, I'm joined by four senior officials from the bureau, a man and three women, some of whom have been involved in Palestinian census taking since its modern reintroduction in 1997. Tea is brought, and we start to discuss the complexities of conducting a census in Palestine.[11]

The greatest challenge for each of the three censuses has been East Jerusalem. After the 1948 war the city was split: Israel in the west and Jordan in the east (a UN plan for an international city came to nothing). After Jordan's defeat in the 1967 war, the eastern part came under Israeli control. At that time, a census was taken by Israel, and Palestinians present were given a status of permanent residence in Israel. Today they are issued with Israeli identity cards and can in theory apply for full Israeli citizenship. Most—reportedly 95 percent—have not. Their status remains somewhat precarious.

The Palestinian Authority views East Jerusalem as occupied Palestinian territory, an integral part of the future Palestinian state; the people living there, then, should naturally be included in the census of Palestine. At the first census in 1997, the Authority set out to do exactly that. It was an act of open defiance against Israel, a continuation of Palestinian resistance by statistical means. The then-head of Palestinian statistics called it "a civil intifada," borrowing the word given to the period of unrest that had been brought to an end with the signing of the Oslo accords. Israel argued that the Authority's actions violated the accords, moving to outlaw Palestinian census taking in East Jerusalem. There was at least one arrest, and the census of East Jerusalem was halted.[12]

In 2017, seventeen arrests were reported of people associated with the Fatah Party, which rules the Palestinian Authority. Israeli police accused them of "taking part in activity related to a population census." At the time, the Palestinian Central Bureau of Statistics denied operating in East Jerusalem and claimed the arrests "had nothing to do with the population census." And yet there in the final census report are census counts for East Jerusalem.[13]

I ask the Palestinian statisticians about this. Their response is one of calculated vagueness, echoing the official denials. (I infer that the enumeration was undertaken by Fatah affiliates already living in Jerusalem, rather than employees of PCBS.) While enumerators used electronic tablets for the rest of the West Bank and Gaza, paper forms were used in East Jerusalem. The questionnaire was shorter than elsewhere in Palestine. These strategies seem designed to avoid drawing too much Israeli attention. Needless to say, this is not a situation addressed in the 299 pages of the UN's *Principles and Recommendations*.

Two other major logistical difficulties confronted the 2017 census takers. The first was the Separation Barrier, which did not exist in 1997 and had grown substantially since 2007. Travel to and from some Palestinian communities is restricted to people who are registered as living there, which makes staffing a census harder. "Mostly we recruit people from the same governorate, from the same locality, especially for localities behind the separation wall," they tell me. The electronic tablets allowed data to be transmitted wirelessly to the head office in Ramallah, reducing the amount of paper shuffling required and eliminating the possibility of seizure by Israeli soldiers. A similar situation held with respect to Gaza: travel back and forth was minimized by hiring local staff and using videoconferencing and other technology. Even with such measures, the 2017 census required, they observe, "emergency plans, all the time."

When the interview is finished, I take the number 218 public bus back to Jerusalem. It passes through the famous Qalandiya checkpoint, which divides Jerusalem from the West Bank. While we wait at the checkpoint, I skim through the official Palestinian census report once again. I make note of the population totals: 2.9 million in the West Bank, including 281,163 furtively enumerated in East Jerusalem; 1.9 million in Gaza; 4.8 million altogether. In many respects it is a typically dry, technical document, replete with obligatory discussions of statistical arcana such as nonsampling error, coverage percentages, and Whipple's index.[14]

But politics is never far away. The census is a "pillar of state building" and "a genuine expression of national sovereignty." Enumeration was impeded by "the procedures of the Israeli occupation and obstacles including the Annexation Wall and settlement expansion." That wall, which looms over the bus as we leave the checkpoint and reenter Jerusalem, "suffocates those living behind it." Even the usually soporific methodology section notes "instability resulting from continuing Israeli aggression, confiscation of land and isolation of the population in Palestinian Localities."[15]

While I do not doubt the statistical rigor of the Palestinian census, its parallel geopolitical purpose is unmistakable. Even the now-predictable arrests play into that: there is no imminent prospect that the Palestinian Authority will actually govern East Jerusalem, so—official denials notwithstanding—its purpose in counting people there seems less administrative than symbolic: to publicly assert its territorial claim. As we pull into the bus station near the ancient Damascus Gate of the old city of Jerusalem, I note, before closing the report, one more potent symbol: fieldwork was completed on December 24, 2017—Christmas Eve.[16]

• • •

Census taking makes sense as a tactic of nation building. The conventional definition of a state under international law requires a permanent population, a defined territory, a government, and the capacity to enter into relations with other states. A census is surely the most direct way to demonstrate a permanent population. It's also evidence of a functional government.

In 1993, in a critique of the first Oslo accord, the Palestinian-American scholar Edward Said called for an immediate census: "not just as a bureaucratic exercise but as the enfranchisement of Palestinians wherever they are…an act of historical and political self-realisation outside the limitations imposed by the absence of sovereignty." Said's qualification—or rather lack of qualification—"wherever they are" was significant. Today there are around thirteen million people who might be considered Palestinian, by virtue of having once lived in historical Palestine or being born to parents or having grandparents who had lived there. Around half live in the West Bank, Gaza, and Israel, with the balance spread between Jordan, Lebanon, Syria, and elsewhere. In holding a census, Said argued, they would "come close to constituting a nation rather than a mere collection of people." But the census that followed four years later in 1997 did not count Palestinians wherever they were. Instead it conformed to international norms, counting people only within the defined territory the Palestinians claimed. It reinforced a particular, concrete assertion of statehood, at the expense of Said's vision of national self-realization.[17]

Census takers are constantly grappling with lines of citizenship, nationality, ethnicity, and race. Citizenship is the clearest of these, while the other categories are much fuzzier, grounded in shared history, culture, and ancestry. Israel itself illustrates this complexity. In 2013, a group of activists petitioned Israel's Supreme Court to allow them to record their nationality as "Israeli" in the state population register. The court declined, concluding that the state of Israel contains within it people of Jewish, Arab, and other nationalities, but nobody of Israeli nationality. It allowed that such a nationality may one day come to exist, but upheld the lower court's ruling that "technical-statistical registration" was not a process that could have this effect.[18]

Arguably, the court was wrong as a matter of fact: history abounds with examples where nationality, race, and ethnicity—far from emerging organically—were assigned, or even created, precisely by "technical-statistical registration." Prior to the widespread use of self-enumeration in 1960, an American's race, on the census, was largely determined by the enumerator—who was, in all probability, a white person. That is no longer the case. Censuses in many countries increasingly treat nationality, race, and ethnicity as a matter of self-identification, refusing to arbitrate or second-guess such slippery categories. Of course, that's not quite right either. A person cannot simply arrive in Israel and successfully self-identify as Jewish. These concepts may not be objective, but neither are they completely subjective.

While I was in Israel, a debate erupted following a statement from the prime minister, Benjamin Netanyahu, that "Israel is the nation-state of the Jewish People—and them alone." Netanyahu was on firm legal ground, having passed a law to that effect in 2018. Israel is now a state in which the Jewish nationality is paramount; there is no Israeli nationality because, by law, the Israeli nationality *is* Jewish.[19]

That doesn't leave much room for a viable one-state solution, but as we discussed this over long days of walking, I found my Swiss companions more optimistic. As they reminded me, national identities are not fixed. In a continent that spent much of its history bloodily rearranging its constituent states along ethnic, religious, and linguistic lines, Switzerland stands as an exception, with four official languages. Roberto, a retired English teacher, German-speaking, but with a name that recalls his family's Italian origins, taught me a word the Swiss use to describe themselves. *Willensnation:* a nation brought into being, and held together, by sheer force of will. It's a hopeful story.

• • •

The Church of the Nativity, in Bethlehem, is the endpoint of the Nativity Trail, by tradition the site of the stable where Jesus was born. To my (and nobody else's) disappointment, Luke doesn't elaborate on how or where the Roman census was taken, or whether the family even made it to be registered, given Mary's presumed state of indisposition and the challenge of caring for a newborn baby. So I too ended my pilgrimage here.

It was unlike any place of worship I had ever visited, not so much a church as a set of interconnected churches—Greek Orthodox, Armenian, and Roman Catholic—all sharing one site. This arrangement, known as the Status Quo, dates back to Ottoman times. It is replicated in miniature in the holiest part of the complex, the Grotto, supposedly the exact place where Mary gave birth. This subterranean space is lit by fifteen hanging oil lamps, whose numerical configuration is specified precisely by the Status Quo: six are Greek, five Armenian, and four Roman Catholic. These proportions have no contemporary meaning that I can discover: they were simply frozen in place, in 1852, by a Turkish sultan tired of religious squabbles. As I read these facts, by the lamplight of the Grotto, I was reminded of another status quo, holding tenuously 150 miles to the north.

Lebanon is the prodigal son of global census taking. Its last full count was in 1932, under French rule. When independence came, in 1943, power was divided between various religious sects on the basis of those decade-old statistics. No individual group—Maronite Christian, Sunni, Shia, and on down a list of seventeen officially enumerated—dominated, though Christians overall just outnumbered Muslims. So Lebanon created its own status quo: top government positions were allocated in proportion to the 1932 population, and the parliament and civil service were established with an exact ratio of six Christians for every five Muslims.[20]

Over time, the ratios between these groups in the population began to drift, even as the 6:5 agreement remained fixed. Quantifying the change and revisiting the agreement was considered too destabilizing, so successive governments, from 1943 until 1975, chose instead to ignore it, refusing to count the people of Lebanon. At the conclusion of the civil war that lasted from 1975 to 1990, the ratio was amended to 1:1, Muslim and Christian parity, reflecting the belief—almost certainly correct, but untested by official data—that the Christian proportion had declined.[21]

You could, reasonably, see this new arrangement as a mere political compromise, divorced entirely from demography, just as every American state receives two senators, regardless of population. But that's not how the people of Lebanon see it: they subscribe to the democratic ideal that political power should reflect numbers. Since in practice it cannot—at least not without the risk of violent conflict—a fresh census would be a provocation. An official, complete count of Lebanon's estimated six million people does not seem likely any time soon.

As I exited the Church of the Nativity and stepped, blinking, into Manger Square, I wondered whether the proponents of a one-state solution for Israel and Palestine imagine that it would turn out more like Switzerland or like Lebanon.

• • •

I return from the Holy Land to the United States on April 1, 2019—exactly one year before this country's next census day. In most decades, by this point, the main parameters of the enumeration—and certainly the questions that will be asked—have been decided. Not this time. A debate is raging over a late order from the secretary of commerce to add one more question to the census, against the near-unanimous advice of Census Bureau experts: *Is this person a citizen of the United States?*

As tends to happen in this litigious nation, the debate has become a lawsuit—actually, multiple lawsuits—appealed all the way to the Supreme Court. The plaintiffs argue that this last-minute addition will dissuade noncitizens, especially undocumented people, from participating in the count. Oral arguments in *Dept. of Commerce v. New York* are scheduled for April 23. In an editorial, the *New York Times* bills it the highest-profile case of the court's term. While I've been looking elsewhere for the story of the census, it has found me in my adopted home.[22]

April 23 arrives, and I read the transcript as soon as it is released. In their attempts to interrogate the legitimacy of the proposed question, the justices grapple with historical and international comparisons. In the first minute, the solicitor-general, presenting the case for the Department of Commerce, declares that such a question "has been asked as part of the census in one form or another for nearly 200 years." He is interrupted by Justice Sotomayor, who contends (correctly) that this is an oversimplification. Later, Justice Kavanaugh observes that many other countries ask about the citizenship of respondents and that the UN includes citizenship among its recommended census topics. "The question," he says, is does "international practice, that UN recommendation, that historical practice in the United States, affect how we should look at the inclusion of a citizenship question in this case?"

This book's answer is yes. A historical and international perspective is essential, not just to understand the issues that were at stake in that now-resolved case but to understand the meaning of the modern census more generally. The census did not appear fully formed in some particular time and place but developed in a slow, continuous interplay of ideas from around the world. The belief that vexes Lebanon, that each census should be followed by a redistribution of political power, is an essentially American idea. The notion that people should be enumerated individually, rather than simply as anonymous members of a household, is Scandinavian. The modern method of testing census accuracy was trialed first in India. Intellectually, the census extends beyond borders, across oceans, and back through centuries, even if individual censuses occur in one place, at one time.

In the chapters that follow, I argue that the census is not just a collection of separate national projects but a human project. My aim is to tell this larger story: to show how the institution of counting people has evolved, how it has changed as societies changed, and how it has sometimes changed those societies in turn. In doing so, I draw on a scholarly movement that, since the late twentieth century, has begun to treat the study of statistics as an object of study itself. This has produced some illuminating academic accounts of census taking in particular countries, but none that attempts, as I do here, to sketch the global history for a nonexpert reader.

Scholars have often cast the census as an instrument of power: as a mechanism of "state formation" and control, following the influential French philosopher Michel Foucault; as an attempt to make society "legible," in the terminology of political scientist James Scott; or as a top-down project of nation building by the "classifying mind of the colonial state," as the anthropologist Benedict Anderson put it. There's a great deal of insight in these perspectives: even the simplest, most essential result of a census—the knowledge of a population's size—can have a kind of power, as the Malthusianism of the nineteenth century and its twentieth-century echo illustrate.[23]

But the census can be a tool, too, of the powerless. It has been embraced, appropriated, and even subverted by those being counted. It has served as a medium for individual and minority self-expression. Even under the strictest regimes—Nazi occupation, for example—people have found, in enumeration, a canvas for protest. Granted, a census is never a blank canvas, but more like a paint-by-numbers in which authorities define, by setting the questions and sometimes the possible answers, both the outline and the palette. Still, by answering questions against expectation, by writing—sometimes quite literally—between the lines, or in the last resort, by absenting themselves entirely, otherwise disempowered people have conspired to reject these impositions. All this is possible because the census has a fundamentally democratizing character: it requires mass participation. It is neither wholly of the state nor of the people but exists as a continuous negotiation between them.[24]

Perhaps the most important phase in that negotiation, achieved in the eighteenth and nineteenth centuries, was the separation of the census from the individual obligations of taxation and military service that so often characterized it earlier. This happened at first casually, almost by accident, but eventually evolved into something closer to a promise. For all the tablet computers and wireless transmissions, this is the innovation that most fundamentally divides the Palestinian census of 2017 from the census of Quirinius on the same terrain, two thousand years earlier. Today the census is something unique: a way for the state to see the people, without seeing any individual person.

That may also be the greatest threat to its continuation, for while the traditional census has shed its role in mediating the relationships between individual citizens and their governments, those relationships have only deepened. Over the twentieth century, individual obligations were joined by individual entitlements arising from the centralized welfare state. As a result, the census today competes with many other sources of information: applications, returns, registrations, records and disclosures, each facilitating some direct relationship between the citizen and the state, each a way to render the citizen "known."[25]

For now the population census still sits at the center of that constellation. But this does not guarantee its future. In a world of driver's licenses and passports, tax returns and benefits checks, fingerprints and retina scans, hourly social media status updates and minute-by-minute location tracking, the traditional census seems increasingly anachronistic—as one group of sociologists put it, "an outdated high modernist invention." It is infrequent, expensive, and bound by strict privacy rules.[26]

Some countries have now abandoned the decennial enumeration altogether. Instead, they maintain population registers, databases of their citizens and visitors that are kept continually up-to-date, so accurate and current as to render a special, once-a-decade enumeration superfluous. This started in the Nordic world and is now spreading to other countries in Europe and beyond. It's very likely that population registers represent the next phase in the long history of counting and classifying people.

For now, though, the traditional census still rules, and it is the heart of this book. There is something special about an actual enumeration, with its proverbial army of canvassers. In 1882, Leo Tolstoy enlisted in one such army, going door to door in Moscow's Khamovnitcheskiy quarter to count its residents. He took his job seriously, coming face to face with every type of working-class Muscovite: "master-artisans, bootmakers, brush-makers, cabinet-makers, turners, shoemakers, tailors, blacksmiths...cab-drivers, young women living alone...female pedlers, laundresses, old-clothes dealers, money-lenders, day-laborers, and people without any definite employment." The census, he wrote, "furnishes...a mirror into which, willy nilly, the whole community, and each one of us, gaze."[27]

Far from a dry statistical exercise, the census is ultimately about people; it is a form of quantitative social history. In 1867, then congressman James Garfield noted that

> till recently the historian studied nations in the aggregate, and gave us only the story of princes, dynasties, sieges and battles. Of the people themselves—the great social body with life, growth, sources, elements, and laws of its own—he told us nothing. Now statistical inquiry leads him into the hovels, homes, workshops, mines, fields, prisons, hospitals, and all places where human nature displays its weakness and its strength.[28]

This is the story, too, of people: those who were counted but also and particularly those who did the counting. You probably imagine this latter group to be like Charles Dickens's character Mr. Gradgrind, "a man of facts and calculations" who cared for little else. Popular culture has not, on the whole, embraced the 2009 prediction of Google's chief economist Hal Varian, that statistician would be "the sexy job in the next ten years." If statisticians have failed to dispel their unsexy image, then government statisticians have done even worse in the popular imagining. They are the grayest of the gray-suited bureaucrats, armed with notebooks, punch cards, calculators, or laptops, as the era allowed. (Arguably they should shoulder some of the blame: in a move entirely worthy of Dickens, the US Census Bureau has been located, since 1942, in a suburb outside Washington called Suitland.)[29]

But the census has always been a vast and intrepid undertaking, and so its agents could be found not only besuited in government offices but crossing the North Atlantic, canoeing up uncharted rivers in the wilds of Alaska or driving for days across the Australian outback. As the function of the census has changed, so have the people behind it; it has drawn in soldiers, clergy, civil servants, scientists, international bureaucrats, and sometimes, today—too often, perhaps—lawyers.

That said, there *are* Gradgrinds. The census invites a kind of obsession, a compulsive drive to count everyone. There is a certain kind of person, recurring in this story, who seeks to arrange the world in neat, numbered boxes. I don't want to leave them out because—and here I confess my lack of objectivity—I empathize with such people. I may even be one. As an economist I have long used census data, and while I've never been involved in running a census, I've spent many hours with the people who have. Still, I've tried my best to climb outside my box, not shrinking, for example, from the abuses and crimes that census takers have abetted.

This is only one story of the long history of counting people, out of many that could be told. In attempting to cover such a broad swathe of history and geography, I have had to be selective. Like the census itself, this book is a series of snapshots, highlighting important moments in the evolution of an underappreciated idea, tracing it backward from its present incarnation: an attempt to count everyone, everywhere. I cannot include every evolutionary step, so instead I have chosen a handful of moments, digressing where necessary to examine the people, ideas, and technologies that shaped them, and the effect, in turn, that they had on the people counted.

Ultimately, it is the distilled essence of the census—the simple idea of counting everyone—that most intrigues me. There is something almost romantic about it. To count is to have value, to matter. To be counted is to be included and, perhaps, to be known. Two thousand years ago, the emperor Augustus decreed "that a census should be taken of the entire Roman world." A count of the entire world: by this standard, the story of the census is one of failure, a story as much of those not counted as those counted. And yet we keep trying. As I write this, the peak years of the next census decennium, 2020 and 2021, are approaching. Across more than two hundred countries, we are attempting, once again, to count every one of our kind. That we will fail is a certainty, but in failing, we may come closer than ever before.

This is the story of how we got here—and where we might go next.

CHAPTER 1

THE BOOK OF NUMBERS

IN 2020, the human population will be just shy of 8 billion, a milestone we'll probably reach in 2023. One century earlier, in 1920, we numbered 1.8 billion. In 1820, just over 1 billion—though the further back we go, the less certain we can be. On sheer numbers, *Homo sapiens* is one of the most successful animal species on Earth. Today even Antarctica, the most inhospitable of places, usually has a transient population of over 1,000. Not quite the most inhospitable: as I write this, there are 3 people located to my north-northeast, 51 degrees above the horizon, about 250 miles above the surface of the planet, aboard the International Space Station.

It wasn't always this way. *Homo sapiens* first emerged under the African sky around three hundred thousand years ago. Up until ten thousand years ago, our ancestors probably never numbered more than about ten million, but what they lacked in numbers they made up for in adaptability. From Africa they dispersed into Eurasia, Australasia, and finally the Americas. Of course, not one of those ten million knew anything of this intercontinental flourishing.

In Genesis, God promises to make Isaac's descendants "as numerous as the stars in the sky" (26:4, New International Version), a metaphor that seems straightforward but is actually as puzzling as it is ancient. The number of stars that are visible to the naked eye is surprisingly small: only around nine thousand. A Stone Age astronomer, looking skyward, would have had no way of knowing there were any more. Before the invention of the telescope, the vastness of the stars in the sky was more an impression than a verifiable truth.

Still, the heavens were teeming compared with the Earth. In the prehistoric world, people were rare. Early humans lived as hunter-gatherers in small groups. No person ever encountered more than a few hundred others over a lifetime. The basic social unit, a band, comprised ten to fifty people, related by ties of kinship. Larger communities, in turn, were composed of several bands, who lived closely and cooperated in activities like hunting. The evolutionary psychologist Robin Dunbar famously observed that humans can maintain only around 150 meaningful relationships. This limit, Dunbar argued, is hardwired in the human brain's neocortex. The amount of gray matter we have dictates the capacity of any of us to maintain close relationships. Dunbar's number is a natural, self-regulating population size, the largest that communities of early humans would have grown without more elaborate social structures. In these tight-knit communities, there was no need to formalize membership or to quantify it. Each person knew each other person. Without much conscious effort, they could keep track of the mutual obligations that are an inevitable part of social living: she shared her berries with me; I made him a spearhead.[1]

Indeed, strict quantification was probably impossible. Some of the most ancient languages lack words for numbers, including those still spoken by the Pirahã of the Amazon and the Warlpiri of Australia's Northern Territory. In an interview for the BBC documentary *The Story of 1,* a younger Warlpiri man, Leo Jampijinpa Wayne, questions an older man, Japaljarri.

"How many grandchildren do you have?" he asks, in Warlpiri.

"Many. Bajan, Parun, Jamarai, Jangan," Japaljarri replies, his right forefinger tracing a stroke in the red desert sand for each name. "Many."

For perhaps 290,000 years this is as close to a census as *Homo sapiens* came.[2]

Eventually things began to change. Larger tribes formed: collections of bands sharing culture and language, governed by a social hierarchy. In Mesopotamia, people domesticated crops and learned to farm, exploiting the fertile topsoil that was deposited by annual flooding of the Tigris and Euphrates rivers. Around six thousand years ago, the earliest agrarian civilizations arose, the independent city-states of Sumer. After another thousand years or so, one of these cities had grown to house more than fifty thousand people within its walls. That city, now vanished, was located midway between modern Baghdad and Basra. It was called Uruk and gave us the name Iraq.

Today, a population of fifty thousand is often used as a lower bound for what is considered a city. For humans alive five thousand years ago, it must have been an almost unimaginable number. But many modern cities are far larger. Fifty thousand people can, after all, be contained in just one structure in a modern city: Yankee Stadium, for example.[3]

In the last few decades, cognitive scientists have begun to study "number sense," our ability to judge numerical quantity. We seem to have a range of cognitive mechanisms available to make such judgments: one for very small numbers (three or four), one for medium quantities (up to perhaps one hundred), and one for larger numbers. But these studies typically focus on how we count simple objects or abstract shapes. Because humans evolved as social animals, it's reasonable to suspect our number sense for people is different than for dots on a screen.[4]

In this specialized case, there's not much research, but introspection is illustrative. It's easy to visualize five to ten people: a sports team, say. Twenty-five people fill a classroom: few enough for a quick estimate of numbers, but not to immediately identify who is present and who is absent (there's a reason teachers take attendance each day). A large movie theatre holds a greater number, a hundred to two hundred fifty people—obviously more than a classroom but still in the realm of a reasonable estimate. Many concert halls are at least ten times larger than that. From the stage, you could probably distinguish the two thousand people in Milan's La Scala opera house from the five thousand filling London's Royal Albert Hall, but any innate sense of quantity you have is now being stretched to its limits.

At the next order of magnitude, the size of Uruk, the scale of stadium crowds and beyond, even our roughest number sense seems to break down. Attendance estimates for Donald Trump's 2016 inauguration ranged from two hundred thousand to nine hundred thousand (setting aside his own inflated claim of over one million). At the battle of Thermopylae, in 480 BCE, it was said one million men marched in the Persian army, although modern scholars believe it was closer to a hundred thousand. Eyewitness accounts of such crowds aren't that useful, because as an observer, you can't directly experience a hundred thousand people. It's a struggle even to fit that many people in your visual field. Whether from the bird's-eye view of the observation deck of the Washington Monument or a mountain overlooking an ancient battlefield, the more distant figures would blur into one uncountable mass. Our hunter-gatherer ancestors simply never needed, so never evolved, the sensory or cognitive capacity to directly grasp such large numbers. We can only do it by shifting from sensing to reasoning: intentional, abstract, methodical counting.

Groups of people at the city scale pose problems not just of comprehension but of coordination. Every society is built on a web of mutual obligations. Among hunter-gatherers, these obligations may be maintained directly, person-to-person. Everyone knows everyone else's business. Debts are self-enforcing. This system of mental bookkeeping can be extended for a while through social substructures—families within a tribe, tribes within a kingdom. But beyond a certain point, more elaborate, abstract, and formal social conventions and institutions are required.

The Sumerian city-states grew prosperous because they enabled specialization and trade: a potter could barter an earthenware dish for grain from a farmer. But certain necessities fall outside this barter structure: things we can't purchase individually but must agree on jointly, like a system of justice, collective self-defense, or the construction of a temple to appease a vengeful diluvial deity.

Everybody in a community benefits from such things, which economists call public goods, whether they contribute or not. But if nobody contributes, they won't be produced. In a village, peer pressure might work to enforce voluntary contributions, but with the city comes the possibility of privacy. In cities, one can hide among the crowd, avoiding purely voluntary civic obligations without fear of rebuke. Instead, governments throughout history have levied compulsory taxes, demanding by threat of force some part of each citizen's product. Taxes might take the form of money or grain or—understood more broadly—the citizen's own labor, as, for example, in the case of military conscription or corveé labor, a kind of civilian conscription for the building of roads, canals, and pyramids. To enforce these formal civic duties at scale, people had to be enumerated, their obligations assessed, and the discharge of these obligations recorded and audited. Effective administration required that the ruler know the ruled, the subjects of the realm. And so the census was born.

· · ·

Were there censuses at the dawn of civilization, in the earliest days of Sumer, at the start of the fourth millennium BCE? Sumerian society enjoyed public goods, including levees and canals for irrigation, so clearly large labor forces were assembled and coordinated. An accurate headcount of residents would have helped with this task. But any such census would have been literally prehistoric, since writing itself was not developed until perhaps 3200 BCE.

Like almost everything in modern society, the census today depends on writing. But a simple kind of headcount is entirely possible without writing. Herodotus, the Greek "father of history," relates a story of the Scythians, nomadic warriors who lived in Central Asia in the first millennium BCE. "Because their king, who went by the name of Ariantas, wished to know how many Scythians there were, he gave orders that each one of them was to bring an arrowhead; and that should anyone fail to do so, then the penalty would be death. A huge number of arrowheads were duly brought, and the king"—presumably having first counted them—"decided to fashion a monument out of them that he could bequeath to posterity." Similar methods were known in precolonial Africa—for example, the use of cowrie shells in the Kingdom of Dahomey (present day Benin) or yams among the Igbo people (of today's Nigeria)—where this object-counting approach also served to avoid a taboo on counting people directly. Such methods of enumeration require no writing.[5]

In fact, proto-literate societies could conduct censuses of great complexity. The Inka, who dominated Andean America at the time of the Spanish conquest in the fifteenth century CE, recorded elaborate census statistics in connection with taxation, despite lacking what we would recognize as writing. Instead they used knots tied in complex bundles of colored strings called *khipu* to encode information. Of the thousand

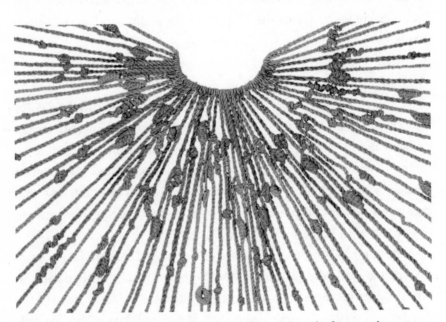

The Inka empire used khipu, arrangements of knotted cords, for recording census results. Although hundreds of khipu survive, most have not been decoded, including this one, which dates from between 1430 and 1530 CE. (British Museum Am1907,0319.286)

khipu that exist in museums today, two-thirds contain numerical data, and at least fifty are thought to pertain to censuses. Unfortunately, our understanding of them is fragmentary. We know how numbers were represented: a decimal system in which a knot with three turns, for example, represents a three (or a thirty or three hundred, depending on position). But we have no understanding of how nonnumerical attributes—for example thread material, spinning technique, color, and left- or right-handedness of knots—should be interpreted. So confirming that any individual khipu contains census data is generally impossible.[6]

Much of what we know of Inka census-taking procedure comes from later colonial accounts. Martín de Murúa, a seventeenth-century chronicler of Peru, wrote:

> They sent every five years *quipucamayos* [khipu-keepers], who are ac-
> countants and overseers, whom they call *tucuyricuc*. These came to the
> provinces as governors and visitors, each one to the province for which
> he was responsible and, upon arriving at the town he had all the people
> brought together, from the decrepit old people to the newborn nursing
> babies, in a field outside town, or within the town, if there was a plaza
> large enough to accommodate all of them; the *tucuyricuc* organized
> them into ten rows ["streets"] for the men and another ten for the
> women. They were seated by ages, and in this way they proceeded....[7]

If the Inka did not require writing to enumerate their population, believed to be ten million when the Spanish arrived, why should the Sumerians? Indeed, many of the earliest preserved examples of Sumerian record keeping relate to accounting. Even before 4000 BCE, clay tokens were used to count, record, and communicate quantities of goods. It doesn't seem such a leap to apply methods of accounting to people.

Yet without written evidence, such early censuses remain highly specu-
lative. (In particular, one oft-repeated claim, dating the "first census" to 3800 BCE in Babylon, seems to have resulted from a misinterpretation by an overzealous early twentieth-century statistician.[8]) Censuses are inher-
ently abstract and—the Inkan quipu notwithstanding—needn't leave

much in the way of physical artifacts, so archaeology can only take us so far. To confirm the invention of the census, we have to await the development of writing—of history itself. Even then, the earliest reports of censuses come not in contemporary accounts but in later (though still ancient) histories, written centuries after the events they narrate.

· · ·

The earliest censuses suggested in writing come not from Mesopotamia but from another wellspring of civilization, China's Yellow River valley. Like Mesopotamia, it provided ideal conditions for settled agriculture, with similar rich alluvial soil. But the floods that gave life could just as easily take it. In Chinese legend, the defining battles of the nation's first dynasty were against nature itself: the mighty Yellow River. The war was finally won around 2100 BCE, under the emperor Yu, a mythological figure awarded the epithet "the Great" for his efforts. Whereas his predecessors had tried and failed to dam the river, Yu succeeded by diverting its waters into irrigation channels. Yu is also credited, in Han era (206 BCE–220 CE) histories, with the first census of the Chinese people. It's quite plausible that the massive earthworks required for early Chinese flood control did demand some sort of headcount, but Yu's census, and its traditional total of 13,553,923 people, is almost certainly a later embellishment. Modern estimates put China's population in that era at no more than 4–5 million.[9]

By the time of the Zhou dynasty in the first millennium BCE—moving from the period of myth to verifiable history—we find the census an established institution of Chinese government. It was a vital part of the machinery of a state that, influenced by Confucianism, emphasized good government, peace, prosperity, virtue, and justice, principles that were given force by a hierarchical bureaucracy and elaborate record keeping.[10]

Confucius himself was said to deeply respect the census. The *Analects* record that, when passing "one bearing the tables of population" upon the road, he would bow forward, in veneration, "to the crossbar of his carriage." Similarly, the emperor himself was said to receive the tables kneeling. Confucian philosophy held that good government would attract citizens through migration, and so the census count was a judgment on not only the prosperity of the state but also the quality of the administration.[11]

While premodern censuses are sometimes dismissed as simple exercises, focused solely on enforcing obligations of taxation and conscription, the Chinese counts were used for more than this. Xu Gan, a philosopher in the Confucian school, wrote an essay on population around 200 CE and included taxation and conscription among a longer list of census uses that included "apportioning land for fields and dwelling areas," "manufacturing implements and utensils," "regulating emoluments and salaries," and "raising numbers of people for hunting and corveé service," as well as legal and ritual practices. These functions—allocation of land, planning of manufacturing, regulation of the economy—go beyond individual obligations and echo the broader purposes described in modern justifications of the census. "Does the significance of population figures, then," Xu asked, "lie just in checking the numbers of people?" (Clearly not.)[12]

These early Chinese censuses appear also to have been remarkably inclusive. Most ancient censuses counted only adult male citizens. But according to one early twentieth-century researcher, the Zhou census counted everyone "from the babe who has teeth up to the man." And it seems to have included both men and women, with documents reporting sex ratios for various provinces.[13]

What the earliest Chinese censuses did not produce—or at least, did not leave to posterity—is reliable population counts. Totals range up to thirty million in 333 BCE and back down to five million in 200 BCE. Since the census was linked to tax collection, underreporting is supposed to have varied as the tax burden rose and fell. Ancient China's vast expanse—not as great as its modern extent, but still around one million square miles—required decentralized governance, and this created opportunities for misreporting. A local official might, for example, downplay the number of households in his purview, submitting only a fraction of the tax collected and pocketing the rest.[14]

This sort of problem was not unique to China. Formal civic obligations became more complex as states grew physically larger and more populous. While population data was used for many purposes, as Xu Gan observed, it tended to be these individual obligations that determined the structure of census taking. Taxation, in particular, was a complex business. Even in a preindustrial economy there were many choices: a direct tax could be assessed on headcount, on the value of land and other property, or as a share of output (what we would today call a poll tax, wealth tax, or income tax respectively). Assessment of a tax liability and collection of the tax itself might be separated, occurring on different cycles. Collection might be delegated to regional leaders or sold as a concession to private interests. These choices were constrained by and, in turn, influenced the political structures a state adopted.

Perhaps the only common feature across ancient censuses is that they were not constructed for the benefit of historical demographers, who now struggle to make sense of the population totals they reveal. Statistical accuracy, in the modern sense, was not the point.

· · ·

Back in Mesopotamia, Sumerian culture continued to dominate for over two thousand years. Eventually it gave way to other civilizations, first to the Babylonians and then, in 911 BCE, to the rising Neo-Assyrian Empire. Over the two centuries that followed, the Assyrians swept across Mesopotamia, eventually reaching the Dead Sea and a pair of western kingdoms where a new, distinct ethnic group was taking shape, possessed of its own census mythology: the Israelites.

This was not a happy meeting. The Kingdom of Israel was destroyed, while its twin to the south, the Kingdom of Judah, survived as a client state of the empire, a fragile preserve of Israelite culture. A century later, Assyria itself collapsed, and around 600 BCE Judah fell to a new Babylonian empire. Its people were driven into exile, where they began to document the stories of their early history. These tales would eventually become the Torah—or, for Christians, the Old Testament Pentateuch books: Genesis, Exodus, Leviticus, Numbers, and Deuteronomy.

That, at least, is the modern historical consensus; the Torah itself tells a rather different story. After the familiar drama of Creation subsides, its main narrative is the Exodus, the foundational myth of the Jewish people, traditionally dated to around 1500 BCE. The Israelites had taken refuge from famine in Egypt, invited by the Pharaoh. There, an original band of seventy had grown to a population of perhaps a few million—a nation—over the span of just 430 years. This very rapid population growth—comparable with the early American colonies or parts of sub-Saharan Africa today—did not go unnoticed by the Egyptians. Feeling threatened, they enslaved the Israelites. It fell to a new leader, Moses, to lead his people to freedom in the Sinai wilderness.[15]

Rather than recounting in detail the presumably monotonous desert journey, the authors of Exodus and Leviticus use this period as an opportunity to establish laws and customs for Jewish life, including most famously the Ten Commandments, and somewhat less prominently, instructions for taking a census. Unfortunately for modern interpreters, and to the confusion of later religious authorities, these instructions lack the straightforward clarity of the Commandments. A census, Exodus notes, should be of those age twenty and older. Each person should pay, as a "ransom for his life," a sum of half a shekel, so that "no plague will come on them" (30:11–16, New International Version). This money should go to the Tabernacle, the portable shrine that God instructs the Israelites to construct in the desert.

Does all this imply, as it was later interpreted, that numbering a population is innately sinful, or the prerogative of God alone, with the tax an atonement in place of punishment? Or is the collection of this tax actually the reason for the census—prudent fiscal management, a balanced-budget measure to defray Tabernacle construction costs? (Crimson fabric and gold clasps could not have come cheap in the desert.) But if so, was it permitted to take a census for purposes less sacred? These ambiguities would have far-reaching consequences.[16]

The interpretive difficulties then compound, because the earliest counts actually described in scripture seem to ignore the Exodus prescription entirely. The first appears in Chapter 1 of the aptly named

Book of Numbers (1:2–3, in the lyrical translation of the King James version):[17]

> Take ye the sum of all the congregation of the children of Israel, after their families, by the house of their fathers, with the number of their names, every male by their polls;
>
> From twenty years old and upward, all that are able to go forth to war in Israel: thou and Aaron shall number them by their armies.

The census is taken, and the counts reported, by tribe. It is taken not as a tax measure but as a military census, a muster, preparation for anticipated resistance as the Israelites moved into the Promised Land. This rather earthbound purpose stands in stark contrast with the description in Exodus; moreover no atonement or ransom is made. And yet no plague follows. But then this census was a direct command to Moses from God, perhaps overriding the law.

Whatever its legal status, the Numbers census is certainly a historical—and statistical—fiction. The population total given is highly implausible: 603,550 men over the age of twenty, implying a total population of 2 to 3 million. By comparison, the Sinai peninsula today, part of Egypt, supports a population of around 1.4 million. It would not have been easy for millions of people to spend decades there without leaving any archaeological evidence. While a distinct Israelite people may just about have existed by 1500 BCE, they were likely living near the Jordan river, unmolested by Egyptian slavers.[18]

Suppose we dismiss the Exodus story—Moses, after all, seems no more a historical figure than Yu the Great—but optimistically imagine that the census took place in the region of the future Kingdoms of Israel and Judah. Even then, two or three million is far too high a number; modern demographers estimate a Jewish population of perhaps ten thousand at that time. What then, explains this ostentatiously exact yet wildly inaccurate passage of Judeo-Christian scripture?[19]

The Old Testament is, of course, prone to numerical exaggeration. By its account, the world was made in six days. Methuselah lived 969 years. Moses himself lived to a generous 120. Scholars and adherents alike have invented theories to rationalize these numerical oddities: errors in interpretation, erroneous transcription, symbolic rather than literal significance.

In the case of the Numbers census, the most enticing theory assumes a mistranslation. The Hindu-Arabic numerals we now use, including the crucial digit zero, had not yet been invented when the Torah was written, so the numbers in Numbers were spelled out: *six hundred and three thousand, five hundred and fifty*. In Hebrew, as in English, a word may have multiple meanings, distinguished by context. And Torahic Hebrew—like modern Arabic—did not record vowels, increasing the scope for confusion. Taking all this into account, some scholars believe that, for the word translated above as *thousand*, a better translation would be *contingent* or *troop*. Under this interpretation, the tribe of Reuben would comprise not 46,500 men, as usually translated, but 46 troops totaling 500 men. Applying this reasoning to each of the twelve tribes produces a total of around 600 troops containing 5,550 adult men—for a total population in the tens of thousands.[20]

This theory, while elegant, does not resolve all the internal inconsistencies, and it remains entirely possible that the numbers are simply ahistorical: symbolic at best and meaningless at worst. The Torah was written at a time with looser standards of numeracy, and a few questionable census results are hardly the least plausible element in a story that involves parting seas and rivers of blood.[21]

Indeed, rather than having absolute significance, this first biblical population total is probably meant to be read in relation to the second recorded census, which comes forty years later and gives—unexpectedly—a slightly smaller count. Previously so fruitful, Israelite fertility has collapsed. But in narrative context, it makes sense. The generation of Moses, lacking in faith, have been condemned by God to die in the desert; only their children will be permitted to reach the land of milk and honey. The demographic stall, echoing the physical stranding of the people, is a somewhat nerdy object lesson in disloyalty.[22]

The census law of Exodus, so far forgotten, does finally resurface, during the reign of King David, some five hundred years later. The story is told twice—in 2 Samuel and in 1 Chronicles—and the two versions agree in almost all the details. David, king of a now-united Israel and Judah, instructs his commander, Joab, to count the people, once again in order to raise an army. Joab, perhaps wary of the Exodus law, objects but is overruled. After traveling the kingdom for nine months, he returns with a tally of 1.3 million able-bodied men. On hearing this pronouncement, David, suddenly and inexplicably en-lightened about his sin, begs forgiveness. God, improvising somewhat, offers David a choice of punishments: three years of famine, three months of defeat by enemies, or three days of plague. David chooses plague. Seventy thousand people die. On all this, the two versions con-cur. But there is one important disagreement: in the first, it is God who inspired David's census, making the divine retribution seem rather arbitrary and unfair. But in the second, the instigator is revealed to be not God but Satan.[23]

This catastrophic count drew, for the first but not the last time, a dark cloud over census taking. With the Torah itself offering no defin-itive guidance, religious authorities developed various hair-splitting interpretations to avoid direct headcounts. If one followed the Exodus instructions precisely, some argued, it would be the half-shekels, and not the people, that were counted. A variant of this argument allowed the counting of body parts—noses, for example—ostensibly in place of the individuals to whom those parts were attached.

But with so many layers of often contradictory guidance on when enumeration was and was not permissible, many Jewish—and later Christian—communities prudently treated the census as taboo. The example of King David was not forgotten: if a census may actually be the devil's work, then it is probably best avoided altogether. Over the next millennium, "the number of the children of Israel" grew to be "as the sand of the sea," as God had promised Hosea (and Jacob before him). But as they multiplied, they remained safely uncounted, like the sand itself, "which cannot be measured nor numbered" (Hosea 1:10).[24]

Another account of an ancient census in the Near East, less detailed but more believable for that, comes again from Herodotus. According to his *Histories*, Egypt conducted an annual census under the pharaoh Amasis II, in the mid-sixth century BCE, around the time the Torah was being written down. Amasis, who reigned for over forty years, "laid it down as a law of the land that each Egyptian, every year, should make a declaration before the governor of his province as to how he derived his living." Omitting to make the declaration was punishable by death. Herodotus applauded these measures, observing that Egypt had reached the height of its wealth under Amasis's rule. The shine of this gilded age rubbed off on the census law itself: Herodotus claimed that Solon of Athens, a reforming lawmaker, took the Egyptian law and imposed a similar one upon Athenians. "Long may it remain in force," Herodotus wrote, "for, as a law, it can hardly be bettered."[25]

Greek philosophers, too, were interested in issues of population, with Plato and Aristotle both writing on the topic in the mid-fourth century BCE. Plato argued that the ideal city-state should have 5,040 citizens (that is, male heads of household): large enough for economic self-sufficiency and defense but small enough for constitutional government. He chose 5,040 exactly because it contains "the greatest and most regular and unbroken series of divisions," meaning that it can be divided evenly in many different ways (modern mathematicians call this a highly composite number). Of these, Plato dwelt particularly on the twice-possible subdivision into twelve (5040 = 12 x 12 x 35). He saw this as useful for social organization. Moreover, the number 12 had special significance to the Greeks, as it did in many ancient cultures. (We retain some of this today: for example, 12 hours on a clock and 12 months in a year.) Presumably he would have approved of the modern reinterpretation of Numbers, which counts 5,000-odd adult male Israelites arranged in 12 tribes. Plato's reasoning is a good reminder that mystical, numerological concerns probably distort many early population counts.[26]

If Amasis's Egypt was, as Herodotus claimed, an exporter of the census idea, then the most important importer was a city-state on the banks of the Tiber, in central Italy. Romans adopted the census late in the city's regal period, shortly before the more familiar republic was declared in 509 BCE. They gave the procedure the name we now use (from the Latin cēnsēre, "to assess"), made it fundamental to their social order, and spread it yet further as their territory grew.

Rome then was not yet the vast empire it would become. At the dawn of the republic, there were around a hundred thousand Romans (excluding slaves), mostly practicing agriculture outside the city, with perhaps twenty-five thousand true city-dwellers. Later Romans gave credit for the invention of the census, as they knew it, to the penultimate king, Servius Tullius. But if the census began in regal times, it was probably as a simple enumeration of military-age men, not unlike the Israelite censuses. It took centuries to develop into the elaborate ritual that marked the height of the republic. By the second century BCE, the census—and the two censors who performed it—had a place of power and centrality unmatched in any civilization before or since.[27]

A twenty-first-century aspirant to the American presidency might serve in the military or join a school board before rising through state politics, and perhaps a US Senate seat, and then finally making a tilt at the highest office. Similarly in the Roman Republic, an aspiring politician would occupy a sequence of public offices known as the cursus honorum (course of offices). It too began with military service, passing through successively senior positions before finally reaching consul, the most powerful executive office in the Republic. But the cursus did not end there: the most senior office, generally held only after the consulship, was that of censor.

The censorship was not directly powerful, as the consulship was; censors did not hold imperium, the power of military or judicial command. Nevertheless, it was the most highly esteemed of the ordinary offices of state. We might think of it as an emeritus position, as today former presidents or prime ministers occasionally lend their moral and political weight to diplomatic efforts or special commissions.

But the censors' role was not merely advisory. They determined each Roman citizen's position in an elaborate class hierarchy. This, in turn, dictated how that citizen and his family lived: how he could dress, how the law treated him, and how he could exercise political power. Over time, as Rome evolved, the old ancestral division between patricians and plebeians grew less important, largely supplanted by an economic hierarchy assessed during the census, with rank determined by the value of a man's property. This was originally assumed to reflect his ability to contribute militarily, but even as the connection to military service weakened over time, the system of property qualifications remained.

The highest classes were senators and *equites* (knights), who had to demonstrate property worth something like five hundred years of wages for a foot soldier. Then came five classes of commoner, the highest of whom might also serve as cavalry, and the lower four, with diminishing wealth requirements, as infantry. At the bottom was the proletariat, the *capite censi,* literally "those counted by head" and not by wealth, of which they had little or none. (Below even those were foreigners—which in 200 BCE meant mostly Italians living outside the immediate vicinity of the city of Rome—and slaves. Neither group was counted in the census.)

In principle, this stratification of Roman society was performed every five years. The two censors, once appointed, would assemble in a building on Rome's Field of Mars. Their dress, the *toga praetexta* with its broad purple stripe, would distinguish them from the masses, as would the ivory-clad *curule* chair upon which each sat, a symbol of office. First the auspices would be read, to confirm that the census had divine approval. Then each head of household would be called upon, in turn, to make his declaration. He would give his full name, that of his father—or patron, in the case of a freed slave—and his age. He would report his marital status and, if applicable, the name of his wife and the number, names, and ages of his children. He would then

The Domitius Ahenobarbus relief is believed to date from about 100 BCE and to depict the taking of the Roman census. The full relief is nearly twenty feet long and shows, in addition, the *lustrum* (the animal sacrifice that marked the close of the census). (Musée du Louvre, LL 399 / Ma 975. Photo credit: Marie-Lan Nguyen / Wikimedia Commons.)

move on to an account of his property. This would proceed by tribe until it was complete. Reported penalties for absence vary from imprisonment through stripping of citizenship, sale into slavery, and even death.[28]

The censors were appointed for an eighteen-month term, and sheer logistics suggest the count must have taken most of this. At its close a total would be announced, and an animal sacrifice—the *lustrum*—performed for the purification of the Roman people. Over time, the word *lustrum* came to refer to the whole census procedure and eventually to the five-year period itself. While *lustrum* did not enter modern English as its Latinate siblings—decade, century, millennium—did, the "quinquennial" (also meaning five-yearly) censuses of countries like Australia, Canada, and New Zealand reflect these classical origins.

The census assessment was far from perfunctory. Romans' fortunes could, and did, rise and fall based on the censors' discretion. As well as fiscal assessors, the censors were moral arbiters in all aspects of Roman life, a potentially intrusive role from which the modern meaning of "censorship" derives. Gellius, a Roman writer in the second century CE, recounts an anecdote in which an unnamed, especially humorless, censor interviews a citizen:[29]

> The man who was to take the oath was a jester, a sarcastic dog, and too much given to buffoonery. Thinking that he had a chance to crack a joke, when the censor asked him, as was customary, "Have you, to the best of your knowledge and belief, a wife?" he replied: "I indeed have a wife, but not, by Heaven! such a one as I could desire." Then the censor reduced him to a commoner for his untimely quip, and added that the reason for his action was a scurrilous joke made in his presence.

This may have been the first recorded joke at a census, but it was not the last. In 2001, in one of the earliest examples of a viral internet phenomenon, people all over the world listed Jedi, a monastic order from the fictional Star Wars universe, as their religion on population censuses: twenty-one thousand in Canada, fifty-three thousand in New Zealand, seventy thousand in Australia, and over four hundred thousand between England, Wales, and Scotland. For some, this reflected a genuine objection to the census or the religion question in particular (although in Australia and Britain the question was optional, and New Zealand provided a specific option to "object to answering this question"). But most participants presumably saw it as a harmless stunt. In response, statistical authorities around the world could do little but issue warning press releases and feign annoyance. More than a few national statisticians may have wished they retained the punitive powers of their Roman predecessors.[30]

• • •

Over the next two centuries, the territory controlled by Rome continued to grow, incorporating most of the Mediterranean coast. While living under Roman rule, the inhabitants of these newly incorporated provinces did not automatically become citizens, although citizenship did expand gradually. But even as Rome's power abroad grew—adding Gaul and Egypt in mid-first century BCE—the republican political system at home was in crisis. In 27 BCE Octavian—soon to be styled Augustus "the Illustrious"—took sole power, inaugurating a new regime: the Roman Empire.

Governance of the empire remained relatively decentralized. Romans tended to preserve local administrative practices in conquered territories if possible. So while the reign of Augustus saw census taking spread across the empire, it varied in form. It probably bore little resemblance to the elaborate ritual conducted in the capital, focusing primarily on tax collection rather than social hierarchy. Some provinces—Egypt, for example—had conducted headcounts before Roman conquest, and these were coopted to collect Roman taxes. In some places, taxation was based primarily on population; in others it reflected wealth or income. These different taxes likely resulted in different census-taking procedures. Nor is it certain that every province had something like a census.[31]

Consequently, there is no record of the complete population of the Roman Empire during the reign of Augustus. There are, however, partial counts. Prior to his death, Augustus left a list of his achievements, to be inscribed and distributed throughout the empire. It was titled *Res Gestae Divi Augusti*—"Deeds of the Divine Augustus." Although the original has been lost, many contemporary copies were made, and some remain, including an almost-complete inscription on the walls of a temple in Ankara, Turkey. It lists many diverse achievements of the emperor, but early among them, that he ordered three censuses, in 28 BCE, 8 BCE, and 14 CE, recording growth from 4,063,000 to 4,937,000 over the period. (As in the Confucian tradition, we can assume that Augustus thought this increase a reflection of his wise rule.) The text makes it clear that these were censuses of citizens only, but the first of these totals is four times higher than the last such totals reported under the republic, only forty years earlier. To explain this, some scholars have argued that adult women must now have been included, though there is no direct evidence for this. Other explanations include the expansion of citizenship that had occurred in the intervening period, as well as better counting, a result of the decentralization of the citizen census procedure in the final years of the republic. Either way, it was still only a fraction of the total population of the empire. Including children, slaves, and—especially—all of the noncitizen residents of outlying provinces, the Roman Empire is believed to have ruled over 40 to 50 million people by 14 CE.[32]

This was one of the largest populations ever to have fallen under the control of a single government in the ancient era, but it was not the largest, even at that moment. In 2 CE, while Augustus was consolidating his legacy, the Han dynasty government was conducting a census of China, now considered the first reliable count in Chinese history. The official total was 59,594,978 people, a number well within the range of modern estimates of 45 to 70 million. It confirmed China's numerical supremacy, a demographic and political reality that had probably already existed for two centuries and would continue to hold, almost without break, for the next two millennia.[33]

• • •

Augustus's forty-year reign spanned the years traditionally marked "BC"— before Christ—and those marked "AD"—*anno Domini,* "in the year of our Lord." (In this chapter, as is increasingly conventional, I use BCE— before the common era—and CE—common era—instead.) It is no coincidence that probably the most famous census of antiquity is supposed to have occurred on this threshold, for it appears as the backdrop to the event that gave us this division. Chapter 2 of the Gospel of Luke, in the New International Version translation, begins so (verses 1–2):

> In those days Caesar Augustus issued a decree that a census should be taken of the entire Roman world. (This was the first census that took place while Quirinius was governor of Syria.)

The translation as "census" is not universal. The original language of the New Testament is believed to be a dialect of Greek, rather than the Hebrew of the Old Testament. The word given in the Greek text, *apographesthai,* is generally translated as "copy," "enroll," or "register," and a direct translation in grammatical context is "that the whole world should have itself registered." The King James version uses "tax," while some modern translators choose "registration" or "listing." But as the reference is to a Roman procedure, the use of "census" seems as reasonable as any.[34]

Luke continues (2:3–7):

> And everyone went to their own town to register.
>
> So Joseph also went up from the town of Nazareth in Galilee to Judea, to Bethlehem the town of David, because he belonged to the house and line of David. He went there to register with Mary, who was pledged to be married to him and was expecting a child. While they were there, the time came for the baby to be born, and she gave birth to her firstborn, a son. She wrapped him in cloths and placed him in a manger, because there was no guest room available for them.

That son, of course, was Jesus of Nazareth. Logically, this event should have taken place in the year designated 1 AD or CE—Jesus being the Dominus of *anno Domini.* In fact, Dionysius Exiguus, the sixth-century monk who designed the BC/AD system, seems to have confused his dates, and most scholars today date Jesus's birth to some time between 6 and 4 BCE. To do so they rely on the 4 BCE death of King Herod, which is assumed to be reliable. Since Herod plays a prominent role in the subsequent story, he must have been alive at the time of the nativity. But resolving this problem creates another, because there was no Roman census in those years.

The Kingdom of Judah had followed a winding path to Roman occupation via Babylonian collapse, Persian conquest, a cameo in Alexander the Great's empire, and a period of autonomous rule. The latter ended in 63 BCE, when Judah was swept into the ever-expanding fringe of Rome. The political chaos in the capital at that time meant that

Roman rule was not fully consolidated until 37 BCE, when Herod the Great, a Jew, was made king of the now-Latinized client state of Judea.

This delegated rule is one reason it seems unlikely that a census would have occurred during Herod's reign: in Jewish law and culture, the memory of King David's disastrous census still loomed large. Other parts of the story also fail to hold up. There were no single simultaneous censuses "of the entire Roman world." Combined with a policy that required registration in one's ancestral hometown, this would have created chaos across the empire. The consensus of historians is that Luke, in placing the nativity at the time of a census, is simply mistaken. Quite possibly, the story of Jesus's birth was entirely invented, crafted to explain how a man known commonly as Jesus "of Nazareth" could be the messiah, whom prophecy stated would come from Bethlehem, a village some seventy miles away.[35]

That said, there was a "census of Quirinius," a decade later in 6 CE. After Herod's death in 4 BCE, his son Herod Archelaus was appointed in his place, but the latter man was unpopular, and Augustus eventually replaced him with a direct administrator. The emperor placed the province in the hands of Publius Sulpicius Quirinius, who was already governor of adjacent Syria. On taking over, one of Quirinius's first actions was to call a census of the province to raise a tax.[36]

The move was not welcomed by the Judeans. Tribute to a remote imperial government is never popular, but in Judea it was doubly incendiary, since it also violated the ancient prohibition on numbering the Jews. A revolutionary, Judas of Galilee, led a movement in dissent, encouraging people to resist registration. The protest would cast a long shadow. The first-century historian Josephus credited Judas with founding the Zealots, a sect whose antitaxation protests eventually led to the First Jewish-Roman War, which ended in 73 CE, with the fall of Jerusalem. That war in turn began a conflict that erupted intermittently until around 136 CE, when Roman legions finally killed or drove from Judea almost the entire Jewish population. Once again, census taking had led, albeit this time by a long and indirect path, to disaster for the Jews.[37]

The story of the nativity, with its time-shifted census, became firmly established in Christian theology as that religion spread. In 337 CE, the emperor Constantine converted on his deathbed, and in 380 CE his successors declared Christianity the official religion of the empire. Virtually overnight, lands as distant as the great wall of Hadrian, on the northern border of Roman Britain, became nominally Christian. The western Roman Empire fell in 476 CE. While population censuses continued elsewhere—in the Islamic world, for example, under the reforming caliph Umar I, who reigned from 634 to 644 CE—Europe witnessed many centuries without them.

Christianity survived the collapse of its imperial sponsor, and while it waxed and waned in the post-Roman period, it retained a tenacious grip on the British Isles. So it was that in 1066, when William of Normandy crossed the English channel to press his claim, he did so as a Christian duke invading a predominantly Christian nation. He was crowned king, symbolically, on December 25, the date the Roman Church had retrospectively fixed as Christmas Day. We know a great deal about William's England, for twenty years later, in 1086, he commissioned a survey of its land and people. The survey or "inquest"— some historians are reluctant to call it a census, although it is popularly understood as such—was unique in Europe at that time. Its results were summarized, and have been preserved to this day, in a contemporary record that became known as Domesday Book.[38]

There are, to be more accurate, two books, Great and Little Domesday, as well as a number of related documents scattered through the state and ecclesiastical archives of England. But despite this wealth of documentary evidence, there is no consensus on exactly how and why the survey was undertaken. Historians do not even agree on whether the books were the intended outcome of the survey or an afterthought. The text itself provides few direct clues, and the mystery has energized scholars ever since.[39]

After the conquest, William was quick to consolidate his rule. He built castles, seized land, and created a new Norman nobility. He carried on the *geld*, the land tax that the Anglo-Saxon kings had imposed for the defense of the realm. He showed little restraint in quashing rebellions: his northern campaign is traditionally blamed for over a hundred thousand deaths and is reflected in the many manors described as "wasted" in Domesday Book.[40]

But despite, or perhaps because of, these measures, his grasp on England remained uncertain. In 1085, King Cnut of Denmark threatened invasion, and William readied mercenaries to defend the realm. These men would have required payment, leading to the longstanding theory that the Domesday inquest was—in time-honored fashion—a tax collection exercise. But the invasion never eventuated, and that it would not was probably clear by the time the inquest got underway. An alternative hypothesis holds that Domesday was a feudal settlement, a renegotiation of rights and responsibilities to recognize and reinforce the changes that resulted from William's own invasion, twenty years earlier: a belated attempt to freeze, in writing, the new "facts on the ground." More recently it has even been described as a kind of reconciliation process, albeit a harsh one, resolving—or cementing—injustices done over the previous two decades.[41]

There is contemporaneous evidence—tantalizingly brief—for the survey's genesis. The *Anglo-Saxon Chronicle,* the most important historical record of the period, notes that William spent midwinter 1085 in Gloucester, a former Roman city. He spent Christmas Day in "very deep consultation with his council, about this land; how it was occupied, and by what sort of men." Nothing more of this discussion is recorded. William's council may have discussed, with relief, the now receding prospect of a Danish attack. Or perhaps the king was besieged by complaints from his advisors of ongoing land disputes, motivating an effort to tie down tenure once and for all. There is simply no way of knowing.[42]

The yuletide timing, however, exactly twenty years after William's coronation, is intriguing. Wander into a church on Christmas Eve, and you may well hear the words of Luke 2:1–7, quoted above. Perhaps on Christmas Eve 1085 that same story, told in carefully enunciated Latin, echoed in the chapel of Gloucester's Kingsholm Palace, itself built upon Roman foundations: *"factum est autem in diebus illis exiit edictum a Caesare Augusto ut describeretur universus orbis."* Perhaps William— born the Bastard, lately the Great, and eventually remembered as the Conqueror—spent a restless night thinking about Octavian, who became the Illustrious. Perhaps William, a man of illegitimate birth and uncertain inheritance, who nevertheless conquered a territory four times larger and more populous than that to which he was born, dreamt that night of the Roman Empire, its rise to greatness, and the ever-present reminders of its fall. Perhaps he woke the next day with thoughts of consolidation—and even of legacy.[43]

Regardless of the motivation, the speed and thoroughness with which the king's wishes were enacted were impressive. By mid-January 1086, the survey was underway. England was divided into at least seven circuits, and commissioners were appointed to supervise collection of information from each circuit. Existing records were likely used, including listings to collect the *geld*. Then the commissioners held special sessions of county courts, during which jurors (half English, half French) were summoned to verify, correct, and augment the information under oath.[44]

The list of topics that the courts aimed to investigate and record was extensive. Ownership of the manor. Population across various feudal categories, from freemen to slaves. Economic resources, from fisheries to mills. Undeveloped resources. All of this was to be assessed at three points in time: the present day (1086) and immediately before and immediately after the conquest (1066). It was exhaustive, and recognized as such. The *Chronicle* observes, "There was not one single hide, nor a yard of land, nay, moreover (it is shameful to tell, though he thought it no shame to do it), not even an ox, nor a cow, nor a swine was there left, that was not set down in his writ."[45]

So detailed was the information initially collected that a series of summarizing steps was required before a complete national record could be compiled. (Little Domesday is thought to be one of these intermediate summaries.) As the information was summarized, it was rearranged; for although the circuits operated geographically, the final summaries were arranged by ownership in the feudal hierarchy, from the king on down. Since large landowners held manors across the country, this collation exercise must have been complex, with many scribes involved. The final summary, however—Great Domesday—is written predominantly in a single hand: one individual, probably English, who worked rapidly to fill 413 leaves of parchment, the skins of some two hundred sheep.[46]

The demographic and economic statistics captured reveal an extraordinary level of numerical detail about Anglo-Norman life: 25,000 individuals recorded by name from 1066, 19,500 from 1086; 270,000 people enumerated but not named; 81,000 plough teams; 2,061 churches; 6,082 mills; 45 vineyards; several mints; and industrial facilities including salt pans, lead works, quarries, and potteries. And although Domesday Book is primarily a book of numbers, small personal details occasionally slipped through the scribe's summarizing filter. A great historical romance remains to be written of the unnamed Breton recorded occupying land in Pickenham without the king's authority because he "loved a certain woman on that land."[47]

Initially the record was called simply the *descriptio*—the same Latin term used in the Vulgate translation of Luke's Gospel, equivalent to the Greek *apographē*. Later it became know as the Book of the Exchequer, after the Norman office of taxation, or the Book of Winchester, after the city where it was kept. As a bound book of complete pages, there was no easy way to amend or update it, and it soon became outdated. Within a few generations, it was, according to one historian, "largely irrelevant to the government of England." Yet despite this, it proved continuously useful in private matters, consulted to demonstrate rights and privileges. By 1179 it had acquired its present ominous moniker, Domesday Book. Domesday, or doomsday, was the biblical day of judgment and did not necessarily have the overtones of destruction and ruin that accompany the word "doom" today. The book was named for it "because its decisions, like those of the Last Judgement, are unalterable." It was relied on in court cases well into the nineteenth century, cited even as late as 1958 in a dispute over a market in Taunton, a town in the west of England.[48]

Perhaps when William looked out to the crumbling Roman walls of Gloucester that Christmas morning of 1085, he glimpsed something of this future. He died less than two years after his survey began. (His death probably brought compilation of Great Domesday to halt, resulting in the incomplete work we see today.) That Christmas in Gloucester, fifty-seven-year-old William was already an old man. His father died at thirty-five, his mother in her forties. Among all the kings of England to that time, only Edward the Confessor had reached his seventh decade. Perhaps William, aware of his mortality, set out quite intentionally to create a kind of *Res Gestae* of his own, an account of whom and what the Conqueror had conquered.

• • •

In 1986, to celebrate the nine-hundred-year anniversary of Domesday Book, the BBC assembled a vast collection of data on the mid-1980s state of the nation. It was recorded using state-of-the-art technology: etched onto plastic-coated aluminum laser discs (similar to compact discs but larger). Less than fifteen years later, the technology no longer existed to retrieve this record. The physical format was obsolete, and the programs to read the data no longer ran on modern hardware. Its eventual rescue took concerted effort by specialist researchers.[49]

Great and Little Domesday, on the other hand, are still quite readable, the technology of abbreviated Latin script on vellum having proved remarkably hardy. The books are usually kept carefully in the National Archives at Kew, accessible only to scholars, but members of the public who are interested can find them online, as both images and translated text. And people, remarkably, are still interested. Domesday Book is seen as one of the foundational documents in England's national story. It remains a matter of pride and excitement for an English family to be able to trace their ancestry to an entry in Domesday—as one historian put it, "the ultimate imprimatur of heritage."[50]

Family history has a long connection with census making. Not far from the biblical reports of Israelite numerical strength, we find extensive genealogies, the chains of begetting that even most dedicated believers skip over today. Indeed, the largest repository of census data anywhere in the world is probably a worked-out quarry, deep within the mountains overlooking Salt Lake City, Utah. There, in the Granite Mountain Records Vault, the Church of Jesus Christ of Latter-day Saints is working to preserve population records from around the world, ensuring that they do not go the way of the 1986 Domesday project. Ancestry is especially important in the Mormon faith, which allows the possibility of posthumous baptism and salvation. Through such baptism, dead ancestors might be reunited with their present-day descendants in the afterlife. Because of the recent and proselytizing nature of Mormonism, those ancestors could include just about anyone who ever lived, so the genealogy project is global. The records kept in Granite Mountain—some 3.5 billion pages—now serve as the basis of online genealogy services such as Ancestry.com, with its more than three million subscribers. In researching this book, I became one of them.[51]

Like many Australians, my ancestors came from Europe, mostly Britain and Ireland. My surname—Whitby—is English, of Viking origin. The town of Whitby, on the Yorkshire coast, is ancient and listed in Domesday Book, but as far as I know, my family has never established a connection to it. In embarking on my own research, I didn't imagine I would find a path to a Norman ancestor, although such a path surely exists, as it does for almost all families present in England before large-scale immigration in the twentieth century.

Upon joining Ancestry, I entered the details of my parents and grandparents (those I remembered, at least). The records that came up initially were sparse: a few Australian electoral roll entries. With additional details gleaned from my parents, like birthdates and birthplaces, my search gained momentum. Most fruitful was the nineteenth and early twentieth century, a period for which detailed British census schedules have now been made public. I found my great-great-grandfather as a nine-year-old in the 1861 census, and his grandfather as a forty-five-year-old in the 1841 census. Earlier, less-detailed censuses were not helpful, but using civil registration and parish records—births, deaths, and marriages—I reached back to 1625. And then the trail went cold.

• • •

It's not surprising that I came to a dead end in my family history research. This is a fairly typical experience for someone of English, or indeed European, background. It was not until the sixteenth century that several countries established mandatory parish registers, the precursors of modern civil registration systems. It was not until the eighteenth century that a procedure known as a census reemerged as an institution of state in Europe.[52]

As it reemerged, it borrowed ideas from the past, most obviously the name. But it also developed features that had never been part of its ancient precursors. While ancient philosophers like Xu Gan may have recognized the value of abstract population data, it usually came as a byproduct of procedures developed for some other purpose. Then, the numbers came second to the procedure, whereas now the procedure follows from the desire for accurate numbers. Following in the wake of the scientific revolution, the census became more scientific.

The reinvented census also discarded some ancient ideas. In the quest for accuracy, it shed the individual civic obligations that usually accompanied it in the ancient world. In Zhou dynasty China, the census was first and foremost a tax collection mechanism. Among the Israelites in the Sinai desert, it served to conscript people into an army. In Rome, it established social and political order, while in the Roman provinces it once again served to support taxation. William's Domesday survey may have done any, or all, of the above. A typical modern census does none of them.

The modern census also had to overcome the taboo, strongly held in the Judeo-Christian tradition but present in other traditional cultures too, against counting people. The elimination of individual obligations probably helped with that—the professed fear of heavenly wrath often masked a more prosaic fear of the tax collector. This demystification of the census did not leave it unchallenged: religious taboos were soon replaced by new fears, of tyrannical governments and total surveillance. In time, the tragedy of King David's census was supplanted by other, even more horrifying stories.

• • •

My search for my ancestors left me with a final, nagging question: How far back does the longest recorded genealogy go? Who is the newest leaf on the tallest family tree, and what great progenitor lies at its root? You might guess it would be some European royal family: descendants of Charlemagne, perhaps, or even of a Roman emperor. But theirs are mere saplings compared with the tallest tree in the human forest. That distinction goes to the descendants of Confucius, the original champion of good government, a man moved to physical deference in the mere presence of the census results.

For most of Chinese history, Confucianism was held in official favor, and so his descendants meticulously, and officially, recorded their descent. When the communist revolution swept China, the state-sponsored branch of the Confucian tree fled to Taiwan. During the early years of the People's Republic, and particularly during the Cultural Revolution, Confucianism came under attack. But millennia-old philosophies do not die easily, and Confucius continued to be celebrated, both inside and outside China. In 1973, an asteroid, 7853 Confucius, was named for him. Today Confucianism is experiencing a resurgence in mainland China.

The current official head of the family of Confucius—written K'ung-fu-tzu in the Wade-Giles system of romanization commonly used in Taiwan—is Kung Tsui-chang, born in 1975. He is not the furthest removed descendant: Guinness World Records recognizes an eighty-six-generation chain in another branch. But because his descent is down the "main line" (a still-impressive seventy-nine generations), he inherited, in 2008, the title of sacrificial official to Confucius. The complete sequence is on Wikipedia. Where a census is a snapshot of a population taken at one time, this is a slice, though time, of one family. Kung Tsui-chang's own son, Yu-jen, the eightieth-generation descendent, was born on January 1, 2006.[53]

Taiwan conducted its most recent census on December 26, 2010, just before Kung Yu-jen's fifth birthday. He was then one of nearly seven billion people who called Earth home. As the result of a mission handover aboard the International Space Station, the extraterrestrial population was temporarily doubled: three Russians, two Americans, and an Italian. From their position in low-Earth orbit, they looked out over a universe far larger than our prehistoric ancestors could have imagined. Scientists now believe there are one billion trillion stars in the observable universe. Those we have counted are recorded in star catalogs, the largest of which contain just a few billion stars, a tiny fraction of the total. Most remain uncountable, beyond the resolution of even our most powerful telescopes. Meanwhile, the possibility of enumerating every single living member of *Homo sapiens* is now within our reach.[54]

In fact, the 2010 Taiwanese census was only a partial survey, relying instead on existing administrative records to enumerate much of the population (just one of the cost-saving tricks census takers in some countries now use). So I can't say for certain whether blank census papers were dropped in the mailbox of the Kung household in late December of that year. But if so, I like to imagine that the young Yu-jen looked skyward, in the general direction of Asteroid 7853, and offered some small gesture of respect, as his father, the newest sacrificial official to Confucius, sat down, rolled up his sleeves, uncapped the requisite blue-ink pen, and began to fill out the form.

CHAPTER 2

POLITICAL ARITHMETIC

IN 1701, the Danish monarch Frederick IV received a desperate petitioner. The man had traveled to Copenhagen from the cold, windswept, North Atlantic territory of Iceland to tell the king that its people—Frederick's people—were starving. Settled by Vikings at the end of the first millennium, Iceland had come under Norwegian rule in the thirteenth century and a united Danish-Norwegian-Swedish crown in 1397, remaining with Denmark-Norway when Sweden broke away in 1521.[1]

Life in the near-arctic outpost had always been tenuous, dependent on grazing livestock and fishing, and subject to the vagaries of climate and active volcanoes. As poet Matthías Jochumsson later put it: "When the grass dies, The beasts die too; First the horse, Then the sheep, Then the cow, After that the beggar, Then the farmer, Then his wife, And finally his child." Despite having a land area larger than its lexical neighbor Ireland, Iceland's population had probably never exceeded seventy thousand and was by then in decline. A global fall in temperatures, known as the Little Ice Age, made the closing decades of the seventeenth century especially difficult for the Icelanders.[2]

There is no record of the petitioner's plea, though it seems to have spurred the king to action, at least for a while. On May 22, 1702, Frederick ordered two Icelandic-born Copenhageners, Professor Árni

Magnússon and Sheriff Páll Vídalín, to make a survey of conditions on the island, including a census of its people. Frederick, widely considered one of the better absolute monarchs of Denmark, was influenced by a German ideology of government known as cameralism. Like Confucianism, it stressed administrative efficiency and a strong state. And as in the Eastern philosophy, cameralism took population growth as a measure of success. The report from Iceland, if confirmed, would therefore be deeply concerning.[3]

The enumeration took place from December 1702 to June 1703, a period that became known as the "census winter." Magnússon and Vídalín relied on the nation's network of county sheriffs and district commissioners, around five hundred people, to make the count. They went to each remote farm, recording every person by name, along with their age, sex, and social status. Most of the population lived on the coast, reachable by sea. But with roads few and far between, those living inland were more easily reached in winter, when snow covered rough lava fields and bogs, and rivers of glacial meltwater were reduced to a trickle. Winter also meant that Icelanders were more likely to be found at home.[4]

In total, 50,366 people were counted. According to the king's instructions, no person should be left out, and almost no person was: even paupers and vagrants were enumerated, listed in thirty-eight special reports. Modern analysis has found that one farm was missed, while 497 people have been confirmed as double counted. A few scholars have argued that some young children were omitted, but the preceding years of harsh conditions could also explain that, through either increased infant mortality or delayed childbearing. Sex was recorded for every person, and age for all but 357. In the annals of enumeration, this was an unprecedented degree of accuracy and inclusiveness; it would more than satisfy a twenty-first-century census taker.[5]

But the Icelandic count of 1703 was modern in a more important way, foreshadowing later developments in census taking. It was not conducted in order to raise a new tax or conscript an army—these would have been pointless, with the island's population barely subsisting. Instead, it was taken to assess, in numerical terms, the state of the nation

The 1703 census of Iceland was the earliest to list every person by name on the territory of a modern state. The first block of entries in the county report for Snæfellsnessýsla is for the Hólmlátur farm. It lists Þorsteinn Sigurðsson, a clerk, carpenter, and builder, as well as his wife, three children, maid, and brother-in-law, along with their ages. (The National Archives of Iceland, 1928-Rentukammer, D1/2-1.)

and the welfare of its people. To achieve this it had to count everyone: male and female, young and old, rich and poor.

It was done presumably with the idea that some action of the king might ameliorate the pitiable condition and increase the dwindling number of the Icelanders. Unfortunately for them, no such action followed. The attention of the Danish court seems to have wandered, perhaps distracted by the death of Frederick's second wife. This groundbreaking enumeration was promptly forgotten, its data lying untouched in a royal archive for the next three-quarters of a century. For Iceland, that century would be among the bleakest in its history. For census taking, it would be a kind of renaissance. In its time Iceland's count was unique, but by the early nineteenth century, similar enumerations had become an important feature of government administration in some of the most powerful countries in the European world.[6]

• • •

By 1703, Frederick was not alone in at least caring about the population of his realm (even if he was ahead in actually measuring it). Population growth was a central tenet of mercantilism, a relative of cameralism that held sway in much of Western Europe from the sixteenth to eighteenth centuries. Mercantilists believed that the state should regulate economic activity, that exports should be promoted and imports restricted, and that the gold and silver that resulted from international trade was a measure of a country's wealth and should be hoarded. A necessary correlate of this, according to the theory, was a large population, essential for the growth of markets and for a strong military capable of projecting power abroad to defend trade.

As European nations began to establish colonies around the world, they were guided by mercantilist beliefs, including on population. The first English colony to survive on North American soil, at Jamestown, Virginia, was really a business enterprise, established in 1607 under the charter of a joint-stock company. Thinly peopled early colonies were quite vulnerable: at the mercy of nature, of justifiably hostile indigenous populations, and, soon enough, of other European powers. Population growth was a defensive strategy, leading imperial powers to take a close interest in the demography of their new possessions.

Seen from the perspective of their indigenous neighbors, these growing colonial settlements were an offensive threat. By 1600, the European-descended population of the Americas was no more than a quarter million, nearly all living in the better-established Spanish and Portuguese colonies further south. Yet they had done hugely dispro-portionate damage, reducing the indigenous population from perhaps forty million or more before 1492 to around ten million by the early seventeenth century. As French, Dutch, and English colonies sprang up further north, the same deadly combination of muskets and smallpox seemed destined to consign the indigenous people of North America to a similar fate.[7]

Not, however, without a fight. The Powhatan confederation, an in-digenous group who lived adjacent to the English colony of Virginia, were keenly attuned to the European threat. They both traded and clashed with the English in Jamestown. In 1616, during a period of peace, they dispatched a diplomatic delegation to London, led by the daughter of the chief, who was known as Pocahontas. This mission disguised another objective. Pocahontas was accompanied by a Powha-tan man named Uttamatomakkin, who had been instructed to perform a kind of demographic espionage, to size up their potential adversary.

As Captain John Smith, a leader and early historian of the colony, wrote a few years later from England: "the King"—of the Powhatan—"purposely sent him, as they say, to number the people here, and inform him well what we were and our state." Uttamatomakkin came with a plan: "Arriving at Plymouth, according to his directions, he got a long stick, whereon by notches he did think to have kept the number of all the men he could see." But according to Smith, the plan proved inadequate to the challenge, for Uttamatomakkin "was quickly weary of that task." Another writer, Samuel Purchas, who had met the delegation, put it more precisely: "his arithmetic soon failed."[8]

It seems unlikely that Uttamatomakkin meant to carve one notch for each person he saw, as is sometimes depicted. Although their population

THE SUM OF THE PEOPLE

never rivaled the great Aztec or Inka cities further south, the Powhatan certainly knew of large numbers, totaling around twenty thousand members in a confederation of a few dozen tribes. They called their land Tsenacomoco, meaning densely inhabited place. While they did use counting sticks, Uttamatomakkin likely planned something more complex than a simple tally. There is evidence from Smith himself, for example, that the Powhatan employed a simple decimal system. In any event, it didn't matter: while Uttamatomakkin abandoned his numerical survey, his qualitative impressions more than sufficed to eventually turn his people against their new English neighbors.[9]

In 1622, the Powhatan launched a coordinated attack on settlements along the James River. A total of 347 English settlers were killed, around a quarter of the population, as well as an unknown number of attackers. A year later the English had their revenge, killing around 250 Powhatan at a so-called peace conference. These attacks triggered a headcount in the colony, one of many conducted in its early years, to assess the fighting strength of those who remained and determine the ongoing viability of the settlement. It also led to the transition of Virginia from a private enterprise to a direct colony of the English crown, consolidating a lasting English beachhead in North America.[10]

Similar mercantilist ideas also prompted a small census of New France (today, Canada) in 1666, which counted 3,215 people. It was less complete than the census of Iceland that would shortly follow. Perhaps a thousand Europeans were missed, living at the edges of a territory that was not naturally constrained as Iceland was. Neither were any indigenous people counted. Still, it was enough to persuade the French intendant responsible for the colony to adopt new measures to increase its population. To correct an imbalanced sex ratio—nearly two men per one woman—some 800 "royal daughters" were sent from France, and intermarriage with Native American women was encouraged. That such active population policies were accepted, at a time when France itself did not even have a census, reflects the different rules that European nations applied to their colonies.[11]

A similar count was made in New York in 1698, and as the eighteenth century progressed, censuses became common in nearly all the British American colonies, organized either for the traditional reasons of taxation and the organization of militias or to satisfy the curiosity of officials in London. By small, ad hoc counts like this, enumeration became relatively well-established in colonial America, even as it remained practically unknown in Europe.[12]

• • •

The lack of comprehensive data on European countries did not stop people trying to make sense of their demography. The most prominent effort came under the banner of "political arithmetic," a discipline defined by one exponent as "the Art of Reasoning, by Figures, upon things relating to Government." The idea of political arithmetic can be difficult to grasp. Today, reasoning by figures is the lingua franca of government, the basis for the budgets, performance indicators, and cost-benefit analyses that underpin efficient administration. But this hasn't always been true: until fairly recently, rulers often made decisions based on the slightest of quantitative information.[13]

Political arithmeticians sought to change that. The pioneers were two Englishmen, William Petty and John Graunt. Both were born in the 1620s to textile merchants in the south of England, but their trajectories soon diverged. While Graunt took an apprenticeship following in his father's footsteps, Petty embarked on a more itinerant, adventuresome existence. An ill-fated stint on a merchant ship saw him injured and stranded ashore in Normandy at age fourteen. There, he charmed his way into a Jesuit college, which gave him introduction to the intellectual community on the continent. He studied and socialized widely before returning to London as a young man in 1646. There, Petty met Graunt, whose thriving textile business had made him a prominent member of the city's mercantile class.[14]

This was a precarious time to be living in the British Isles. The English Parliament was at war with its own king, Charles I, who also held

the crowns of Scotland and Ireland. But while the country was in tur-
moil, Petty and Graunt found in London a vibrant intellectual community, a group of thinkers, experimenters, and inventors at the
forefront of what would eventually be called the scientific revolution.

The revolution's greatest victory, at that time, was the radical new
understanding of astronomy that had emerged over the past century. In
1543, Copernicus had published his heretical model of a heliocentric
universe, in which the planets revolved around the sun, rather than the
other way around. Inspired by this work, the Danish noble Tyco Brahe
spent several decades making observations of celestial bodies, using
instruments of his own devising, unprecedented in their accuracy.
From this data, Brahe's assistant Johannes Kepler was able to deduce
the final puzzle piece that had eluded Copernicus: the planets followed
not circular but elliptical orbits. Kepler's three laws of planetary motion were published between 1609 and 1619. In a period not much
longer than a single lifetime, thousands of years of accepted wisdom
had been overturned. To Petty and his London circle, it was proof of
the revolutionary potential of this mode of reasoning, empirical and
mathematical.

But could it be applied to the tumultuous society in which they
found themselves living? Theories of society and its government
abounded, from the philosophy of Aristotle and Plato, through Machi-
avelli, to the mercantilism that was then dominant. But social and economic data were scarce. The most basic facts, including population
totals, were often unknown. It was as if instead of the consistent, rigorous work of Brahe, Kepler had had to rely on a grab bag of observations: a few unconfirmed rumors of a comet, the position of the moon
one night in Prague, and a week's worth of observations of Mars from
Copenhagen. Without better data, nobody could tell whether mathematical principles might rule not just the heavens, but humankind
itself.

Petty would soon have a chance to find out. By 1652, Cromwell's
army had overthrown the king, had seized control of England, and was
in the process of doing the same in Ireland. Petty accepted a lucrative

commission as physician to the English army in Ireland, abandoning professorships in Oxford and London to do so. There, he found success as, in effect, a colonial administrator. He maneuvered into the leadership of an ambitious survey of the lands expropriated in the occupation, an opportunity to apply the tools of empirical science to public administration. He was well suited to the task: the diarist Samuel Pepys later called him "one of the most rational men that ever I heard speak." As surveyor, he found opportunities for private land speculation and became a wealthy man. His survey was not limited to land, though: in 1659, he organized a partial census of the country, probably in order to levy a poll tax, before returning to England. When the monarchy was restored in 1660, Petty managed, despite his association with Cromwell, to ingratiate himself with the new king, Charles II. He was knighted in 1661, his ascent in society complete.[15]

John Graunt had none of Petty's swashbuckling flamboyance, but the following year he too achieved a degree of fame, publishing a painstaking analytical treatise entitled *Observations on the Bills of Mortality*. The eponymous bills had been introduced in London some seventy years earlier, to track mortality during an outbreak of plague. But since they also recorded less pestilential ends—among them such causes of death as fright, grief, and lethargy—they offered a valuable, albeit incomplete, record of overall mortality in London. It's not clear how or when Graunt first became interested in this record, but his business success had given him the toolbox—"shop arithmetic," he called it— needed to analyze the bills and answer simple questions of birth and death.[16]

One such question was the size of the population itself. Once, he wrote, he had trusted "men of great experience" who asserted London's population to be in the millions. He grew doubtful, and it occurred to him that he might do what these voices of authority had not and apply his "shop arithmetic" to the question. Before he began, though, he explained, he paused to consider the "example of David," the plague that followed that biblical king's numbering of the people. It was, he concluded, "misunderstood." Whether this reflected a

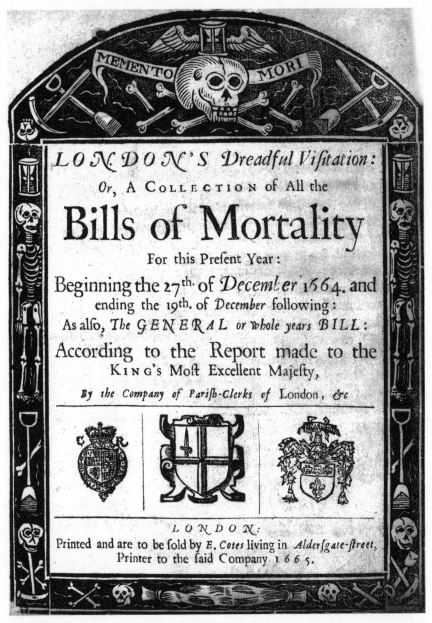

London's Bills of Mortality listed deaths and their causes for London from around 1600 until 1858. John Graunt used them to estimate the city's population, long before any census had been taken. (*London's Dreadful Visitation: or, a Collection of All the Bills of Mortality* [London: E. Cotes, 1665], frontispiece. Credit: Wellcome Library.)

genuine concern—quite possible, given plague was a constant presence in Graunt's source material—or was merely a reassurance to his readers is hard to tell. In any case, he then set out, logically and comprehensively, to determine what the Bills might imply for the city's population.[17]

Graunt's method was to triangulate different sources: estimates from the bills, reasoned assumptions, and more than a few wild guesses. His "shop arithmetic" was what we might today call back-of-the-envelope calculations. In one approach, for example, he guessed that one in ten adults die each year, and finding 10,000 adult deaths per year in the Bills, he surmised that London's adult population must be around 100,000. His final and preferred estimate was higher, 384,000, but reached by a very similar style of reasoning. This was well short of the sophistication of Kepler's orbital mechanics, but it was the first serious analysis of population data in English history.[18]

Observations was the pinnacle of Graunt's life, often now considered the first work of statistical demography. He was nominated to the Royal Society at the personal request of the king ("if they found any more such tradesmen, they should be sure to admit them all, without any more adoe"). But just a few years later, in 1666, tragedy struck, when Graunt's business was destroyed in the Great Fire of London. Petty came to the assistance of his old friend, but Graunt never recovered. His final years were weighed down by bankruptcy and religious persecution (he was a Catholic convert), and he died in 1674.[19]

Petty, ever the survivor, lived a further thirteen years. With his reputation established and financial independence guaranteed by his Irish landholdings, he continued to ponder the application of scientific methods to the art of government. Sometime around 1672 he coined the term "political arithmetic" to describe this, in an essay of the same name. Like Graunt, Petty was interested in questions of population, births and deaths. But some of Petty's writings had a narrower and decidedly self-serving aim: the stability of the Irish land settlement that he had helped create and that had earned him his fortune. His flagship

policy was "transplantation," the forced migration of population between Ireland and England through which, he supposed, the Irish
would become English by intermarriage. He didn't hide his bigotry. He
called for the "obliteration" of Irish place names. In a companion essay,
he wrote of "political anatomy," which he thought might be tested on
Ireland for the same reason that medical students "practice their inquiries upon cheap and common Animals." These schemes, amounting
to ethnic cleansing, were considered ambitious, though not necessarily
immoral, when Petty proposed them.[20]

Petty died in 1687. That same year saw the publication of Isaac
Newton's *Principia Mathematica,* containing the celebrated law of
gravitation. This single equation explained the planets' motions, bril-
liantly unifying Kepler's laws, and for that alone it would be justly famous. But the law of gravitation applied to not just the very large, but
also the small, and everything in between—even the proverbial apple
falling from the tree. It secured the role of applied mathematics in the
natural sciences forever, the strongest demonstration yet that nature
was amenable to numerical reasoning.

A year later, the civil and religious strife that had defined the lives of
Graunt and Petty was finally put aside. It was the beginning of a new
form of constitutional government, in which the monarch would be
constrained by laws made in Parliament. The English philosopher John
Locke supplied an intellectual framework for this moment in a simple
but startling idea. Governments, he reasoned, draw their legitimacy
not from heavenly mandate, the divine right that King David, Caesar
Augustus, and William the Conqueror would have claimed, but from
the consent of those governed. Locke's idea was soon swept into the
movement that would become known as the Enlightenment, eventually expanded into the notion of a "social contract," between ruler and
ruled.[21]

Meanwhile, in this more peaceful world, the practitioners of political arithmetic quietly shed Petty's overt political agenda. Ireland remained under occupation, the land settlement held, and Petty's most

radical ideas were not needed. What Petty's followers retained was his mode of reasoning. "Instead of using only comparative and superlative Words, and intellectual Arguments, I have taken the course," he had written, "to express my self in terms of Number, Weight, or Measure"— a biblical phrase—"to use only Arguments of Sense, and to consider only such Causes, as have visible Foundations in Nature." It was this incantation—number, weight, or measure—that became the basis of political arithmetic in the eighteenth century. Graunt's work, soon misattributed to the more famous Petty, was also incorporated and further neutralized political arithmetic's colonial beginnings.[22]

Yet despite this effective rebranding, the unsavory interventionist side of political arithmetic—statistics as surgery rather than science— was never quite eliminated. The idea that in numbering, weighing, or measuring a people, the state could gain the means of control over their very persons, was a powerful one. It came to sit, alongside the religious taboo, as a powerful argument against census taking.

•   •   •

The English method of political arithmetic soon crossed into Europe. In Sweden its practitioners found both demand for their services—a liberal constitutional monarch concerned about the country's sparse population—and a supply of source material, including a long-standing system of parish registers, which tracked births, deaths, and marriages, as well as people entering and leaving the parish. From this material, the mathematician Pehr Elvius fashioned a report on the population of Sweden, using methods similar to Graunt to make various findings about births and deaths and arrive at a total of 2.1 million. Elvius considered this a preliminary estimate and advocated for a more official system to update it.[23]

His wish was granted in 1748, when a law was passed for making annual records of the population. This burden fell to the clergy, who soon campaigned to have it reduced to a triennial process. Every three years they compiled parish records, which by progressive summarizations for ever-larger districts eventually reached a committee of scientists for a final account of the national total. In 1756 that committee became permanently instituted as the Table Commission—the first national statistical office.[24]

As well as containing the final summaries, the reports of the Table Commission included commentary on the data. They observed that many deaths seemed to be avoidable, urging the public provision of medicine and inoculation against smallpox. They noted a shortage of physicians and regretted that so many people lived as paupers. These early reports were offered as counsel to the government and were not published, treated instead as state secrets. But eventually that changed, and from 1762 the commission began producing a regular public report—a summary, at least, of its work.[25]

Things worked out differently in Britain, where the threatening potential of political arithmetic was evidently still a recent memory. The English government proposed a census in 1753. It reached Parliament by way of a bill for "taking and registering an annual Account of the total number of people." This would, its proponents claimed, "ascertain the collective strength of the nation," determining how many men might be called upon for military service. It would allow government administration "upon certain and known principles." It would encourage trade and industry. But not everyone agreed.[26]

In the system of English legislation, the bill had to be read and debated repeatedly before a final vote could be taken. On the first reading, it passed with only a single voice in opposition. For the majority, including the member Matthew Ridley, it seemed "a matter of very great indifference...a satisfaction to the curiosity of those gentlemen who love to deal in political arithmetic." But the single opposing voice, William Thornton, the forty-one-year-old member for York, was formidable. Thornton employed the full rhetorical force for which the English parliament is famous. He was "astonished and alarmed" that such a bill would be proposed, that would "molest and perplex every family in the kingdom," merely to determine "questions in political arithmetic." Thornton did not buy the arguments of scientific government: "Can it be pretended, that by the knowledge of our number, or our wealth, either can be increased?"[27]

And so just as the enduring rationales for a census had been laid out at the beginning of the third century by the philosopher Xu Gan, so now were the major objections enumerated by Thornton, establishing a template for opposition in centuries to come. He argued it would reveal numerical weakness to enemies abroad. He invoked popular fears of divine retribution: "when the Census is once taken, a Lustrum"—the Roman postcensus sacrifice—"will certainly follow." He managed to attach to the proposal that most offensive (to the English) of labels: that it was a French idea. And looking to that still-absolutist kingdom across the Channel, he proclaimed that it would lead to tyranny: "To what end then should our number be known, except we are to be pressed into the fleet and the army, or transplanted like felons to the plantations abroad?" These specific threats, echoing the schemes of William Petty, were not so far from reality as to be implausible to the average English person. In those years, the "press gang" forcibly recruited thousands of men each year to serve in Britain's growing navy, while transportation of convicts to the American colonies was routine.[28]

He concluded that the proposal was "totally subversive of the last remains of English liberty" and promised disobedience to the law if it passed. "If any officer, by whatever authority, should demand of me an account of the number and circumstances of my family, I would refuse it; and if he persisted in the affront I would order my servants to give him the discipline of the horse-pond." One can imagine cheers from the benches as Thornton invoked this proverbial public humiliation, which involved ducking the unfortunate victim in a body of water used for washing and watering horses. His appeal found converts, and what started as a solitary protest became two members against, then seventeen, then fifty-seven.[29]

Of his many arguments, it was the religious objection that roused the public's attention in this still-devout nation. By the third reading of the bill, a month later, Matthew Ridley had defected to Thornton's side. He reported—just a touch too self-defensively—that though *he* was not superstitious, "people every where look upon it in this light, which has... filled them with imaginary terrors." He worried, he said, that should the bill pass and then "be accidentally followed by any epidemical distemper, or by a public misfortune of any other kind, it may raise such a popular flame as will endanger the peace, if not the existence of our present government."[30]

Despite this growing opposition, the bill passed the House of Commons after this final reading. It died, instead, in the House of Lords, whose aristocratic members, though less sensitive to popular superstition, were more so to the threat of increased taxation that a census might carry with it. An enumeration would have to wait: for the remainder of the century, Graunt's shop arithmetic was the best English political arithmeticians would manage.

• • •

One man who well understood the limitations of shop arithmetic was Benjamin Franklin, self-described printer and son of a Boston soap and candle maker. In 1755 he published his own *Observations Concerning the Increase of Mankind*, which he had written four years earlier. In it, he argued that "tables... formed on observations made upon the Bills of Mortality... of populous cities, will not suit countries; nor will tables formed on observations made on full settled old Countries, as Europe, suit new Countries, as America." Extrapolation, in other words, should be excluded as a method of studying the population. Interesting though limited studies like Graunt's might be, what was true in one place might well not be true in another—especially in the unique circumstances of the New World. No general statements could be made that would apply in all places and at all times. The only route to sure knowledge was to survey the people of each place directly. Franklin was a strong proponent of collecting population data.

Indeed, by the middle of the eighteenth century, censuses were more abundant on his side of the Atlantic than the other. Most such counts were incomplete; Americans were not immune from the biblical fears of their European cousins. But there was enough data for Franklin to apply some shop arithmetic of his own. What he observed was stark. Having subdued the early native opposition, Europeans were settling comfortably, and fruitfully, into the new continent. Land was plentiful in America, so marriages occurred earlier and produced a greater number of children than in crowded Europe. Based on a loose argument (more shop arithmetic) Franklin reckoned that the population was doubling every twenty years and would, in the future, continue to do so every twenty-five. This led him to a remarkable prediction: that people of English descent in America "will in another Century be more than the People of England, and the greatest Number of Englishmen will be on this Side of the Water." The center of the English-speaking world was moving rapidly westward, across the Atlantic. Benjamin Franklin saw this earlier than most, but others soon joined him.[31]

As the balance of population between England and its American colonies shifted, the relationship became strained. Colonial settlement in North America had convincingly overcome its precarious start. By 1750, as Franklin observed, there were more than a million British subjects in America. In population, it was comparable with Scotland, which had united with England in 1707 to form Great Britain. But while Scotland had then gained representatives in Parliament—forty-five members in the House of Commons and sixteen peers in the House of Lords—the American colonies had none.[32]

Under the influence of mercantilist thinking, Britain continued to treat its colonies as profit centers, destinations for exports and sources of raw materials, rather than political entities worthy of a say in their own affairs. When colonial censuses were conducted, the results were delivered to the Board of Trade in London. Following the end of the French and Indian war in 1763, new taxes were instituted to recoup the British outlay in defending the colonies. When these were imposed on a variety of everyday goods—sugar, paper, glass, and most famously tea—dissent intensified. The voices against "taxation without representation" grew deafening.

By 1775, Americans had had enough. War broke out. A quarter century earlier, when Franklin made his predictions about population, he envisioned an America perhaps united, and more populous than Britain, but still firmly inside its empire. But now that future looked untenable. "There is something very absurd," wrote Thomas Paine in early 1776, "in supposing a continent to be perpetually governed by an island." The island's 8 million people still outnumbered the continent's 3 million (of which 2.5 million were British subjects). But the idea now arose that America might challenge that dominance. Six months later, the colonies claimed their independence, and in November 1777 the Second Continental Congress approved the Articles of Confederation, beginning the process of union. By 1781, with French help, the war was over. When peace was finally concluded two years later in Paris, Benjamin Franklin was a signatory, joining John Adams and John Jay in representing the new nation.[33]

The celebrations did not last long. The articles, drafted quickly amid war, proved inadequate to the task of managing a newly victorious but heavily indebted confederation. In 1787 a convention was called to revise the articles. This was not the first such attempt at revision, and several delegates who had arrived early gathered one evening in Franklin's dining room and made a momentous decision. They would start over. The convention would not merely revise the articles but construct a wholly new government based on a new constitution.[34]

The war with Britain had been triggered by the link, or lack thereof, between taxation and representation, so that link would be central in the new constitution. It would, moreover, be established in terms of population, on an unambiguously numerical basis. When the document was finished, article 1, section 2, clause 3 read:

> Representatives and direct Taxes shall be apportioned among the several States which may be included within this Union, according to their respective Numbers, which shall be determined by adding the whole Number of free Persons, including those bound to Service for a Term of Years, and excluding Indians not taxed, three fifths of all other Persons.

The constitution went on to describe how Congress should ascertain those Numbers:

> The actual Enumeration shall be made within three Years after the first Meeting of the Congress of the United States, and within every subsequent Term of ten Years, in such Manner as they shall by Law direct.

The decennial census was born.

• • •

The paragraph above is today known as the "census clause," yet the word *census* does not appear anywhere within it. The only occurrence of *census* in the constitution comes later, in section 9, clause 4, which limits the direct taxing power of the federal government. In the crucial passage that commands that everyone should be counted, the framers chose instead the biblically intoned "Numbers" and "Enumeration." That choice seems noteworthy.

In debating the new constitution, the delegates had taken inspiration from the classical world, from Aristotle's ideas about government and from the structure of the Roman Republic. They were, no doubt, familiar with the Jewish and Roman censuses. Many of them were educated in Latin and Greek, and Gibbons's *Decline and Fall of the Roman Empire* was one of the literary sensations of the decade. The framers embraced this classical inheritance—adopting terms like "Republic" and "Senate"—and the new country's census clearly owed something to the Roman tradition. So why not use the word?

It's not that the founders thought it inapplicable: it seems to have been their term of choice in the convention debates, appearing dozens of times in Madison's record; it also appears in later personal correspondence. They may have considered it obscure, since its usage up to this time was nearly always in specific reference to the Roman institution. But then the 1777 constitution of New York had used it freely. The 1776 Pennsylvania constitution had even created a Council of

Censors, further mimicking the Roman Republic. And the framers of the US constitution were, after all, happy to deploy "census" in section 9 of their document. Yet the first implementing act, passed in 1790, avoids the word once again.[35]

Perhaps the framers were actually trying to distinguish their enumeration from its Roman precursor: to make it as much a rejection as a reflection of the classical idea. For while the new nation would not be a pure democracy, neither would it be the inegalitarian layer-cake society constructed, at each lustrum, by toga-wearing censors. Gone was the Roman combination, carried into medieval times, of counting with judging: the "assessing" that gave the procedure its Latin name. In the United States of America, the equivalent institution would be a simple and pragmatic tally.

But if that was their intent, they failed, because the census clause did, in fact, delineate different classes of people—four in total.

First were free persons. These were the majority, numbering around three million.

The second group, to be counted with the free, were "those bound to service for a term of years," indentured laborers who had traded their service to an employer for a fixed term and who—unlike modern employees—were not free to break this arrangement. They constituted around 10 percent of the free population, though since this was usually a short-lived status, the proportion of people who had ever been indentured was higher. Benjamin Franklin himself had been apprenticed to—and later absconded from—his older brother.[36]

Third were "Indians not taxed," who were not to be counted at all. Since they were not, it is now hard to say how many such Indians lived within the borders of the United States of 1787. Modern estimates suggest there were fewer than a million Native Americans spread across the continent by then, so presumably at most a few hundred thousand east of the Mississippi, the western boundary of the new nation. Still, that would mean perhaps one Native American for every ten European Americans. In principle, the state laid no claim on them, arguing that Indian tribes were sovereign and not subject to the authority of the

United States—neither to its tax collectors nor to its enumerators. The norm that a census should count everyone present in a place, regardless of status, had not yet developed, so there was no contradiction in omitting them.[37]

It is the fourth group that is the most problematic: "all other persons," each to be counted as three-fifths of a free person. That anodyne phrase conceals another word that the framers avoided: slaves. The new republic was born with nearly 700,000 black slaves: men, women, and children who themselves, or whose recent ancestors, had been transported against their will from Africa to the Americas (some of a total 12.5 million who were brought this way). Within the United States, the majority of slaves lived in five Southern states: Maryland, Virginia, North Carolina, South Carolina, and Georgia. They comprised between a quarter and one-half of the people in those states.

Their status presented a conundrum for the framers. A census might serve to inform political representation, taxation, or both. In law slaves were not quite people, considered, as Madison wrote, "in some respects, as persons, and in other respects as property." How, then, to count them in a census? The question had arisen repeatedly since the Articles of Confederation were drawn up in 1777. Then, Franklin himself, a recent convert to the abolitionist cause, had offered one way to distinguish people from property: "sheep," he observed, "will never make any insurrections"—while slaves did, repeatedly.[38]

But on that occasion the issue was tabled, and instead each state was given exactly one vote, a coarse but practical kind of representation, given ongoing hostilities with the British. Taxation, meanwhile, was effectively left to the states, with each state's quota based on an assessment of land and buildings within its borders. In practice this didn't work: it was simply too hard to value property for taxation, and the contributions from states were effectively voluntary. In 1783, Congress debated moving to a tax based on population, raising, once again, the question of whether that should include slaves. With the focus on taxation, the Northern states favored counting everyone, free and enslaved, an approach that conveniently shifted the tax burden onto

Southern states. The Southern states, unsurprisingly, opposed this. A compromise was reached, but the amendment had still not been ratified by 1787, so the point was moot.[39]

Instead, when the convention revisited these questions, the delegates chose to address them jointly: the same basis would be used to apportion both representation and taxation. This changed the calculus of the jockeying states. Taxes, in general, were low compared with today, and direct taxes—the kind that might be apportioned based on population—were rarely used, ad hoc measures to cover extraordinary expenses such as war. The benefit of greater representation clearly outweighed the theoretical risk of greater tax liability, and the two sides now switched positions.

Northern delegates like Elbridge Gerry, representing Massachusetts, argued for omitting slaves entirely—giving them a weight of zero—while the Southern delegates, for example those from the Carolinas, argued for counting them one for one with free people. The number finally voted into the draft, three-fifths—that is, three free persons counting the same as five enslaved persons—was based on the ratio suggested by Madison and adopted, but never implemented, in 1783. It was almost entirely arbitrary: ratios of one to two, two to three, and three to four had also been considered. It was simply the end result of an argument in which one side started at zero, the other at one, and agreement inevitably lay somewhere in the middle.[40]

The resulting "three-fifths compromise" is now infamous: oft-cited and sometimes misunderstood. It was not a statement about the political or other rights of slaves (which were practically nonexistent), so much as a struggle between landed white men in the North and landed white men in the South. To the extent that black slaves were counted, it was as objects rather than political subjects in their own right. Nor did this counting rule have any particular symbolic significance to the framers. The reversal in positions between 1783 and 1787 shows that most delegates were willing to entertain any ratio, as long as it served their parochial interests.

It is unclear what slaves themselves and free black Americans made of the clause. In reality, it had little direct effect on either group. Slaves could not vote anywhere, while free black men were increasingly disenfranchised even as qualifications for white male participation were eliminated. In 1860, Frederick Douglass, himself a former slave, called the clause "a downright disability laid upon the slaveholding States," in a generous and perhaps over-optimistic assessment. He argued that "taking it at its worst, it still leans to freedom, not slavery," precisely because it would reward, with greater representation, any state that freed its slaves. But this is a view with seventy years of hindsight: in the 1787 debate about counting, considerations of emancipation barely featured, let alone black political power.[41]

On September 17, 1787, the constitution was read aloud for the first time. James Wilson offered a statement on behalf of his fellow Pennsylvanian Benjamin Franklin, the elder statesman of the convention, who was in poor health. "Mr. President, I confess that there are several parts of this constitution which I do not at present approve, but I am not sure I shall never approve them." He counseled compromise, "because I think a general government necessary for us. . . . I doubt, too, whether any other Convention we can obtain may be able to make a better Constitution. . . . Thus I consent, sir, to this Constitution, because I expect no better, and because I am not sure, that it is not the best."[42]

What was true for the whole was true for article 1, section 2, clause 3. Writing five months later in support of ratification, James Madison called the tying of both representation and taxation to population—and implicitly, the three-fifths compromise that it entailed—"the least objectionable among the practicable rules." Alexander Hamilton of New York and Gouverneur Morris of Pennsylvania—opponents of slavery—agreed. Lawyers, historians, and politicians have argued ever since over whether they were right.[43]

Unquestionably, the three-fifths rule was a betrayal of the "Enlightenment values" that the Declaration of Independence espoused and that the framers are sometimes supposed to have embodied. Of the many such betrayals, it was hardly the greatest. But it was a potent, explicit symbol: an obvious asterisk on "all men are created equal" that has still not been fully erased. It was a reminder that when the doctrine of number, weight, and measure was applied to human beings, nothing in the method itself guaranteed that the same measure be applied to each. It was what happened when ancient political phenomena—power, powerlessness, compromise—were rendered in an increasingly numerate society. Politics as arithmetic.

. . .

The arguments of Madison and his fellow federalists won the day, and the new constitution was ratified by the states, taking effect on March 4, 1789. The following year, a bill to conduct the enumeration was debated in Congress, its terms illustrating the variety of attitudes that still existed toward census taking. The constitution required only a minimal tally, with the status of enslavement or freedom as the sole essential attribute: a purely political instrument, albeit informed by Enlightenment ideas of representative government. Madison, taking the part of political arithmeticians, proposed a deeper inquiry, including age, sex, race, and occupation. The last was struck by the Senate, whose members considered it, in Madison's words, "a waste of trouble... materials for idle people to make a book," but age, sex, and race remained in some form. This concession, a little more than the bare minimum, offered something to those who, like Madison, wished to be acquainted with "the real situation of our constituents." The bill was finally authorized on March 1, 1790, the sixth act of the first Congress. Census day was set for August 2 of that year.[44]

Congress gave responsibility for organizing the count to the US marshals, lawmen appointed to support federal judicial districts (which then closely aligned with states). Since the federal government initially had little footprint outside the capital—then, New York—the marshals had quickly taken on various nonjudicial duties. Across the country, they appointed 650 assistants to do the actual enumeration, who would

The Return for SOUTH CAROLINA having been made fince the foregoing Schedule was originally printed, the whole Enumeration is here given complete, except for the N. Weftern Territory, of which no Return has yet been publifhed.

DISTICTS	Free white Males of 16 years and up-wards, including heads of families.	Free white Males under fixteen years.	Free white Fe-males, including heads of families.	All other free per-fons.	Slaves.	Total.
Vermont	22435	22328	40505	255	16	85539
N. Hampfhire	36086	34851	70160	630	158	141885 ·
Maine	24384	24748	46870	538	NONE	96540
Maffachufetts	95453	87289	190582	5463	NONE	378787
Rhode Ifland	16019	15799	32652	3407	948	68825
Connecticut	60523	54403	117448	2808	2764	237946
New York	83700	78122	152320	4654	21324	340120
New Jerfey	45251	41416	83287	2762	11423	184139
Pennfylvania	110788	106948	206363	6537	3737	434373
Delaware	11783	12143	22384	3899	8887	59094
Maryland	55915	51339	101395	8043	103036	319728
Virginia	110936	116135	215046	12866	292627	747610
Kentucky	15154	17057	28922	114	12430	73677
N. Carolina	69988	77506	140710	4975	100572	393751
S. Carolina	35576	37722	66880	1801	107094	249073
Georgia	13103	14044	25739	398	29264	82548
	807094	791850	1541263	59150	694280	3893635

Total number of Inhabitants of the United States exclufive of S. Weftern and N. Territory.	Free white Males of 21 years and up-wards.	Free Males under 21 years of age.	Free white Females.	All other Per-fons.	Slaves.	Total
S. W. territory	6271	10277	15365	361	3417	35691
N. Ditto	—	—	—	—	—	—

The United States constitution instituted enumeration as a means of distributing political power. George Washington and Thomas Jefferson thought that the results of first US census, shown here, understated the new nation's population. Jefferson made his own additions, handwritten in red ink, to copies he gave to others. (US Census Bureau.)

each on average have counted around 6,000 people, paid at a basic rate of $1 per 150 people counted (or $1 per 300 in urban areas). No special forms were provided, so the enumerators were free to collect the information as they wished. In the end, it took some eighteen months. Since there was no census office yet, the returns were delivered directly to the president's office. Not until October 1791 could President George Washington finally report the new country's population to Congress: 3,929,214.[45]

Benjamin Franklin, "the first American" and perhaps the first American demographer, was not among them. He had died on April 17, 1790, just months before the census. Franklin's daughter Sally inherited his Philadelphia house and continued living there with her family. She was recorded in the census, though not by name. Only heads of household were named, and the head of Sally's household was her husband, Richard Bache. Alongside Richard, the census listed two other free white males of sixteen years and upward, two free white males of under sixteen years, two free white females, one "other free person" (probably a black servant), and one slave. Women were not divided by age; nonwhites were not even divided by sex. From the household to the national level, this was the sum total of information reported.

Compared with later counts, it was a remarkably limited exercise. And yet the first census of the United States added several crucial innovations. It was integrated into the mechanism of representative government. It was mandated by law. It was periodic (the framers had debated five-, seven-, fifteen-, or even twenty-year periods, before eventually settling on ten). These were features that had not been seen since the Roman census fell into disuse nearly two thousand years earlier.

It also elevated accuracy and completeness in a way that no large census before it had done—not so much in its implementation, the sworn oath of enumerators to make "a just and perfect enumeration and description of all persons," but in its institutional structure. Like the 1703 count in Iceland, and notably unlike the census of Rome, it did not create or enforce personal obligations on the part of those counted. It was linked to taxation, of course: any federal direct taxes would be "apportioned among the several States...according to their respective numbers." But the link was indirect, via state population totals, rather than to individuals directly. This weakened the individual incentive to hide from or lie to the census takers.

Even more cleverly, the constitution had a check built in against the kind of official corruption that was said to have affected many earlier censuses of large polities—for example, ancient China. If local officials were tempted to downplay the population of any state to avoid taxes, then they would lose representation in equal proportion. The census count determined both. As Madison had argued: "By extending the rule to both objects, the States will have opposite interests, which will control and balance each other, and produce the requisite impartiality."[46]

Yet for all this, the first census of the United States was far from perfect. When the result was returned, many people, Washington and Jefferson among them, suspected an undercount. There is some evidence for this. Two of Benjamin Franklin's granddaughters, for example, seem to have been omitted from the household of Sally and Richard Franklin Bache—from the very home where the idea of a new constitution was born, in the heart of the nation's soon-to-be temporary capital. That said, comparison with subsequent censuses suggests that the 1790 count was fairly accurate overall. For the most part, unreasonable expectations, rather than errors of enumeration, were responsible for the perceived undercount. Accurate or not, the new nation had, finally, a number. It now remained simply for Congress to reapportion itself accordingly.[47]

But simple this was not. The inaugural House of Representatives had 65 members, apportioned according to numbers negotiated by the framers and specified in the constitution. The reapportionment rule stated that the "number of Representatives shall not exceed one for every thirty Thousand, but each State shall have at Least one Representative," without actually fixing a number. This meant anything from one member per state—15 members total—up to an absolute maximum of one member per 30,000 "people" (remembering that slaves counted as three-fifths)—120 total—might be allowed.

And while the principle of proportionality seemed clear, the framers had overlooked—or at least breezed past—the intricacies of integer arithmetic and the indivisible nature of human beings. Starting with any total size of the House—say 120, as Hamilton did—and applying strict proportionality would produce nonsense. New York, for instance, would be owed 11.004 members—perhaps a reasonable answer for a chemist weighing reactants but not for a political scientist numbering people. Even a country willing to entertain the possibility that one person should count as three-fifths of another could not actually send four one-thousandths of a representative to the Capitol. It had to make a choice: 11 or 12. A scientist or engineer confronted with this problem would simply round the number, taking fractions greater than one half up and those less than one half down. This is what Hamilton proposed.[48]

But in politics, unlike science, arithmetic is rarely guided by logic alone. Jefferson immediately objected to his rival's proposal to use what he called the "difficult and inobvious doctrine of fractions." The constitution, he argued, did not mention fractions, and so Congress too should ignore them. He then rather undermined his objection by proposing an alternative that can only be described as even more difficult and inobvious, involving rounding all the allocations down and seeing if they still added up to 120 (invariably, they would not); adjusting the divisor (30,000 in this example); and repeating the process as many times as necessary until they did. Jefferson's method did, however, have the rather obvious advantage of giving his home state of Virginia an extra seat.[49]

The argument went on for six months. A bill supported by Hamilton was passed in March 1792 but vetoed by Washington, in the first use of that power. A second bill, more in line with Jefferson's proposal, was finally passed on April 14, 1792, expanding the number of members to 105, 15 short of the allowed maximum. This new, arithmetic approach to allocating political power might be more fair, but it was also unexpectedly complex.[50]

• • •

From America, revolution spread to France, exploding onto the streets of Paris even as the US Congress was calmly debating the finer points of arithmetic rounding. The French Revolution went far beyond its American counterpart. For a brief moment, nothing seemed beyond challenge: tradition, religion, and monarchy alike. Freed of all constraints, the philosophers of the Enlightenment were at last able to put into practice a century's worth of new ideas, and little escaped their rationalizing, improving gaze. The calendar was redrawn. Clocks were built with a new system of decimal time, rejecting the awkward and superstitious reliance on multiples of twelve. A commission of esteemed scientists recommended a new measure of distance, the meter, and a new measure of weight, the kilogram. The Marquis de Condorcet, a member of the commission, called it a system "for all people, for all time."[51]

Condorcet had earned his early renown as a mathematician, but his interests always straddled mathematics and politics. He called the combination social mathematics and founded a scientific journal of the same name. As France's heir to the ideas of Petty and Graunt, he was instrumental in the founding of a Bureau of Political Arithmetic in the French treasury. In the heady atmosphere of that time, Condorcet favored revolutionary change. He advocated mass education, social insurance, equality of the sexes, and the abolition of slavery. Where Petty had thought to reason about society by number, weight, and measure, Condorcet aimed to reinvent it, beginning with those very concepts.[52]

But if the revolution was the culmination of the Enlightenment, it was also its death. By 1793, polite debate in the salon had been replaced by violent action in the public square. That fall, as the Reign of Terror got bloodily underway, Condorcet found himself a fugitive, ensconced in a cramped room above the streets of Paris. His aversion to violence, even as it became the currency of politics, was legendary: it is said that he joined the militia carrying only an umbrella. But his nonviolent stance condemned him when he refused to support the execution of King Louis XVI. An arrest warrant was issued in July 1793, and Condorcet was forced into hiding.[53]

From his top-floor window, if he dared stretch his neck out, he could have seen the nearby Jardin du Luxembourg, whose trees were beginning to change color and whose open spaces he could no longer risk visiting. A small plaque marks his brief stay at number 15 Rue Servandoni, known then as Rue de Fossoyeur—Gravedigger's Street. Many a night Condorcet must have imagined his own meeting with the gravedigger, by way of the guillotine's blade. Heads fell nearly as quickly as leaves that sanguinary autumn.[54]

For a man once lauded as a hero of the French Enlightenment it must have been miserable. But Condorcet's misery emerged, in literary form, as something else altogether. From his refuge, by candlelight, he set down in words an outrageously optimistic vision of human progress, an encapsulation of the spirit of improvement that had developed over the past century. Alas, Condorcet's own situation did not improve. In March 1794, a decree formally outlawed him. No longer safe in Paris, he fled to the nearby town of Bourg-la-Reine, where he was arrested, dying in mysterious circumstances just days later.

The following year, Condorcet's widow, Sophie, an accomplished intellectual in her own right, published the introduction to his book— all that was complete—giving it the title *Sketch for a Historical Picture of the Progress of the Human Mind.* It is essentially a work of history, much of which Condorcet had written before going into hiding. But as the revolution closed in on him, he added a sweeping final section describing the "future progress of mankind." The term *progress* has since accrued layers of significance, but for Condorcet its meaning was quite precise: "the destruction of inequality between different nations; the progress of equality in one and the same nation; and lastly, the real improvement of man."[55]

He saw science and technology as the forces that would drive this improvement: "Industry awakes; the arts already known, expand and improve." He went on to consider the consequences: that "as the means of living become less dangerous and less precarious, population increases; agriculture, which can provide for a greater number of individuals upon the same space of ground, supplies the place of the other sources of subsistence; it favours the multiplication of the species, by which it is favoured in its turn." Confined to a single room, Condorcet saw a future without limits. "The perfectibility of man," he concluded, "is indefinite."

• • •

Across the Channel in England, the Reverend Thomas Robert Malthus read those words, just a few years later, with exasperation. Condorcet's *Sketch*, he complained, was "a singular instance of the attachment of a man to principles, which every day's experience was so fatally for himself contradicting." Like other conservatives of the day, Malthus was deeply skeptical of the path the revolution had taken and philosophically opposed to Condorcet and British radicals of the same persuasion. But in the Frenchman's *Sketch*, he identified a more specific flaw: population.[56]

Malthus had studied mathematics at the University of Cambridge. He grew to favor social applications, avoiding a fate as a pure theorist (in his father's derisory description, a "mere speculative algebraist"). So it was natural for him to express his objection to Condorcet's forecast in the abstract language usually reserved for physical, mechanical phenomena. He did so in his *Essay on the Principle of Population*, which was first published in 1798.[57]

In an ideal, unconstrained state, he argued, population would grow "geometrically," doubling in any fixed period. Such was assured, he wrote, by "the passion between the sexes." The natural period of doubling Malthus claimed, twenty-five years, was the same one once predicted by Benjamin Franklin, based on evidence from North America.

Then, the complication: new mouths required more food, and while America's unmapped expanse had proved equal to the task so far, no country's food supply could forever match the growth in population. Malthus argued that agricultural output grew at most "linearly," adding a fixed amount each time period. He provided little direct evidence for this claim, considering it self-evident.

According to these rules, if there was just enough food for the population in 1800, then a century hence population would be sixteen times as large, having doubled four times, while the food supply would be only five times as large, having grown each period by addition, not multiplication. "The power of population," Malthus wrote, "is indefinitely greater than the power in the earth to produce sustenance for man." Population would be checked by misery—famine, plague, war; by vice—prostitution; or by "something else unnatural," a veiled reference to birth control. This, he believed, was an insurmountable mathematical certainty. Condorcet's ideal state was impossible. "Man cannot live in the midst of plenty," Malthus declared with finality.[58]

Humankind perhaps could not, but Malthus himself surely did. He lived comfortably as curate—priest-in-training—of Okewood Chapel in Surrey, twenty miles to the southwest of central London. The chapel itself, a modest building, is hidden down a long, narrow lane lined with blackberry bushes and bracken. When I visited, only the occasional aircraft passing overhead interrupted the chirping of birds and buzzing of insects. I was not long escaped from London's rush hour, and my strongest impression was not of misery or vice, of people or populousness, but of nature, peace, and solitude.

Noting this, scholars have long speculated about the origin of Malthus's ideas. Okewood and its pleasant surrounds seem a direct rebuke to his dismal forecast: it's hard to imagine life there was ever less than idyllic. But a biographer of Malthus describes "the hard grind of subsistence farming" that faced most of the clergyman's parishioners in late eighteenth-century Surrey. One traditional theory has it that Malthus's views on population came directly from his role as curate, performing more baptisms than funerals, but a leaflet left in the chapel, presumably as a courtesy to infrequent tourists, dismisses this. Such explanations seem unnecessary anyway: Malthus's thesis was grounded less in personal experience than in the logic of numbers—what applied mathematicians today might call his model. Malthus no more needed to experience the grim life his calculations foretold than Isaac Newton had needed to visit Jupiter in order to predict its orbit, a century earlier.[59]

But abstract mathematical reasoning, applied to society, was still in its infancy. Not every reader would be convinced, so Malthus filled his

Essay with secondhand demographic observations of a world that, for Europeans, had recently grown much larger. He wrote of Pennsylvania and New England, China and Indostan (by which he probably meant the entire Indian subcontinent). Naples, he observed, was "very populous, notwithstanding the repeated eruptions" of Vesuvius. Of Lima and Quito, Spanish capitals in the New World, he wrote "no settlements could well have been worse managed."[60]

This breadth of examples served a specific purpose. Malthus wanted his readers to understand that the principle of population was universal, like Newton's law of gravity, dooming Egypt as thoroughly as England. That Malthus does not mention Iceland can only mean he did not know of its circumstances. If he had, he would have seen its desperation and its stagnant population as the natural and unalterable order of things. *Count them if you like,* he might have advised the Danish king Frederick IV, a century earlier, *but there's nothing you can do to help them.* The world predicted by Condorcet's *Sketch* would never arrive. Not in France, or Britain, or America. Not anywhere. Social improvement was not possible. The most that could be expected was misery and vice.

• • •

The contrasting lives and ideas of Condorcet and Malthus form a neat tale of two philosophers: the Frenchman an eternal optimist, even as the Damoclean blade hangs over him, and the Englishman an implacable pessimist, living in the midst of Arcadia. But their political and dispositional differences were less important, less influential, in the long run, than what they shared: a profound belief that society could be understood, that it could be reasoned about and even—at least for Condorcet—improved by the application of numerical reasoning.

To the frustration of those wishing to engage, in such terms, with Malthus's argument, Europe was still almost bare of social and demographic numbers. Even as the United States committed itself to a complete decennial census, enumerations of any kind remained rare in Europe. Sweden was the clear exception: it had continued its census taking every three years until 1775 and then every five years thereafter (although some of the earlier abstracts had been lost). Denmark-Norway had conducted counts in 1769 and 1787. Spain too made a rough one-off count in 1787, as did the French-dominated Netherlands in 1795. But no other country had followed Sweden's lead in adopting a regular census in eighteenth-century Europe.[61]

In particular, there had been no comprehensive, nationwide census of either France or England, the two great powers as the century came to a close. When it was published in 1798, Malthus's *Essay* joined raging and often speculative debate about the size and change in the British population. Nobody knew what it was or whether it was rising or falling. Across the British Isles, the landscape of demographic data was much the same mess that had confronted Graunt and Petty more than a century earlier.[62]

The time was ripe for this, at last, to change. A degree of skepticism had already crept into religious thinking, a challenge to superstition. Britain had watched the enumeration of its recently escaped American satellite with interest. Several million people—people until quite recently British subjects—had been numbered, and no plague or other biblical calamity had followed. To the contrary, the United States of the 1790s seemed to be flourishing, its population growing by more than 30 percent over the decade. Perhaps John Graunt had been right, and the example of David had been misunderstood.[63]

Meanwhile, there was less to fear from earthly authorities. Political arithmetic had been cleansed of Petty's radically coercive agenda. Memories of the failed 1753 census proposal had faded, and with them William Thornton's evocation of tyranny and disaster. There was a growing belief that political arithmetic might even disperse political power, a role it seemed to play in the United States, albeit with serious caveats. A census might be a way to mediate the social contract that was now thought to underpin legitimate government: an enumeration not of subjects but of citizens.[64]

Moreover—and more immediately—ignorance of population now seemed imprudent. If Britain was on a path to Malthusian catastrophe, with population outpacing production, then surely the people and their leaders should know of it. And if, to the contrary, earlier claims of decline were true, that too seemed worthy of confirmation, lest the country suddenly find itself unable to field an army. An increasingly belligerent Napoleon Bonaparte had seized power as first consul of France, and the English Channel felt suddenly narrower. The remote prospect of tyrannical rule by an English government was subsumed by the real threat of the same by a French one.[65]

A young magazine writer named John Rickman seized on this heightened atmosphere to publish an essay, written four years earlier, calling for a "General Enumeration." Rickman painted the undertaking as a grand national project, in continuity with the enumerations of Augustus and William the Conqueror. He ended on a patriotic note, confident that a count would show that "the industry and value of our countrymen, is double that of our rivals, the French." In the space of fifty years, the census had gone from being a suspiciously French-sounding import, which might reveal weakness, to a means of showing strength against France.[66]

Rickman's essay was read by a member of Parliament, Charles Abbot, who took the idea to his colleagues. "It has long been a matter of surprise and astonishment," he said, perhaps exaggerating just how long, "that a great, powerful and enlightened nation like this should have remained hitherto unacquainted with the state of its population." The new bill he introduced "for taking an Account of the Population of Great Britain, and of the Increase or Diminution thereof" passed quickly, with no opposition. Like the corresponding clause in the American constitution, the word "census" did not appear anywhere within it.[67]

Unlike in the United States, where marshals had had to quickly recruit a census workforce, the British census took advantage of a more established network of local public officials. In England and Wales, forms and directions were distributed, via justices of the peace, to the "Overseers of the Poor." These were officials appointed to each Church of England parish to administer the Poor Laws, an early system of social support dating back to 1601. In Scotland, which had its own system of Poor Laws, schoolmasters acted as enumerators. In some remote places, the duties were filled by a "substantial householder."[68]

The official returns did not list households, as in the United States, but only totals for each "parish, township or place." The instructions to overseers did not specify any particular methodology for gathering these totals. Some clearly took the task seriously, with some dozens of individual or household listings having been discovered in local archives. Others, presumably, were less diligent.

Details reported included the number of houses, families, males, females, and the total population. No age information was collected, so the census could not really serve as a measure of military potential, as Rickman had proposed. A broad classification of occupations was, however, applied, with overseers required to report the number of people involved in trade and manufacture, in agriculture, and in other work. They also reported the number of baptisms and burials at ten-year intervals since 1700, in order to estimate the change in population, and the number of marriages annually since 1754. Rickman himself was appointed to "digest, and reduce into order" the returns.[69]

In his speech introducing the bill, Abbot had complained that extant estimates of the English population ranged anywhere from 8 to 11 million, with the latter number, he thought, the result of "a more correct train of reasoning"—a view also held by Rickman. In the event, the count that came in was, like in the United States, at the low end of expectations: 8.3 million for England, with a further 2.1 million between Wales and Scotland. Making an allowance for Ireland, which was not enumerated, Rickman estimated that the population of the British Isles had, over the preceding century, increased from 8.1 million to 15.1 million.[70]

• • •

The year 1801 turned out to be a banner one for census taking. France, under Napoleon, finally conducted its first real census, after a decade of revolutionary dithering. Its results were questioned (perhaps unfairly), and another was taken in 1804, though that count's results were never published. Denmark-Norway also took a census in 1801. It followed largely the form of the 1703 census of Iceland but covered nearly the whole kingdom. The official order noted that "the population number in a country when it is known quite accurately is used in several ways for statistical, political and economic calculation."[71]

That census, covering an entire sovereign state and—unlike the British or American censuses—recording everyone by name, has a good claim to the first modern census. But then so too does Iceland's 1703 count, which had many of the same features. In counting everyone by name in a defined geography, in not taxing or conscripting them as it did so, and in privileging accuracy, it certainly prefigures many technical changes that would otherwise only emerge a century later elsewhere. But since it was initiated at the command of a distant monarch, it might better be placed in the line of mercantilist, colonial censuses that both preceded and succeeded it, rather than the more democratic, public enumerations that later emerged. And if we are to allow that, then New France's census of 1666 may also be a contender, albeit in the flyweight division.

But although they were relative latecomers, America's 1790 and Britain's 1801 censuses were more influential than any of the above. In the eighteenth century, only Sweden had conducted a regular, repeating census. Now, at the beginning of the nineteenth century, it was joined by Britain, the dominant world power, and the United States. While the latter country would eventually succeed Britain, its influence in the world of census taking was felt long before that. In 1847, Alexandre Moreau de Jonnès, director of the French bureau of statistics, wrote that "The United States presents in its history a phenomenon without parallel: that of a people who instituted the statistics of their country, the very day they founded their society, and who regulated, in the same act, the census of their fellow citizens, their civil and political rights and future destiny of the country." America was a counterargument, too, to William Thornton's concerns: it demonstrated that there was no inherent contradiction between regular census taking and liberty.[72]

Together Britain and the United States brought new momentum to the census undertaking, setting in motion a tradition in each country that continues, repeating every decade, to this day. In the

United States this had always been the intent: the second American census was already underway even as Britain's parliament voted to hold its own. But it was not obvious that the British census would be repeated consistently in the decades to come. And yet when 1810 came around, a new bill was debated and passed to undertake an 1811 census of Britain. And again, for an 1821 census, and nearly every decade since. The United States has now conducted a population census every ten years since 1790—twenty-three in total—while the United Kingdom has missed only one since 1801, during the darkest days of the Second World War.

These patterns were soon adopted by other countries. As constitutional government grew in popularity, nations looked to the American document, often adopting the decennial census requirement (for example, Argentina in 1853, Canada in 1867). Today, the constitutions of fifty-four countries mention a census. The standard recommended by the United Nations is to hold a census every ten years, in years ending in zero. Most countries follow this "American standard." Meanwhile, coordination among Britain's nineteenth-century colonies led them to take censuses in years ending in one, and many of their successor states—including India, Australia, Canada, and South Africa—still do (for five-yearly countries, years ending in six also).[73]

Regularity in census taking, and the flood of data that resulted, began to change the way people looked at population and societies. Thomas Malthus, whose work had motivated the first British census, was now influenced by it in turn. He released five further editions of his essay, each updated to reflect new data. This revealed a mixed picture for his theory. England saw no more famine: agricultural output grew faster than Malthus had predicted. Iceland's population finally began to grow again, doubling over the century. But Ireland, still a subordinate member of the United Kingdom, suffered greatly, with a million people dying in the Great Famine from 1845 to 1849.

These various fates made clear that the principle of population, if there was one, was more complex than Malthus had initially supposed. In some places it seemed to hold, while in others something had changed, allowing societies to escape the Malthusian trap. As the economist Paul Krugman has written, "Malthus was right about *the whole of human history up until his own era*" (emphasis in original). If this is a defense of Malthus, it is also an admission that human populations are not systems of interacting masses, subject to Newtonian laws that apply in all places and at all times. Malthus himself increasingly recognized this complexity: by the *Essay's* second edition, in 1803, he introduced a third check he called "moral restraint"—late marriage or abstinence—that was neither miserable nor immoral and might after all admit the possibility of improvement.[74]

It is the barnstorming first edition, though, with its confident pessimism, its judgment, and its appearance of mathematical authority, that is remembered today. If Graunt's *Observations* had begun the study of population, then it was Malthus's 1798 *Essay* that made it a field unto itself, a topic large enough to warrant a whole book. His ideas also informed economics and ecology. His vision of a world always on the precipice of disaster, of individuals inevitably dragged toward death by famine or war, directly inspired Charles Darwin's theory of natural selection. Malthus's own death came suddenly but peacefully in 1834. According to his epitaph in Bath Abbey, he had lived a "serene and happy life."

Political arithmetic itself was changed by the flood of new data. No longer the domain of singular, inspired essays, it increasingly became an everyday mode of reasoning. Even before Britain's census, the field had been splintering into new disciplines. The publication of Adam Smith's *The Wealth of Nations* in 1776 saw political economy established as a separate subfield—albeit one suspicious, like Smith himself, of political arithmetic's empirical tendency. The word "statistics," borrowed from German, outgrew its qualitative origins and came, by the 1820s, to describe the empirical side of political arithmetic, the collection of numerical facts about the state. In 1834, the year Malthus died, "demography" entered the English lexicon, carving off the part of political arithmetic that focused specifically on population. By the end of that decade, a new term, "social science," began to gain ground, eventually coming to reunite all these emerging, overlapping subfields under one umbrella. As usual, Condorcet had been in the vanguard, using the term four decades earlier in his *Sketch*.[75]

The vanguard is a dangerous place to be. After Condorcet's death in prison, he was the subject of a crude and hurried cover-up. He was buried a commoner in the town's cemetery, his death hidden for another seven months and his grave lost to posterity. The French Revolution had devoured its children, and the Enlightenment itself seemed to flicker out. The whole notion of rational improvement, beloved by Condorcet and his fellow *philosophes,* was rejected by a new counter-Enlightenment movement. So too was the mechanistic worldview of Malthus, with its geometric and arithmetic growth rates.

Despite this turn, the empirical and mathematical mode of reasoning about society, the thread that linked Graunt and Petty, Franklin, Condorcet, and Malthus, was never really threatened. The census too was secure. In the United States it was once again linked to the very structure of government, as it had been in the Roman Republic, with a decennial enumeration written into the very heart of the new US Constitution—but on new, more democratic (though still imperfect) terms.

Even in countries where this was not the case, an accurate census was accepted as an invaluable tool of administration. With access to more data, political arithmetic, the art of government by numbers, was growing more powerful. Meanwhile, increasingly centralized states had more need for such methods than had earlier, more devolved feudal societies. Census taking took root in Britain and France and, as the nineteenth century unfolded, many other European countries besides. There were still many developments ahead, particularly in methodology and technology, but the essential role of the census in the modern world was now established.

CHAPTER 3

A PUNCH PHOTOGRAPH

IN THE FALL of 1889, a contest was taking place that pitted human against machine. It was split between Washington, DC, and Boston, happened behind closed doors, and received little attention at the time. Its purpose was to save the US census from its own success, and while it did that, it also changed the world.

Over the century since the first US census, the procedure had become routine. It had become more scientific and, increasingly, comparable with the enumerations of other countries. It attracted greater interest from an increasingly numerate public, curious about the quantifiable aspects of the nation. More and more questions had been included, and the process of summarizing all the answers—an activity known as tabulation, performed by row upon row of clerks working mostly by hand—was taking longer, and costing more, than ever before. With the 1880 count, a breaking point had been reached: the American census ran out of time and money. Some new method of tabulation, faster and therefore cheaper, had to be identified.

The 1889 contest was an attempt to do that, with three teams competing. Two were made up of human contestants, hard at work in Boston. The third team, far more consequential, combined human and machine, and was based in Washington, in a room of the Atlantic Building. This prestigious new commercial development—one of the first in the city to feature

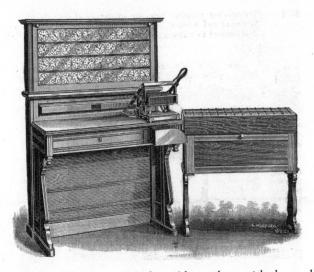

The Hollerith Electric Tabulating Machine (shown here with the card press and sorting box) was invented to address the difficulties the US census office had faced in processing the 1880 returns. (T. C. Martin, "Counting a Nation by Electricity," *Electrical Engineer* 12, no. 184 [November 11, 1891]: 525. Credit: New York Public Library.)

1	2	3	4	CM	UM	Jp	Ch	Oc	In	20	50	80	Dv	Un	3	4	3	4	A	E	L	a	g
5	6	7	8	CL	UL	O	Mu	Qd	Mo	25	55	85	Wd	CY	1	2	1	2	B	F	M	b	h
1	2	3	4	CS	US	Mb	B	M	O	30	60	O	2	Mr	O	15	O	15	C	G	N	c	i
5	6	7	8	No	Hd	Wf	W	F	5	35	65	1	3	Sg	5	10	5	10	D	H	O	d	k
1	2	3	4	Fh	Ff	Fm	7	1	10	40	70	90	4	O	1	3	O	2	St	I	P	e	l
5	6	7	8	Hh	Hf	Hm	8	2	15	45	75	95	100	Un	2	4	1	3	4	K	Un	f	m
1	2	3	4	X	Un	Ft	9	3	i	c	X	R	L	E	A	6	O	US	Ir	Sc	US	Ir	Sc
5	6	7	8	Ot	En	Mt	10	4	k	d	Y	S	M	F	B	10	1	Gr	En	Wa	Gr	En	Wa
1	2	3	4	W	R	OK	11	5	l	e	Z	T	N	G	C	15	2	Sw	FC	EC	Sw	FC	EC
5	6	7	8	7	4	1	12	6	m	f	NG	U	O	H	D	Un	3	Nw	Bo	Hu	Nw	Bo	Hu
1	2	3	4	8	5	2	Oc	O	n	g	a	V	P	I	Al	Na	4	Dk	Fr	It	Dk	Fr	It
5	6	7	8	9	6	3	O	p	o	h	b	W	Q	K	Un	Pa	5	Ru	Ot	Un	Ru	Ot	Un

Each 6⅝-inch-by-3¼-inch card used in the 1890 US census represented one person. The boxed areas correspond to questions; answers were marked by holes punched in the card. For example, the third field from the left at the top indicates race: Jp, Japanese; Ch, Chinese; Oc, Octaroon; In, Indian; Mu, Mulatto; Qd, Quadroon; B, Black; and W, White. (L. E. Truesdell, *The Development of Punch Card Tabulation in the Bureau of the Census, 1890–1940* [Washington: Government Printing Office, 1965], 47.)

a passenger elevator—backed onto Ford's theatre, where Abraham Lincoln had been shot. Directly to the northeast lay a block that Washington's master planner, Pierre L'Enfant, had intended as a place to inter the good and the great of the new nation. Fittingly, for a country of inventors, this Pantheon became, instead, the Patent Office.[1]

The Atlantic Building room, number 48, was rented to Herman Hollerith, an engineer originally from New York. Inside, he had assembled a strange-looking invention. It was about the size of a writing desk, with a tall cabinet stacked at its rear, giving it the overall shape of an upright piano. Its polished oak would not have looked out of place in a nineteenth-century parlor, but Hollerith's device was more steampunk than salon. The cabinet displayed forty dials arrayed in four rows and ten columns. Each dial had one hundred subdivisions and two hands, like a clock, which together could count up to ten thousand.[2]

The machine was not fully automatic. Seated in front was a clerk, trained by Hollerith in the machine's operation. At the clerk's right, on the desk's surface, lay a sturdy contraption with a smooth wooden handle, which Hollerith called the press. At the left was a stack of stiff cards, each one 6⅝ inches by 3¼ inches with round holes punched out seemingly scattershot. In fact, the holes were arranged in a precise grid, and the presence or absence of each was carefully determined. Each card represented one person, and the grid positions represented different characteristics of that person: black or white; male or female; single or married; "maimed," "crippled," "bedridden," "idiotic," "insane."[3]

The operator placed each card, in turn, on the lower surface of the press and then pulled firmly down on the handle. As the jaws of the press came together, spring-loaded pins pushed down against the card. Some were blocked, while others passed through holes, making contact with cups of mercury below, closing electric circuits and advancing dials corresponding to the holes. If a second device, the sorting box, was connected, then one of twenty-six lidded compartments would spring open, indicating where the processed card should be placed.

For Frederick H. Wines, a census employee who later saw the machine in operation, this process of counting and sorting people by electricity approached a religious experience. "Under the mysterious influence of the electric current running through the machine, they organise themselves, as though possessed of volition.... I can compare this current to nothing less intelligent and powerful than the voice of the archangel, which, it is said, will call the dead to life and summon every human soul to face his final doom."[4]

. . .

When the contest's judges came to observe Hollerith's machine in action, sometime in October, it was not heavenly judgment that concerned them but a much more prosaic source of doom. By the late nineteenth century, the census was in trouble. Part of the challenge, of course, was the sheer number of people to be counted, more than ten times as many as in 1790. By itself, that problem could have been managed by hiring more staff. The bigger problem was there were too many questions.[5]

For the first few decades after 1790, the US census had stayed true to its narrow origins, recording the numbers necessary for reapportionment, with only very basic demographics. Political arithmeticians might have preferred more detail, but the simple needs of the state took precedence. As political arithmetic was subsumed within statistics, however, its influence grew. The 1830s saw a rash of new statistical societies, including the Statistical Society of London (founded in 1834) and the American Statistical Association (founded in 1839). There was a corresponding trend among European countries to establish permanent statistical offices to conduct the census and other inquiries: for example, Prussia in 1805, the Netherlands in 1826, and France in 1833.[6]

In the United States the census office remained an ephemeral thing, reconstituted every decade for each count. But the influence of statisticians was still keenly felt. Joined by other stakeholders of the now-established decennial enumeration—businessmen, publishers of almanacs, social reformers—they demanded that it be expanded to consider ever more areas of life. Beginning in 1840, these ancillary topics proliferated. How many persons were engaged in industry? How many had disabilities? How many were illiterate? The census was increasingly being used to monitor the health—both physical and social—of the population, rather than just its size. It had grown to be a once-a-decade review of all aspects of the nation.[7]

This expansion of topics invited a new type of analysis—cross-tabulation—that focused on not just individual variables but the relationships between them. This could paint a much richer picture of society. For example, a simple count could say how many blind people lived in a city or how many children lived in that city. But neither of these figures could tell a mayor whether the city should build a school for the blind. To answer that, one would need to "cross-tabulate" blindness with age, calculating the number of blind children—that is, people who are both blind *and* children.

Such questions were difficult to answer from the early censuses because of the way the schedules were constructed. Each page was divided into rows, one for each household the enumerator visited. Reaching a household, he would record the name of the head of the household at the left and then work along the row, writing a number in each column to record the number of people living there who met the criteria described in that column's heading. A column might be simple—"total," which would count all the persons living in the household—or it might be some complex combination of attributes. Each person could be counted in multiple columns. An enumerator might record that a household contained one free white male age twenty to thirty, one free white male age five to ten, and one blind white person. But once the information was summarized like this, there was no way of knowing whether it was the child who was blind or the adult.[8]

If the designers knew in advance which particular cross-tabulations were important, they could expand the schedule accordingly. The "deaf and dumb" column in 1840, for example, was further subdivided into three age groups, allowing the enumerator to distinguish between a deaf person under fourteen and a deaf person over fourteen. But this only went so far. If, after the enumeration was complete, somebody wanted to analyze the data differently—to examine, say, deafness by sex

Left page of schedule

Right page of schedule

Up to 1840, only the head of household was named on the US census schedule. The line excerpted here shows the 1840 household of Frederick Douglass, comprising three people: himself (twenty-three or twenty-four years old), his wife, Anna (twenty-five years old), and his daughter, Rosetta (nine months old). The numbers directly below the column headings are subtotals carried over from the previous page. Each double-page spread was thirty-seven inches wide by sixteen inches high. (National Archives and Records Administration.)

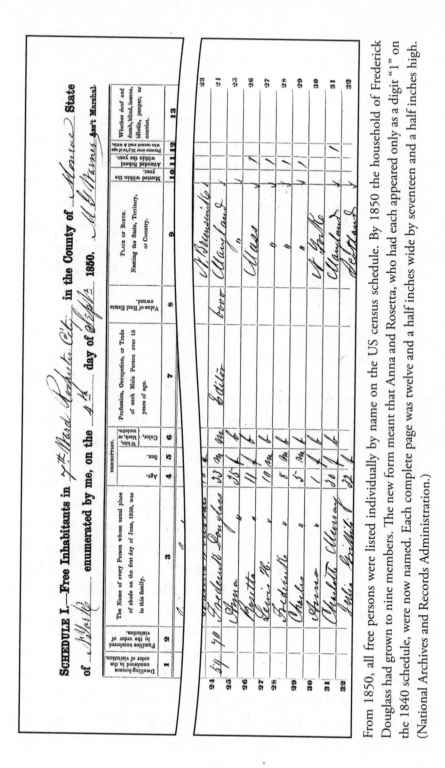

From 1850, all free persons were listed individually by name on the US census schedule. By 1850 the household of Frederick Douglass had grown to nine members. The new form meant that Anna and Rosetta, who had each appeared only as a digit "1" on the 1840 schedule, were now named. Each complete page was twelve and a half inches wide by seventeen and a half inches high. (National Archives and Records Administration.)

instead of by age—it was not possible. The schedule itself dictated the limits of analysis, and the only way to add more cross-tabulations was to add more columns.

The outcome was that by 1840, the schedule contained nearly eighty columns, making the enumerator's task difficult and error prone. This had serious consequences. In 1842, a curiosity was found in the recently released census results. The proportion of the black population recorded as "insane and idiots" was ten times higher in the North than in the South—with no similar pattern in the white population. Here was proof, claimed advocates of slavery, that black people were better off in Southern bondage than in the freedom they enjoyed further north. In fact, it was proof of nothing but poor questionnaire design and sloppy enumeration. More careful investigation quickly surfaced obvious errors, including 133 black people recorded living in an all-white lunatic asylum in Massachusetts. But the damage was already done.[9]

Clearly, a solution had to be found for this proliferation of columns. To find it, census officials could look to Denmark, France, and Great Britain, all of which had already adopted a better system. Those countries treated each individual person, rather than each household, as the unit of record in each row, a so-called nominative rather than numerical census. Structured like this, each column could refer to a single attribute, rather than some combination. This design greatly simplified the enumerator's job. Instead of having to locate a particular relevant column heading among many, he could simply record each person's exact age in a column marked "age," note their sex in a column marked "sex," and so on. The 1850 census schedule, the first in the United States to adopt the nominative approach, had only thirteen columns, one-sixth as many as 1840.[10]

As well as being easier for the enumerators and more accurate, nominative enumeration had another side effect. In the numerical census of 1840, precious column space was saved by collecting less detail on nonwhites—only six age categories for free colored people, for example, instead of thirteen for white people. But the row-oriented nominative census used from 1850 onward imposed a limited kind of equality:

the same columns applied to each free person, regardless of what might be written under "color." At the same time, it persisted an old inequality: on the separate slave schedule, the name recorded against each person was not their own but that of their owner. Each owner's slaves were identified only by number, from one upward.[11]

Nominative enumeration did not come without a cost. Since the enumerators now started a new row for each person rather than each household, they recorded many more rows than in 1840. In effect, some of the processing workload was deferred, shifted from enumerators in the field to clerks in Washington. The simpler schedule structure also freed Congress to add even more detailed questions. By 1880, the census was asking twenty-two questions per person, rather than roughly eight topics covered in 1840. An average household would now generate over a hundred data points, up from just five in 1790. In combination with population growth, this meant the total number of individual data items flowing into the census operation grew four-hundred-fold, from around three million in 1790 to over one billion in 1880.[12]

It's no wonder that analysis of the 1880 census had taken nearly the whole succeeding decade. Congress had provided supplemental funding in 1881, 1882, and 1884, but ever more reluctantly. The final two appropriations were accompanied by demands that further tabulation should cease, and eventually it did, with the last volume published in 1888 and the planned program of analysis unfinished. Statisticians could forget about the exciting potential of cross-tabulation: some variables, like conjugal condition, were never tallied at all, let alone in combination with others. "Today we do not know what proportion of the population is married or single!" lamented one journalist after the work was terminated.[13]

Yet Congress was quick to forget, and despite the problems with the 1880 tally, it demanded a still-more-elaborate population census in 1890. There was to be a new question on Civil War service history and a baroque new racial categorization: "white, black, mulatto, quadroon, octoroon, Chinese, Japanese, or Indian." The questions were to be asked of a population that had grown by a quarter over the decade. Without some breakthrough in tabulation technology, a repeat of the 1880 fiasco was certain.[14]

The man officially charged with identifying such a breakthrough was John Shaw Billings. A surgeon and Civil War veteran, he ran the census's Division of Vital Statistics, overseeing the quantification of birth and death that had once occupied John Graunt. He had been appointed chair of the commission tasked with finding and testing new methods of tabulation for the 1890 census.

Billings had long been interested in improved methods of tabulation. He was a supporter and mentor of Hollerith, so the latter man's machine probably went into the contest a favorite. But there's no indication that the competition was rigged in Hollerith's favor or taken less than completely seriously. Machines, especially new machines, could fail in any number of ways, and Hollerith had yet to prove that his would not. Moreover, his fellow contestants, Charles Pidgin and William C. Hunt, were also insiders. Pidgin and Hunt had worked together on the widely admired 1885 state census of Massachusetts and had already been drafted to work on the 1890 federal census—Hunt as head of the all-important Population Division. Indeed, Hunt had originally been part of Billings's commission, stepping down so that he could enter his own method in the contest. The two Bostonians proposed similar manual systems of tabulation: Pidgin's, based on the 1885 state census, used specially designed cards of various colors, which he called "chips," while Hunt's used slips of paper in combination with different colored inks.[15]

All three systems shared the common idea of representing a single person on each physical card, chip, or slip. As such, tabulation by any of these methods occurred in two distinct phases. First, entries from the handwritten schedules were transcribed into the intermediate form. Then these intermediate objects were counted one by one, paying attention to the characteristics recorded. During a real census, transcription would happen only once, but counting would be repeated over and over again for all the different subgroups on which the census reported: once for men, once for women, once for those native-born, once for those foreign-born, and so on.[16]

The rules of the competition were simple. A selection of returns from the 1880 census—representing citizens of St. Louis, then the country's sixth-largest city—had been dug out of storage. Each man should use his method to transcribe and then count these returns. Whichever technique performed fastest, without sacrificing accuracy, would be judged the winner and receive the recommendation of the commission for use in the upcoming 1890 census.[17]

By October 1889, Billings and his fellow commissioners had already visited Boston to see the two manual systems in operation. While that work continued, they returned to Washington to observe Hollerith's system. It had already taken an early lead in the transcription phase, finishing in seventy-two and a half hours, one-third faster than Pidgin's method and twice as fast as Hunt's. But the real test—counting—lay ahead. To succeed, Hollerith's method would have to be fast, but speed meant nothing without accuracy. Acknowledging this, Hollerith had lately connected a bell that would sound each time a record was successfully processed, to guard against operator error. Now, with the second phase underway, the hallway of the Atlantic Building rang out with a carillon of counting, as each of 10,491 St. Louisans passed through the machine.[18]

• • •

The nineteenth century was the great age of mechanization. Task after task, once the preserve of skilled artisans, fell to machines, with their gears and belts and hissing steam. This wasn't always well received, and the century saw sporadic outbreaks of conflict or sabotage by workers who felt their livelihoods were threatened, most famously the Luddites, who in the 1810s smashed machinery in the textile mills of England's north. "The instrument of labour," wrote Karl Marx, in 1867, "when it takes the form of a machine, immediately becomes a competitor of the workman himself." Mechanization was the dominant economic force of Hollerith's lifetime.[19]

One example of this general conflict is reflected in the American folk ballad of John Henry. As the story goes, Henry was a "steel-driving man," a construction worker involved in railway earthworks. Nitroglycerine or dynamite did most of the work, but these explosives needed to be detonated from deep within the rock. The job of a steel-driving man was to drill the hole in which the explosive charge could be sunk. One man would hold a steel chisel, while another swung an eight-pound hammer down on it. A skilled pair could burrow through solid rock surprisingly quickly, each hammer blow ringing out before the previous echo had died away.[20]

But despite the power of high-explosive chemistry, sculpting the landscape remained the slowest part of railroad construction, holding back the iron highways that were spreading across the country at otherwise breakneck speed. In the 1860s, several inventors developed machines that could speed up the drilling—at least in theory. But these early steam drills were difficult to use and unreliable. It took a decade until they became good enough to challenge manual teams. And so, by the 1870s, the stage was set for one unnamed foreman to mount a contest between a steam drill and a drilling team, with John Henry swinging the hammer:

> *John Henry hammered on the right-hand side.*
> *Steam drill kept driving on the left.*
> *John Henry beat that steam drill down.*
> *But he hammered his poor heart to death, Lord, Lord,*
> *He hammered his poor heart to death.*[21]

So ended the life and parable of John Henry, a martyr for the cause of humankind against the rise of the machines. It was a Pyrrhic victory in more ways than one: the machines kept getting better, and hand drilling was all but extinct by the 1920s—a perfect demonstration of Marx's argument.

Today there is no question that machines perform better than people in tasks of strength or speed. That battle was lost long ago. The

front has moved, with machines now encroaching on purely intellectual labor, a possibility Marx could not have imagined. Such machines
process information rather than materials. Yet still we thrill and terrify
ourselves at public, head-to-head demonstrations of their superiority—
Garry Kasparov versus IBM's Deep Blue, Ken Jennings versus IBM's
Watson, Lee Sedol versus Google's AlphaGo.

Although the contest to prove its superiority was not public,
Hollerith's device was among the first such machines, the manipulators
of bits rather than atoms. This has earned it a prominent place near the
entry of the Computer History Museum—not far from Google's headquarters in Mountain View, California. Unfortunately, the machine, a
replica, is no longer functional. According to the curator, the open
cups of toxic mercury would be a safety hazard. Perhaps that explains
the hallucinatory religious visions that Frederick Wines experienced in
working with the machine.[22]

. . .

The inspiration behind the tabulating machine lay in a conversation
between Hollerith and Billings one summer evening in 1881. Both
were then working on the 1880 census. Hollerith was a twenty-one-
year-old graduate of New York's Columbia School of Mines, forerunner of Columbia University's School of Engineering. He had an
inventor's disposition and the good fortune to be born into a time and
place that rewarded invention. With the chaos of civil war behind it,
the United States was emerging as an epicenter of dynamism in what
Vaclav Smil, a historian of technology, has called "the most inventive
decade in history."[23]

That August, the spark of electricity captivated the public imagination. Steam power, the violent, dirty, dangerously pneumatic force that
had bested John Henry, was just beginning to yield to this new source of
energy: silent, clean, invisible, mysterious. In Paris, the first International Exposition of Electricity had just begun, with exhibitors including
Alexander Graham Bell and Werner von Siemens. But while scientists mingled with statesmen and nobility in Paris, a very different city

of lights was under construction in Menlo Park, New Jersey. There a new industrial laboratory was turning out invention after life-changing invention.[24]

Four years earlier, Thomas Edison, a former telegraph operator, had stepped quite suddenly into the limelight with his invention of the phonograph, the first means to record and reproduce sound. In 1879, Edison had demonstrated the first commercially viable incandescent electric light bulb. In 1880 the first electric utility, the Edison Illuminating Company, was incorporated, and by 1882 it would open New York's first commercial power station at Pearl Street in Manhattan. A new age of electricity beckoned.[25]

No doubt all this ran through Hollerith's mind that late summer's night, as he reflected on the evening's conversation. Billings had mentioned, over dinner, a deep frustration. Not even one year in, the 1880 census analysis was far behind schedule. It was distinctly, worryingly possible that the next census would be underway before analysis of the 1880 data was complete. "There ought," mused Billings, "to be a machine for doing the purely mechanical work of tabulating population and similar statistics."[26]

While its methodology and content had been updated repeatedly since 1790, the collection and processing of the census had barely changed. Enumerators filled in forms by hand and then returned them to the superintendent in Washington, where they were tallied by hand into the various categories required for reporting. The switch to nominative enumeration had meant a slight reorganization, but the work itself was essentially unchanged, employing complex tally sheets to record intermediate results. The latest advance was an ingenious contraption that organized these sheets in a more ergonomic manner, using an elaborate system of rollers to bring related but physically distant columns closer together, as one might temporarily hide columns in a computer spreadsheet today. It was an incremental innovation at best. In its essential technology, nothing about the 1880 census would have surprised Benjamin Franklin.[27]

The suggestion to use mechanical—perhaps even electrical—power to augment human labor in this process would have seemed natural to Hollerith. His own role in the 1880 census involved collecting statistics on steam and water power, and he had come of age on the cusp of a world lit by electricity. Once Billings suggested it, Hollerith adopted the census-processing problem as his own, throwing himself at its solution. As his work on industrial statistics wound down, he requested a transfer to the Population Division so that he could better understand the problem.[28]

Compared with the wonders unfolding in Paris and Menlo Park, Hollerith's government office in Washington, then a city of just a hundred fifty thousand people, must have felt like a backwater. A talented engineer, he might have applied to work for Edison, as the young Henry Ford would a decade later. But perhaps even then, Herman Hollerith sensed that his destiny lay not in the dawning age of electricity but in the information age that would follow.

• • •

If the technology of the 1880 census would not have surprised Benjamin Franklin, then neither would the results. Over the ninety years since 1790, the US population had risen more than tenfold, doubling on average every 24.5 years—astoundingly close to the 25-year prediction made in Franklin's 1755 essay.

Admittedly, things hadn't played out exactly as Franklin had predicted. Immigration, in particular, had played a larger role than he had anticipated. Of the fifty million people counted in 1880, nearly seven million were foreign born—not just British, but Irish, German, and Scandinavian. There were also still many Americans who had been born in various parts of Africa, a legacy of the slave trade.[29]

It was not just the population of the United States that was growing. Over the same period, the country itself grew, incorporating new states and expanding its territory fourfold. These two parallel expansions were only loosely connected. There was little in the way of population pressure. At the time of the first census in 1790, the original thirteen states were lightly populated by Old World standards. They had just four million residents between them: about the same as Ireland, but with twenty-six times as much space. Nor were American cities yet crowded: New York, the largest at that time, had just thirty-three thousand people. By contrast Beijing, then likely the world's largest city, already had more than one million residents.[30]

Instead, the borders of the United States proceeded west across the continent in advance of any crowding. The path was set with the purchase of the Louisiana territory from France in 1803. President Thomas Jefferson had authorized his ambassador, Robert Livingston, to negotiate terms to acquire the strategic port of New Orleans from the French. When Livingston instead came home with a deal for the entire Louisiana territory—a transfer of land three times the size of France itself—Jefferson went along with it, despite harboring concerns about his constitutional authority to do so.

It might have seemed an extravagance: the country had no need, yet, for such a large additional territory. But one day, perhaps, it would. Two years before the purchase, not long after taking office, Jefferson had used results from the first two American censuses to update Franklin's calculations. He found that the doubling time of the US population was just twenty-two years. He was already then familiar with the arguments of Thomas Malthus, having encountered and been unimpressed by the first edition of the *Essay*. But shortly after the purchase was ratified, Jefferson found himself reading the newly published second edition of the *Essay*. He judged it now "a work of sound logic." As Jefferson contemplated the vastly larger territory over which he now presided, perhaps Malthus's words reassured him: soon enough, the power of population would vindicate his decision to double the territory of this fledgling nation.[31]

As the 1800s proceeded, robust population growth continued, but a spate of further territorial additions ensured that, at any time during the century, some large swathe of the United States remained beyond the limits of European-American settlement. Texas joined the union in

1846, the same year that the Pacific Northwest was absorbed in a division with Britain. In 1848, following two years of conflict, Mexico ceded what is now California, Nevada, Utah, and parts of Arizona, New Mexico, Colorado, and Wyoming. By midcentury, the United States stretched from coast to coast.

But a frontier of settlement persisted. It was not yet *the* frontier— the Wild West of popular culture, of outlaws and rogues, Davy Crockett and Daniel Boone—but a simple statistical classification. The census office declared an area "unsettled" if the population density was below two persons per square mile, "the petty population that lies beyond being made up of the solitary ranchman, trapper, or fisherman, or of mining parties, lumber camps, and the like." The line, it said, "which limits the average density of two to a square mile, is considered as the limit of settlement—the frontier line of population."[32]

The report of the 1880 census included maps showing population density for each decade since 1790, revealing the relentless westward expansion of the population. On the final map in the series, showing 1880 data, the frontier seems to be a ragged north-south line, cutting through Dakota, Nebraska, Kansas, Oklahoma, and Texas. Beyond this to the west are isolated patches of settlement amid a vast area left unshaded by the cartographer to reflect its emptiness in the eyes of the census, which still did not count "Indians not taxed" among the general population.[33]

• • •

Far from this frontier, Hollerith continued to think about the tabulation problem. In 1882 he finished his work as a census agent and moved to Boston, where he was appointed an instructor at the Massachusetts Institute of Technology (MIT). It was well suited to his needs, founded to advance the "practical application of science in connection with arts, agriculture, manufactures and commerce." There he began to grapple with the details of the machine he envisioned.[34]

Hollerith was far from the first to think of automating the mental labor of manipulating numbers. Simple, general-purpose calculation aids such as the abacus had existed since antiquity, and far more complex devices were developed to support astronomical predictions. In the early 1600s, the Scot John Napier discovered the logarithm, a mathematical transformation that allowed rapid, approximate multiplication and division. Logarithms could be precalculated and compiled into tables for easy reference. Soon a device called the slide rule was invented to make Napier's method easier and more portable, at the cost of some precision.

Around 1820, the first practical mechanical calculator, the arithmometer, was invented—though it took another thirty years' refinement to put it into commercial production. By the turn of a handle, the arithmometer could be made to perform addition, subtraction, and multiplication with nearly as much ease as a modern electronic calculator, though division remained somewhat more involved. By 1880 over a thousand of the machines had been manufactured for the use of government departments, railways, banks, and insurers as well as scientific and professional users. If Hollerith had not encountered such machines before, he certainly did in the census office.[35]

But clever though the arithmometer was, it solved a different problem from the one that interested Hollerith. It performed basic arithmetic operations between pairs of numbers, handling results of up to twenty digits. This was a mathematical problem, the kind that scientists and engineers routinely encountered in their work. Census tabulation, however, was less a mathematical problem than a data problem.

Consider the census enumeration schedules. From 1850 onward, they contained very few numerical entries amenable to arithmetic, and instead consisted mostly of either yes/no questions ("Single?") or what statisticians today would call "categorical" questions ("Place of birth?"). By a simple transformation, even categorical questions could be transformed into binary yes/no questions ("Born in England?" No. "Born in Ireland?" Yes).

As a result, the arithmetic side of census processing was very simple: add one if a person answers yes to a particular characteristic; otherwise add nothing. But this had to be done repeatedly for each person and in many different configurations—for example, to produce summaries for a city, a county, a state, and then the nation as a whole. The entire procedure depended far more on record processing—sorting and grouping and selecting—than on arithmetic. For the census Billings didn't need a calculator but a new kind of machine: a tabulator.

The difference, Hollerith saw, was storage. An arithmometer did not store data. If the operator needed to retain a value, he or she would copy it, digit by digit, from the device's numbered wheels onto scrap paper. Data had been stored in essentially this way since Sumerian accountants started keeping records on tiny clay tablets five thousand years earlier. With flexible papyrus and animal skin parchment came larger, more practical writing surfaces. But these materials were difficult in their own way, vulnerable to physical damage and humidity. This was resolved by gluing pages together into a scroll or, later, binding them into a book. Both approaches locked everything in place: information was inked immutably onto pages, which were themselves fixed into an unchanging order by glue or stitches.

Books and scrolls worked well for a finished narrative, the Bible, or *Hamlet,* and for certain kinds of records in which entries were recorded chronologically and rarely edited—for example, accounting ledgers. But they were less useful for working records, for storing information that needed to be reused and manipulated in different ways. Wax tablets had long served this need, as they were cheap and easily reused by smoothing out the surface using heat. The scribes working with the Roman censors may well have kept notes on such tablets, before transcribing records to parchment. But this very mutability made wax tablets inappropriate for long-term record keeping, and their dimensions made them, like clay tablets, unsuited to large collections. Still, for a long time, there was nothing better.[36]

By the late medieval period, a new possibility emerged. Paper, a Chinese invention, brought to Europe via the Islamic world, had fallen in cost to the point where it could be used for working records. It was not exactly reusable, but it was cheap enough to be disposable. With the explosion of printing and literacy in the centuries that followed, paper became a routine tool of administration for everyone from government ministers to shopkeepers.[37]

Perhaps the pinnacle of paper record keeping was pioneered by Carl Linnaeus, a Swedish botanist. Linnaeus aspired to organize all known species in a single taxonomy. As he worked, he soon discovered that the taxonomy itself was a living thing: a single newly discovered species could upend the whole structure, requiring him to revise previously settled relationships and classifications. To solve this problem, he used standardized slips of paper to record each species, settling on a size of 5.1 inches wide by 3 inches tall. It was a brilliant system, and other than employing a stiffer cardstock, index cards today are not much different from those of Linnaeus, right down to the 5-by-3-inch size.[38]

For working records, index cards have many advantages. They are more durable than ordinary paper. Their small size and stiffness allow them to stand loosely but upright in drawers, where they can be searched and rearranged as needed. New cards can be inserted in any position, and old ones simply removed. Small amendments can be made directly on the card, but if that is insufficient, any card can quickly and easily be copied with alterations and replaced, unlike a page in a book.

During the nineteenth century, cards like these had been adopted widely by libraries to catalog the contents of their shelves. Card catalogs were part of an explosion of filing methods, driven by the administrative needs of both governments and businesses.[39]

By the 1880s, the best ideas for manual census processing, the methods of Pidgin and Hunt with which Hollerith was now competing, involved some variation on index cards. By transferring data off the paper schedules and onto cards or slips, it became easier to manage, as Linnaeus had discovered. More work could be handled by fewer people. But some number of people would always be required because index cards, like all earlier technologies, could only be read by human eyes. Hollerith wanted to avoid relying on people altogether, if possible, or at least reduce their presence to a minimum, and so he needed a medium that could be read directly by machine.

There were several precedents for such technology, all of which worked by treating paper not simply as a substrate for ink but as a material that could itself be physically modified. While a machine could not (yet) hope to read a letter or digit drawn upon paper, a carefully calibrated device could detect a hole or a notch cut in the medium itself. Charles Wheatstone's automatic telegraph of 1858 used a ribbon of punched paper tape to store and relay the contents of a message. An 1874 description of this apparatus identifies immediately the key advantage: "the perforated slip of tape, as long as it is kept whole, may be used for any number of circuits over which the message has to be transmitted, thereby saving a great amount of time and labour."[40]

That reusability was precisely the feature Hollerith needed to make the many overlapping tabulations in a census, so while at MIT he began to experiment with paper tape. In 1883, he left Massachusetts and made a strategic return to Washington, DC, taking a job at the Patent Office. He stayed less than a year, just long enough to understand how the system of legal protection for inventions worked. He then filed his own first patent for a tape-based tabulator in 1884.[41]

But paper tape, while ideal for the sequenced stream of data produced in telegraphy, proved impractical for tabulation. As Hollerith later put it, "The trouble was that if, for example, you wanted any statistics regarding Chinamen, you would have to run miles of paper to count a few Chinamen." Hollerith had been trying to use a scroll when what he needed was a set of index cards. The solution was to take the holes, which a machine could read, and put them in cards.[42]

Later in life Hollerith would claim that he came to this conclusion while traveling by train. "I was traveling in the West," he wrote, "and I had a ticket with what I think was called a punch photograph.... The conductor...punched out a description of the individual, as light hair, dark eyes, large nose, etc." This method had been invented to prevent passengers from reselling tickets, much as airlines check that boarding passes match identity documents today. "So you see," Hollerith continued, explaining his own census cards, "I only made a punch photograph of each person."[43]

This story notwithstanding, Hollerith probably took more direct inspiration from two other inventions. In 1804, the Frenchman Joseph Marie Jacquard had demonstrated an automatic loom that used holes punched in cards, chained in sequence, to represent intricate weaving patterns. By the late eighteenth century these looms were common enough that an engineer would have known of them, Hollerith especially, since his brother-in-law worked in the silk-weaving business.[44]

Even more influential would have been the ideas of the English mathematician Charles Babbage, regarded today as the father of the computer. In the nineteenth century—indeed well into the twentieth—there was no convenient way to calculate the many mathematical functions needed by engineers and scientists to complete their work, such as sine, cosine, and logarithm. Instead, books of such functions were produced and sold, consisting of hundreds of pages of laboriously hand-calculated solutions to these functions for different inputs. Babbage's first invention, the Difference Engine, was designed to automate these calculations and make the production of these books faster and more accurate. An 1830 design called for twenty-five thousand parts weighing fifteen tons and was never completed.[45]

Somehow this failure inspired Babbage to even greater heights of imagination, a machine he called the Analytical Engine. This was to be a programmable digital computer, equivalent in a theoretical sense to a modern electronic computer—an astonishing feat given that it was to be entirely mechanical and powered by steam. To store programs for the computer, Babbage borrowed Jacquard's punch card idea. Unfortunately, his design genius far exceeded his organizational and fundraising abilities, and like the Difference Engine, this machine was never completed, dying with Babbage in 1871. It was, however, still well known in Hollerith's time.[46]

Whatever his true inspiration, Hollerith was soon experimenting with punch cards. Their only downside was that unlike tape, cards could not be fed continuously from a spool, so a clerk was still required to place each card in the press and remove it afterward. (It would be another decade before Hollerith perfected an automatic card feeder.)

Hollerith tested and refined his new design on a few small projects before submitting another patent application in 1887. While it shared a title with the 1884 filing, "Art of Compiling Statistics," it was a very different machine.[47]

The patent was granted in January 1889, official recognition of the invention's novelty. No part of the machine itself was particularly new: not the counters, which kept and displayed the tallies; not the method of storage, the punch card; and not the electrical logic that connected everything together. Hollerith's contribution was in the *art:* working out how to combine these pieces and apply them to a general problem of information processing.[48]

With patent in hand, Hollerith turned to sales. He hoped that his old employer, the US census, would be the company's first serious customer, but Hollerith's ambitions were much larger. Over the course of the nineteenth century, censuses had become a regular event in dozens of countries. Soon he was seeking contracts in Austria, Italy, Canada, and Russia. If the tabulator could succeed in the United States, a world of opportunities would be waiting.[49]

• • •

Censuses had not just spread but begun to converge in methods and content. This was partly a consequence of a world in which states themselves were converging in form, if not in size, wealth, or power. Railways and the telegraph accelerated a process of centralization already underway: national capitals grew more powerful and important—and greedy for information. But this convergence in census taking was also the result of an intentional effort: government statistics had become the focus of an international project.

The person most responsible for this project was Adolphe Quetelet, a Belgian statistician whom Florence Nightingale called "the founder of the most important science in the whole world." Quetelet was born in 1796 in Ghent, in what was then French territory. Like Condorcet and Malthus, his prodigious interests spanned both mathematics and the humanities from an early age. But Quetelet's career took a different path, one that reflected a broader change in the organization of science over the generation or two that separated them.[50]

The scientific revolution had been a time of singular individuals, Galileo staring through his telescope or Newton pondering the prism. But the late eighteenth and nineteenth centuries saw the beginnings of state-sponsored institutional science. Today we take this for granted: the 2012 academic paper announcing the discovery of the Higgs boson lists around three thousand coauthors, while the Large Hadron Collider facility that made its detection possible is a multibillion-dollar pan-European collaboration. These are extreme examples, but even minor discoveries these days usually involve several collaborators, institutional laboratories, and multiple government research grants.[51]

Quetelet arrived just at the beginning of this change. Its most obvious manifestation was the great scientific expeditions of people like Captain James Cook, Alexander von Humboldt, and Darwin. Such voyages needed the kind of financing that only imperial states, keen to expand their global footprints, could provide. But institutional science was growing on shore too. Quetelet's first exposure to this was his campaign, in the 1820s, for the construction of an astronomical observatory in Brussels, which was by then under Dutch rule.[52]

Over the same period Quetelet's interest in society and government grew, a pursuit he called "social physics," echoing Condorcet's "social mathematics." In this field, too, he saw the need for large-scale collaborative effort. Just as astronomy needed observations gathered by teams located across Europe and around the world, so social physics required large, organized teams to collect its raw material. He lobbied for a census of the United Netherlands, which went ahead in January 1830, just before Belgium split from the union.[53]

Over the next decades, Quetelet's international standing grew. He attracted particular renown for his 1835 book, *A Treatise on Man and the Development of His Faculties,* which attempted to quantify practically every facet of its subject. He covered not only more traditional topics like birth and death, but also height, strength, power, respiration, intellect, morality, and criminality. Whereas his predecessors like

Malthus had reasoned mathematically, by analogy with astronomy, Quetelet went beyond this. He applied the specific statistical methods of that field, in particular the Gaussian law of errors, to his fellow citizens. He found that many attributes of human beings—height, for example—behaved just like the observations of planetary motion that the mathematician Carl Friedrich Gauss had analyzed a quarter century earlier. Measurements from a group of people tended to fall in a bell curve around an average.

This much is broadly true. But Quetelet made further unscientific claims, imputing meaning—a kind of truth and beauty—to this phenomenon. "If the average man were completely determined," Quetelet wrote, we might "consider him as the type of perfection; and every thing differing from his proportions or condition, would constitute deformity and disease; everything found dissimilar, not only as regarded proportion and form, but as exceeding the observed limits, would constitute a monstrosity." This equating of average with correct generated considerable controversy, even within his own lifetime.[54]

From his position in newly independent Belgium, Quetelet used his international reputation to champion the cause of statistics across Europe. He was instrumental in the founding of the Statistical Society of London in 1834, alongside other luminaries including Malthus and Babbage. He was the first foreign member of the American Statistical Association. Throughout his life Quetelet was a prolific letter writer, corresponding with mathematicians, statisticians, and politicians around Europe and beyond (indeed, in 1835 he was the first to hear, in writing, of Babbage's plans for the Analytical Engine).[55]

In 1851, during the Great Exhibition in London, Quetelet moved to formalize this network, proposing an international congress on statistics. It took place in 1853, hosted, naturally, in Brussels. International was a relative term: aside from the three-person American delegation, two Egyptian astronomers were the only participants from outside Europe (the total of twenty-six countries was inflated by the abundance of small German and Italian states then existing). At this first congress, Quetelet gave an address outlining its aim of "introducing unity into the official statistics of the different countries and...rendering the results comparable." Without this, he claimed, "there could be no progress in the sciences of observation."[56]

The next two decades saw eight further congresses. Although all were held in European capitals, they became slowly more diverse, with representation from Brazil, Japan, and British India, among others. These efforts to make statistics more comparable and more scientific paid off. James Garfield, a correspondent of Quetelet's and a future president of the United States, was among those convinced. In 1867, Congressman Garfield chaired a committee on the future of the American census. "This is the age of statistics," he declared, arguing that the census "should serve the country by making a full and accurate exhibit of the elements of national life and strength, and it should serve the science of statistics by so exhibiting general results that they may be compared with similar data obtained by other nations."[57]

The eighth congress, held in St. Petersburg in 1872, was Quetelet's last. Age had not diminished his passion, and the seventy-six-year-old Belgian was appointed honorary president of a subcommittee that made new recommendations for census taking. A census, it announced, should collect data on named individuals; be taken in a single day, or as near to this as possible; and be made every ten years, in years ending in zero. It should gather, at a minimum, name, sex, and age; relation to head of household; civil or conjugal state; occupation; religion; language spoken; ability to read; origin, place of birth, and nationality; usual residence; and any disabilities.[58]

On their return, the American delegates presented these recommendations to Congress, endorsing them with some caveats. They noted, a little smugly, that the decennial rule "harmonized with the custom of the United States." But they disagreed with a recommendation that people should be counted in the place where they were present on census day—a "de facto" census. American enumerations had always counted people at their usual residence—a "de jure" census. To do otherwise, they felt, would be too unreliable in a nation as mobile and dynamic as the United States, where "every day and every night there are hundreds of thousands of persons traveling the whole day or the whole night in railroad-cars and steamboats, without stopping or sleeping in any town." In fact, many censuses today capture both present location and usual residence.[59]

They also drew lawmakers' attention to questions recommended by Quetelet's subcommittee that were not asked in the United States, including each person's relationship to the head of the family, conjugal condition, religion, and language spoken. All of these, except religion, eventually made their way onto the 1880 and 1890 question lists, part of the explosion of detail responsible for the crisis in processing that Hollerith now aimed to solve.

• • •

By November 11, 1889, the census contest was over. The members of Billings's commission had seen enough. Neither Charles Pidgin not William Hunt had been able to present a John Henry, some champion clerk who could outpace Hollerith's machine using their manual methods. Hollerith's tabulating machine completed the counting stage in just five and a half hours, trouncing Pidgin's and Hunt's methods, which took forty-five and fifty-five hours respectively. The tabulator was also, they concluded, "decidedly more accurate." It was a rout.[60]

The commission estimated that using the machines, rather than one of the manual methods, would save nearly $600,000 in reduced manpower—even assuming a very minimal program of tabulation. Robert Porter, the politically savvy superintendent of the census, was more circumspect about the labor impacts in his report to the secretary of the interior. He wrote that use of the tabulator "will not, however, dispense with the labor of clerks so much as it will render the same more efficient and available for the intellectual work of the census."[61]

The census office ordered an initial fifty machines, rented for $1,000 per annum, later expanding the order by another forty at a 50 percent discount. Considering the expected savings, this was a remarkable deal

SCIENTIFIC AMERICAN

[Entered at the Post Office of New York, N.Y., as Second Class Matter. Copyrighted, 1890, by Munn & Co.]

A WEEKLY JOURNAL OF PRACTICAL INFORMATION, ART, SCIENCE, MECHANICS, CHEMISTRY, AND MANUFACTURES.

Vol. LXIII.—No. 9.
Established 1845.

NEW YORK, AUGUST 30, 1890.

[$3.00 A YEAR.
Weekly.

THE NEW CENSUS OF THE UNITED STATES—THE ELECTRICAL ENUMERATING MECHANISM.—[See page 132.]

Scientific American celebrated the counting of the census by "electrical enumerating mechanism" on its front cover on August 30, 1890. Top-right shows cards being prepared on the pantograph punch. (*Scientific American* 63, no. 9 [August 30, 1890]: 127. Credit: Library of Congress.)

for the government. As nearly fifty thousand enumerators fanned out across the country in the spring of 1890, Hollerith tabulators were being assembled in the Inter-Ocean Building, a brand-new edifice not far from Hollerith's old office in the Atlantic Building. Shortly after census day, June 1, completed schedules started pouring in to Washington's Union Station.[62]

First a rough count of population, without any attributes, was made directly from the schedules, using special numeric keypads hooked up to the tabulators. A single operator could count fifty thousand people a day in this manner. Next the schedules were transferred onto punch cards. This was done using a device Hollerith called the "pantograph punch," which worked like a typewriter, except that rather than imprinting a letter on a page, each key press punched a hole in a card. It was a slower, more careful process, with each clerk producing around seven hundred cards a day.[63]

Once prepared, the cards were processed by the tabulation clerks, many of whom were women; in the words of Washington's *Evening Star*, "nice-looking girls in cool white dresses...at work at the long rows of counting machines." For each round of counting, the machines would be configured to produce a particular cross-tabulation—for example, occupation by sex and race. As each card was counted, a compartment would open in the sorting box, into which the operator would deposit the card. In this way, the cards could be sorted in preparation for the next round, even as the current count was underway.[64]

In total, the clerical workforce, split evenly between men and women, peaked in May 1891 at 3,143. This was twice as many as in 1880, proving Superintendent Porter's claim quite correct. Most would never have sat at one of the ninety tabulating machines but worked on supporting tasks. It took, for example, around five clerks producing cards using pantograph punches to keep up with one tabulator.[65]

The whole operation made a strong impression on observers. "As one enters, the ear catches the sound of crisp bell ringing, for all the world like that of sleighing," wrote T. C. Martin, reporting for a technical journal. He counted "81 clerks at the machines, and their work showed 434,493 cards counted and 121,853 sorted, a total of 556,346 for the day." Each day this amounted to "a stack of cards nearly as high as the Washington Monument"—around five hundred feet.[66]

For Frederick Wines, the census employee who took charge of statistics on crimes and pauperism, the cards themselves came alive. They became endowed "with all the attributes of living beings, whose life experience is written upon their face in hieroglyphic symbols resembling in significance the traits of human countenance. A card which means nothing to the uninitiated is converted into a pauper or a criminal whose sin and suffering are as palpable as if the man himself were bodily present in the room."[67]

The rough count was announced on October 28, and the official count, for apportionment, just a month later. Of course, there were many more tabulations and cross-tabulations yet to be made; the published results of the 1890 census eventually ran to more than twenty-one thousand pages. But already the contest commission's faith had been repaid. As Martin, the journalist, put it, the machine "works as unerringly as the mills of the Gods, but beats them hollow as to speed." When all was done, Hollerith's invention was estimated to have saved the office two years and $5 million. The American census was never again compiled by hand.[68]

• • •

When the bells fell silent and the 1890 census tabulations were complete, they showed a maturing nation, one vastly different from the one enumerated a century earlier. The population was aging. Marriages were less frequent. The birth rate was falling. The overall total of sixty-three million was lower than expected. The *Times-Democrat* of New Orleans declared that "Dr Hollerith's figures confirm the theory that we have already announced, that the tendency of all civilized countries toward the slower increase of population . . . would be entirely so but for immigration. No Malthus will ever be needed in this world, unless conditions greatly change."[69]

And though Malthus had been held at bay, one hundred years of population growth had reshaped the nation and its relationship to the continent

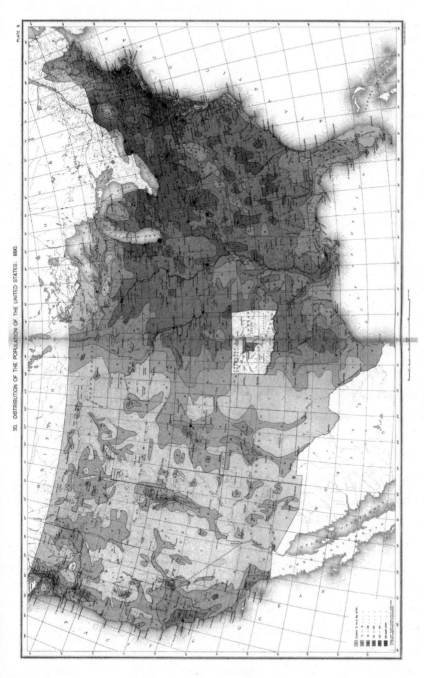

According to US Census superintendent Robert Porter, a frontier of population, evidenced in previous counts, was no longer apparent in the distribution of population revealed by the 1890 census, shown here. (Henry Gannett, *Statistical Atlas of the United States, Based upon the Results of the Eleventh Census* [Washington, DC: Government Printing Office, 1898]. Credit: Library of Congress, Geography and Map Division.)

it now dominated. Porter, the superintendent, noted one change in particular. "Up to and including 1880 the country had a frontier of settlement," he wrote, "but at present the unsettled area has been so broken into by isolated bodies of settlement that there can hardly be said to be a frontier line. In the discussion of its extent, its westward movement, etc., it can not, therefore, any longer have a place in the census reports."[70]

The population maps produced by the census office offer some support to this claim. On the 1880 map, it is possible to draw a north-south line through the United States—roughly at the Kansas–Colorado border—so that it passes only through "unsettled" areas. On the 1890 map, that's no longer possible: the patches of settlement in the west have started to coalesce. While there's still an abrupt drop-off in population density from east to west, as there still is today, the wide, "unsettled" swathe is gone.[71]

But if we examine even later maps—an advantage Porter did not have—it is equally easy to make a case that a statistical frontier persisted for some time after 1890. It was not, for example, until 1910 that the settled areas actually linked up from coast to coast. Porter, a former newspaperman, had an ear for rhetoric, and the temptation to make such a call on the occasion of the nation's centennial census must have been great. It was less an unambiguous observation than a subjective assessment. Rather than finding the frontier closed, Porter himself closed it by sheer declarative power—driving a metaphorical Golden Spike into the settlement of the United States.[72]

The declaration did not go unnoticed. It directly inspired the historian Frederick Jackson Turner, who interrogated it further in a seminal 1893 paper delivered to the American Historical Association. Turner's argument has become known as the frontier thesis: that America the land gave birth to Americans the people; that the country developed unique institutions and cultural values precisely because of this crucial period of boundary pushing by the men—for Turner, this was a male phenomenon—of the frontier: fur traders and Texan ranchers, Mormon pioneers searching for Zion and Yankee forty-niners trying their luck with pick, shovel, and pan.[73]

A PUNCH PHOTOGRAPH

. . .

Even as the western frontier of the United States had closed, or was closed, another had opened far to the north, in Alaska. The territory had been purchased from the Russian Empire in 1867. There was no pressing need to enumerate it: Alaska was not a state and had no congressional representation, and nearly its entire population was excluded anyway as "Indians not taxed." Still, America's lawmakers, and its people, were curious about this vast new territory, so in 1880 and 1890, it was surveyed, with results published in a special census report.

The man responsible was Ivan Petroff. Petroff was exactly the kind of frontiersman Turner conjured in his essay: resourceful and unafraid of risk. He was also a rogue, a three-time army deserter chased out of journalism amid accusations of plagiarism. Still, in his census work, Petroff seemed finally to have found a measure of stability. Even as the rough count was being made in the fall of 1890, he remained in the field, sending dispatches back to Washington.[74] For example:

> After arriving at Nushegak I administered the oath of office to Mr. Frank E. Wolff, the special agent appointed to assist me. . . . I purchased two skin canoes, laid in a small supply of provisions, and engaged the services of four natives to carry me up the Nushegak river to a point from which I could effect a portage to the Kuskokvim river.[75]

Like many of his plans, this one failed; but Petroff did eventually reach the Kuskokvim, hitching a ride along the coast aboard a government steamer. There he proceeded upstream, "burdened with cumbersome packages of census schedules" that forced him "to leave behind a large portion of my personal baggage, clothes, etc." He set off with "no supplies beyond a little tea and sugar, some graham flour, and ammunition for my shot-gun." By such arduous journeys, Petroff and his local assistants eventually counted an Alaskan population of 32,052.[76]

Through his reports, Petroff almost single-handedly defined Alaska for its new owners, for whom names like Nushegak, Yukon, and

Kuskokvim would otherwise have been completely unknown. The work restored his tarnished reputation for a time. But ignominy pursued Petroff: in 1892, while working on a diplomatic matter as a Russian translator, he was discovered to have taken rather too much editorial license. As scandal once again enveloped him, the name Ivan Petroff was stripped from the 1890 census report on Alaska (though a picture that includes him was kept as the volume's frontispiece).[77]

To this day both his 1880 and his 1890 reports remain disputed. One historian calls them an "indispensable reference work," while another notes that Petroff "holds the distinction of probably telling more lies about Alaska that were believed for more years than any other person in history." Likely, both are correct.[78]

• • •

Men like Ivan Petroff make for colorful stories, but today historians are more critical of Turner's triumphalist frontier thesis. As an overarching theory of the American character it ignores more than it explains, including the role of women and Hispanic and French colonists, as well as the vast nation-shaping forces of urbanization, slavery, and the Civil War. Turner could only describe the West as "an area of free land" because he treated as unimportant, like the census on which he relied, "Indians not taxed." Nevertheless, his ideas held sway for the better part of the twentieth century, and their influence on the American self-image is undeniable. Some of his observations still ring true, among them that Americans are possessed of a "practical, inventive turn of mind."

That turn of mind is perhaps best exemplified by Thomas Edison, widely considered America's greatest inventor, whose incandescent light bulb has become a metaphor for inspiration itself. But while we remember Edison for that single invention, it was really his successful creation of an entire system, from power stations to domestic lighting, and the business models that supported them, that ensured his long-term impact. My electricity is still delivered by the Consolidated Edison Company.[79]

The same can be said of Hollerith. While the tabulator itself worked well enough, it was just one of the many devices that he, and the company he soon founded—the Tabulating Machine Company—eventually developed. It was the whole system—the paper cards, the pantograph punch, the tabulating machine, the sorting drawer, and, importantly, the procedures for organizing the work—that brought success in 1890.[80]

Even before then, Hollerith was working on new accessories. In time, his system would be extended with typewriter-like keypunches, automatic card feeders, adders, sorters, collators, card punchers, and duplicators—a complete set of machine tools for the knowledge factories of the twentieth century. It was extended, eventually, to include true computers, the electronic successors of Babbage's Analytical Engine. With the punch card as their common, machine-readable language, these devices dominated information processing well into the 1970s, filling the so-called unit record shops of corporations and government departments, including statistical bureaus.

It's not surprising, in retrospect, that these innovations came out of the census. From their origins in antiquity, until perhaps the 1950s, national censuses produced the largest collections of structured data in existence. They were the original big data, unchallenged in scale until the Second World War, when atomic research and code-breaking created new frontiers in information processing. When the world's first commercial electronic computer, UNIVAC I, came to market in 1951, its first customer was the US Census Bureau.

• • •

The nineteenth century made the census what it is today. Increased numeracy and the professionalization and internationalization of statistics gave it greater relevance than ever before. Process improvements, including nominative enumeration, made counting smoother and more accurate. But of all these changes, it was the invention of electronic tabulation that would have the widest impact.

The punch card changed the relationship between the individual and central government. For thousands of years it was possible for a person to remain effectively invisible to distant seats of power. If, in

1880, a politician or bureaucrat in Washington, DC, wanted a list of every noncitizen living in the United States, it simply wasn't possible, at least not without dedicating a substantial workforce to sort, by hand, through millions of written census returns. After 1890 it became a theoretical possibility, and by the middle of the twentieth century, a real one. Where once an insurmountable technical barrier stood in the way of centralized mass surveillance, after Hollerith only legal and ethical restraint remained to prevent it.

Even before its wider impacts were felt, Hollerith's machine brought well-earned success to its inventor. The census itself charts his rise: in 1880, fresh from Columbia's School of Mines, he gives his occupation as "mining engineer"; in 1900, having found his calling, he is a "statistical engineer" (a unique occupation in that census); by 1910, his business success assured, he is a "general manager." We might suppose that his name, or that of the Tabulating Machine Company, would be as widely known as Edison's.[81]

But in 1911, age fifty-one, Hollerith sold his firm. He stepped away from business, retiring a millionaire, and giving his occupation, in 1920, as "none." The firm merged with three others that made complementary equipment, becoming, for a time, the Computing-Tabulating-Recording Company. That name, always awkward, was soon inaccurate too. Punch card tabulation found opportunities far beyond the census and quickly became the conglomerate's main business line. In 1924, the company adopted a sleek new name, befitting a new global century. Henceforth it would be known as International Business Machines—IBM.

CHAPTER 4

PAPER PEOPLE

TWENTY-ONE-YEAR-OLD Robbie Cohen was flying his Mosquito lower than ever before. Low enough, he marveled, to "count the buttons on the jackets" of the Dutch farmers who waved as the squadron passed overhead. Low enough to clear the German radar. It was Tuesday, April 11, 1944, and Cohen's first daylight bombing raid. The six De Havilland Mosquito fighter-bombers had taken off from Royal Air Force Station Swanton Morley, in the east of England, at 1:05 p.m. Greenwich time. Despite some cloud, the midday sun left them exposed. But, flying fast, they reached the Dutch coast around half an hour later. As they did, the lead aircraft, piloted by squadron leader Robert Bateson, turned northeast, toward the Hague, where their target lay.[1]

The last time Cohen had seen this coast, nearly three years earlier, was over his shoulder, as he paddled a canoe away from the Dutch town of Katwijk—and the Nazi occupation. It was a reckless thing to do. German patrols and one hundred unforgiving miles of open water made escape by sea unlikely: of the thirty-three *Engelandvaarders* ("England sailors") who attempted the crossing from Katwijk that summer, only eight made it. But for Cohen, a Jew, remaining in occupied Europe must have seemed just as dangerous. Anyway, Cohen's odds of reaching Britain were better than average: he was joined in the vessel by a champion rower, Coen de Iongh. The pair set out in the early hours of July 20, 1941, and reached the coast of East Anglia some fifty hours later. From there, both joined the Royal Air Force. De Iongh flew Spitfires until his death in 1943, shot down while escorting American B-25s near Ghent.[2]

German air power had greatly diminished since then. Antiaircraft guns were still a threat, but the raiders remained undetected on their approach. As Cohen flew over the Hague, he saw smoke rising near the distinctive, oddly menacing tower of the Peace Palace. The palace had been built thirty years earlier to house international institutions intended to end war; it made an incongruous final waypoint for the bombing mission. It's doubtful Cohen had time to let that irony register as he lined up his target: the Kleykamp building, a stately four-story former art museum across the road from the palace. The lead aircraft had already dropped high explosives, blasting the building open. The following planes carried incendiary bombs, intended to set everything inside alight. But Cohen's bomb release jammed. Unable to drop his ordinance, frustrated, he pulled back on his plane's control stick and climbed to safety. As he did, he captured several frames of film showing the damage wrought by the earlier aircraft.[3]

On the ground, the villa was, in Cohen's own words, a "sea of flames." Sixty-two people lay dead or dying. From open cabinets, thousands upon thousands of paper files spewed out and fueled the fire. As the blaze grew intense, these file cards, each with a photograph placed neatly at its center, burst into flames. The heat rising from the inferno lifted half-burned records high into the air, and they settled in the surrounding streets, the whorls and loops of inked fingerprints crumbling away as the paper smoldered. While the fire brigade worked to extinguish the fire, police forced some passersby to rescue what records they could. Others surreptitiously did the opposite, moving files further into the flames.[4]

Other Allied bombing missions that week went after aircraft or vehicle factories, aiming to destroy buildings, machinery, equipment, supplies—typical objectives at this stage in the war, as the Allies prepared to land ground forces at Normandy. Cohen and his fellow airmen, though, were tasked with the destruction not of property or people but of information itself: records of the entire Dutch population.

The Kleykamp building became a military target because the Nazi regime had made population data a weapon. In Germany, the Netherlands, and other occupied countries, censuses and other records of population were drafted into battle. To some extent, this happened in the Allied countries too: domestic populations were issued with identity cards; conscription systems were reactivated; visiting foreigners became enemy aliens and were registered as such.

But in Nazi Europe, census takers were asked to help reshape the very populations they were accustomed to counting and measuring. That they did was a betrayal of trust and a moral failure. To understand exactly why, we have to return to the start of the twentieth century, when the relationship between states and their citizens, statisticians and their statistical subjects, was being renegotiated.

• • •

As the twentieth century got underway, census taking was significantly more complex than it had been a century earlier. It was now supported by innovative data processing equipment, improved methodologies, and dedicated, permanent statistical workforces. There had been an evolution in what information a state might reasonably ask of its citizens, but also in what it could do with that information. A body of laws, institutions, and norms had evolved that both enabled and limited census taking.

Hollerith technology had matured into a multimillion-dollar industry, with commercial customers increasingly important. By 1930, Hollerith machines—now made by IBM—were being sold by subsidiaries or agents in Britain, Germany, and France. IBM was no longer alone in the market: the Remington Rand / Powers and Bull companies had joined with similar machines of their own. The cards themselves could store more data, having grown from twenty-four to forty-five and then eighty columns, but the capability to record alphabetic data, such as names and addresses, was still in its infancy. The system was still better suited to narrow, one-off processing tasks, like censuses, than long-term, general record keeping. For that, written files, including index cards, retained a slight edge.[5]

Government statistics had itself matured. In 1902, the United States finally established a permanent Census Bureau, joining the ranks of European nations that had done so over the course of the nineteenth century. The structure of these offices varied between countries: census taking in Germany, for instance, was far more decentralized than in Britain or the United States, reflecting that country's late unification from independent states. But everywhere, permanent offices allowed the development of an institutional memory, a deepening of knowledge and sharpening of technique. Permanence created a cadre of dedicated professionals whose lives were governed by the decennial rhythm of the population census but who had plenty of other work scheduled in the off years: surveys of manufacturing, studies of trade, and so on.[6]

By the early twentieth century, census taking was ruled, in a word, by bureaucracy. German sociologist Max Weber described bureaucracy, in a 1922 essay of the same name, as a process of rationalization. He saw it as something that "develops the more perfectly the more it is 'dehumanized,' the more completely it succeeds in eliminating from official business love, hatred, and all purely personal, irrational, and emotional elements which escape calculation."[7]

Weber likened bureaucracy to a machine. Once set in motion, it would go wherever its operator pointed it. "The mechanism," he wrote, "is easily made to work for anybody who knows how to gain control over it. A rationally ordered system of officials continues to function smoothly after the enemy has occupied the area: he merely needs to change the top officials."[8]

Weber died in München in 1920 (the essay on bureaucracy was published posthumously). That year, a minor political party, the National Socialist German Workers' Party, was founded in the same city. Weber couldn't possibly have known that just over a decade later, that group— its long name soon abbreviated to the Nazi Party—would put his theory to the ultimate test.

For the average person, the most significant change to census taking over the late nineteenth and early twentieth centuries was the incorporation of a formal notion of privacy. Censuses in the early nineteenth century were accompanied by a loose understanding that they were in some way limited, that governments would not use them directly to tax or conscript individuals, as they had in antiquity. But this was not privacy: up to and including 1840 in the United States, census schedules were publicly displayed in each town for error checking. And it was not a guarantee. If anything, it was simply the default way of working for statisticians, for whom the individual data point had little value anyway.[9]

Confidentiality, when it arose as an issue, did so first in relation to commercial and industrial surveys. Business owners worried that enumerators might share sensitive information with their competitors or customers or use it for taxation purposes. As population censuses began to ask more detailed and obviously invasive questions, this concern spread to individuals, worried about the reputational consequences of reporting a disability or "idiotic" family member. In America, the practice of posting schedules was discontinued in 1850, and in 1870 enumerators were told that returns should be "treated as strictly confidential."[10]

At first, such undertakings were less about some abstract right to privacy than a necessary means of ensuring data quality. When the 1890 census asked new questions about "debts and diseases," the *New York Sun* labeled it "an outrageous invasion of the personal and private business of the citizen." But the census statisticians were probably more sensitive to the *Boston Globe*'s observation that "reports based on the evasive and incorrect replies that will be made in probably the majority of cases will, of course, have no real statistical weight or value whatever."[11]

This was a serious concern. The census relied on the trust and cooperation of the public, and while the government might try to compel participation—there were sixty arrests for census noncompliance in New York City alone in 1890—it could not really compel honesty. To elicit voluntary disclosure, at a time when societal notions of privacy were developing rapidly, the census had to offer something in return, a promise that data would only be used for official purposes.[12]

The census in Britain operated under an even stronger commitment. Not only would responses be protected from the prying eyes of neighbors and competitors, but the state itself would strictly limit the uses it would make of the data. The epidemiologist William Farr, who dominated British census taking in the mid-nineteenth century, announced in 1861 that "the whole of the facts...are to be treated as confidential, and neither to be used to a person's disadvantage nor to gratify 'idle curiosity.'" America had reached the same point by 1910, with President William Howard Taft proclaiming unequivocally: "The census has nothing to do with taxation, with army or jury service, with the compulsion of school attendance, with the regulation of immigration, or with the enforcement of any national, state, or local law or ordinance, nor can any person be harmed in any way by furnishing the information required."[13]

In other words, private data would enter the census office but would never leave, except in an anonymous, aggregate form that could do no harm to an individual. This idea is now known as "statistical confidentiality." Although that term came later, the concept itself was becoming established in the increasingly international norms of official statistics by the early decades of the twentieth century. It was increasingly codified in law, too, as part of the growing recognition of moral and legal rights to privacy.[14]

• • •

From the security of a permanent footing, government statisticians grew increasingly ambitious. The pace of life was accelerating. Modern transportation was increasing mobility. Across Europe and North America, people were pouring into industrializing cities, and international migration was at an all-time high. Faced with such dynamism, a once-a-decade census hardly seemed up to the task of accurately reflecting society. The twentieth-century state—larger, more interventionist, more information-hungry—needed something better: not snapshots of society spaced ten years apart but a motion picture, a twenty-four-frames-per-second record of a changing population.

As early as the mid-nineteenth century, statisticians had suggested a way of doing this, a kind of continuously updated census called a population register. This idea owed something to ecclesiastical registries of vital records, which for several centuries had recorded births (or baptisms), marriages, and deaths (or burials) as they occurred. But a population register would go further, tracking at least the arrival, departure, and changes of address of its subjects, so that at any moment it provided a perfect record of how many people there were and where they lived. Even as he championed decennial census taking in the 1830s and 1840s, Adolphe Quetelet pushed for countries to adopt municipal registers. The countries most under his influence, Belgium and the Netherlands, soon did.[15]

Registration, especially as it grew more comprehensive, sat uneasily alongside the emerging norm of statistical confidentiality. Unlike censuses, registers were meant to be used as a day-to-day tool of administration, consulted continuously by officials to verify citizen identities, determine eligibility for pensions or indigent assistance, record military service, manage school enrollment, and more. The whole point of a register was to be a single source of data on residents that could be used throughout government. Consequently, registries were often coordinated not by the census or statistical office, which might be burdened with promises of confidentiality, but directly by the Interior Ministry or equivalent. Moreover, they were often decentralized, with the actual files kept locally in each district.[16]

Unlike censuses, registers put the onus of enumeration on the individual. At a time when a census usually meant enumerators visiting residents, registries required the opposite: residents were expected to keep police or other officials appraised of relevant changes. This didn't always happen smoothly, so early implementations were often inaccurate, double-counting or losing track of people. By the end of the nineteenth century three countries—Belgium, Italy, and the

Netherlands—had established legally mandatory registration in order to address this problem.[17]

Still, progress was slow, as the case of the Netherlands illustrates. Registers did not replace censuses so much as complement them. Dutch censuses continued roughly every ten years up to 1930. Inaccuracy of the population register continued to be a problem, exacerbated by its decentralization. The Netherlands had not so much a single register as a set of registers, each maintained separately at the municipal level, bound into unwieldy books with one page dedicated to each family. When members left or joined a family, or an entire family moved, the change somehow had to be reflected in these family books.[18]

A better alternative had been obvious for decades: to switch from family registration books to individual index cards. Rather than details being inaccurately copied from one book to another, a person's card would follow them wherever they moved, removed from one municipality's file and replaced in another's. But lack of agreement hampered its adoption. Some cities, including Amsterdam and Rotterdam, had started using card files, but in other places officials dragged their feet, worried that cards would be lost or misplaced.[19]

The man who overcame this reluctance, and finally achieved a uniform card file in the Netherlands, was a civil servant named Jacobus Lambertus Lentz. Lentz joined the Hague's registry as a seventeen-year-old clerk in 1907 and rose quickly. In 1932 he was appointed to lead the National Inspectorate for Population Registries, a new agency spun out of the Central Bureau for Statistics to oversee population registration. By this time middle-aged, serious, and balding, Lentz embodied Weber's ideal bureaucrat. He was experienced, capable, and diligent—a true expert in his field.[20]

Lentz could be found in his office at all hours, "wedded to his work," according to his civil service boss. Soon enough he was unwedded in life—he neglected his family, and his wife left him. He was obsessed with perfectly solving the problem of registration. Had he been born a century or two earlier, in the age of Linnaeus or Darwin, he might have cataloged plant species or collected butterflies. Instead, he cataloged people—but the approach he took was not much different. The population register, he wrote, should be "a collection of paper people, that represents the natural man in all central points, to grant the authority any information desired about his person."[21]

In 1936, Lentz wrote a three-hundred-page manual on the Dutch registration system, entitled *Population Accounting*. It opened with a short verse of his own composition, a whimsical statement of his aspiration:

In administration
The paper man
Is the surrogate
Of the natural man.[22]

With Henri Methorst, head of the Central Bureau of Statistics, Lentz published summaries of the system in leading German and American statistical journals.[23]

From the beginning the register included traditional census topics, such as age, sex, occupation, and religious denomination, but Lentz predicted that it might eventually encompass everything from firearms permits to alimony obligations, vehicle registrations to cause of death. "From a theoretical point of view," he wrote, "the collection of data concerning each person can be increased to such perfection that the paper man gives a clear picture of the natural man." By analogy with the "totalitarian" form of government then developing in Europe, Lentz's objective could be similarly described as total registration. The Italian dictator Benito Mussolini famously described the former as "everything within the State, nothing outside the State, nothing against the State." Lentz's ambition was that everything be known to the state.[24]

It did not occur to Lentz that his system might be abused. It's not clear that he considered abuse a relevant concept; as long as an application was sanctioned by the state, it was legitimate. His system left no room at all for people who might fear or object to having such exact

THE SUM OF THE PEOPLE

paper surrogates of themselves in official hands. He was not alone in this oblivious optimism. As the historian Adam Tooze writes of the interwar period: "Across the world, bureaucrats were inspired to dreams of omniscience.... For the first time it became possible to conceive of an entire nation recorded in a single database instantly accessible by means of mechanical handling equipment."[25]

Lentz's system did not, in fact, use mechanical equipment—not yet, and not ever in any central way. But around the same time, the United States was pioneering an expansive new use for Hollerith machines: Social Security. This New Deal system employed the latest machines from IBM, recording employee wage contributions on punch cards. It was not fully automated; employee addresses, somewhat beyond the capabilities of the machines, were still stored in a separate written file. To link everything to the individual, the now-ubiquitous Social Security number was invented. By the end of 1937, the first full year of operation, thirty-seven million such numbers had been issued.[26]

That year, the *American Sociological Review* published a glowing appraisal of Lentz's book by Dorothy Swaine Thomas, a noted sociologist:

The aim of the New Deal in Dutch registration is to produce a paper surrogate for every living inhabitant. During his residence or lifetime in the country, the paper man follows the natural man in all his migrations, and, though the natural man may emigrate and must die, the paper man is assured statistical immortality in the archives of the Department of the Interior.... With Mr. Lentz' book as a guide, there should be no excuse for the misuse of the new Dutch population data.[27]

By misuse, Thomas meant *statistical* misuse, technical errors such as may arise from a misunderstood definition or misapplied technique. And yet, this breezy commentary is sandwiched between reviews of books with titles including *Under the Swastika, Under the Axe of Fascism, Europe Under the Terror,* and *Hitler.* In such a moment, statistical misuse was the least of concerns.

In 1937 only Germany was yet under the swastika, but the aspirations of the remilitarizing Nazi regime were no secret. Hitler's own inclinations were known since at least 1925, when he published *Mein Kampf*. They rested on his twinned intentions, reflected in the Nazi slogan of "blood and soil," to reshape the population of Germany according to a racist ideology (blood) and to reshape the territory of Germany through conquest (soil).

To justify territorial expansion, Hitler drew on the concept of lebensraum, the idea that the German people needed "living space" into which to expand. "Our movement must seek to abolish the present disastrous proportion between our population and the area of our national territory," he wrote. Although Germany's population had grown rapidly since the country's unification in 1871, its population density was still less than Britain's, and considerably less than that of England, Belgium, or the Netherlands. But as Hitler saw it, those countries already had lebensraum in their colonial empires. With Germany's overseas empire dismantled after the First World War, Hitler instead took the United States as his model. He imagined Eastern Europe as Germany's own American West: frontier lands to be conquered and incorporated into a greater German Reich.[28]

Hitler's racial ideology established an elaborate hierarchy, with Europe's Jews as the bottom rung. This drew, in part, on a long history of Jewish persecution and religious conflict in Europe. Hitler also embraced a myth, then popular, that Jews were responsible for the German defeat in World War I. But it was not religion or some particular alleged betrayal that mattered: it was the nebulous idea of blood. He likened Europe's Jews to "tuberculosis bacilli that could infect a healthy body." Since the largest number of European Jews lived in Poland and the Soviet Union, they were an obstacle to his plans of eastern expansion—the problems of blood and soil were linked.[29]

This ideology and the Nazi "race science" that developed to provide its pseudoscientific backing were not an entirely German phenomenon. Of course, Hitler's views were seen as extreme and repugnant by many

THE SUM OF THE PEOPLE

at the time, both inside and outside Germany. But anti-Semitism was casually accepted, to varying degrees, in much of the world then. Meanwhile, the idea of the population as a body whose health could be measured and manipulated was also promoted in Britain, the United States, and beyond, under the guise of eugenics.

Eugenics is the now-controversial science of manipulating human populations to improve their genetic "quality." The term was coined in 1883 by Francis Galton, an English polymath and another classifier of people. As well as inventing eugenics, Galton published the seminal text on fingerprints, building the scientific foundation for their use in forensics and identification. But he is best known as one of the founders of modern statistics. Because of the influence of Galton and his intellectual descendants, the history of statistics is inescapably entwined with that of eugenics.[30]

Galton was one of the founders of a new mathematical approach to statistics. Around the same time Graunt and Petty pioneered the simple numerical analysis of social data, the Frenchmen Blaise Pascal and Pierre de Fermat invented a new branch of mathematics, probability, to describe games of chance. This theory was deductive, used to answer questions about specific future events. For example: If one flips a fair coin ten times, how likely is it that it will come up heads every time? (Probability says we should expect it to happen—on average—once in every 1,024 attempts of ten flips.)

In the nineteenth century, statisticians realized that probability theory could be applied in reverse, inductively, working from specific, already-observed events to general truths about the world. Again: If a coin has come up heads ten times running, how likely is it that the coin is fair? (This is a more complex question, depending, for example, on how common we think unfair coins are in the wild.) This process became known as inference.[31]

Galton began to use these new mathematical methods to formalize the kind of analysis Quetelet had included in his *Treatise on Man*. Like his predecessor, Galton studied all manner of human differences, from simple physical traits like height, weight, and fingerprint morphology to more complex and ambiguous phenomena like criminality and intelligence. He developed new statistical tools—correlation and regression analysis—to examine the connections between these traits. These tools were to inferential statistics what cross-tabulation had been to descriptive statistics. They allowed him to quantify the underlying relationship between two variables, to make precise the obvious pattern that emerged when one cross-tabulated—for example, height with age.

But whereas Quetelet had conceived average as a kind of perfection, Galton saw it as mediocrity: something that should, and could, be improved. In his *Sketch,* Condorcet had written, somewhat fancifully, of the "organic perfectibility of man." Malthus had countered that there was no clear mechanism to support such a idea: while he acknowledged the selective breeding of animals and plants, he did not see its application to people. To his credit, Malthus saw a moral quandary: the "human race…could not be improved in this way, without condemning all the bad specimens to celibacy." Moreover, like most of his contemporaries, he thought selective breeding quite limited. "Were the breeding to continue for ever, the head and legs of these sheep would never be so small as the head and legs of a rat."[32]

In 1859, all that changed. Galton's half cousin Charles Darwin published *The Origin of Species by Means of Natural Selection* (inspired, in part, by Malthus's work). Darwinism implied almost unlimited possibilities for breeding; a sheep could indeed become a rat, given enough time. A decade later Darwin followed up with *The Descent of Man,* in which he explicitly applied evolutionary theory to the human species and touched upon the idea of *unnatural* selection. Galton, less conservative than Darwin, saw unnatural selection at work all around him—by, for example, migration, war, and social customs. Since it was happening anyway, Galton advocated that it be "intelligently directed." In 1883 he published *Human Faculty and Its Development,* in which he proposed incentives to encourage the production of children by "superior strains"—what would now be called positive eugenics. In so doing, Galton carried the project of social improvement radically beyond knowledge, culture, and institutions to the gene pool itself.[33]

There's no question that eugenics benefited from this early association with the pioneers of mathematical statistics; the latter was proving increasingly useful across a variety of fields. Statistical inference allowed statisticians to make principled decisions based on experiments and on data drawn from partial samples of the things they were studying. This was an alien concept for census takers, who were used to collecting data on every person, but it was a common tactic in commercial settings. In industry there was often little alternative: the Edison company, for instance, could not test every bulb for failure. This practical utility allowed statistics to grow well beyond its origins in public administration.

The first academic department of statistics was established at University College London by Galton's student—and fellow eugenicist—Karl Pearson in 1911. This new scientific, inferential statistics borrowed language from the older descriptive science: a "population" was the entire set of relevant subject units, whether people or light bulbs or something else, and a "census" was data collected for the entire population (as opposed to a sample). But otherwise, the academic science had little connection to what was practiced in government offices. All the way to the 1940s, government statistical offices owed more to Hollerith than Galton, using very little of the new theory but continuing to count, measure, and classify as they always had.[34]

Meanwhile, eugenics traveled in the opposite direction, growing from intellectual, theoretical origins to become a mainstream issue of public policy. By the first years of the twentieth century it was widely accepted in Britain, anchored by the statistical work of Galton and Pearson, and endorsed by figures as diverse as H. G. Wells, Winston Churchill, Sidney and Beatrice Webb, and John Maynard Keynes. And while eugenics was framed, in Galton's initial work, as encouraging valued traits, it soon slipped into a negative mode, the discouragement or outright prevention of reproduction by those bearing supposedly undesirable traits. In the United States it was used to justify the forced sterilization of mental patients, the "idiotic or insane" people who had been enumerated in censuses since 1840. American eugenics disproportionately targeted African American, Native American, and immigrant populations (it gave, for example, a new pseudoscientific underpinning to old anti-miscegenation laws). In Germany, eugenic ideas under the euphemism of "race hygiene" motivated Nazi targeting of those they considered genetically inferior, including disabled people, gay people, Sinti, and Roma.

But Hitler's own particular obsession remained the Jews. Eugenic ideas framed his vision of a world in which Aryans and Jews were in an existential, Darwinian struggle. This worldview was incoherent and pseudoscientific, not least the attempt to define races. A joke of the time, whispered in German, went that an Aryan was blond like Hitler, tall like Goebbels, and slim like Göring (these Nazi leaders being, respectively, brunette, short, and fat). Neither did the Jewish "race" of Hitler's imagining really exist: no single clear definition could encompass what was, by then, a complex community, diasporic in origin yet long-established in Europe.

• • •

Unlike the other major monotheistic religions, the Jewish faith has not, at least in the last millennium, been one of proselytism. The most common way to be recognized as Jewish is by birth to a Jewish mother—matrilineal descent. This rule is not universal; some communities recognize patrilineal descent, and conversions, while rare, are quite possible. Still, the Jews of early twentieth-century Europe could trace their ancestry—albeit with considerable intermarriage—to people who once lived in the Middle East and had, over centuries, migrated into Europe, bringing with them a distinct literature and culture.

Migration like this is the rule, not the exception, in human history. The Angles of England and the Turks of Turkey were both originally from somewhere other than their names now suggest. Christianity and Islam spread far beyond their own Middle Eastern origins, a result of both migration and conversion. The central European Jews—the Ashkenazim—differed only by arriving in smaller numbers and in peace, living alongside preexisting communities rather than conquering or converting them. But neither were they fully absorbed into these predominantly Christian communities, maintaining, to different degrees in different places, a distinct cultural identity.[35]

By the early 1930s, there were over nine million Jews in Europe, and their situation varied markedly by country. In Western and Northern Europe, Jews were often culturally assimilated, living freely and without much distinction among their compatriots. While anti-Semitism persisted, the Jews of Germany, Britain, France, and the Netherlands—over a million people—were integrated into national cultures and nominally enjoyed the same legal rights as anyone else.[36]

But the majority of European Jews, over 6 million, lived further east, the majority in Poland and the Soviet Union. The legacy of discrimination under Russian imperial rule meant that the large Jewish communities in these countries—although theoretically granted the same rights as non-Jews—remained separate, segregated into clearly defined Jewish quarters and maintaining a distinct language and modes of dress. In Poland's 1931 census, for example, 2.5 million people reported Yiddish as their mother tongue (nearly as many as the 3.1 million who reported Jewish religion). These differences would soon have significant implications for how Jewish populations fared under Nazi occupation—not least in how they were identified in the first place.[37]

In invoking a Jewish "race" Hitler was flattening a blend of religion, ethnicity, community affiliation, custom, and ancestry into a monolithic supposedly biological group of his own invention. The question of "Who is a Jew?" was not one to which Jews themselves had a consistent answer, and it was certainly not scientific. So before the Nazis could set about destroying the Jewish race, they had to construct it.

• • •

Hitler was appointed chancellor of Germany in January 1933, quickly assuming dictatorial powers. He took Max Weber's observation—that bureaucracy would serve any master, that he need only "change the top officials"—to heart. On April 7, a law was passed dismissing civil servants of non-Aryan descent, including those working in statistical offices. Around the same time, the president of the Reich Statistical

Office was fired; a new man, Wolfgang Reichardt, was appointed shortly thereafter.[38]

For the statisticians who remained, 1933 signaled the start of—in the words of one historian—a "statistics boom," which would see Reichardt's office double in size over six years. The boom started with a census. One had been planned for 1930, under the Weimar Republic, but was repeatedly postponed because of the difficult fiscal situation of the German states, which still bore the burden of census taking. Under Nazi control, these objections were swept away. On April, 20 1933, a special law ordered that the census should proceed the following June, conducted by the states but under the close supervision of Reichardt's office.[39]

Most of the census's planning predated the change of government, but one late procedural modification hinted at a quiet change in the role of official statistics. In past censuses, states would often dispose of the voluminous census returns as soon as statistical tabulations were completed. This now changed: an order was issued that original returns could only be destroyed with the consent of the central Reich Statistical Office. Already, perhaps, the Nazi regime anticipated additional uses for these records.[40]

The census went ahead on June 17, with several hundred thousand enumerators enlisted, including civil servants, teachers, and even police officers. Under the decentralized processing model, only the state statistical office of Prussia and the Reichardt's central office used Hollerith machines. Nonetheless Willy Heidinger, the chair of Dehomag (IBM's German subsidiary), was clear about the role his company could play amid the new boom in statistics and record keeping. In a January 1934 speech he explained, "We are recording the individual characteristics of every single member of the nation onto a little card... so that our physician [Hitler] can determine whether... the results calculated in this manner stand in a harmonious, healthy relation to one another, or whether unhealthy conditions must be cured by corrective interventions."[41]

Among the results that were of greatest interest to the Nazi authorities was the size of the Jewish population. Before the census, Joseph Goebbels, the Reich minister of propaganda, had claimed that as many as 2 million Jews lived in Germany. But the final count of 67 million Germans included just 505,000 people classified as Jewish. That classification was based on a long-standing religion question, which depended on formal membership in a congregation. Goebbels's claim was vastly exaggerated, but it was true that the census had not counted somewhere between a quarter and half a million nonpracticing Jews, or people of mixed descent, in its Jewish total.[42]

It took time for the race scientists of the Reich to agree on a broader definition that could encompass such people. They finally did so with the passing of the Nuremberg Laws in 1935, which stripped Jews of citizenship and forbade marriage between Jews and non-Jews. These high stakes now demanded that clear lines be drawn, so the laws established a new definition of Jewishness based on ancestry. A person would be considered Jewish if three or all four grandparents had been born into Jewish communities. A person with only one or two such grandparents was considered to be a *mischling*—of mixed blood.[43]

Over the years that followed, various organs of the state and the party, in both local offices and Berlin, began to assemble lists of Jews and non-Jews sorted according to these definitions. Names of prominent or politically active Jews were quietly collected by the Gestapo, Germany's secret police. Jewish and Christian religious institutions shared data under various degrees of duress, the latter to identify Jews who had converted through baptism. At first these records were consulted directly, but soon they were copied wholesale onto index cards—the Jewish Index—for more convenient access.[44]

By 1938 the authorities had access to many sources of data, overlapping and incomplete, on Jews in Germany. That year, over two days beginning November 9, Jewish homes, businesses, and synagogues were attacked, and hundreds killed, in an orchestrated campaign of terror known as the Night of Broken Glass (*Kristallnacht*). This escalation of violence was a demonstration of how vulnerable many Jews were, even in the absence of the complete lists the Nazis sought. A synagogue was an obvious, public building and couldn't simply blend into the background. The intention of this violence was to encourage the self-deportation of Jews. But behind closed doors, those partial lists were being tested: in the immediate wake of the violence, some thirty thousand Jewish men were rounded up and incarcerated in camps.[45]

As the prospect of war drew closer, Nazi efforts to improve their systems of population control accelerated. Over 1938, a series of decrees established a population register (*Melderegister*), imposing a duty of registration on residents and collecting information that included grandparents' religions, in line with Nuremberg Laws. It was held in police stations and organized alphabetically. In April 1939, yet another district-level population register—the *Volkskartei* or People's Card File—was established, building upon the *Melderegister*. This index was organized by age, designed primarily to support enlistment during the anticipated war. It included fields like foreign languages spoken, time spent living abroad, and any specialized skills of military use. Residents were to fill out their own cards at police stations. Links to identification papers, work permits, and ration cards would make it difficult to evade.[46]

But enrollment in the *Volkskartei* was delayed until later in the year. In the meantime the highly anticipated census of 1939 was expected to produce a new, definitive list of Jews in Germany. In addition to the regular schedule, a so-called supplementary card was delivered to each household. This card focused on just two additional topics: occupation (for military mobilization) and ancestry. The latter operationalized the Nuremberg race definitions, asking for each person in the household, "Were or are any of the grandparents full-Jewish by race?" with a column for each grandparent. The card includes example rows to make clear how households should respond. The fate of the fictional, perfectly Aryan Schmitz family (*nein—nein—nein—nein*) would be very different from that of their imaginary neighbor Solly Cohn (*ja—ja—ja—ja*). Once completed, each card was to be placed in a sealed envelope, a show of confidentiality that belied the murky reality of statistics in the Third Reich.[47]

As soon as the supplementary cards had been collected, statistical offices found themselves deflecting requests from various authorities intent on using them to improve their lists of Jews. The official line was that statistical processing was to take precedence. This time, the records for the entire country were processed by machine tabulation in Berlin, a reflection of increasing centralization under the Reich Statistical Office. A rough count was completed by March 1940, with a final total reported a year later. The census had counted 331,000 full Jews and around 115,000 mixed Jews, a marked decline since 1933 (albeit the numbers are not directly comparable).[48]

With statistical tabulation complete, the supplementary cards were immediately repurposed—not to satisfy ad hoc requests but for a more systematic project. From around April to September 1941, they were used to check and update the files of the *Volkskartei*. Neither race nor religion appeared as a standard entry in that register, but its operators began marking the cards of Jews: first with a black letter *J*, then later with a black tab affixed to the top edge—the better to efficiently find the Jewish cards when needed.[49]

Even once this was done, the Nazi state had two further uses for the supplementary cards. First, they were passed to the Reich Office for Genealogical Research, an agency that made detailed case-by-case investigations and final determinations on the Aryan ancestry of individuals (some proof had to be offered, for example, to retain a civil service job; even more to join the SS). Second, they were processed again by the Reich Statistical Office, to build yet another register, the so-called Ethnic Card File (*Volkstumskartei*). Completed by the spring of 1940, it included all those who were not of Aryan ethnicity and was probably the most comprehensive listing of Jews yet.[50]

These two enumerations, 1933 and 1939, were the only official censuses conducted in Nazi Germany. Historians still argue about exactly what role they played in the identification, deportation, and murder of Germany's Jews. They were not the only sources of information and were processed slowly, so that many addresses would already have been out of date by the time they found their way to the Gestapo or other authorities involved in arrests and roundups.[51]

But trying to apportion blame between the many overlapping censuses, registers, and other lists in Nazi Germany seems to miss the point. This apparently chaotic approach to information gathering was itself a mechanism of control: lying to the authorities in one registration was all the more hazardous if one's name might appear on some other list anyway. In the same way, failing to wear an identifying mark was risky when identity papers, clearly marked with a *J* for Jews, might be demanded at any time. Each system acted as a check on all the others.

Any attempt to draw a clear dividing line between, for example, the 1939 *Volkskartei* registration (run by police) and the near-simultaneous 1939 census (ostensibly run by statisticians) is artificial. Ordinary people did not appear to make such a distinction. By then, the formerly professional, scientific, independent statistical services of Germany had been subverted to the purposes of the Nazi regime. The separation between official statistics and systems of surveillance, the tracking of individuals and businesses, had been eliminated entirely.[52]

In 1940, Wolfgang Reichardt finally recognized this. In that year, his eighth as president of the Reich Statistical Office, he contributed a rather unexpected essay to a volume in honor of Friedrich Zahn, then Germany's most esteemed living statistician. As president of the German Statistical Society, Zahn had enthusiastically committed his discipline to the cause of the Nazi party, of which he was a member. "In its very essence," he wrote, "statistics is closely related to the National Socialist movement." Unlike Zahn, Reichardt had never joined the party, but his career had benefited from its rule, so the elegiac tone of his essay, bordering on critical, is quite surprising.[53]

Reichardt noted what had changed since the Nazi seizure of power and what had been lost:

> At all times in the civilized world, the reliability of official statistics has been founded on the conviction amongst the population being questioned that their returns are protected by so-called 'statistical confidentiality', i.e. that their individual returns are made only to the statistical authority and only for statistical purposes, and may never be used for administrative measures against the individual respondent.[54]

The historian Adam Tooze describes Reichardt's essay as "a brave defence of liberal principles," though arguably Reichardt was actually defending the principles of scientific integrity, which just happened to align with those of liberty. This same motivation can be seen in Reichardt's approach to the 1939 supplementary cards: he did not exclude nonstatistical uses but merely subordinated them to the statistical uses. Reichardt's principles were fatally compromised; in his post since 1933, he had himself been party to the "great, far-reaching changes to the nature, constitution and organization of the official German Reich statistics," of which he now wrote despairingly.[55]

Still, unlike so many civil servants in Nazi Germany, Reichardt did, eventually, reach a breaking point. Unhappy with plans to increase the influence of the Nazi party in selecting personnel for his office, Reichardt resigned. According to the official history he "retired to private life in 1940 as a sick man."[56]

• • •

On September 1, 1939, Germany invaded Poland, and the Second World War officially began. "In the occupied countries," write the historians Goetz Aly and Karl Heinz Roth, "census takers filed in immediately behind the German army." So it was in Warsaw. By the end of September the city had fallen, and paramilitaries entered the city to establish administrative control. They immediately established a Jewish council and appointed as its chair Adam Czerniakow, a nonobservant Jew who had been active in city politics. During the war and immediately afterward, Jews in such positions were dismissed as collaborators. But Czerniakow's diaries, which survived the war, tell a more complex, sympathetic story.[57]

Among Czerniakow's earliest tasks was to enumerate the Jewish population of Warsaw. On October 4, just days after the city fell, he was intercepted by the security police and brought to their headquarters. Two issues were discussed: the structure of the Jewish Council and preparations for a census. The logistics of this count consumed much of his next three weeks, his diary entries filled with references to census questionnaires, census stations, census commissioners, and census expenses. It took place on October 28, and within three days there was already an initial count of three hundred sixty thousand Jews.[58]

It is unclear to what extent the census, so urgently called, was used to identify Jews. The Jewish community in Warsaw was more distinct and already more localized than in most German cities. Even as Czerniakow prepared his report, the Nazi occupiers were working to construct a ghetto to further segregate the Jews from the broader city of Warsaw. Soon signs went up around its borders: "Warning! Epidemics. Entry forbidden." Many Jews already lived in the district chosen for the ghetto. But many did not: the creation of the ghetto involved an exchange of over a hundred thousand Jews and Poles. The census may have played a part in this.[59]

One thing it would certainly have been used for is administering the ghetto's prison economy. For around eighteen months following the invasion, the Nazi occupiers used the captive Jewish population as a source of slave labor. While rations in the ghetto were at starvation levels, even this required careful planning, given that links to the outside had been severely curtailed.[60]

Warsaw's Jews were themselves uneasy about the census and uncertain as to its purpose. Chaim Kaplan, another ghetto diarist, records for October 25, "Another sign that bodes ill: Today, notices informed the Jewish population of Warsaw that next Saturday there will be a census of Jewish inhabitants.... Our hearts tell us of evil—some catastrophe for the Jews of Warsaw lies in this census. Otherwise there would be no need for it." On the day of the census, he reiterated the thought: "The order for a census states that it is being held to gather data for administrative purposes. That's a neat phrase, but it contains catastrophe.... We are certain that this census is being taken for the purpose of expelling 'nonproductive elements.' And there are a great many of us now.... We are all caught in a net, doomed to destruction."[61]

Perhaps there are echoes of the ancient biblical prohibition on numbering the Jews in Kaplan's apprehension. But his fears were soon proved more than superstition. The final "administrative purpose" to which the census was put was to schedule enough trains, with enough boxcars, to completely empty the ghetto. That final catastrophe was slow to unfold, but on July 22, 1942, the deportations began.

• • •

Eight months after the first shots were fired in Poland, Germany took the war west, invading France, the Netherlands, Belgium, and Luxemburg on May 10, 1940. Once again would-be census takers followed in the tracks of the panzer divisions. But the Jewish populations they encountered presented a more difficult target than their counterparts to the east. The Jews of Western Europe were more assimilated and could not easily be corralled in ghettos. Before they could be deported, they would have to be identified and extracted from among the general populations.

The whole approach of the invading Germany army was different. In the Nazi racial hierarchy, the Slavs of Eastern Europe ranked near to the bottom—above the Jews, but hardly worthy of much better treatment. That was not the case for many people the Nazis encountered as they swept westward. Some, like the French, they considered inferior but not so far inferior as to be subhuman *Untermenschen,* as they labeled those in the east. Some, like the Luxembourgers, might even be considered Aryan.

A tiny country wedged between France and Germany, Luxembourg stood no chance of resisting invasion. The grand duchess and her family fled into exile in England, and German paratroopers faced only light resistance. Germany had occupied Luxembourg in 1914, too, but then the objective had been military: to gain a position from which to invade France. This time, Germany's leaders were motivated by a grander aspiration: to create a Greater Reich that would incorporate all Germanic peoples.[62]

Their immediate priority was dealing with those who would have no place in the future Reich: Luxembourg's 3,500 Jews, some of whom had already escaped Nazi persecution further east. In September 1940, the Nuremberg Laws were extended to Luxembourg, and 2,500 Jews fled, mostly to France. With the Jewish population thus diminished, the occupiers worked on drawing the remaining ethnic Luxembourgers closer to the Reich. Joseph Goebbels suggested that a "census" be used to affirm their German character. Given the chance, the Nazis assumed, Luxembourgers would surely follow Austria's example and join the Reich with enthusiasm. The census included three specific questions, the responses to which would conclusively demonstrate the people's desire to be German: nationality, mother tongue, and ethnicity. To each, the expected answer—the correct answer—was "German."[63]

It failed spectacularly. In advance of the October 10, 1941, census date, the still-embryonic resistance mounted an underground leafleting campaign. It entreated people to answer the census questions *dräimol Letzebuergesch*—three times Luxembourgish. As early sample counts came in, it was clear that the people—over 95 percent—had done so, overwhelmingly rejecting German identity. The occupation leader, Gustav Simon, monitored the results through the night, his consternation growing. At four a.m. the next morning, a telegram was sent to newspapers: "the filling in of the census cards must cease."[64]

For the resistance, the failure of the census was a propaganda victory. It was a clear rebuke to Goebbels and a decisive rejection of the Greater Reich. Writing immediately after the war, the historian Paul Weber called it "the only day of unmitigated jubilation during the five long prison-years of the war." Luxembourg would remain occupied, but Luxembourgers had withheld their consent. They remained, defiantly, three times Luxembourgish.[65]

Simon, furious, was quick to enact reprisals: within days further repressive ordinances were enacted, and mass arrests followed. Symbolism could not save Luxembourg's remaining eight hundred Jews; in fact, it may have brought forward their fate. They were rounded up and interned, eventually to be loaded onto trains to camps in the east. On October 17, 1941, just a week after the census, Luxembourg was declared free of Jews.[66]

The Netherlands, larger and better defended than Luxembourg, held out for five days against the German invaders, until aerial bombardment of Rotterdam forced surrender on May 15, 1940. As in Luxembourg, the Dutch queen Wilhelmina and the government were evacuated to London. For a moment, it looked as if occupation might be short-lived. But with the Allies' disorderly evacuation from Dunkirk just a fortnight later, it became clear that there would be no quick liberation.

The Nazis considered the Dutch, like the Luxembourgers, to be a Germanic people. Rather than a military leader, an Austrian civilian, party member Arthur Seyss-Inquart, was appointed to head the occupation. He inherited a Dutch bureaucracy more or less intact. The government in exile had left orders that secretaries-general of the ministries should continue in their roles "in the interests of the state." Though Seyss-Inquart gave them the option of resigning, few did. When civil servants were asked to sign a document attesting to their Aryan ancestry, almost all complied. Was it not a civil servant's duty to remain at his post, even if he served a new master?[67]

If that moral dilemma weighed on Jacobus Lentz, whose system of total registration now came under Gestapo control, it didn't show. By all accounts, Lentz was not ideologically a Nazi or particularly anti-Semitic. He was, however, an authoritarian and pro-German in a general way. The respect was mutual: the Security Service of the SS was impressed with his work on the population registry, which exceeded anything Germany had. There was no need here for a hurried census; Lentz's card file was already quite comprehensive. But could he also, they wondered, design a photographic identity card to accompany the register?[68]

Lentz had suggested such a card system before German occupation, in 1939 and again in March 1940. He had been thwarted by the Dutch cabinet, whose members viewed the proposal as illiberal, seeming to treat ordinary citizens as criminals. Mere months later, in August 1940, with that cabinet in exile, the occupying Germans were offering Lentz an opportunity to at last realize this ambition. He held nothing back, traveling to Berlin to confer with German experts on the latest anti-forgery techniques. (He soon wrote a second book, another four hundred pages, on this system.)[69]

The new identity card was issued to all Dutch citizens over the course of 1941. Dutch Jews were the first to be enrolled, beginning in January. This was accomplished quickly and completely: nearly 160,000 presented themselves at registration offices. Their cards were stamped unmistakably with a large, black letter *J*. Thus marked, Jews were now subjected to a range of anti-Semitic measures that were aimed, along similar lines to those in Germany, at social isolation and economic exclusion. They were banned from cinemas, public parks, swimming

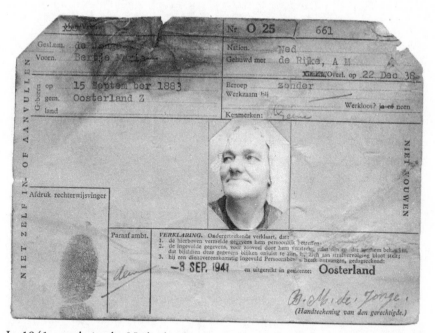

In 1941 people in the Netherlands were required to register for a new identity card, designed by Jacobus Lentz. The registration receipts, including this one for Bertje Maria de Jonge, were forwarded to the central population registry. Many were later damaged or destroyed in the aerial bombardment of the Kleykamp building in 1944. (Credit: Luuk Brand.)

pools, and some professional occupations (having already, by then, been expelled from the government administration).[70]

The introduction of the identity card increased the importance of Lentz's central registry. According to his 1936 manual, only files for people not covered by a municipal registry were kept centrally. But as the countrywide reregistration took place over 1941, duplicates for every person were forwarded to the registry in the Hague. Those copies, supervised by the compliant Lentz, were much more accessible to the occupying Nazis

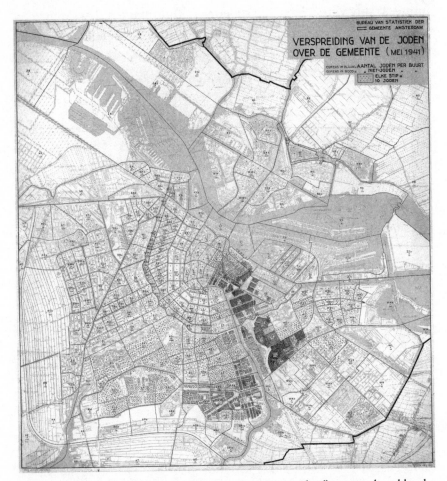

This map, entitled "Distribution of Jews in the Municipality," was produced by the City Office of Statistics of Amsterdam based on the January 1941 registration of Jews. The legend notes, "Every dot = 10 Jews." (Resistance Museum, Amsterdam.)

than the originals, which were distributed across multiple municipal of-fices. A few months after the initial registration of Jews, a member of the SS requested that Lentz compile an alphabetic punch card index from the duplicate files, to more efficiently search for different subgroups.[71]

The following year on July 4, letters were mass-mailed to Dutch Jews at their registered addresses, requiring them to assemble for de-portation.[72] In her diary, Anne Frank records her family receiving such a letter the following day:

> Margot appeared in the kitchen doorway looking very agitated. "Fa-ther has received a call-up notice from the SS."...I was stunned. A call-up: everyone knows what that means. Visions of concentration camps and lonely cells raced through my head.[73]

Concentration camps and lonely cells were just the beginning, as Lentz and his compatriots must soon have known. On July 29, 1942, Radio Oranje, the official station of the Dutch government in exile in London, made a broadcast that placed these "call-ups" in European context: "Just how does it help the German war effort to herd together thousands of defenceless Jewish Poles and do away with them in gas-chambers? How does it help the war effort when thousands of Jew-ish Dutchmen are dragged out of their country?" (Dutch Jews them-selves would have missed this warning: any not already interned were forbidden by this time from owning radios.)[74]

• • •

In his 1922 essay, Max Weber wrote that "bureaucracy is among those social structures which are the hardest to destroy." Lentz's Dutch regis-tration bureaucracy proved especially resilient. Across occupied Eu-rope, forgery was the preferred method to defeat identity cards. By obtaining a forged identity card, a Jew could adopt an Aryan-sounding name or make a stamped *J* vanish. An outlawed member of the resist-ance might assume a new identity entirely. Fake German identity cards were notoriously common in occupied Poland.[75]

Not so in the Netherlands. The quality of Lentz's card, with multiple antiforgery devices, made counterfeiting a more dangerous proposition. In such circumstances, the safest form of forgery was an original. The resistance had infiltrated local registration offices, and smuggled authentic blanks could be used to produce convincing fakes. It might even be possible, if risky, to have a sympathetic clerk slip a matching file into the local registry, so that a police check on a suspicious identity card would find nothing amiss. But Lentz's system created one more barrier to such an attempt: the duplicate files kept by the central population registry in the Hague. That anyone at all succeeded in using fake cards was only because these additional checks were not always made.[76]

The Dutch resistance tried in vain to defeat this system. They sent death threats to Lentz and denounced him in underground newspapers. This nearly worked: he tried to resign but instead accepted the offer of a bodyguard from the occupation authorities. So the resistance fighters tried sabotage. They successfully bombed local municipal registries, including in Amsterdam. But the damage was minimal—the files were kept in steel cabinets—and the effect even less, since a local register could always be reconstructed from the central duplicates. Meanwhile, the Kleykamp building in the Hague, home to the duplicates themselves, was too well-defended to make a promising target for saboteurs.[77]

Toward the end of 1943, a new measure was announced that was designed to flush out any fake identity cards. New ration cards would be issued to each person—but only upon presentation of his or her identity card. This would enable officials to carefully check, and place a new stamp, on the identity card. With its members threatened by this plan, the Dutch resistance appealed to London for a bombing raid on the factories that produced the new cards and the authorizing stamps. A few weeks later, Kleykamp itself was added to this list of potential targets. The message was sent to London on December 16 by Pierre Louis d'Aulnis de Bourouill, who had been trained by the British Special Operations executive:

Above: The 1944 raid on the Dutch population registry was well planned. A detailed model was built to brief the squadron. The arrow points to the target, the Kleykamp building. At the left is the Peace Palace. (Imperial War Museum MOD 152.)

Below: A low-level oblique photograph taken during the raid shows the Kleykamp building a "sea of flames." The angle is from the right of the model above, looking back toward the tower of the Peace Palace. (Imperial War Museum C 4320.)

Permanent forgery of the personal identity cards impossible because a governmental inspection department, manned by German sympathizers, of the population registry holds copies of all real data. It has been established that these copies are exclusively and completely saved in a housing in The Hague, destruction of same not possible by us. In case RAF destroys these archives, we will be able to forge the municipal registry which will make many persons legal.[78]

On Tuesday, April 11, 1944, the Royal Air Force gave the Dutch agent his reply. The six Mosquito bombers, squadron leader Robert Bateson in the lead and Robbie Cohen bringing up the rear, left the Kleykamp building in flames. It was later described by the British Air Ministry as "probably the most brilliant feat of low-level precision bombing of the war."[79]

Around sixty Dutch citizens died that day, civilians cut down in the middle of their work day (and not all were German sympathizers, as d'Aulnis de Bourouill had supposed). The British and Dutch mission planners had anticipated such a death toll. A calculation had been made. The raid had had to occur in daytime, during office hours, to ensure that the file cabinets were open and their contents vulnerable to destruction. The exact time was chosen in the hope that civilians would be off the streets, at lunch, but casualties in the building itself were all but guaranteed.[80]

In the end, fewer than half the records were destroyed—a seemingly poor result given the high cost in Dutch lives. And yet it was probably enough to make a difference to the resistance. With even a quarter of the records destroyed, every fourth identity card in the country—whether real or forged—could no longer be centrally verified. Suppose a suspected resistance member were arrested, their (forged) papers checked, and no central duplicate found. So what? Many law-abiding people would have been in the same position. The Kleykamp attack didn't need to destroy everything to be effective, but just enough to cast doubt on the whole system.

Quite aside from the deaths of his colleagues, it must have infuriated Lentz to see his collection disordered and crippled in such a fashion. Indeed, he never really recovered from the campaign against the population registry. A few months after the Kleykamp bombing, Allied troops landed in Normandy and began advancing up the coast toward the Netherlands. In August 1944, when Paris fell, the outcome of the war must have been obvious to even the most ardent believer. Soon, the anonymous resistance fighters who had threatened and attacked Lentz and his system would be the victors. By that time Lentz was, in the words of historian Louis de Jong, "broken and trembling, chained to the system that he had designed four years earlier with so much devotion and satisfaction."[81]

• • •

For Dutch Jews, the attacks on the population registry came too late: the deportations had, by and large, already happened. A Jewish population of around 160,000 (including 20,000 of mixed descent), registered in 1941, was reduced, by 1945, to around 35,000. Around 73 percent of Dutch "full Jews" were killed, the highest proportion of any Western occupied country. The fatality rates for the Jews of neighboring Belgium and France were 40 percent and 24 percent respectively. With so much else in common between those countries, historians have pointed to the cooperative bureaucracy and uniquely effective Dutch registration system as key factors explaining the different outcome.[82]

In France as in the Netherlands, Nazi administrators attempted to exploit population registration as a tool of genocide, but their attempts were less successful. France did not have an existing system to draw on, and the civil servants who offered to build one, using the very latest punch card technology, proved far less cooperative than Jacobus Lentz.

France had been one of the first countries after the United States to adopt Hollerith's tabulating machines, using the system for census processing in 1896. But French statisticians found the system cumbersome and did not return to it immediately. It took until the early 1920s for the technology to reestablish itself in France, first in commercial use and then in government. By the mid-1930s the national government was again the largest French customer of machines from both IBM and its competitors. As war approached, the most advanced government punch card project was a register of conscripts and military personnel, headed by René Carmille, an army officer.[83]

In June 1940, France fell to the invading German army and was divided into two: an occupied zone in the north and a client state in the south, administered from the city of Vichy. Under the terms of the armistice, the French army was reduced to a hundred thousand men. Suddenly Carmille found himself living in the Vichy state, his conscription project canceled. He offered instead, in August 1940, to create a new population register of all Vichy residents—under the cover of which he planned to create a covert file for future mobilization of a French army. What he proposed was more sophisticated even than Lentz's Dutch registry. Each person's file would include one written file, with multiple photographs, but also two punch cards—one containing demographic details and one encoding name and address. The government agreed, and in November Carmille was appointed head of a new Vichy Demographic Service.[84]

Meanwhile attempts began to identify and isolate French Jews. The Nuremberg Laws were extended to occupied France in May 1941. Implementation was more difficult, however, than in Germany or the Netherlands. France was a staunchly secular state and had no up-to-date information about its population of Jewish citizens; the last census including a religion question had been in 1872. There were, however, perhaps two hundred thousand foreign Jews living in France, refugees from further east. These were more easily identifiable and less able to blend in to the French population, and the French authorities were less inclined to protect them. An early mandatory registration was decreed in September 1940, resulting in a written file containing names, addresses, and professions of a hundred fifty thousand Jews, of whom sixty-four thousand were foreign-born. Based on this, 6,494 summonses were delivered to the homes of Jews in Paris, mostly foreigners, in May 1941.[85]

From having not much information on its Jewish population, France soon had a surfeit. In early summer 1941, Carmille was planning a census of the professional skills of people age fourteen to sixty-five in the Vichy zone, clearly designed to support his covert mobilization file. At the same time, the recently appointed general commissioner for Jewish questions in Vichy, Xavier Vallat, was planning a census of Jews in parallel with a similar census in the occupied zone. Carmille suggested these efforts be coordinated. He added to his census of professions a question (number 11) asking Jews to identify the religions of their grandparents, in line with the Nuremberg definitions.[86]

In working with Vallat, Carmille saw an opportunity to increase the financial, human, and tabulation resources available to him. He offered to handle processing of both censuses, including the returns from occupied France. The offer was accepted. Indeed the German occupiers must have been impressed by Carmille's ambition: in October 1941, he was appointed head of a new National Statistical Service, which took responsibility for all statistics in both the occupied and Vichy zones.[87]

The new service merged several existing agencies, including the country's oldest statistical office, the Statistique générale de la France, which had a pedigree dating back to 1833. Apparently the merger caused consternation among the conservative statisticians of the Statistique générale, who had internalized the notion of statistical confidentiality and were worried about the consequences of moving from purely statistical processing to maintaining administrative files. Carmille had no such concerns. He embraced Lentz's aspiration of creating a paper man. "We are no longer dealing with general censuses," he wrote to Vallat, "but we are really following individuals."[88]

But for all his promises, as soon as Carmille had custody of the census returns, his operation went quiet. He offered various excuses. The boxes of schedules had been delivered to him incomplete. He struggled to acquire sufficient tabulators. But a year later, still no results had been produced. Vallat had not received the lists of Jews he sought—either from his census of Jews or from question 11 of Carmille's own census.[89]

In November 1942 Germany formally occupied the whole of France, bringing an end to the Vichy regime. The occupying administration soon became suspicious of Carmille's inexplicably inefficient operation. A German intelligence officer, captured after the war, explained that his office received, in 1943, "information about a special bureau in Lyon which, under the cover of a census of the population, was in fact a secret mobilization office."

Following this tip, Gestapo agents secretly obtained a sample of Carmille's punch cards. These confirmed their suspicions. As the intelligence officer explained, Carmille's office "could find, in a matter of moments, using special cards, all the specialists (Aviators, Tank Drivers, Mechanics, etc. . . .) needed to make up organized units." Surprisingly, the German authorities did not act immediately on this information. Compromised as it was, Carmille's work was still important to the war effort. He remained at liberty for almost a year before SS security officers finally arrested him in February 1944.[90]

As for the lists of Jews, according to the later testimony of his son Robert, Carmille never intended to produce them. As a young man, Robert had assisted his father in the tabulation effort. In 2001, then about eighty, he was interviewed by Edwin Black, author of *IBM and the Holocaust*. He insisted that the statistical service, far from collaborating, had sabotaged the tabulations, intentionally failing to punch the information on religion. Black asked him how he could be so certain.

"We never punched column eleven!" Carmille responded, meaning the column that would indicate religion. "Never."[91]

It's unclear exactly what Robert Carmille was referring to. Question 11 on the census of occupations—which did identify Jews—would not necessarily have corresponded to column 11 on a punch card. The punch card used in the census of occupations had two places in which Jewish race might be marked, neither of which is column 11. Perhaps after more than half a century, he was simply confusing the questionnaire itself and the punch card.[92]

· · ·

Ultimately seventy-five thousand French Jews were rounded up and deported to concentration camps in the east, even without the acceleration promised by Carmille's punch card operation. For most, their final destination was the complex at Auschwitz, in Poland, the largest of the Nazi camps, responsible for the greatest number of deaths (around one million in total). There they mingled with some of the hundred seven thousand Dutch Jews transported east, as well as some of those removed from Luxembourg, Germany, and Poland itself. Although Jews comprised the largest number, ethnic Poles, Roma and Sinti, Soviet prisoners of war, gay people, and political prisoners were all dispatched to camps across Europe.[93]

The scene that unfolded at Auschwitz is now darkly familiar from memoirs, literary accounts, and films. Victims disembark trains. Possessions are confiscated. Families are separated. Human beings are stripped naked, heads shaved, bodies tattooed with a number. A long process of dehumanization ends as it has begun, with registration. The process of genocide has passed through systematic phases of isolation, exclusion, deportation, and imprisonment. By stages, human beings have been reduced to mere sets of discrete characteristics: male/female, Pole/Jew/Gypsy, fit for work/unfit for work. Passing under the infamous gates, these are no longer people but things to be processed: ingested, selected, enumerated. And, once no longer useful, destroyed.

But Auschwitz was not typical of the Holocaust as a whole. Over a million victims in Eastern Europe never reached a camp and were simply shot or gassed near where they lived. Close to a million died in ghettos, some from acts of violence, but many from starvation and disease. Moreover, Auschwitz was, in part, a work camp: one reason it resonates in memory today is that it lasted the war. It had survivors who could be liberated and who could eventually tell their stories.[94]

This was not how things ended for the Jews of the Warsaw Ghetto, including the three hundred sixty thousand enumerated by Adam Czerniakow's October 1939 census. From July to September 1942, those who had not already succumbed to starvation and disease were transported a short distance by rail. They arrived in Treblinka, the final destination for perhaps a million people: over nine hundred thousand Jews from all over Europe, as well as an unknown number of others. It was an extermination camp: a facility constructed for the pure pursuit of industrial-scale murder. Unlike work camps, extermination camps like Treblinka, Bełżec, Chełmno, and Sobibór had only a minimal permanent population. There was no selection and no registration; nobody was tattooed on arrival. There was no point: nearly all were dead within hours, dumped in mass graves.

Treblinka was a model of efficiency, processing up to fifteen thousand people per day. Once they stepped off the trains, the victims were not so much counted as massed and measured: so many cubic meters in a gas chamber, so many in a burial pit. When their purpose had been served, extermination camps were dismantled and the evidence of their existence hidden or destroyed. In the spring and early summer of 1943, the eleven burial pits at Treblinka were transformed: bodies exhumed and then incinerated, crushed, mingled with sand, and reburied. All that remained of a million human beings was ashes.[95]

• • •

This is where the story might end, a horrific account of overenthusiastic, morally oblivious bureaucrats blithely supporting a charismatic dictator with genocidal intent. And indeed this is where it would end, were it not for the dogged work of a pair of American historians, Margo Anderson and William Seltzer, who in the early years of the twenty-first century unearthed a discomforting cross-Atlantic parallel to the moral failures of Europe's Nazi-era census takers.[96]

Following the Japanese attack on Pearl Harbor of December 7, 1941, President Roosevelt issued an executive order that authorized the internment of Americans with Japanese ancestry, two-thirds of whom were born in the United States and therefore citizens. More than a hundred and ten thousand mainland Japanese Americans were relocated away from the presumed front on the West Coast to secure camps in the interior.[97]

This history is well known, but less so is the role the US Census Bureau played in helping to enforce this order. Rumors that the Census Bureau had released names and addresses of Japanese Americans to military or law enforcement authorities were long met with official denials. There was evidence that aggregate data from the 1940 census, revealing in general terms where Japanese Americans lived, was provided to officials in western states to support "mopping up" operations. This was arguably within the bounds of prewar commitments about statistical confidentiality. But for decades, there was no public evidence that the bureau had gone any further and compromised individual data.[98]

Nonetheless, it seemed quite likely. In 1939, the director of the census, William Lane Austin, had resisted congressional attempts to use the upcoming 1940 census to register illegal aliens, citing the legal mandate of confidentiality. But when Austin reached retirement age in 1941, a new director, James Clyde Capt, was appointed. Capt was a political functionary and lacked his predecessor's four-decade-long association with the census. He was not a statistician at all and was much closer to the administration. In January 1942 he expressed, in a private meeting, a willingness to sacrifice confidentiality: "We're by law required to keep confidential information by individuals. But in the end, [i]f the defense authorities found 200 Japs missing and they wanted the names of the Japs in that area, I would give them further means of checking individuals."[99]

In 2007, Anderson and Seltzer finally found confirmation: a series of 1943 memos in federal government archives. They related to a Secret Service investigation into a threat against the president reportedly made by a man on his way to an internment camp. The threat was quickly dismissed, but it triggered a wide inquiry. Treasury secretary Henry Morgenthau requested from the Census Bureau the names and locations of people of Japanese ancestry living in the Washington, DC, area—who, living far from the West Coast, had not been subject to internment. Just seven days later, the bureau provided a list of seventy-nine Japanese Americans in the area, including name, address, sex, age, marital status, citizenship status, status in employment, and occupation and industry. Seltzer and Anderson argue that this rapid reply is indicative of an already-established administrative process. In all likelihood, 1943 was not the first time the bureau had received and honored such a request.[100]

Such disclosures, in fact, had been legal since 1942. A provision of the Second War Powers Act allowed the secretary of commerce to break confidentiality, as long as it was "for use in connection with the conduct of the war." The likelihood that it would be used to target Japanese Americans was noted at the time by the *New York Times*. Internment too was legal, upheld 6-3 by the Supreme Court in a 1944 decision, *Korematsu v. United States*. This, however, provides little comfort: actions of the Nazis in occupied Europe frequently took place under the veil of legality. While camps like Treblinka and Auschwitz cannot be equated with the relocation camps of the US interior, the mechanisms of identification, registration, and control that brought people to them were more similar than we might like to admit.[101]

In 1980 a congressional commission declared that the *Korematsu* decision had been "overruled in the court of history." In a 2018 decision, *Korematsu* was overruled in law, too, explicitly repudiated by the Supreme Court. Justice Antonin Scalia, who died in 2016, was not part of that decision, but he had already spoken against internment in a 2014 speech. Even as he did, he issued a warning: "You're kidding yourself if you think the same thing will not happen again." He quoted the Roman statesman Cicero: "*Inter arma enim silent leges.*" In times of war, the laws fall silent.[102]

• • •

Since the early 1990s, and especially since the 2001 publication of Black's *IBM and the Holocaust,* the focus of this story has often fallen on the role of punch card tabulation and its lead supplier, IBM. That's something of a red herring. There seems little question that IBM was too close to the Nazi regime and that it continued to do business in Germany, at least indirectly, long after it should have stopped (although IBM officially disputes Black's account). But that is more useful as a moral accounting than as an explanation of the Holocaust.[103]

Tabulation technology played a role, of course, but it's easily overstated. First, as tabulation was used in Germany's 1933 and 1939 censuses, it did not allow the recording of names or addresses, or easy tracing back to the schedules that did. The critical population data systems, including those that drew on the 1939 census, used not punch cards but traditional written files, which retained the advantage of flexibility well into the 1930s. The armies of clerks needed to operate these manual systems were not a major hurdle for a militarizing totalitarian government. Second, inasmuch as basic punch card tabulation was used throughout the government and commercial sector for accounting purposes, that's because it was, by then, a decades-old technology, widely used in many countries.[104]

From a twenty-first-century perspective, it is not the hard technologies of punch cards and tabulators that stand out as decisive, but softer factors. Social norms encouraged participation in censuses and other schemes of registration. Authorities were trusted not to abuse this public cooperation. Statistical confidentiality was assumed to be stronger than it was. Bureaucrats turned out to be more compliant than might have been imagined. Punch card technology has been irrelevant since the 1980s, but these other factors remain central to any discussion—past, present, or future—about census taking and population data.

In 1947, twenty-three doctors were tried at Nuremberg for war crimes, including human experimentation and mass murder dressed up as euthanasia. Seven were acquitted, seven were executed, and the remaining nine received prison sentences. Out of the so-called Doctors' Trial emerged a set of ten principles for human experimental research, known as the Nuremberg Code, which has been highly influential in establishing ethical norms for medical and other human subjects research. These principles are designed to ensure the preservation of the basic humanity of experimental subjects: human beings first, even as they are abstracted as cases and controls, blinded and double-blinded.

No statistician stood trial at Nuremberg. For the most part, the men who, in the words of Dehomag's Willy Heidinger, were called to "dissect, cell by cell, the German cultural body" for Adolf Hitler faced no indictments. Wolfgang Reichardt died in 1943, a few years after resigning. But other key figures in the Nazi-era statistical establishment were quickly rehabilitated and returned to government or academic service.

Jacobus Lentz was punished, as he had feared he would be—but lightly. He was sentenced in the postwar Netherlands to three years in prison (the prosecutor had asked for twelve). The indictment emphasized his willing opening up of the population register, rather than the consequences of that choice.[105]

Adam Czerniakow did not live to see the fall of the Third Reich. For him, the beginning of mass deportations from the Warsaw Ghetto was the last straw. Czerniakow wrote his final diary entry on July 23, 1942, and then swallowed a cyanide pill that he had kept since the earliest days of the German occupation. He left a letter to his wife and one to the Jewish Council. He is said to have written: "They are demanding that I kill the children of my people with my own hands. There is nothing for me to do but die."[106]

Nor did René Carmille survive the war. After his arrest in 1944 he was transferred to Dachau, where he died on January 25 the following year as prisoner 76608, missing by just a few months liberation by American troops.[107]

It is difficult, at three-quarters of a century's remove, to make confident moral judgments about these men and the decisions they made. Lentz seems the embodiment of Hannah Arendt's concept of the "banality of evil": neither sadistic nor brutal, just a functionary following orders. After the war, an official described him in these terms: "I would like to imagine that if tomorrow morning Lentz received the assignment to make his own death warrant, he would make it so there was no possibility he would escape through a loophole." The others—Reichardt, Czerniakow, and Carmille—offer only moral ambiguity. Each collaborated in his way, until he found a line he would not cross.[108]

Unlike medical doctors, statisticians rarely encounter their subjects face-to-face. Their job is to provide data and analysis to others who make and implement policy. Their moral failures, therefore, are marked not by mutilated and disfigured bodies, but neatly typed numerical tables, columns of figures revealing the progressive, orchestrated destruction of a people. Such crimes are abstract, cold, and deniable. The practice of statistics necessarily relies on this abstraction: on classification and the reduction of people to categories and numbers. Abstraction is the source of its power. Yet there is a fine line between abstraction and dehumanization.

The custodians of paper people never really faced the public reckoning the medical profession had. No code of statistical principles emerged from Nuremberg. The American Statistical Association began a conversation on statistical ethics in 1949, but it met with limited support from members, and it was not until the early 1980s that the organization finally adopted a code of ethics. The International Statistical Institute published a "Declaration on Professional Ethics" in 1985. The UN Statistics Commission, which comprises the leaders of the statistical offices of member states, adopted a set of "Fundamental Principles of Official Statistics" in 1994. The most recent version, adopted by the UN General Assembly in 2014, includes as Principle 6 a version of statistical confidentiality.[109]

These ethical codes and principles are an important first line of defense against wrongdoing. But ethical codes can be breached. The technical infrastructure that enabled the rapid corruption of the census in Nazi Europe continues to exist: it remains as easy today to set a flag in a database row as it once was to punch a hole in a Hollerith card. We may take comfort that the legal and political context is different, but those can change with remarkable rapidity. Bureaucracies, on the other hand, are resilient. Information, once collected, is hard to destroy. The only sure way to prevent its misuse is not to collect it in the first place— a reality that should weigh on census takers everywhere.

And yet the longevity of information cuts both ways. In 1946, Robert Kempner published an article outlining the many systems of wartime German population control. Kempner had once been a legal advisor to the Prussian police in the Weimar Republic, but he was a Jew, so in 1933 he was fired and, in 1935, expelled from the country of his birth. A decade later he returned as a prosecutor at Nuremberg. He wrote his 1946 article, urgent and specific, to let his new colleagues know where they might find surviving evidence of the Nazi genocide. He advised them to turn to the registries, full of paper people, immortal though their natural counterparts were gone: "Kings, dictators, Nazi bosses, buildings, factories, and monuments might disappear—administrative files and records remain."[110]

CHAPTER 5

A WORLD CENSUS

IN THE DECADES following the Second World War, the specter of Thomas Malthus rose triumphant, from his grave in Bath Abbey, to make regular guest appearances in the opinion columns of major newspapers and on late-night television.[1] It was an improbable second act. Malthus had been influential, without question: his style of analysis had been absorbed into the new fields of demography and economics. But his main thesis—that population growth necessarily led to misery—had fallen out of favor, seemingly undermined, or at the very least postponed, by the transformative effects of the industrial revolution. Between 1801 and 1901, the population of England had nearly quadrupled, yet the descendants of Malthus's parishioners in Surrey lived lives no worse, and in some ways much better, than their great-grandparents had.[2]

But the twentieth century brought about a gradual revival of Malthusianism. The march of technology and two world wars had created a new sense of population awareness, not merely international but global. This sense was buttressed by new, concrete knowledge, comprehensive demographic data that now embraced the whole of humanity. By the middle of the century, the global population was established as a well-defined object of study, measured every decade in an orchestrated

---

See note 1 for sources of population totals and related statistics presented in this chapter.

ritual of worldwide census taking. It is not surprising, then, that global population finally became an object of policy, too.[3]

The idea of actively controlling population had been gestating on the margins of polite society for decades, the subject of academic discussion but not political action. Discussions of population control inevitably led to the fraught issue of birth control, which remained taboo—privately practiced, perhaps, but publicly condemned. Even as birth control became more acceptable, it remained a matter of private choice rather than public policy. In 1959, President Eisenhower examined the issue of population control, eventually declaring it "not a proper political or governmental activity."[4]

Just ten years later, everything, it seemed, had changed. In July 1969, President Nixon described population as "a world problem no-one can ignore." He placed responsibility for addressing this world problem on the nearest thing there was to a world government: the United Nations (UN). That organization had long been divided about taking a role in the population debate, but at the end of the 1960s it finally did so. A flurry of activity followed, including the creation of a new UN Population Fund. In 1970, the UN General Assembly designated 1974 as "World Population Year."[5]

One book, more than any other, has come to represent this cultural and political moment: 1968's *The Population Bomb*. It was written by Paul R. Ehrlich, a Stanford professor who had begun his career studying insect biology. But as the title suggests, this was no dry academic tract. "The battle to feed all of humanity is over," it begins. Over the following pages, Ehrlich lays out the blueprints of the eponymous population bomb: a straightforward Malthusian scenario of too many people and not enough food.[6]

The Population Bomb was already a best seller when, on February 9, 1970, Ehrlich was interviewed on Johnny Carson's *The Tonight Show*. This forty-five-minute appearance—difficult to imagine today—propelled Ehrlich to public intellectual status, the leading voice on the hot topic of global overpopulation. *The Tonight Show* received over five thousand letters from viewers. Ehrlich was chosen as the subject of

Playboy's featured interview for August 1970, coming in sequence between singer Joan Baez and actor Peter Fonda. Now a cultural icon in America, Ehrlich went on tour. In 1971, he visited Britain, not merely as a guest academic lecturer, as he had been on a previous visit in 1969, but as a television personality. In advance of an Australian visit, he was profiled in the popular *Australian Women's Weekly.*[7]

Ehrlich's message succeeded because it was simple, anchored in easily verifiable facts about population. Recall that 10,000 years ago, Earth's population was perhaps 10 million people, a number that had been reached at a glacial pace, over hundreds of thousands of years. By 1 CE, humanity numbered around 250 million individuals, the growth to that point still imperceptible to those living through it, a doubling of population every 3,000 years. By the 1650s, we were 500 million, having doubled again in around 1,500 years. Then things really accelerated. The 1 billion milestone was reached in around 1800: a doubling in only 150 years. Two billion came in 1927, just over a century later. By the early 1970s, the world's population was on the cusp of 4 billion, a number it would reach in 1974. This last doubling had taken not even 50 years.[8]

Extrapolating this acceleration, Ehrlich forecast a bleak future. He reckoned that the next doubling would take just thirty-seven years. He wanted his readers to understand viscerally what that meant. "If growth continued at that rate for about 900 years,"—an "absurd assumption," he acknowledged—"there would be some 60,000,000,000,000,000 people on the face of the earth." Not shy about taking this absurd assumption to its vivid—but equally absurd—logical conclusion, Ehrlich observed that "such a multitude might be housed in a continuous 2,000-story building covering our entire planet" with "three or four yards of floor space for each person." It was a horrifying, dystopian image: a hive, not a home.[9]

Still, he assured readers, long before this came to pass population growth would stop, by one of two means. One was the "birth rate solution," in which we find ways to lower the birth rate. The other was the "death rate solution," in which ways to raise the death rate—war, famine, pestilence—find us.[10]

If this all feels quite familiar, it should, as an almost blow-for-blow restatement of Malthus's main argument in his 1798 *Essay on the Principle of Population*. Long before Ehrlich, Malthus had invented the genre, deploying the same rhetorical technique of extreme and absurd extrapolation. Suppose, Malthus wrote, a world population of "any number, a thousand millions, for instance" and a twenty-five-year doubling period. Then in "two centuries and a quarter"—around 2023, given when he was writing—the population would be 512 billion. Remarkably, Ehrlich fails to credit his predecessor anywhere in the 198 pages of his book.[11]

Of course, there were differences, too, between the two books. In 1798, Malthus had faced a paucity of data; he was forced to lean heavily on his theoretical model. Since that time, estimation of global population had become an enormous, official, coordinated effort. Where Malthus had little more than anecdote, Ehrlich could point to more than a century of increasingly reliable census data to support his claims. Ehrlich also offered a sliver of hope that Malthus could not. The explosion might yet be interrupted, its effects contained. Between Malthus and Ehrlich humankind had invented modern contraception and a loose system of international governance by which it might be deployed to every part of the globe. Ehrlich and his contemporaries took a step that Malthus never had: from measurement of population to management of population.

• • •

That Malthus had even a rough sense of the global population, in the eighteenth century, is surprising. In fact his offhand estimate of "one thousand million" was almost exactly right. This was more a fluke of timing than any particular demographic virtuosity: he simply chose a round number for ease of exposition. That said, in choosing a round billion, Malthus wasn't making a totally uninformed guess. By the 1790s, he could draw on several sensible, if conflicting, estimates of world population.

Certain facts, or at least impressions, had been understood since antiquity: the high population density of China and India, the

emptiness of the Sahara. The great voyages of the fifteenth and sixteenth centuries had filled in this sketch. By about 1600, learned Europeans could possess a broadly accurate picture of the continents, their
relative sizes and configuration (with the exception of lightly populated
Australia and unpopulated Antarctica).

In 1661 an Italian Jesuit, Giovanni Battista Riccioli, combined
these impressions to calculate that the total population of the world
could be as large as one billion. The truth then was probably about half
that, according to modern estimates. Riccioli's biggest error was the
two hundred million that he assigned to the Americas. The New World
had probably never been as populous as the old, and European contact
had reduced it to perhaps twelve million by then. Still, the Italian's estimate was a remarkable effort: he probably deserves recognition alongside his near-contemporaries Graunt and Petty as a founder of
demography. Petty, for his part, offered a rather less satisfying global
total, credited only to "learned men," of three hundred twenty million.
Gregory King, another English political arithmetician, made a better
estimate of around seven hundred million in 1696, using similar logic
to Riccioli (it was probably about six hundred million by then).[12]

In 1721, the French philosopher Montesquieu set off a debate in
Europe's intellectual circles, claiming that the world's population
had fallen to one-fiftieth its total in Roman times. He was wrong on
this point. Moreover, the "world" he considered—Europe and the
Mediterranean—was an increasingly archaic and irrelevant concept. By
the end of the eighteenth century, the coastlines of the populated continents had been mapped in detail. European traders and colonists were
beginning to venture into the most populous parts of the world, including India and China. They brought back to the West a much firmer—if
still anecdotal—base of knowledge. In 1775, Johann Peter Süssmilch, a
German pastor, produced the definitive eighteenth-century account of
world population. It was from Süssmilch that Malthus adopted his total
of one billion.[13]

After Malthus's *Essay*, demographic knowledge grew even faster.
Modern census taking was spread by Adolphe Quetelet and his

international meetings. National headcounts became more frequent and more accurate, and these were quickly used to update global estimates. The 1891 ninth edition of *Encyclopaedia Britannica* listed twenty successive claims about world population from 1804 onward. The earliest are too low, but they eventually converge on an accurate total: by the 1880s, around 1.4 billion.[14]

The study of global population had made the transition from informed guesswork to science. Even by 1880 some guesswork remained—over half the world's people had still never been included in a census—but with each year, and every new census, that was changing. The need for estimates or guesses was receding. After the 1890 American census, Superintendent Robert Porter calculated that the entire world could, in principle, be tabulated by Hollerith machine in under two hundred days.[15]

For Porter, this was a mere thought experiment, an illustration of the power of Hollerith's technology. But for another statistician, Hungary's Joseph Körösi, counting everyone, in every country, was a serious goal—his life's mission. In 1885, the International Statistical Institute was established as an enduring successor to Quetelet's statistical congresses. Through it, Körösi argued tirelessly for a "project for a census of the world." He saw national censuses "no longer as a goal, but as a means... towards a higher goal, the supreme goal of demography: to arrive by national censuses of peoples at an international census of the world, at a general knowledge that embraces all humanity—or at least all civilized humanity!"[16]

That final qualification was important: throughout this period and well into the twentieth century, the "international" statistical community still hailed almost exclusively from Europe and the United States. But while these men (also still nearly always men) came from narrow origins, they shared an increasingly global outlook. As the nineteenth century ended, vast swathes of the world came under European control, involuntarily swept onto the fringes of Körösi's "civilized humanity." For census takers, colonialism and spreading European influence created opportunity. The skills of counting and categorizing were sought after in places like Borneo, Morocco, New Caledonia, and Palestine. Even those countries that had already escaped the colonial yoke, or never experienced it, were adopting European models of statehood and statecraft, including the model of census taking promoted by European statisticians.[17]

Altogether, these changes meant that by 1890, around 60 percent of the world's population lived in a place that had seen a census in the past century. Some, like the British, had been counted many times. Others, like the Peruvians, had been counted only once. Perhaps half of all people were visited by a census taker in the final decade of the 1800s. Many participated voluntarily. Some, no doubt, were enumerated at the point of a bayonet.[18]

. . .

Probably the greatest feat of near-simultaneous, worldwide enumeration prior to the Second World War was the 1911 census of the British Empire. It was a feat that took many decades to achieve. The empire was constructed of dissimilar parts, and census taking initially developed in the same fragmented way, springing from local initiative and reflecting local concerns, rather than from any explicit goal to enumerate the whole.

From the 1840s onward, the British government made increasing efforts at coordinating the empire's disparate counts, influenced by the recommendations from Quetelet's congresses. But harmonization was slow, and through the nineteenth century the censuses of British possessions remained separate, based on different questions and published in individual reports. It was not until 1906 that, for the first time, an official consolidated *Report on the Census of the British Empire* was published. It was based on 1901 data and included tables comparing the empire's many peoples by age, marital status, occupation, birthplace, religion, education, and disabilities.[19]

Impressive though this was, the report was an ex post attempt at unification; the 1901 censuses themselves were still quite separate, overlapping in only some of their topics. The report noted, for example, that 9.3 percent of men in Scotland were employed in "Metals, Machines, Implements, and Conveyances," whereas only 0.4 percent were in Ceylon—the result of successful adoption of a uniform occupational classification. But it could not answer how many schoolchildren the empire had in total—a seemingly simple question. Moreover, some very populous parts of the empire remained beyond the enumerators' reach: outside of Lagos, for example, Nigeria's population was not counted (it was estimated to be in the range of fifteen to twenty-five million). If anything, compiling everything into one volume simply showed how inconsistent the efforts at harmonization had been.[20]

The result of the 1906 report was a renewed effort at harmonization. Following its publication, a plan for true uniformity emerged. In 1911, finally, something like an empire-wide census became a reality. It was held in most places within a few months of April 1. In India alone, more than two million enumerators went about counting the three hundred million subjects of the king-emperor George V. Those counted did not always share the enthusiasm of those doing the counting. *National Geographic* reported, of the Indian enumeration:

> Some of the people seemed to think it a joke if they could manage to
> have some in their house escape the eye of the enumerator. Children
> had to be dragged from dark corners and older persons from cattle
> sheds, in order that the list might be made complete. If any one es-
> caped entirely he was the hero of the day in his village the next
> morning.[21]

Indeed, with children dragged from dark corners across the empire, this became the most complete imperial census yet: the enumerators missed only Sarawak (now Malaysian Borneo) and the interior of Somaliland.

Another small but significant group of people was missed much closer to home. In Britain, the 1911 census became the focus of a campaign by suffragettes, who argued that women—who did not count for the vote—should not allow themselves to be counted in the census.

Two years later, Emily Wilding Davison would become famous as a martyr of the movement, killed by the king's horse as she attempted to interrupt the Epsom Derby. But on Sunday, April 2, 1911, she was engaged in a much less visible protest, hiding from the king's census takers, in her own dark corner of—of all places—the Houses of Parliament. She had probably been there since the previous day. As the suffragettes' newspaper later recounted it: "Armed with some provisions, Miss Davison took up her position in a cupboard of about 5ft by 6ft . . . In this small dark place, taking only occasional walks in the crypt, Miss Davison remained until Monday morning."[22]

Davison was no more able to escape the census than the villagers of India. She was discovered on Monday and briefly detained by police. While in custody, a census schedule was completed in her name (in fact she was double-counted, also recorded by her landlady in her absence). An estimated three to four thousand other protesters were, however, successful in their boycott. Others failed to escape enumeration but used it as an opportunity to record statements of resistance. Miss Sarah Bennet, sixty-one years old of Finchley, London, for example, returned a blank schedule with the note "I am denied the full rights of citizenship, so I will not perform the duties of a citizen. . . . I refuse therefore to answer the Census questions."[23]

The outbreak of the First World War in 1914 delayed, and then permanently ended, the compilation of an integrated, empire-wide report of the 1911 census, as had been made in 1906. While the British empire persisted for another three decades, no such ambitious publication was ever again produced.[24]

• • •

The war left more than fifteen million dead. Its impact was felt across the globe, and it was soon recognized as a "world war." The influenza epidemic that followed, spread in part by troop movements, took an ever greater toll, killing an estimated fifty million. Some blamed the devastation on population pressure. With every piece of land that could be discovered having been discovered, and every place that could be colonized having been colonized, the world—at least the world of great European powers—had no room to grow. The inevitable result, according to this logic, had been a Malthusian check of global proportions.

For the living, the war led to renewed vigor in the measurement of world population, now increasingly cast as a "population problem." Before the war, national population totals had been assembled into world totals, from time to time, by staff of the International Statistical Institute. Now this task was taken over by the League of Nations, a new multilateral institution charged with maintaining world peace. The result was the first consistent, rigorous, annual estimates of world population, published in a series of year books covering the years 1926 to 1944.[25]

The books showcased the growing international success of census taking. By the start of the 1930s, three-quarters of the world's population lived in a country that had held an official headcount, most as recent as the last ten years. A billion people—half of humanity—were enumerated in 1930 and 1931 alone. Of large countries, only China lacked a census total acceptable to the league's statisticians. The country's various governments had tried to take censuses, in 1909–1911, 1912, and 1928, but each was beset by political instability. The vast distances and enormous population of China meant that only a secure, consolidated government could hope to make a comprehensive enumeration. So the League of Nations listed China's population as four hundred fifty million, a rough estimate with "a very considerable margin of error."[26]

In 1932, a new milestone was recognized: two years earlier, the league declared, the world's population had passed 2 billion people. Of those, slightly more than half—1.1 billion—lived in Asia. But despite this, the broader picture was of a European world. The continent's share of population had grown from around a fifth, in 1750, to a quarter in the first decades of the twentieth century—despite an enormous out-migration to the Americas over that time. Moreover, another quarter or so of the world's population lived in Europe's scattered colonies.[27]

Those figures hold up well to modern scrutiny. Today's estimates place the two billion milestone only a few years earlier, in 1927. That year witnessed another landmark of a different kind: the first World Population Conference.

• • •

For demographers, the conference was the meeting of the decade. It was held in Geneva, diplomatic capital of the world and home of the League of Nations. Attendees came from twenty-nine countries, including China, India, Japan, and Brazil. They heard from leading experts on population in all its aspects—"biological, social, economic, medical, statistical, and political"—including biologists Alexander Carr-Saunders, Raymond Pearl, and Julian Huxley (the former two protégés of Karl Pearson, the last the brother of novelist Aldous Huxley) and statistician Corrado Gini. The one person they did not hear from was the person who had made it all happen, the chair of the Organizing Committee, Margaret Sanger.[28]

Sanger, born in upstate New York in 1879, was a socialist and advocate for women's reproductive rights, radicalized by her experiences as a nurse in the slums of Manhattan's Lower East Side. These neighborhoods were the center of a garment industry that supplied the entire United States. Its workers—Sanger's patients—were predominantly young women, often immigrants. They were women for whom an unwanted pregnancy could mean destitution or even death. By the time patients reached her, Sanger realized, it was too late: much earlier intervention was required, in the form of what she first, euphemistically, called "family limitation."

Family limitation—or birth control, as it later became known—has a long history. Many writings on population note that the ancient custom of "exposure," infanticide by abandonment, and various methods of abortion were practiced. The contraceptive effect of breastfeeding was probably long known and widely used. The withdrawal method appears in Genesis. Contraceptive devices, by the nineteenth century, included cervical caps, early condoms, and spermicides. These methods had varying degrees of efficacy and risk to the user. Even before his marriage in 1804, Malthus knew enough of such "unnatural" checks and "improper arts" to condemn then in his writing.[29]

These methods became increasingly effective, well known, and used over the nineteenth century. At least, historians assume they were used—nobody was taking surveys of sexual practices in the 1800s. Fertility in the United States and much of Europe fell dramatically over that period. Since it seems unlikely that the "passion between the sexes," as Malthus had delicately put it, had dimmed, something else must have been going on to limit births. (Malthus's preferred solutions of marital delay and abstinence can only explain so much.)

But knowledge of birth control remained unevenly distributed in the early twentieth century. It was generally considered sinful by established churches. Its promotion in the United States was effectively outlawed by the Comstock Act, which prohibited the mailing of obscene material. In 1914 Sanger set out to challenge this law, starting a monthly newsletter to promote contraception and publishing a short brochure on the same topic. As she wrote, "It is only the workers who are ignorant of the knowledge of how to prevent bringing children in the world to fill jails and hospitals, factories and mills, insane asylums and premature graves." Sanger attacked that ignorance with sixteen pages of detailed description and anatomically explicit illustrations. As she had probably intended, she was shortly indicted. She fled to Britain, leaving a trail of publicity in her wake.[30]

Sanger used this brief exile well, building a network of overseas contacts, beginning with the members of the international neo-Malthusian movement. The movement had its origins in the Malthusian League, a nineteenth-century English group that borrowed Malthus's name and his analysis to campaign for contraception (something that would have horrified the reverend). In the neo-Malthusians, Sanger found influential fellow travelers who were sympathetic to her aims. She established her own position within the group rapidly, chairing a session at their fifth conference in 1922—which, under her influence, became the

International Neo-Malthusian and Birth Control Conference—and then hosting the sixth in New York, in 1925.[31]

Sanger proposed a seventh Neo-Malthusian Conference, to take place in Geneva in 1927. Instead it became, at the last minute, the first World Population Conference, with the "viewpoint... of the scientific laboratory or the study, rather than that of the pulpit or the hustings." To some extent, this change served Sanger's objectives: it would attract a wider audience to what remained a fringe cause. But it was also a rejection: her co-organizers were men who claimed scientific authority, whereas Sanger's natural environment, by then, *was* the hustings (she was, according to opponents, an "indefatigable propagandist"). And along with the new name, certain controversial elements were banished from the program: birth control and Margaret Sanger herself.[32]

The opening address was delivered by Pearl, who spoke on the mathematics of yeast cells multiplying in a petri dish and fruit flies breeding in a sealed bottle. Darwin's revolution had swept biology, placing humankind properly within, rather than apart from, the natural world. Humans were to fruit flies as fruit flies were to yeast: more complex but bound by the same essential rules, living on the surface of our own near-spherical petri dish. Discussion at the conference anticipated the coming (in actual fact, already arrived) two billion population milestone. The idea of overpopulation was ever-present.[33]

Conversation inevitably bled into eugenics. Nearly all conversations among population experts did, at that time. With the need to curtail population growth taken for granted, it was quite natural to ask how, and to whom, to target such curtailment. Eugenic questions, if not eugenic answers, were unavoidable. Sanger's reputation has suffered, perhaps unfairly, for this: eugenic beliefs formed a spectrum, and Sanger's were far removed from some of her more enthusiastic colleagues, let alone the noxious racial theories that were motivating the Nazi party in Germany.[34]

For advocates of birth control, the conference was, in the end, a failure. Sanger's movement was not embraced by "scientific" demography but remained separate. She went on to cofound the action-oriented Birth Control International Information Centre, a forerunner of the International Planned Parenthood Federation. Separately, the demographers formed the measurement-focused International Union for the Scientific Investigation of Population Problems. Despite this nominal separation, however, the two fields remained closely linked. The measurement of population could never quite escape questions about the mechanisms of its control.[35]

· · ·

In 1937, the League of Nations finally agreed to embark on its own program of work to address the population problem that it had thus far only measured. But by then the league itself was largely defunct. With Europe again on the brink of war, the core of the league's demographic program was relocated from Geneva to a new home at Princeton University, led by American demographer Frank Notestein.[36]

When peace returned in 1945, the world had changed. A terrible new weapon, the atomic bomb, had left Hiroshima and Nagasaki shattered beneath mushroom clouds. Much of Europe, too, was devastated, leaving only two global powers, the United States and the Soviet Union. The League of Nations, a demonstrated failure, was succeeded by the United Nations, which settled, in 1952, in a headquarters built on the banks of the East River in New York, the new "capital of the world." As demographers resumed their prewar activities, they found population data, in Notestein's words, "in a chaotic state." The conflict had interrupted the prewar rhythm of census taking. Many population counts were now well out of date. Even the United Kingdom had, for the first time, skipped a census, the year 1941 having presented more pressing concerns.[37]

The UN quickly picked up where the League of Nations had left off, creating in 1946 two bodies, composed of member country representatives, to coordinate international statistics. The Population Commission would compile population statistics, as the League of Nations had done. It would also—in principle—advise on "policies designed to influence the size and structure of population." The Statistical Commission, meanwhile, would coordinate other international statistical efforts. Economic measurement in particular had flourished over the prior decade, with new concepts like Gross National Product (GNP) invented to regulate the wartime economies.[38]

Each commission was supported by a permanent staff within the UN Secretariat in New York: the Population Division, headed by Frank Notestein, and the Statistical Office (later the Statistics Division). The former soon got to work updating the League of Nations' population statistics, and starting in 1948 the two departments jointly published a *Demographic Year Book,* similar to the league's yearbook but growing vastly more detailed over time. Together, the commissions encouraged every country to take a new census. They published a new two-hundred-page book of recommended enumeration methods in 1949. This period also saw the establishment of a convention that is still followed: censuses in the decennium of 1945 to 1954 were considered part of an international census "round" centered on the year 1950.[39]

The Population Commission did not immediately embrace the more advisory role envisioned at its founding. But it nonetheless set the terms for the global population debate by beginning, in 1949, to publish future projections of world population. Serious demographic forecasting had started in the nineteenth century as an academic endeavor. Between the wars, it was adopted as a tool by planning agencies in individual nations. Now, for the first time, the same methods were applied to the entire world, stamped with the official emblem of the UN. As the world entered the second half of the twentieth century, the UN offered three scenarios for world population: in the highest it would reach 3.6 billion by 1980; the middle projection reached 3.3 billion; the lowest, 3 billion. At the time of publication in 1951, the world population was already 2.5 billion. The projections indicated only moderately higher growth than in the past, and they attracted limited attention.[40]

Meanwhile, hopes that the United Nations might take any more active role on population policy began to fade. The Population

Commission did not take it up. Neither did the new World Health Organization, which could in principle have examined the health dimensions of birth control. The issue was simply too fraught to pursue directly in these forums.[41]

To supporters of a more active role, UN demographic experts were peacekeepers just as much as the "blue helmets" that were first deployed to conflict zones in 1948. Even in the atomic age, the population problem remained a threat to world peace. There was, as the Indian demographer Sripati Chandrasekhar put it in 1952, a need for "demographic disarmament."[42]

But there were powerful interests aligned against such a role. The Anglican Church had given guarded approval to birth control in 1930, but the Catholic Church continued to resist it entirely. The Vatican carried influence in the UN through Catholic-majority countries and later more directly as an observer state. The Soviet Union and its fellow Eastern bloc states also rejected the population agenda, opposing the very idea of the Population Commission. The early Soviet state was overtly pro-natalist in its own policies. Communism rejected Malthusian doctrine: Marx himself had penned a scathing critique of the *Essay*, calling it a "schoolboyish superficial plagiary."[43]

Soviet leaders had, in fact, a rather difficult relationship with population statisticians. When the 1937 Soviet census turned in a number eight million short of projections—and nearly twenty million short of what had been implied by statements made by Joseph Stalin—the officials responsible were arrested. Olimpy Kvitkin, leader of the Census Bureau, and Ivan Kraval, head of the Central Office of Statistics, were shot. A replacement census, held in 1939, produced a total that was, mysteriously, eight million higher. No further census of the USSR was held until 1959, six years after Stalin's death.[44]

This strange alliance between the Catholic Church and the communist bloc meant that in the early 1950s, there was still no concerted global agenda to limit population growth. Measurement, however, continued apace.

• • •

In 1953, the largest unknown in the global population sum was finally resolved, with the first complete census of China. It had, despite the timing, little to do with the newly established international statistical machinery. When the UN was founded, the Republic of China was admitted as a member state. Almost immediately, a simmering conflict in the country grew to all-out civil war, with the Communist forces of Mao Zedong attempting to overthrow the Nationalist government of the Republic. In 1949, the Communists succeeded, gaining control of mainland China and driving the remaining Nationalist forces onto the island of Taiwan. Both sides—the Taiwanese Republic and the communist People's Republic—now claimed to be the legitimate government of all of China, but for the time being, it was the government in Taiwan that occupied China's seat at the United Nations. The much larger mainland was not represented.

Because of this complex political situation, much remains unclear about this large and historically important census. One contemporaneous Western report claims it was ordered "in preparation for nation wide elections," though the subsequent history of China does not bear out this democratic rationale. The census's reference date was July 1, 1953, although the 2.5 million enumerators took another twelve months to bring in all the results. Reportedly, 98 percent of the population was "directly surveyed," with estimation applied mainly to remote areas like Tibet. But unlike most censuses elsewhere at the time, Chinese people were required to travel to a census-taking center to be registered. The information collected was minimal: name, age, sex, nationality, relationship to head of household, and whether the enumeration location was urban or rural.[45]

In November 1954, the government announced the total: 582 million for the mainland. The complete official count included indirect estimates of another 8 million people living outside the control of the People's Republic in Taiwan and 12 million diaspora Chinese. The figure came as a shock in the West. League of Nations publications had been reporting 450 million as the best estimate as late as 1945; this new total was around one-third higher. Still, the result was generally accepted. Modern UN estimates of mainland China's population in 1953 are actually even higher, at 593 million (excluding Taiwan).[46]

With the completion of the 1953 Chinese census, nearly every part of the world had now been enumerated at some point. The UN's call for a new international census round centered on 1950 had been convincingly answered. Around 170 present-day countries took part (though, still on the eve of widespread decolonization, these comprised only around 80 sovereign states). Around two billion people, representing 82 percent of the world's population, were counted. Writing in 1955, the UN's statisticians observed with satisfaction that "a tremendous statistical task has been accomplished. . . . The censuses since 1945 more nearly approach a 'world census' than at any other similar time period in the history of the world."[47]

That record was soon broken again. With the end of hostilities in the Korean War, the world settled into a period of relative stability. Between 1955 and 1964, census takers nearly everywhere could go about their work in peace. They counted nearly 95 percent of people on the planet. Finally, Josef Körösi's vision of "an international census of the world" had been achieved. But as the enumerators returned from the field, and statisticians tabulated their findings and forwarded them to the UN Population Division, a disturbing new picture emerged. Finally possessed of what Körösi called "a general knowledge that embraces all humanity," the demographers began to worry: the population problem was beginning to look like an explosion.[48]

• • •

In 1958, the Population Division announced a dramatically revised projection. Its demographers were now predicting 4.2 billion people in 1980, nearly a billion greater than their equivalent middle forecast of just a few years earlier. For the first time, too, they extended their horizon to the end of the century, predicting a population in 2000 of

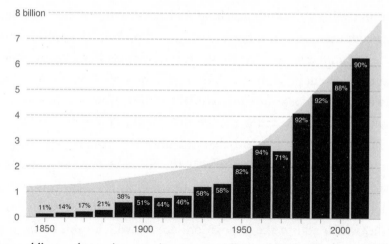

The world's population (gray area) grew especially quickly after the Second World War. By the 1960 census round, the number of people enumerated each decade (black bars) caught up, and something close to a world census was finally achieved. The 1970 round was less successful—marked by the absence of China's eight hundred million people—but since then around 90 percent of people have been counted each decennium. (See note 1 to this chapter for sources.)

6.3 billion. With these new, larger numbers came a shift in tone, less matter-of-fact and more sensational. In the preface to their report, they wrote that "in 600 years the number of human beings on earth will be such that there will only be one square metre for each to live on."[49]

The new data on China had challenged the models of the UN's demographers. China's population total, unexpectedly large compared with earlier partial enumerations, suggested that it was growing faster than previously believed. As the census results flowed into New York from around the world, the same phenomenon appeared elsewhere. The assumptions that the demographers had been making, especially concerning mortality, looked suddenly outdated.[50]

Over the 1930s, the world population had grown around 1 percent a year. Superficially, growth in the 1940s appeared similar, but the sixty to eighty million casualties of the Second World War (about 3 percent of the world population) masked an underlying trajectory of acceleration. By 1950, world population was growing by an estimated 1.8 percent a year and still accelerating, reaching 2 percent by the mid-1960s. Some large countries grew even faster through this period: China, India, Bangladesh, Indonesia, and Brazil all reached population growth rates of near to 3 percent per year—as, indeed, did the United States. An annual growth rate of 3 percent equates to a doubling of population in about twenty-five years: the fastest growth that Malthus thought possible.

But of course much had changed since the time of Malthus, not least the methods of demography itself. To make sense of population growth, demographers had learned to break it down into its components. Population change, growth or decline, reflects three things: births, which add to the population; deaths, which subtract from the population; and migration, which can go either way. The fundamental equation of demography states that this year's population equals last year's population, plus natural increase (births less deaths) plus net migration (inward less outward migration).

The components of this equation are usually presented as rates, proportions of the base population: the (crude) birth rate and (crude) death rate and net migration rate. For the globe as a whole, with zero net migration, only birth and death rates matter. The same is approximately true for countries with low net migration rates (for example, China or India in the 1950s). In India, the death rate declined from a high of over 40 per 1,000 at the start of the twentieth century to an average of 25 over the 1950s. But the crude birth rate had barely budged since 1920, hovering around 43 per 1,000 through the 1950s. The difference, the rate of natural increase, was around 18 per 1,000, or 1.8 percent. It wasn't that more people were being born than before—at least as a proportion of the population—but that far fewer were dying. As Julian Huxley described it, India, and countries like it, had achieved "death control" without "birth control."[51]

This "death control" was mostly the result of effective public health interventions. In the late nineteenth and early twentieth century, infection, then the leading cause of death, came under sustained attack. Public sanitation, draining of swamps to eliminate mosquito-borne diseases, better nutrition, vaccination, and, eventually, antibiotics all contributed to the decline of infection. These changes came to the richest countries first, but by the 1930s and 1940s they were spreading to poorer countries like India, China, and Brazil.[52]

The conquest of common yet deadly infections like cholera and tuberculosis was surely something to be celebrated. Yet not everyone saw it that way. In 1967, for example, the brothers William and Paul Paddock—an agronomist and retired diplomat, respectively—published a book titled *Famine—1975! America's Decision: Who Will Survive?* In it, they wrote approvingly of an anonymous ruler of an unnamed developing country who "held back spending tax moneys on public health," in order to prevent fast population growth. This particular story may be apocryphal, but the sentiment it expressed was not so taboo as to prevent its occasional airing in the postwar period. Until the birth rate could be brought under control, this logic went, public health improvements would only lead to temporary gains, soon offset by overpopulation and famine.[53]

• • •

In fact, the crude birth rate, though easy to measure, is not the best way to understand changing childbearing patterns within a population. It is a single quantity driven by two quite different things: the number of women of childbearing age and the number of children each such woman has. Of these two components, only the latter—the fertility rate—can actually be influenced by current policy. The number of women of childbearing age living today is determined by births that already happened decades ago, a tendency known as population momentum. Momentum represents growth (or decline) that is already "baked in." Because of it, the birth rate alone can provide a misleading or, at best, delayed picture of a changing population.

Considering fertility as well provides a more complete picture. There is more than one way to calculate and represent it, but the most common is the total fertility rate. This rate reflects the average number of children (technically "live births") a woman would have, over her lifetime, if current trends continued. The most important fertility threshold is what demographers call replacement fertility: the number of children who must be born to each couple, so that exactly two children survive to reproductive maturity and "replace" their parents. In countries with low child mortality, replacement fertility is around 2.1, while in countries with high child mortality, it is higher.

The total fertility rate and the crude birth rate usually follow the same ups and downs. Population momentum may cause them to diverge for some time, but if the average woman has fewer children over her lifetime, then the birth rate will eventually fall to reflect that, as will population growth (holding death and migration rates constant). If fertility falls below replacement, growth will eventually become negative, and population will decline.

Demographers, armed with this conceptual toolkit, were able to easily diagnose the population problem as a problem of high fertility: a rate of somewhere around five to six children per mother in countries like India, Brazil, and Indonesia during the 1960s. Two centuries earlier, Western countries like the United States, Britain, and France had had similar high fertility, but by the 1920s it had fallen to around two to three. These countries had somehow found a path to low fertility that other countries might follow. Yet nobody was absolutely certain why fertility had fallen in rich countries. The fall had been gradual and, it seemed, spontaneous. One leading demographer attributed it to the "competitive, individualistic, urban" societies that arose from industrialization. But that was hardly a concrete policy prescription.[54]

The great and celebrated exception to this pattern was Japan. In the decade following its defeat in World War II, Japan had slashed its fertility rate from around five to three—a transition that had taken the better part of a century in England. But for those worried about global overpopulation, Japan was not an easy example to follow. Its initial decline in birth rates relied heavily on increased rates of abortion, a solution unlikely to appeal in Catholic Latin America. Nor was it viable in poor countries like China and India, which had many fewer trained medical professionals (given their larger populations).[55]

The same need for specialized expertise plagued the most effective forms of contraception, such as the diaphragm, cervical cap, and surgical sterilization. The contraceptive pill, developed at the end of the 1950s, offered initial hope, but it proved less revolutionary in poor countries than in rich ones, requiring a commitment to small family size that was often absent. An improved intrauterine device showed promise, but it too required medical expertise, and early versions caused side effects and complications.[56]

Contraceptives also continued to face religious objections. In 1963, Pope John XXIII established a pontifical commission to reconsider these objections in the light of the new contraceptive pill. It looked, for a moment, like the church might at last reverse its position. But John died later the same year, and his successor, Pope Paul VI, changed course. In 1968, Paul overruled the commission's recommendation, issuing a new encyclical, *Humanae Vitae* ("Of Human Life"), which reconfirmed the church's anti-contraceptive position. It was a major blow for birth control advocates.[57]

• • •

With official action on population stalled, a group of mostly American business leaders, philanthropists, and internationalists began to direct financial resources toward research on, action to address, and public awareness of world population growth. In 1952 John D. Rockefeller III, heir to an oil fortune, established the Population Council, a New York–based nonprofit, to fund research on and programs of population control. In 1954 a private foundation financed by the industrialist Hugh Moore published *The Population Bomb*, a pamphlet whose title Ehrlich would later borrow. It was widely distributed, mailed first to notable and influential Americans and eventually reaching 1.5 million people.[58]

Although it had been coined earlier, the term "population explosion" itself exploded in use from the mid-1950s onward, increasingly embraced by the mainstream media. In 1959, nearly twenty million people watched a documentary broadcast on CBS entitled *The Population Explosion*. The same phrase reached the cover of *Time* magazine in January 1960. Books like 1965's *The Hungry Planet* and 1967's *Famine*

1975! pressed the point. By the time the king of late night anointed Paul Ehrlich as America's pessimist in chief in 1970, the explosion imagery had become the default way of discussing population.[59]

The United States was itself experiencing rapid population growth. The postwar baby boom had driven the fertility rate from a prewar low of near-replacement to a high, by 1960, of above 3.5 (at a time when Japan's was 2.0). But the attention of American campaigners was always on the growing populations abroad. Population was not a localized problem, something that could be contained country by country. Whether through refugees fleeing famine, destabilized governments falling to communism, or the outbreak of World War III, overpopulation anywhere in the postwar world would eventually affect the West. Controlling population was seen as a geopolitical imperative.

The same conclusion was reached, from a completely different direction, by adherents of the emerging environmental movement. Modern American environmentalism is often traced to the early 1960s, in particular Rachel Carson's 1962 book *Silent Spring,* which described the damaging effects of pesticides on ecosystems. Pesticides were a largely local problem, but there were other environmental problems that were unavoidably global. Ehrlich himself noted, presciently, "the greenhouse effect . . . being enhanced now by the greatly increased level of carbon dioxide in the atmosphere." That there was only one, shared atmosphere, enveloping one, shared planet was a fact reinforced when the first images of the whole planet from space appeared in the late 1960s. In 1927, Raymond Pearl had imagined the Earth as a petri dish. Forty years later people didn't need to imagine: they could see the whole fragile dish, viewed from afar, in full color. On spaceship Earth, it was self-evident that isolationism was no answer.[60]

In the United States, and at the United Nations, this burst of publicity created a popular movement that could finally rival the religious conservatism that had long held back policies of population control. In 1965, President Lyndon Johnson committed his administration to "seek new ways to use our knowledge to help deal with the explosion in world population." The National Catholic Welfare Council objected, but as *Life* magazine wrote, "the statistics now outweigh political pressure." In 1966, the UN General Assembly passed a resolution emphasizing a new interest in the population issue, and the following year the secretary-general, U Thant, announced a voluntary fund for population control programs. This fund became, in 1969, the UN Fund for Population Activities (UNFPA). In April of the following year, the next World Population Conference was called for 1974, the year in which world population was expected to pass four billion. It was to be designated "World Population Year."[61]

For an international system used to moving slowly, or not at all, on population policy, this was a major shift. Unquestionably, a genuine expert concern lay at the heart of it, a studied reaction to an accumulation of data. But cautious experts had been sounding the alarm for some time; it was not until this alarm was taken up by private campaigners and amplified in the popular press that the United States and the UN took concerted action. Once population growth had been framed as an explosion, it was impossible to ignore.[62]

• • •

Since moving to New York, I've often wondered just how much of the growing panic about overpopulation in the 1960s and 1970s was a reaction to cities, sprawling and unnatural—and to this one in particular.

One of the most quoted passages of Ehrlich's book was a scene he witnessed in Delhi: "People eating, people washing, people sleeping. People visiting, arguing, and screaming. People thrusting their hands through the taxi window, begging. People defecating and urinating. People clinging to buses. People herding animals. People, people, people, people." This, he claimed, is when he came to know "the feel of overpopulation." But the feeling he experienced was less a result of population than of population density: the close quarters of a poor city. The difference is subtle but important. Delhi had fewer than three million people when Ehrlich visited it. He might have experienced the same "hellish aspect" in London in 1700, long before anyone was talking about global overpopulation. Or indeed, in New York in 1850.[63]

Between 1830 and 1860, the population of New York City quadrupled. As census innovator Herman Hollerith departed for Washington, DC, in 1879, he left a city growing into its own population. It was a metropolis on the cusp of a golden age. A boom in skyscraper construction began to sketch out its famous skyline. By the 1920s, New York was probably the largest city on earth. Tokyo overtook it sometime in the early 1950s, but even by 1960, the world had only three urban agglomerations with over ten million people—so-called megacities—of which only New York was located in the developed world. It was home, fittingly, to much of the influential "population establishment"—the United Nations, the Rockefeller and Ford Foundations, and the Population Council—along with a large part of America's media elite.[64]

But by the end of the 1960s, these and other New Yorkers might have been forgiven for thinking that such an enormous concentration of human beings was a terrible mistake. In 1965, the governor of New York, Nelson Rockefeller, described the Hudson River as "one great septic tank." A smog event in 1966 led to an estimated 166 deaths. Industry was in decline, the garment factories that had provided Margaret Sanger's clients relocating to cheaper shores. The city saw repeated riots, as unaddressed issues of social justice burst onto the streets. Between 1960 and 1974 the murder rate quadrupled. Gotham was in crisis.[65]

In 1966 a pulpy science fiction novel titled *Make Room! Make Room!* extrapolated these trends three decades into the future: "Manhattan has writhed upward, feeding on its own flesh as it tears down old buildings to replace them with the new, rising high and still higher—yet never high enough, for there seems to be no limit to the people crowding here." The story ends on New Year's Eve 1999, in Times Square, with "the glaring screen of a gigantic TV" announcing the United States' new population of 344 million (in reality, it reached around 280 million that year).[66]

More serious commentators echoed these doubts about urbanization. The World Population Conference in 1965 noted the special problems of urbanizing populations. Ehrlich addressed them directly:

"Are we living in a deteriorating 'psychic environment'? Riots, rising crime rates, disaffection of youth, and increased drug usage seems to indicate that we are." He cited fellow biologists who, he wrote, believed "that mankind's genetic endowment has been shaped by evolution to require 'natural' surroundings for optimum mental health."[67]

On the edge of midtown Manhattan, the delegates and staff of the United Nations were suffering from their own deteriorating environment. The headquarters of the League of Nations had been a sprawling, palatial complex set among green space, with views of Lake Geneva and the French Alps. The UN headquarters was a stark contrast to this: unapologetically modern and metropolitan, all steel, glass, and concrete, stacked vertically on the site of derelict slaughterhouses and tenements. At its founding, the organization had 51 member states. Its headquarters were designed to accommodate expansion up to 75 members. But by 1970, UN membership had grown to 127 states, most of the additions being newly independent former colonies in Africa. Thirty-nine floors of fading midcentury optimism, crammed with a representative (at last) mix of nationalities, looking out over the endless flat sprawl of Brooklyn and Queens: it was not a bad metaphor for the world as the 1970s began.[68]

Perhaps the world's leading population specialists would have had a more sanguine view about "third world" cities, if only they had felt like the "first world" had any sort of handle on its own greatest concentrations of people. How would Delhi cope with ten million people when not even New York could?

• • •

The new sources of money unlocked by public concern about population flowed mainly to programs of aggressive action: birth control schemes, rolled out hurriedly and often controversially, with little concern for individual rights, across the world. But some of the influx found its way to fund demography itself. UNFPA, the new Population Fund, quickly assumed a prominent role in worldwide census taking. The need was great, especially among the new postcolonial countries, the indigenous populations of which had never, in some cases, been properly enumerated. By 1973 UNFPA was working on requests for technical assistance from twenty African countries, seventeen of which had not had a census since independence. The head of UNFPA, Rafael Salas, described this as a "Population Fund Explosion." At the 1974 World Population Conference, he reported that the agency had grown its resources from US$3 million to US$175 million and now worked in ninety countries.[69]

The conference, held in Bucharest, had been organized to establish an international consensus on population. Under consideration was a World Population Plan of Action, containing strict targets to reduce population growth. But the hoped-for consensus did not eventuate. The Chinese delegate Huang Shuzhi—new to these sorts of events, since communist China had only recently replaced Taiwan at the UN—took particular issue with the Malthusian assumptions underlying the proposal. Imperialism and capitalism, he argued, rather than overpopulation, were the causes of underdevelopment. The proposed plan was simply another manifestation of those same forces. Each country should instead decide its own policy; moreover, he explained, "Revolution plus production can solve the problem of feeding the population."[70]

This claim was disingenuous—at least based on China's recent experience. The country had experienced the largest famine of the twentieth century, possibly of all time, as it attempted an abrupt industrialization under Mao's "Great Leap Forward" policy. The scale of this disaster was concealed at the time, but historians now believe that from 1959 to 1961, somewhere between fifteen and twenty-five million people starved to death. Whatever the benefits of revolution, feeding the population was not among them.[71]

It was a lesson the Soviet Union had already learned, found reflected in the quickly suppressed census of 1937. Perhaps looking to avoid the same embarrassment, China became increasingly secretive about its population starting in the late 1950s. A 1964 census counted a mainland total of 695 million, but China hid the survey's very existence from the world until the early 1980s and did not rush to take another count. A record number of countries participated in the 1970 census round, but without China, the proportion of people counted globally fell to 71 percent.[72]

Still, even as it protested on the international stage, China was taking domestic action on population, which its leaders had come to recognize as a serious threat. The Bucharest statement echoed an outdated orthodoxy, a position taken by Mao in 1949. China's 1953 census result had raised concerns inside the country, just as it had outside. In 1956, China's premier, Zhou Enlai, spoke of "the desirability of adopting measures favoring birth control," and the following year all restrictions on sterilization and abortion were abolished. From 1970 contraceptives were provided for free. In 1973, a year before it rejected population growth targets at the Bucharest conference, China quietly adopted its own internal population targets. China's real objection was not to population control itself but simply to internationally mandated population control.[73]

In fact, China soon became the face of population control in its most draconian form. In 1979 it introduced the infamous one-child policy, under which women were required to submit to mandatory contraception or sterilization after the birth of their first child and faced serious penalties including loss of employment, health, and education benefits if they did not. Couples who did have a second child faced further penalties.[74]

China was not alone in adopting more coercive population policies in the late 1970s. More liberal developing countries did too—most notably India, which used a variety of inducements to encourage sterilization. These programs, bordering sometimes on compulsion, were assisted and encouraged by wealthy countries and international organizations, whose electorates and stakeholders, caught up in the population hysteria, were unlikely to challenge them. Could any policy really be too strict, when the promised alternative was mass starvation?[75]

• • •

REN KOU PU CHA YOU LI YU KONG ZHI REN KOU ZENG ZHANG

人口普查有利于控制人口增长

上海市人口普查办公室

"The census helps control population growth." China's 1982 census came at a controversial time, just a few years after the one-child policy began. It showed the country beginning to address its population growth. The UN Population Fund's support of the census incited American political opposition. (International Institute of Social History / Zuster Mart Nienhuis Stichting.)

Although the most extreme population control programs came after 1974's World Population Year, it marked, in retrospect, the beginning of the end of widespread population concern. Well before the delegates assembled in Bucharest, major demographic changes were already underway. Censuses were slow to show this; spaced, most commonly, at ten-year intervals, they only write the story of one decade a few years into the next.

In 1982 China held what is sometimes considered to be its first modern census following international standards. It was the first since the 1964 enumeration (still then unknown outside China) and the first since its major efforts on population control—though the government had used household records to make population estimates in the mean-time. The count employed a workforce larger than the populations of many countries. Five million enumerators gathered responses, passing them to one hundred thousand clerks, who processed the returns into the databanks of twenty-nine mainframe computers.[76]

Some twenty-one of these were IBM machines provided by UN-FPA as part of a wider program of cooperation with China. This association would soon lead to criticism of the UN agency, as news of abuses justified under the one-child policy leaked out of China. The computers themselves were not spared condemnation, alleged to have been used to calculate quotas for the enforcement of the policy.[77]

When the mainframes finished counting, they reported a total of 1,008,175,288. It was the first time a single census had counted over a billion people. But even as it reached that milestone, China's annual population growth had declined to 1.4 percent. Whatever China was doing, argued its defenders, it seemed to be working. Fertility was falling elsewhere, too. The American baby boom had ended as quickly as it had begun: by 1976 total fertility had fallen to a record low of 1.74. Other populous countries—India, Brazil, Indonesia—all showed steady declines in fertility over the 1970s.[78]

In the West, public concern about population, and support for its control, dissipated even before these falls were fully apparent. *The Population Bomb*'s runaway success—two million copies sold by

1974—inspired a raft of similar titles, but none were as successful. For books published in English, the terms "overpopulation," "population problem," and "population explosion" all peaked in usage between 1970 and 1973, before retreating rapidly. Ehrlich's last appearance on *The Tonight Show* came in 1981.[79]

The slide continued through the 1980s. As the most alarmist predictions of disaster failed to eventuate, people lost interest. Then, as the excesses of population control programs were exposed, indifference turned into outright hostility. In the United States, a turn toward smaller government and a rise in religious conservatism fueled a rejection of population control, now seen as an intrusion on individual liberty. In 1985, amid a warming cold war, the Reagan administration withheld funding for UNFPA, citing the agency's earlier support for Chinese policies.[80]

By the 1990s, population control had almost vanished as a singular global issue, replaced by a broader concern for development. In 1994, what would have been the third UN-sponsored World Population Conference became, instead, the International Conference on Population and Development. The conference, held in Cairo, adopted a "Programme of Action" focused on individual rights, particularly of women, and specifically rejecting demographic targets. A few months later, the UN's Population Commission was renamed the Commission for Population and Development. When the UN voted on global development goals, in 2000 and again in 2015, reducing population growth was not among them—but gender equality was.[81]

Meanwhile, the most draconian national policies were moderated. By 2015, population growth had fallen so low in China that its leaders relaxed its one-child policy (already by then full of exceptions), allowing all families to have two children. It wasn't a complete reversal, but with fertility rates in the rest of East Asia having already fallen, more freely, to just above 2.0, and a small family norm now embedded in Chinese culture, the new policy is unlikely to constrain more than a small minority of parents.[82]

Why did population growth slow? Top-down planning unquestionably played some role. In countries like India and China, government attention had focused on reducing population growth long before Paul Ehrlich declared the battle lost. India had been the first country to adopt an official policy of population limitation, in 1952, stepping up efforts considerably through the 1960s. Even before the UN got involved, private foundation money flowed to such initiatives.[83]

The earliest "supply side" policies, designed to make birth control more accessible and available, were probably necessary but rarely sufficient in reducing fertility. In many places they were eventually complemented by "demand side" policies: public campaigns and financial incentives to encourage the uptake of family planning. Some argue that these actions, illiberal though they could be, were central to fertility declines. Even the strongest critics of population control accept they had some effect.[84]

The role of the most coercive measures—for example, the one-child policy in China—remains controversial. These extreme and blunt manifestations of population control often came too late to have played an important role. Virtually the whole of China's decline in fertility, from above six to below three, happened between 1965 and 1979— before the one-child policy was instituted. Moreover, it was not long before the same pattern was seen in countries that had not adopted such measures. Altogether, global population growth had peaked at about 2.1 percent in 1968. In 1971, growth began to decline, reaching about 1.8 percent in 1977. It held steady for a decade before entering in 1988 another period of steep decline, which continues to this day.

In the long run, more important than specific population policies were the underlying drivers of demand for birth control, the social and economic factors that had always affected childbearing choices. In rural areas, large families were beneficial, as children provided additional farm labor, but as people moved to cities, this was no longer a consideration—in fact children might become an expense. In traditional societies, children often cared for aging parents; but the development of social welfare systems reduced the pressure for parents to make this "investment." Falling mortality, the original cause of the population explosion, also helped end it: once people were assured that their two or three children would all survive to adulthood, they stopped having more. The decision to have children is a complex one, affected by many factors besides government targets, campaigns, and incentives.[85]

One factor in particular has been emphasized in recent decades: education. The connection between girls' education and fertility was recognized (at least, by female researchers) even in the 1950s, but it was not until the late 1970s that it began to receive serious attention. By the 1990s the notion that "education is the best contraceptive" was part of conventional wisdom in development. There are many reasons why education has this effect. Women who remain in school are more likely to delay marriage until after the age of eighteen and are more likely to learn about contraceptive options. Education raises the earning potential of women, so the opportunity cost of time off work to have children becomes higher. Education also raises the status of women within the household, giving them more power over their reproductive choices.[86]

For the suffragette Emily Davison, hiding out from the 1911 census of Britain, this would have been a welcome recognition, if rather late coming. Prior to her activism, Davison had attended the University of Oxford, among the first generation of women to do so. She excelled in her exams but—as a woman—was denied a degree. She eventually earned her degree from the University of London instead. In the meantime she taught at two girls' schools and privately as a governess. When her census schedule was completed, against her will, by the clerk of works for the Houses of Parliament, her occupation was listed as "school teacher."[87]

· · ·

As fears of overpopulation receded, the census takers in many places began to observe another phenomenon entirely: population decline. It wasn't unexpected or entirely new. Even against a backdrop of strong population growth, there had always been local pockets of decline; a changing climate made agricultural land unproductive, or a mine or fishery was exhausted, or a plague or war or natural disaster laid waste to a city. These pockets multiplied as countries industrialized, and people departed the countryside en masse for growing cities. But after a century or more of falling fertility, that local phenomenon began, by the twenty-first century, to affect entire regions of the world. In 2020, some thirty countries will have declining populations. Europe as a whole will begin to shrink a year or two later.[88]

By then, more than half the world's population will live in countries with below-replacement fertility: nearly all high-income countries and a majority of middle-income countries. The total fertility rate for the United States fell below replacement in 1972; only continued immigration keeps America's population from falling. China's fertility is now also well below replacement; on present trends, its population will begin to decline in the 2030s. India is poised to overtake China as the world's most populous country, a momentous event currently projected to occur in 2026 or 2027. Indian fertility is right at replacement, but momentum will carry its population upward for a while longer, to a peak somewhere in the late 2050s. By that decade, according to current projections, nearly one hundred countries will be losing people, and the populations of three continental regions—Europe, Asia, and Latin America—will be declining overall.

The exception to this trend, for now, is Africa. Over the first half of the twentieth century, Africa, like Asia, moved into a regime of low mortality and high fertility. In 1960, the population of Africa was below three hundred million. But high fertility persisted much longer in most African countries than in those of Asia. Of the eleven countries with fertility rates still above five, all are in Africa. The continent reached one billion people in 2009 and will be one-third larger again in 2020. By 2100, it could be about as populous as Asia, home to anywhere from three to six billion people.[89]

Unsurprisingly, Africa is now the focus of most international attention on population—albeit moderated by the lessons of the last century. Once again, that attention takes the form of both interventions to reduce population growth and programs to measure it. Of the twenty-one countries that did not conduct a census during the 2010 round, nine are in Africa. In a world now flush with data, these countries strike a sharp contrast. With donors keener than ever to see the impact of aid quantified, terms like "data deprivation" and "data poverty" have entered the development lexicon.[90]

The UN Population Fund, UNFPA, spent over $200 million supporting 130 countries through the 2010 census round, with the largest share going to eastern and southern Africa. The World Bank also provides census funding, contributing, for example, $34 million for Sudan's census in 2008. Many donor countries support census taking in Africa directly; the US Census Bureau has a significant program of international assistance that has operated in more than a dozen African countries since 2010.[91]

But lack of resources is not the biggest problem. Consider the two most populous African countries, Nigeria (estimated at 206 million people in 2020) and Ethiopia (115 million). Until recently, income per capita in Nigeria had kept pace slightly above India, and while Ethiopia is much poorer, it is comparable to India in the early 1990s. Rather, it is political instability that disrupts the plans of Africa's census takers. Nigeria's last census—of which many observers were skeptical—was held in 2006. A new census expected originally in 2016 has still not been taken as of 2019. Political rivalries between the north and south of the country mean that, as in Lebanon, a proper count could be destabilizing. Ethiopia's fourth national census was meant to have been in 2017, was postponed to 2018, then set for April 2019, only to be postponed once again amid security concerns, just a couple of weeks before it was to have taken place.[92]

These failures are reminiscent of China's three unsuccessful attempts to enumerate itself in the first half of the twentieth century. No amount of money or technical assistance can make a census happen if security concerns or political incentives work against it. Techniques not available in the early twentieth century, like sample surveys and satellite imagery, can help keep track of population growth even in the absence of a full count. But if too much time elapses between actual enumerations, the world's demographers might one day discover, with surprise, a couple of hundred million extra people, as they did following China's 1953 census.[93]

• • •

Fifty years on, *The Population Bomb* still divides opinion. It pits the children of Malthus against one another. Economists are more likely to believe it was all an alarmist fantasy, based on naive forecasts and a failure to recognize that people, even parents, respond to incentives and that functioning markets can solve many resource constraints. Ecologists and environmentalists are more likely to believe that Ehrlich was fundamentally correct, that disaster was averted only by coordinated, top-down action, and—what's more—that we're not yet out of the woods.

To credit Ehrlich, the growth in population was only a little slower than his book predicted (reaching seven billion in 2011, rather than 2005, as it would have if his thirty-seven-year doubling time had held). But even with this substantial growth, global disaster was avoided. The battle to feed all of humanity was not in fact over, lost, and hopeless, as Ehrlich declared in 1968. Although there have been occasional famines in specific regions since 1970, the widespread shortages of *Famine 1975!* never happened, in 1975 or any year that followed.

Instead a set of technological innovations known as the Green Revolution swept agriculture, pushing food outputs higher than midcentury pessimists believed possible. Working in Mexico over the 1940s and 1950s, an American agronomist named Norman Borlaug developed new varieties of wheat that yielded more harvestable grain for each acre planted. Similar improvements soon followed in other staple crops. Irrigation, mechanization, fertilizer, and pesticide technologies were improved and introduced to parts of the world where they had not previously been used.

Ehrlich might have seen this coming: by the time he wrote his book, wheat yields in Mexico had already doubled. In December 1970, less than a year after Ehrlich's appearance on *The Tonight Show*, Borlaug received the Nobel Peace Prize for his work. Asked about the Green Revolution in 1971, Ehrlich replied that it would only "guarantee that we'll have a much larger population to starve a little bit later." Nearly fifty years later—with much larger populations—both India and China are more or less self-sufficient in food production.[94]

By the 1980s another Nobelist, the economist Amartya Sen, argued that famines, at least in modern times, were not even the result of insufficient food production. As a nine-year-old boy, Sen had witnessed close-up the Bengal famine of 1943. His later study of the actions of the British administrators of India led him to the view that famine was a political failure, rather than an agricultural or a demographic one. Famine, he argued, would not occur in a functioning democracy. More recent instances of food insecurity—for example, Ethiopia in the early 1980s or Darfur in the early years of the twenty-first century—tend to bear this out, taking place amid violent conflicts.[95]

It remains, however, impossible to dismiss Ehrlich completely. His intellectual heirs argue today that the advances of the Green Revolution have been unsustainable, dependent on a continual draw-down of finite resources and therefore putting off, rather than avoiding, a final reckoning. The extent to which this is true is hard to determine (one can never be sure what is, and is not, sustainable, until it can no longer be sustained). But at least one case of unsustainability has the near universal agreement of scientists: climate change caused by the emission of greenhouse gases. Half a century after Ehrlich's first appearance on *The Tonight Show*, this remains his most potent rejoinder.

One could argue that population has not, as yet, been the central factor in climate change: around two-thirds of accumulated carbon emissions have been due to a small minority of people, living in rich countries in Europe and North America. But the fact remains that— holding other things equal—carbon outputs really do scale with population, while the capacity of the planet to absorb them appears relatively fixed. The rising middle classes of countries like China quite reasonably aspire, and are beginning to reach, the same living standard—and hence the same carbon footprint—as their peers in the West.

Of course population may yet offer a solution to climate change. Among these additional billions of carbon-producing consumers are also the scientists and engineers who will invent the solutions to decarbonize the world's economies. But to treat that as prophecy, rather than recognize it as hope, would be foolish. Midcentury fears of a population explosion were overplayed, but they were not completely unfounded. To suppose that problems simply solve themselves, as critics of Ehrlich sometimes do, would be to take exactly the wrong lesson from that period. After all, the work of Norman Borlaug and the other Green Revolutionaries did not come along by accident: it was funded and supported by the same organizations then sounding the alarm about population, among them the Rockefeller and Ford Foundations and the United Nations.

• • •

The world as a whole is now following the same urbanizing path that Europe and the United States did in the nineteenth and early twentieth centuries, having crossed the majority-urban mark—according to UN definitions—in 2007. It hasn't been easy. A present-day traveler to Delhi will probably encounter many of the same sights, sounds, and smells that so perturbed Paul Ehrlich during his 1960s trip. Somehow, though, that city has continued to expand, growing tenfold since then to nearly 30 million today. It is on a trajectory to overtake Tokyo by 2030 and head a list of megacities that now includes Shanghai, São Paolo, Mexico City, and Cairo. Meanwhile New York has been pushed down the ranks of the world's largest cities, no longer even making the top ten. But even New York, after static and sometimes declining population from 1960 to 1980, has grown over the last two decades (albeit at the time of writing, growth had turned negative again; it remains to be seen if this is a lasting development).[96]

Cities—at least the big ones—are ascendant in the twenty-first century. Once associated with smog and unclean water, urban density is now lauded for its small carbon footprint. Heaving urban populations are no longer seen as fomenting vice, but creativity and dynamism.

Hubs of knowledge work have risen from the ashes of industrial decline. A new theory in economics recognized that people might not be merely a drain on resources, but a source of ideas, the kind of world-changing ideas that Norman Borlaug had. Cities, with their "people visiting, arguing, and screaming," are now seen as the heart of this process—or perhaps more accurately, the brain.[97]

Of course cities still have their problems. Smog and unclean water remain features of many of the world's largest cities. A cleaner New York or London is at least partly the result of a dirtier Shenzhen or Chongqing; a consequence of global trade shifting polluting industries away from the penthouse apartments of the world's rich and powerful. In wealthy countries, the recovery of cities, and accompanying gentrification, has pushed established communities to the margins, even as signs are emerging that their great engines of social mobility may be stalling. City-country divides are stressing aging political structures, pitting increasingly progressive and diverse urban populations against rural areas that often lean conservative and wield disproportionate political power.[98]

But for better or worse, global urbanization shows no signs of slowing down. Meanwhile, the world's rural population will probably peak around 2020 at about 3.4 billion people. In the years that follow, on current trends, it will begin to decline.[99]

• • •

The latest estimates from the UN Population Division show a world population on July 1, 2020, of 7.8 billion people. None of the experts I spoke to would commit to an error range for that figure, but it's likely to be small, probably less than 5 percent. Since 1980, every census round has covered around 90 percent of the word's population. Even for large countries with patchy census records, like Nigeria, the proliferation of household surveys means that official population estimates are likely to be relatively sound for now. Today, we know the number of people on this planet with greater certainty than ever before.

What that number will be beyond the next few decades is much more difficult to say. The great mistake of demographic pundits, from Malthus to Ehrlich, has always been to assume that current trends must continue. The very concept of doubling times, used to describe population growth since before Benjamin Franklin, creates an unjustified sense of certainty. A "twenty-five-year doubling time" suggests that growth will be consistent over twenty-five years. At least for human populations, nothing is ever quite that stable.

Some part of population growth is fairly stable, at least over the space of a few decades, as a result of momentum. (Although Malthus's positive checks of war, famine, and epidemic disease can still quickly decimate populations today.) But the underlying drivers of demographic change—technology, politics, and culture—are not fixed. Fertility, in particular, can change dramatically in a very short period. Future population now depends less on the unremitting "passion between the sexes" than on the private childbearing decisions of a billion or so couples around the world. Those decisions are not as predictable as Ehrlich imagined when he wrote, in 1968, that "people *want* large families." Forecasting long-term population change is now at least as much a job for anthropologists, cultural critics, and science fiction writers as it is for political arithmeticians and their descendants. Demography may be destiny, but not much is predestined about demography over the long run.[100]

Acknowledging these uncertainties, the UN continues to publish population projections using various scenarios, revising them every two years to account for new censuses and other demographic data. The latest high scenario shows population continuing to grow, doubling again to sixteen billion by 2100, with no peak in sight. The medium scenario shows slowing growth and a peak of around eleven billion, arriving just after 2100. In the low scenario, the peak comes in 2054, at not quite nine billion people. When forced to choose a single scenario, UN publications favor the medium one, but many outside experts lean toward the low end.[101]

The best guess—allowing that it really is a guess—is that human-kind will reach a peak population probably sooner than 2100 and with fewer than eleven billion people. If so, then for a time—possibly for decades, possibly for centuries—the population of not just one city or one country but our entire species will decline. After dutifully record-ing centuries of unrelenting growth, the world's census takers will in-stead face what the poet Robert Frost described, in 1923's "The Census-Taker," as

The melancholy of having to count souls
Where they grow fewer and fewer every year[102]

It needn't be such a dismal prospect. If we, as a species, can get through the next few decades of population growth and avoid the worst consequences of climate change, then perhaps the melancholy of the late twenty-first-century census taker will be offset by the richer, health-ier, happier families they enumerate. And then, perhaps, the ghost of the Reverend Thomas Robert Malthus will finally get some rest.

CHAPTER 6

THE UNCOUNTED

As the cartoonist known as Zapiro correctly surmised, neither Mark Orkin (depicted left) nor Pali Lehohla (right) relished the task of explaining the revised census total to South Africa's minister of finance, Trevor Manuel. ("Ministry of Finance" © 1998 Zapiro. Originally published in *Sowetan*. Republished with permission. www.zapiro.com.)

How do nearly 3 million people suddenly appear out of no-
where? That was the question Trevor Manuel, South Africa's minister of finance, was asking in September 1998. It was two years after
South Africa had conducted, with great fanfare, its first census as a
postapartheid, democratic country. Midway through the previous year,
what had then been called the Central Statistical Service had announced
a preliminary population total of 37.9 million. Now Mark Orkin, head
of the service, was telling Manuel that the true number was over 40
million.[1]

There was a rational explanation, of course, as Orkin was trying to
make clear. But the minister clearly felt blindsided. "He was absolutely
incandescent" with rage, Orkin explains, in a biography of Manuel.
"He...just blew up."[2]

Orkin wasn't the only one in the firing line. He had brought along
his deputy, Pali Lehohla, who was in charge of the census. Also with
them was an advisor, Julia Evans, from the Australian Bureau of Statistics. The Australians had been providing technical support for the census; they had a particular, long-standing expertise in dealing with a
problem that afflicted censuses everywhere: their troublesome tendency
to simply overlook people. At that moment the three people sitting opposite South Africa's finance minister might well have wished they, too,
could vanish. "Julia was sitting behind me and Mark when [Manuel]
rose," Lehohla remembers. "She just disappeared into the wall....I
couldn't see her. She just disappeared!"[3]

The revision to the preliminary estimate might have been manage-
able if it had been distributed equally across the country. At 2.7 million
people, or 7 percent of the population, it was high by international
standards but not embarrassingly so. The difficulty was that most of
these newly discovered people were living in rural areas in the predominantly black provinces of the nation. While the population figures for
these areas had been revised upward, by as much as 10–20 percent,
those of Gauteng and Western Cape, the two wealthiest provinces,
with the largest white populations, had not. The population of Gauteng
was only marginally higher, while that of Western Cape had actually

been reduced, by over 150,000 people. For a country in the midst of dismantling a racial caste system, still feeling its way toward a fragile new democratic compromise, this was a potentially explosive situation. To skeptics, it would appear that Nelson Mandela's new, black-led government was fiddling the numbers to its own advantage.[4]

"How do I face the president and this nation and tell them this?" yelled Manuel. "I'll have to resign."

"Minister," offered Orkin, "I'll have to resign before you do."[5]

• • •

Population censuses have always made mistakes. It has been an open secret: well known, certainly, to enumerators and statisticians, sometimes explained to the public and politicians, but just as often dealt with in breezy introductory caveats or relegated to footnotes. People were recorded in the wrong category or place. Others were counted twice. Many more were not counted at all, accidentally or intentionally escaping the attention of enumerators. And this is not even to consider the monumental, systematic screw-ups: boxes of records lost, enumerators who simply made up their data, coding errors that could add or subtract a million people at a keystroke. As in any complex human enterprise, error is an ever-present possibility. No census of any size is, or ever was, a true count of the population.

For a long time, genuine mistakes were the least part of the problem. The vast bulk of "miscounting" historically resulted not from incompetence but from intentional discrimination: legal and political decisions about who should count in the first place. Censuses in antiquity often counted only adult men or only adult men of a particular class. Those early censuses, if we allow them that label—and some scholars quite reasonably do not, for exactly this reason—didn't even begin to attempt to count everyone.

But the modern era of census taking, from the early nineteenth century, was meant to be different. As professional statisticians took the reins and framed counting people as a technical enterprise, a consensus emerged that the census should count everyone. To do otherwise would be unscientific. By the end of the century, a basic structure for global enumeration was taking shape: a world divided into territories, with each territory enumerating its entire population every ten years, such that in principle those counts, summed together, would include every single person on earth. As the Hungarian statistician Josef Körösi wrote in 1887:

> Battalions of this army of enumerators will invade again every inhabited place, from the snow clad peaks of Alaska and of Iceland, to Cape Town and even to the South of Australia.... Patrols of this great army will penetrate anew into the palaces of the great capitals of the world, and into the lonely shanties of the squatters in the wilderness; they will omit neither the tents of the Bedouins, the huts of the Eskimo, nor the wigwams of the Indians.[6]

But even if statisticians felt that way—and not all did—censuses were constrained by cultural and political realities that did exclude people, as, for example, "Indians not taxed," who were still not included in the official count in the United States. For those who shared Körösi's vision, such exceptions must have chafed; over time census takers often found ways of counting excluded groups all the same.

In the 1880 US census, special provision was made, for the first time, to count those Native Americans still in the "not taxed" category. The census office published two different population totals: an official one, for the purposes of apportionment, without "persons in Indian territory, on Indian reservations, and in Alaska," and another, more scientific one that included them. Such auxiliary totals, special reports, and supplementary tables, set aside from the main work of the census, didn't exactly signal inclusion, but they were a step in the right direction.[7]

As time went on, political developments—for example, slave emancipation and the expansion of women's suffrage—challenged exclusionary notions of membership in society. In many areas of life, racial and other hierarchies persisted and even flourished. But inclusion in the census was the most basic recognition by society: according to the international conventions of counting, it should be blind to those hierarchies, reflecting not social standing, the right to vote, or even citizenship but the simple fact of being a person who spent a particular day or night in a particular place.

The United States continued to use a slightly different rule, counting those who were "habitually resident" in a place and ignoring anyone who was simply visiting on census night. But interpreted sensibly, even that rule was incompatible with the exceptional treatment of Native Americans. Their exclusion was finally ended—rendered void—in 1924, when all those who were not already citizens were made so by an act of Congress. The language of "Indians not taxed" still exists unamended in the constitution, but it now signifies an empty category.[8]

Today the only people within the borders of the United States on April 1 who are excluded from the census are short-term visitors from other countries. Everyone else is counted: black, white, Native American, citizen, noncitizen, documented, and undocumented.[9]

• • •

A similar evolution in counting took place in Australia, although it began later. Australia's indigenous population comprises two distinct groups: (1) the Aboriginal people of the mainland and Tasmania and (2) Torres Strait Islanders, the traditional inhabitants of the islands that lie in the narrow strait separating the state of Queensland from Papua New Guinea. When the British colonies that spanned the continent federated in 1901, their new constitution echoed its American predecessor, stating in section 127: "In reckoning the numbers of the people of the Commonwealth, or of a State or other part of the Commonwealth, aboriginal natives shall not be counted."

As in the United States, the intent was to exclude indigenous people from the calculations that would allocate power among the separate colonies, now states. Initially, "aboriginal natives" were not included in census publications at all. States and localities, however, often made their own estimates for administrative purposes, and by the 1920s the federal Bureau of Census and Statistics was including these totals in its publications.[10]

As in the United States, the excluded category was progressively narrowed. Queensland lobbied successfully for Torres Strait Islanders to be reclassified as Pacific Islanders and therefore subject to ordinary enumeration. Meanwhile, "aboriginal" was reinterpreted so that eventually only "full-blood Aboriginals" were excluded. Like their American counterparts before them, Australia's census takers felt bound by the language of the constitution to include these Australians in separate tables: counting them but not including them in the final "reckoning of numbers."[11]

This was the status quo when the civil rights movement reached Australia in the late 1950s: a statistical bureau still excluding a part of its population from overall counts and detailed tabulations—and making a less than concerted attempt to enumerate them. To be clear, the numbers involved were small: Australia's indigenous population had probably never exceeded one million, and as in the Americas, it was devastated by disease and violence following colonization. Moreover, despite widespread prejudice and occasional legal prohibitions, intermarriage had begun to blur race lines. By the 1961 census, the bureau reported only 40,081 "full-blood Aboriginals." Ninety percent had been actually counted, with the balance reflecting estimates made by state authorities. But small though this number was, it was highly symbolic.[12]

Whereas successive American governments could gradually erase the exclusion of Native Americans through administrative and legislative decisions, the unambiguous language of the constitution made this approach impossible in Australia. In the late 1950s a movement arose to find a constitutional solution. Section 127 was one of two in Australia's founding document that specifically referred to Aboriginals. The other was similarly technical, relating to state powers. Neither was the sort of thing that would be expected to inspire a popular campaign. But a broader narrative quickly took shape. An amendment that eliminated these provisions, it was widely believed, would bring myriad benefits: granting Aboriginals citizenship rights and ending discrimination.[13]

Legally, none of this was true, but the public debate was not conducted in legal terms. The exclusion of Aboriginals from Australia's "reckoning of numbers" was a powerful symbol and a damaging one for a young nation looking outward. By the early 1960s, decolonization and civil rights movements were together bringing increasing attention to the rights of indigenous people everywhere. With pressure mounting both inside the country and out, the government agreed to hold a referendum on May 27, 1967. Those campaigning in favor of a pro-amendment Yes vote focused on the theme of inclusion. The repeal of section 127 was a matter of "treat[ing] Aborigines as people," according to a leading newspaper.[14]

The amendment passed overwhelmingly, with just over 90 percent of voters and clear majorities in all states approving the measure. It remains the most decisive referendum vote in Australia's history. Over time, it has come to be seen as a turning point for racial equality, for Aboriginal rights, and for progressivism in Australia. The relatively technical focus of the changes that resulted is largely ignored or forgotten in public discourse, replaced by general ideas—and myths—about citizenship granted and equality won.[15]

For activists, this perception, and the totemic status of 1967, can be frustrating, suggesting that a single legislative gesture half a century ago, heavy in symbolism but light in substance, could be thought to have solved racial inequality in Australia. The constitutional changes of 1967 had far less impact on the lives of Australia's indigenous people than many less-celebrated reforms. And yet this stubbornly rooted narrative shows just how potent the symbolism of counting, and not being counted, is.

• • •

In South Africa, progress toward an inclusive census came even later and by a much more circuitous route. As long as it had existed, the country had been ruled by its white minority, to the exclusion of others:

black Africans; "coloureds," or people of mixed descent; and "Asians," descendants of indentured laborers transported from the Indian sub-continent. And just as Australia and the United States began to grapple with racial inequality, South Africa doubled down on it. The national-ist government elected in 1948 introduced a new system to support segregation: apartheid.

Initially, the apartheid system empowered census takers, and far from being ignored or uncounted, nonwhites were of great interest—both statistically and individually—as objects of control. During a re-cent visit to Pretoria, the country's administrative capital, I was reminded forcefully of this history. I arrived the morning following Human Rights Day, and various posters and notices still advertised the previous day's commemorations. The event marks one of the darkest moments in the country's apartheid history, a massacre that took place on March 21, 1960. That day, a large crowd gathered outside a police station in the township of Sharpeville to protest apartheid and, in par-ticular, the "pass laws," under which all black South Africans were re-quired to carry an elaborate identity document, which determined where they could work, travel, and live.

Pass requirements actually predated apartheid. They were instituted as early as the eighteenth century to control the large black population that supplied labor to agriculture and, from the mid-nineteenth cen-tury onward, in South Africa's gold and diamond mines. But when the policy of apartheid was adopted, passes were woven into a network of measures designed to enforce separation and maintain white control. The Sharpeville protest was the culmination of a campaign that focused on these "unjust laws."[16]

As the day wore on, the crowd grew, with people publicly burning passbooks and defying the police to arrest them. Eventually a scuffle broke out, protestors began throwing stones, and police opened fire in response. Sixty-nine people were killed. The massacre initiated a new era in South Africa, one of harsher oppression and more violent resistance. It established the pass book as the symbol of apartheid, and brought international attention—and condemnation—to the elaborate system of control that had been established over the previous decade.[17]

At the center of this system was a short piece of legislation called the Population Registration Act, passed in 1950. As the Nazis had discovered in Germany, racially discriminatory measures require an operational definition of race and a classification process to apply it. Who better to turn to for such a classification than the census office? The Population Registration Act instructed the director of the census to use the next count, 1951, as the basis for a population register, with racial classification at its heart. The director, Jan Raats, was well-equipped to do so, having earlier toured postwar Europe to learn about the registration systems still in place there.[18]

According to the 1950 law, each person was to be classified as "a white person, a coloured person or a native, as the case may be." The definitions provided were vague and sometimes circular: "white person," for example, meant "a person who in appearance obviously is, or who is generally accepted as a white person." So the job of actually classifying individuals fell to the census enumerators, mostly local white people, untrained and otherwise unemployed.[19]

A person who felt he or she was incorrectly classified might appeal this decision. Then an array of dehumanizing methods would be applied to make a conclusive determination of race. The most infamous was the so-called pencil test: if a pencil threaded into the hair of a racially inconclusive person fell to the floor, he or she was designated white; if not, coloured or black. Officials also examined noses, ears, and veins for telltale markers of race. A contemporary *New York Times* article reported that Raats himself "personally classified 700 persons after separate interviews." A critical account in a left-wing South African newspaper described the bureaucrats involved as having "all the makings of good Nazis."[20]

The registration was soon complete. Raats's tenure as director of the census ended in 1956, and by the 1960s, responsibility for maintaining the population register had been transferred to another department. The importance of the census diminished, with the last unified count of the whole country under apartheid taking place in 1970.

At around that time, South Africa's leaders developed a new approach to segregation. Since the beginning of apartheid, various areas of the country had been carved out into "homelands" along rough ethnolinguistic lines. From the 1970s, the South African government declared these homelands either fully independent or self-governing. The residents, including many who had been forcibly resettled there over the preceding decades, were stripped of their South African citizenship. Anyone black and living outside his or her designated homeland was henceforth considered a foreign guest worker rather than a South African citizen.

The homelands were never recognized internationally. Outside observers saw them for what they were: puppet states completely dependent on South Africa. But to maintain the fiction of the homelands' independence, the South African government excluded their newly created populations from central statistics, devolving statistical responsibility for the homelands to their governments. The consequence was that for the next quarter century, censuses proceeded in a messy, piecemeal fashion.

The last apartheid-era census, in 1991, exemplifies this approach. In predominantly white areas, enumerators visited houses and surveyed residents as usual. But many of the crowded, underdeveloped, black-majority settlements adjacent to South African cities, the so-called townships, were declared inaccessible, too dangerous to enter. There was truth to this: toward the end of apartheid the African National Congress (ANC, the party of Nelson Mandela) adopted a strategy of making the townships "ungovernable" through violent resistance. But an accurate count of such places was, in any case, not a priority. The million-strong population of Soweto, for example, was estimated from the safety of the sky, by counting the structures visible in aerial photographs.[21]

Meanwhile, few of the homeland governments actually had the capacity to run a proper census, still depending on South Africa's Central Statistical Service for support and ultimately employing similar aerial and sample-based methodologies. One exception was the so-called

Republic of Bophuthatswana, an infeasible collection of seven physic-ally disconnected enclaves of Tswana-speaking black South Africans. It was here, more than a decade before he found himself on the defensive in Trevor Manuel's office, that Pali Lehohla was introduced to the art of census taking.[22]

• • •

I meet Lehohla at his house, in a pleasant Pretoria suburb not far from the city's botanical gardens. According to the 2011 census, the sur-rounding area is majority white and Afrikaans-speaking, so Lehohla, a black speaker of Sesotho, finds himself in the minority. I've arrived slightly ahead of our already-early appointment, and while I wait, I wander a little. This is the kind of neighborhood census enumerators dread: not because of civil unrest, as in the townships of the 1980s and early 1990s, but because of its counterpart: imposing spiked stone walls, steel gates, and electronic intercoms. In areas with such defenses, trying to take a household survey can be a disheartening experience.[23]

When he opens the gate for me, I half expect Lehohla to be wearing his famous canary yellow suit. A sartorial trademark he adopted during the 2011 census, it echoed the yellow vests worn by the enumerators and made him instantly recognizable to television audiences across the country—he became a genuine census celebrity. To my disappoint-ment, he is dressed more casually, although as I step inside I note that the number on his gatepost is that same yellow. We settle in his living room, where we are surrounded by mementos of his time in govern-ment, including a framed newspaper profile from 2002, headlined "The Man Who Really Counts."[24]

Counting came early to Lehohla. He was born in 1957 in what was then the British colony of Basutoland, an enclave within South Africa that would become, in October 1966, the independent country of Le-sotho. A census was scheduled shortly before independence, to estab-lish a baseline of reliable data for the government that would take over. It was the first time that eight-year-old Lehohla had heard of such a thing, and the idea fascinated him. When his father, a teacher, came home one day with a new ox, the family decided to name it Census in celebration of the coming events.

(Lehohla, like many South Africans, seems interested in words and their meanings—perhaps an inevitable consequence of living in a country with eleven official languages. When the statistical bureau's new steel-and-glass headquarters opened near the end of Lehohla's tenure in 2016, it was named ISIbalo House: *isibalo* means "sum" in the Nguni language, while the first three capitalized letters are an affectionate nod to the International Statistical Institute.)[25]

As an undergraduate student, Lehohla studied economics and statistics before enrolling, in 1980, as a graduate student at the University of Ghana. A prestigious institute for demography had been established there, in 1972, with support from the UN Population Fund. Shortly after completing his graduate work, Lehohla's statistical career took an unexpected turn. At independence Lesotho had been a multiparty democracy, but it had since become increasingly authoritarian. In 1982, Lehohla helped a friend flee the country and, as a result, soon found himself having to do the same. Crossing into South Africa, he stayed for a while in Mmabatho, then the capital of Bophutatswana. While there he applied for, and was appointed to, a job in the homeland's statistical office.[26]

For Lehohla, this decision was not free from tension. The legitimacy of Bophutatswana, like all the homelands, was questionable at best. Its autocratic leader, Lucas Mangope, was widely viewed as an apartheid collaborator and his rule had been condemned by the ANC. When Lehohla left Lesotho, he had not been heading for Bophuthatswana at all but Botswana, its neighbor to the north, which had become a haven for South African dissidents. "All my years at university, including when I was at the University of Ghana, [I attempted to] discourage anyone trying to come to South Africa," he tells me. "I said, 'How do you go to this apartheid system?' A few months later I found myself deep in that system."

In the Bophutatswana statistical office, Lehohla quickly encountered the practical side of census taking often overlooked in university study. For example, none of the staff had a driver's license—a serious impediment to conducting a field survey across this archipelagic terri-tory. The work gave him an appreciation for the logistical and organi-zational challenges of collecting statistical information. He led the homeland census in 1985 and again in 1991.

By the time of this latter count, Nelson Mandela had been released from prison, and negotiations to end apartheid were underway. Amid the transition, in June 1991, the hated Population Registration Act was repealed. It was the last of the major pieces of apartheid legislation to go. For the first time in forty years, South Africa was without a for-mal, legal structure for racial classification. "Now it belongs to history," the president, F. W. De Klerk, told Parliament. "Now everybody is free of it."[27]

The homelands, too, belonged to history. But before Bophuthatswana was dissolved, Lehohla used his position there to agitate for change in the South African statistical system. After the election of Mandela's new postapartheid government in 1994, pressure to reform the Central Statistical Service grew. Its professional staff was almost uniformly white, with many reluctant to embrace the new "rainbow nation" that South Africa was becoming. Conflict was inevitable: Lehohla recalls one occasion when he was actually locked out of a meeting in the Pre-toria headquarters.

A new leadership team was sought and found in Mark Orkin, who had previously run a nonprofit social research organization, and Le-hohla, who became his deputy. For the staff of the Central Statistical Service the duo's appointment was a shock: a black troublemaker, pre-viously persona non grata at the service, teamed with "perhaps the one Marxist in the ANC who still believed in numbers," in Orkin's self-description.[28]

As the two men took control in June 1995, they embarked on an intimidating program of work. New employees had to be recruited to replace apartheid-era bureaucrats unwilling to serve under the new regime. Economic statistics required expansion and methodological improvement, to facilitate the flood of investment unlocked as international sanctions were lifted. Most critically, the country needed a new census of its population—its entire population. This would inform the enormous tasks required to build a democratic South Africa and give the public its first glimpse of the new nation.

Arrangements for a mid-decade census were already underway when Orkin and Lehohla took over. But they found it "poorly planned, behind schedule and apartheid-ridden." They decided, effectively, to start over. Fighting back demands for an almost immediate count, the pair won themselves about a year for new preparations—hardly more reasonable. As Orkin put it to me: "Australia takes seven years to plan its five-yearly census. It's planning the one even before it has administered the prior. So to do it in a year was nothing short of a bloody miracle!" They did it, he added, by working "like lunatics from the word 'go.'"[29]

And this, of course, returns us to the rushed preliminary result, the subsequent revision, and that tense meeting in the office of the minister for finance. Their real mistake, Lehohla explains, was not that the initial count was low—a common enough occurrence in most countries—but in announcing the preliminary figure, in 1997, before all the analysis was done and all the checks complete. Their international advisors had cautioned against it: if the preliminary and final results differed by much, the advisors feared, it could threaten public confidence in the new nation's statisticians and, by implication, its government. But in the euphoric, chaotic, insurgent mood of mid-1990s South Africa, Orkin and Lehohla ignored the advice. In their eyes, they had already achieved the impossible. "We were so eager...and bravado...it blinded all of us," recalls Lehohla. "We were feeling so victorious.... It was the urge, the eagerness, to get the numbers that count for the nation, to the nation, in preliminary form.... It came to burn us really badly."[30]

• • •

For most of the history of the census, large revisions of this kind were unthinkable. The total was the total. It was not subject to appeal.

Enumerators went about their work, schedules were completed, subtotals were tabulated, and then a grand total was announced. There wasn't much room for debate. Statisticians might recheck some of the intermediate sums, or even go back and reexamine the schedules, but barring a major miscalculation the result was unlikely to change by much.

The difference between the rough count and the official count in the 1890 census of the United States was about one quarter of 1 percent. But this didn't mean that those early numbers were correct. Many people expressed severe doubts about the 1890 result, as indeed Washington and Jefferson had questioned the total a century earlier. Among statisticians there was a general suspicion that censuses tended to omit people, resulting in an overall, or net, undercount. But there was no feasible way to confirm or quantify these suspicions. These omissions, if they were occurring, were occurring in the field. Statisticians could retabulate the results as many times as they liked: that could never find people enumerators had missed while canvassing. The results had to be accepted on faith, because no one knew how to properly double-check a census from beginning to end.[31]

The problem is that the census is already the gold standard in measuring a population: it is supposed to be a best-efforts attempt to count every person living in a particular territory. Against what could you compare that? The most obvious option would be to simply run another census. This is, after all, how you might double-check counts in daily life: the cash in your wallet or the playing cards in a deck. But for a population of millions, counting everyone once is difficult and expensive enough, let alone doing it twice.[32]

If accurate vital and migration records were available, demographers might try to build a model of the population, updating a past census total to account for the births, deaths, immigration, and emigration that had occurred in the intervening years. This relied on the same "cohort-component" method used to create population projections, but in the census-checking context it became known as "demographic analysis." Depending on the level of detail available in those records, totals could be estimated for different subgroups, then compared against the actually enumerated totals. But poor tracking of international migration made this method unreliable until the mid-twentieth century.

Another possibility arose as governments began to register people for purposes outside the census. An investigation of the accuracy of the 1940 American count, for example, compared census subtotals for young men with estimates drawn from conscription registrations. This confirmed the suspicion that censuses tended to omit people. Across the country the census total was about 3 percent lower than the count of registrations. The study also revealed a new issue: at 13 percent, the net undercount for black men was much higher than for the nonblack population.[33]

These methods gave useful hints as to the accuracy of the census and the errors it contained, but each relied on the ad hoc availability of supplementary data. What statisticians needed was a truly independent method of evaluating census results that could cover the whole population: one akin to taking a second complete census but without the duplication and expense that would entail. The answer was to be found in sampling, a technique that was increasingly popular in statistical offices by the 1940s.

The idea of sampling is quite intuitive. Suppose you have a bag containing thousands of marbles, identical in every way except that some are red and some black, and you wish to calculate what proportion of the marbles are red. You could tally every marble by color and arrive at an exact answer: that's a census. (It might take a long time, though.) Another approach would be to shake the bag vigorously, then draw some smaller number, say a hundred, and tally only those: a sample. Suppose you find that forty out of the hundred marbles are red. You can then reasonably deduce that 40 percent, or two-fifths, of all the marbles in the bag are red. Of course that probably won't be exactly right, but unless you're exceeding unlucky—or failed to mix up the marbles properly—it will be a good estimate.[34]

That simple logic is probably ancient: John Graunt used a version of it in his seventeenth-century estimate of London's population. But the mathematical revolution in statistics had offered an improved frame-work for understanding sampling. Using the techniques of inference, a statistician could take that estimate—40 percent red—and quantify exactly how good it was. (What "good" means here can get quite technical: for the example described above, a standard analysis would conclude that the true proportion of red marbles very likely lies between 30 and 50 percent.)

Government statisticians in the United States began to experiment with sampling methods in the 1930s as a way of collecting data more frequently than the decennial enumeration allowed. A monthly sample survey of a few thousand households, carefully selected to be representative, could be used to track the rate of unemployment in the whole population. Sampling was a valuable addition to the toolkit of official statisticians and outside census years, it now represents most of what they do. But it wasn't immediately obvious how it might be used to estimate the total size of a population, which is what seemed to be required in order to independently double-check the census. Population size is not an attribute of a sample. One hundred marbles drawn from a bag tell us nothing about how many still remain in the bag.[35]

The key insight came from an unexpected direction: ecology. If counting humans seems hard, imagine the challenge of counting fish in the murky waters of a lake. This was the task facing Carl Georg Johannes Petersen, a Danish biologist working in the 1890s. Petersen wanted to estimate how many plaice were living in Limfjord, a shallow, almost-landlocked channel in the north of Denmark.

He devised an ingenious method to do this. Working with local fishermen, he would first land a catch of fish and mark each one by punching a hole through its dorsal fin. He would note how many had been marked and then release the whole catch back into the fjord. He would then wait some time—long enough for the marked fish to mix with the unmarked fish—and then make another catch. By observing the proportion of the fish in this second catch that bore the fin marking, he could estimate the total population without actually counting every fish.[36]

Suppose Petersen's team marked and released a thousand fish and then in a subsequent haul of five hundred fish found ten that were marked, a proportion of one in fifty. By assuming that this second catch—this sample—was representative of the whole population, he could deduce that one in every fifty fish in the entire fjord must be marked. Since he knew that the number of marked fish was exactly one thousand, the total population must be fifty times greater: fifty thousand.

In ecology, this became known as the capture-recapture method, and it is still used, in some fashion, to count wildlife populations today. It was introduced to demography in 1949 by the Indian demographer Chidambara Chandrasekaran and the American William Edwards Deming. They used the idea to study birth registration in India, comparing births recorded by the official registrar with those counted in an independent survey. Of course, babies could not be marked like fish, but the statisticians could use identifying details like given name and village for the same purpose, to see if births recorded in the survey had already been noted by the registry. Since the capture stage and the re-capture stage used these two different systems, the technique became known, in demography, as "dual system estimation."[37]

Statisticians realized that the same approach could be scaled up to double-check an entire national census. Soon after enumeration was complete in the 1950 American census, an independent sample survey was taken. In most respects it resembled the census itself, though on a much smaller scale and using only interviewers "of top competence" who possessed exceptional "meticulousness and persistence." Of course in an ideal world, all the original census interviewers would have met those standards, but recruiting 140,000 equally meticulous people for a few months of work is not easy. So instead, this elite group of super-enumerators was dispatched to a sample of enumeration areas and instructed to climb over fences, knock on doors, and brave guard dogs that their predecessors might have passed by. This process became known as a postenumeration survey.[38]

Once it was complete, the two independent lists of people—from the census and from the postenumeration survey—were compared. Statisticians could then identify who was correctly enumerated by the census, who was omitted, and who, if anyone, was erroneously included, and from that they could derive a measure of net undercount for the areas sampled. As long as those areas had been chosen carefully, the results could be extrapolated to the country at large. Because the census and survey recorded a wealth of demographic detail, the undercount analysis could be conducted for different subgroups to identify what kinds of people were missed (and perhaps even why they had been missed).

Today postenumeration surveys are the preferred method of evaluating censuses worldwide—around 70 percent of countries used one in the 2010 census round. Around 40 percent used demographic analysis, which has become more reliable as its inputs—migration statistics especially—have improved. Some countries used both.[39]

As statisticians became increasingly comfortable with measures of census undercount, a logical next step beckoned: adjusting the officially reported totals to reflect those measures. There is something odd, after all, in reporting to the public a population of 100 million and a 3 percent undercount, rather than simply giving an adjusted total of 103 million. With a higher undercount of, say, 5 or 10 percent, it seems downright negligent: the adjusted number is, after all, the statistician's best estimate of the truth.

Australia was an early adopter of this adjustment procedure, beginning to apply it in 1976. Twenty years after that, Australia's statisticians advised their counterparts in South Africa to follow this same approach, making South Africa the first African country to use sampling to adjust its census totals. Technically, this was an admirable achievement, as Mark Orkin and Pali Lehohla tried to make clear to South Africa's furious finance minister that September day in 1998. But as they discovered, explaining to a curious public the complex and not entirely flawless process they had used was another challenge entirely.[40]

In the United States, these new techniques for quantifying census error came along just in time to inform an unfolding debate about political representation. The constitution mandated that representatives should be "apportioned among the several states...according to their respective numbers," but it was silent on how congressional districts should be drawn within each state. This had led to some severe disparities—in the early 1930s, for example, New York's most populous district had 799,407 people, while its least populous had only 90,671. Unsurprisingly, these smaller districts were disproportionately rural and white. In the 1960s, the Supreme Court finally began to crack down on such unequal districts, recognizing a general principle of "one person, one vote."[41]

As the most egregious breaches of this principle were rectified, attention turned to subtler forms of electoral inequity—including the perpetual census undercount. Had the undercount been purely random, distributed evenly across the country and throughout the population, it would not have had much political significance. But the Census Bureau's own figures showed that it was far from random. There was, as it came to be known, a *differential* undercount. In 1960, 9.5 percent of black Americans were missed in the census, compared with only 2.2 percent of those who were white. A similar pattern was found for other disadvantaged minorities. The census may have seemed objective and nondiscriminatory, but it was perpetuating inequality.[42]

The reason omissions and other errors systematically affect particular groups—often already-disadvantaged groups—rather than striking at random, has to do with the way censuses are planned and conducted. A census begins with geography. A country is divided up into enumeration areas, the basic work unit of census taking. Each of the areas is the responsibility of just one enumerator. By dividing the entire country in this way, nobody should be missed. And as long as none of the enumeration areas overlap, nobody should be double counted. As the US Census Bureau describes it, the census should count "everyone once, only once, and in the right place."

But enumerators can't simply walk the streets of their assigned areas, tallying the people they encounter. They have to knock on doors. Houses, and their addresses, are a critical part of census geography. The census reaches individuals in their houses, whether by an enumerator visiting in person or a form slid under the door or placed in a mailbox. This is why many countries hold a joint census of housing *and* population: enumerators have to list and potentially visit every house anyway, so they might as well record its physical characteristics, such as the presence of an electricity connection, as they do.

But making houses and households so central to the enumeration process creates sources of error. Some houses may be unknown to postal authorities or hard for census takers to identify—for example, a basement rented to a lodger. Not everybody lives in a house. Some people are homeless, sleeping on sidewalks or in vehicles. Some people live a traditional nomadic or seminomadic existence, perhaps driving herds of animals to higher ground in summer and living in tents. Some people live in institutional settings: prisoners, residential university students, refugees in camps, military personnel living on base.[43]

People may be away from their house, absent when the census taker comes calling or, if self-enumeration is used, when a family member fills out the census form. Business or recreational travelers may spend census night in a hotel, not a house. Fishermen or merchant mariners may be at sea. These itinerant individuals could be easily missed without special efforts to enumerate them. Or they might be double-counted, as Emily Davison was in 1911, recorded both at the Houses of Parliament (where she was) and by her diligent landlady at her home (where she was not).

Because of the focus on households, census officials do not necessarily encounter and lay eyes on every single person they enumerate. Interviewers will usually speak with one person in each household, the head of household or (more neutrally) the reference person, trusting that person to report all those with whom they live. Even in the case of self-enumeration, it's common for a single person to fill in all the details for the household. It may seem surprising, but evidence suggests that, especially with complex family or household structures, people are sometimes overlooked in this process.[44]

Finally, and perhaps most challenging of all, some people choose not to be enumerated. They may be undocumented, refugees, or stateless persons, wary of any interaction with agents of authority. They may be perfectly legal citizens of a place who object to the census on philosophical or political grounds. They may simply be too busy to respond or consider the census unimportant. They may be wealthy enough to surround themselves with walls, gates, and barbed wire, making it physically difficult for enumerators to reach them.[45]

These groups are not spread evenly throughout a country—for example, homeless people may congregate in cities—so the undercount is different for cities and suburbs, for urban states and rural states. And because race tends to correlate with social, economic, and cultural factors, the undercount usually varies by race. In fact, the census undercount varies according to every demographic attribute for which it can be calculated. Race and ethnicity are simply the most salient; they receive the most attention because they reinforce existing and historical disadvantage. (People are not, on the whole, concerned about extremely wealthy people being omitted from the census, although they probably are.)

• • •

Having developed effective measures of census undercount, and with growing political pressure to address it, census takers began to devise ways of reaching people who might otherwise be missed.

In the United States, one of the most important measures to increase participation was a gradual reduction in the size of the census questionnaire. In the first few decades of the twentieth century, when census interviewers still visited every house, each adult was asked around thirty questions. In 1940, the Census Bureau experimented with using sampling as part of the census, with interviewers asking every twentieth person they encountered a handful of additional questions. In 1950 the use of sampling was expanded, and the number of questions asked of every adult fell to only sixteen.[46]

By the time the Census Bureau moved to self-enumeration, in 1960, the form mailed to every household contained just five questions for each person: relationship to head of household, age, sex, color or race, and marital status. This mail-out census was a risky new approach, and keeping the standard questionnaire—the short form—as simple as possible helped mitigate the risk of nonresponse. After the initial census was complete, enumerators delivered a further questionnaire—the long form—to one in every four households. This general system was used for the next several decades, with the short form never exceeding ten questions per person. Canada adopted the same approach, but many other countries, including Australia and the United Kingdom, did not, even as they too switched to the mail-out enumeration.[47]

While census takers around the world worked to maintain response rates across the entire population, they also began prioritizing those groups that were most often omitted, developing methods to improve enumeration of these difficult-to-enumerate groups.

Following the formal inclusion of Aboriginals in Australia's censuses after 1967, the Bureau of Census and Statistics began to work harder to fully enumerate them. In 1971, entire communities that had previously been overlooked were included for the first time. From the 1980s onward, the bureau adopted an intensive strategy that included using special forms, employing indigenous enumerators (in their own communities whenever possible), allowing a longer time for enumeration, and taking, overall, a much more flexible and pragmatic approach.[48]

Properly counting indigenous Australians remains a challenge. Australia's population is extremely concentrated, with nearly 90 percent of people living in urban areas and two-thirds in just a handful of state capitals. Around 80 percent of the indigenous population also lives in urban areas. But the other 20 percent includes people living in settlements that are among the most isolated in the world. An enumerator's account from 2001 reports "a special trip involving two days' driving to an Aboriginal-owned cattle station...on advice that several Aurukun people"—from a community in far north Queensland—"were resident there; in the event however, only two people were enumerated."

Unsurprisingly, that year the cost of the census was about ten times higher, per person, in remote indigenous communities than elsewhere. For Australia, that is the cost of finally counting everyone.[49]

As South Africa embarked on its first census as a democratic country in 1996, it too adopted such strategies. In a way it was ironic. Census takers were breaking away from the patchwork approach that had characterized South African censuses in the past. But experts had come to understand that in a heterogeneous country, a good census requires a patchwork of methods. The difference lay in the motivation: a drive to include, rather than to exclude, ignore, or control.[50]

At its most basic, inclusion meant translation: the census form was prepared in all eleven official languages. But more elaborate measures were taken too, reflecting specific, local circumstances. For instance, a substantial number of South Africans—mostly black men—lived in workers' hostels, a form of institutional housing developed to serve the mining industry. These workers would not be counted in a house-by-house enumeration, so a special set of forms was used and delivered to the chiefs of the hostels. A special effort was made, too, to enumerate homeless people, the first time this had been attempted in South Africa. In total, three additional questionnaires, along with the general form, were used to capture these special populations.[51]

Despite these efforts, the count was still incomplete, as Orkin and Lehohla had known it would be. As their advisors recommended, they embarked upon a postenumeration survey, to measure exactly how incomplete the initial enumeration had been. Six weeks after the census, over one thousand of the most experienced interviewers once again donned their distinctive yellow fishnet vests and set out to "recapture" the people living in around 1 percent of enumeration areas.[52]

Not everything went to plan. In a measure designed to allay fears about confidentiality from a public still somewhat suspicious of census takers, the census questionnaire had only recorded people's first names or initials. Since street addresses were also unreliable in areas of informal housing—the townships, for example—the statisticians soon encountered problems matching the original census records against the postenumeration survey. Deriving a proper measure of the undercount was going to take much longer than expected.[53]

So Orkin and Lehohla make a fateful executive decision: instead of waiting for the results of the full dual-system estimation, the preliminary population estimate would be adjusted for undercount using a simpler method. That method suggested a net undercount of only 6.8 percent; the full method would eventually find a much higher undercount, 10.7 percent—a difference of 1.6 million people. A second error—also the result of an attempt to save time—reduced the preliminary total by another million. Eventually these errors were discovered, but not before that preliminary total had been announced.[54]

Pali Lehohla's regret is still palpable as he describes these errors to me, more than twenty years later. Government statisticians are usually cautious to a fault. To rush out incorrect results is inexcusable, the kind of thing one might still regret twenty years later. That the history of census taking is—as I argue—a litany of such errors isn't much consolation. Neither is the fact that the mistakes were eventually corrected. If you're the Man Who Really Counts, or indeed any of the thousands of men or women who help count, the one thing you're supposed to do right is count. It was, he admits, "a terrible mistake."[55]

In the end, though, nobody—not Lehohla, who ran the census, nor his boss Mark Orkin, nor Trevor Manuel, the minister responsible— had to resign. After that first, dramatic meeting, the statisticians took their time to carefully review their work and develop a communications strategy to explain the new population total. On Tuesday, October 20, 1998, Manuel presented the final census report to President Nelson Mandela in front of an audience of several hundred distinguished guests. In his speech, Mandela declared the census "one of the defining milestones in the building of our new nation."[56]

The president confidently dismissed the revisions controversy with a few sentences: "It is in keeping with the spirit of openness of our democracy and the early need for information that preliminary estimates were for the first time shared with the public. And it is also in the nature of such information that it might need a revision, as indeed proved to be the case." Mistakes, he seemed to be saying, were an inevitable consequence of trying audacious things.

A few days after interviewing Lehohla, I watched a grainy video of that event, which he had sent to me. I wasn't expecting much, having already reviewed an official transcript. But President Mandela strayed well beyond his official published remarks, offering a strident defense of the achievements of his government as well as an admission of its missteps and imperfections. As Mandela finally concludes his remarks, nearly twenty minutes later, Pali Lehohla can be seen in the background (not yet possessed of the yellow suit for which he would become famous). He is grinning. In those few frames, I can feel his relief. Nelson Mandela, more than most, knew what it meant to forgive a mistake.

• • •

In the United States, the opening years of the twenty-first century saw a new twist in the story of the census undercount. The Census Bureau had worked hard on outreach, cooperating closely with community groups and embracing paid advertising, culminating, in 2010, in a thirty-second commercial during the Super Bowl (part of a $2.5 million package). To a casual observer, it might have looked like the bureau had succeeded in solving the problem of the undercount. It was 1.6 percent in 1990, falling to -0.5 percent—a net *over*count—in 2000, before settling at -0.01 percent—statistically equivalent to zero—in 2010.[57]

But this apparently perfect total obscured, once again, a differential undercount. "While the overall coverage of the census was exemplary, the traditional hard-to-count groups, like renters, were counted less well," observed Robert Groves, the director. And, he added, "because ethnic and racial minorities disproportionately live in hard-to-count circumstances, they too were undercounted relative to the majority population." The zero net error was something of a fluke, with undercounting in some populations balanced out by double-counting in others (for example, residential college students, who are often counted both by their parents and in their residences).[58]

Despite all the effort on outreach, the American census still fails to accurately reflect the underlying population. The one tool that might actually fix that—census adjustment—seems out of reach of the Census Bureau. Though it pioneered the postenumeration survey, the United States has never used the results of such a survey to adjust the official census total. Because black people and other Americans of color vote disproportionately for the Democratic Party, any adjustment that improved their representation in the census would, via redistricting, have partisan effects. Proposals for adjustment throughout the 1980s and 1990s invariably became mired in controversy. A legal challenge to compel adjustment for the 1980 census failed in the Supreme Court. The issue was revisited both before and after the 1990 census and before the 2000 census.[59]

By then, the topic of census adjustment had become hopelessly politicized, with high-minded statistical arguments hard to disentangle from naked partisan interest. The linking of the census to representation, a true innovation in 1787, was now an impediment to further innovation. Every methodological proposal would unavoidably create political winners and losers. With today's polarized politics, every major census decision now attracts criticism.

It would be wrong, however, to dismiss the argument about adjustment as purely partisan and ignore the philosophical dimension. Adjustment is theoretically attractive, the right choice statistically, if one is attempting to estimate the true population. It acknowledges the impossibility of ever actually counting every single person in a country as large, varied, and—frankly—oftentimes uncooperative as the United States. Done properly it should result in a more accurate total.

But the quantitative measures of undercount on which adjustment relies are also imperfect. Postenumeration surveys, for example, invariably miss some of the same people as the original census. They have the potential to introduce new errors, as South Africa discovered in 1996. Depending on how they are constructed, they may improve the total but decrease its distributional accuracy. That makes some statisticians wary about adjustment. In the 2010 census round, 90 percent of countries performed a quantitative evaluation of their census results—either a postenumeration survey or demographic analysis—but only one-quarter of those actually used it to adjust the results. Adjustment necessarily requires many small methodological judgments, each subject to dispute. It is difficult to understand and explain, with nuances that seem beyond the grasp even of Supreme Court justices.[60]

There is a virtue to simplicity, especially for a process so integral to the distribution of political power. And a raw, unadjusted count is simplicity itself, a straightforward stocktaking. Or at least it can be presented that way.

Moreover, some legal scholars believe that the constitution's use of the phrase "actual enumeration" excludes statistical sampling. That argument is controversial, since the discipline of statistics didn't exist when that phrase was drafted, let alone sampling theory in its modern form. So far the Supreme Court has found ways to avoid ruling on this point.

The question of adjustment was not revisited at the 2010 census, the bureau presumably still exhausted by the legal battles of the past few decades. The official announcement stated simply that "the 2010 Census showed the resident population of the United States on April 1, 2010, was 308,745,538." As I read it now, that strikes me as an absurdly precise statement, even given the zero net undercount. It would, perhaps, be more honest to say the population was 308 million, plus or minus a million or two (probably plus). But such a concession seems to go against the grain of even the most statistically minded census taker. Even when we know better, the temptation to view the census as truth can be inescapable.[61]

• • •

The rejection of statistical adjustment in the United States—for now—has closed the door to esoteric arguments about different methods of adjustment that might favor one party over another. A postenumeration survey will be conducted soon after the census in 2020, but it will once again only be used to report on any under- or overcount, rather than to rectify it. The count will stand, unadjusted, for all purposes. But this outcome has made possible a different kind of political manipulation: the weaponization of the undercount itself.[62]

This, at least, is how many observers interpreted reports, in late 2017, that the Justice Department was requesting an addition to the 2020 census questionnaire on the topic of citizenship. The news drew an immediate reaction. There are believed to be some eleven million people living in America without citizenship or other legal immigration status, most, originally, from Latin America. Opponents of the question argued that it would depress response rates among those people—who, according to the constitutional rule, should be counted in the census, their status notwithstanding—and among other immigrants and Latinos with whom they may share housing. The plan was, according to one community advocate, "a recipe for sabotaging the census."[63]

In March 2018, Wilbur Ross, the secretary of commerce (whose role includes responsibility for the Census Bureau) submitted a list of census questions to Congress that replaced one already submitted

Is this person a citizen of the United States?

☐ Yes, born in the United States

☐ Yes, born in Puerto Rico, Guam, the U.S. Virgin Islands, or Northern Marianas

☐ Yes, born abroad of U.S. citizen parent or parents

☐ Yes, U.S. citizen by naturalization – *Print year of naturalization* ↘

☐ No, not a U.S. citizen

In 2017, a question about citizenship was controversially proposed for the 2020 census of the United States. It was eventually defeated in the Supreme Court in 2019. (US Census Bureau, "Questions Planned for the 2020 Census and American Community Survey," Washington, DC, March 2018, 7.)

and contained the exact form of the proposed question: "Is this person a citizen of the United States?" Less than a week later a coalition of states, counties, and cities, led by New York state, brought suit in federal court. They argued that they stood to lose representation and funding if the undercount increased among Latinos and immigrants. They were soon joined by a group of civil rights organizations.

The administration's official excuse for requiring the question—to analyze and enforce the prohibition of racial gerrymandering under the Voting Rights Act of 1965—struck many observers as unlikely. For decades, the data necessary for that task, consisting of citizenship, race, and age, had been gathered by the Census Bureau using sampling—first using the long-form census and then by its successor the American Community Survey. But now the Justice Department—which had not, in fact, embarked on any relevant enforcement actions since the change of administration—was claiming that the sample-based estimates were inadequate.

As the legal process of discovery proceeded, a more complicated picture emerged. Documents showed that the idea of a citizenship question had been pushed by immigration hardliners within the administration since its earliest days. The request to the Census Bureau, ostensibly from the Justice Department, had, in fact, been solicited by the secretary of commerce himself. The trial judge in the New York case, Jesse Furman, declared this convoluted approach to be "pretextual," in violation of administrative law that prohibited "arbitrary and capricious" decisions—and vacated the order to add the question. The stated purpose of voting rights enforcement, he concluded, was a "post hoc rationale." He did not, however, reach a conclusion on Secretary Ross's real rationale.[64]

The Census Bureau was once again caught in the middle. The evidence showed that it had repeatedly tried to deflect the secretary's request, warning that it would harm the quality of the census. It recommended an alternative method to improve on sample estimates, by using administrative data held by the Social Security Administration and other agencies. If the question went ahead regardless, the bureau's statisticians advised, it would increase the nonresponse rate for noncitizen households by 5.8 percentage points. This was later revised to 8.0 percentage points, equivalent to a 2.2 percentage point drop in self-response across the whole population. This was commonly misreported as a prediction of undercount, though it was not: increased nonresponse would, inevitably, lead to some increase in the net undercount, but that would be mitigated by follow-up field work. The researchers predicted that this extra work would cost $121 million but gave no estimate of the final effect on the undercount.[65]

The government appealed Furman's decision directly to the Supreme Court, arguing that the pressing timelines of the census required a speedy final resolution to the case. Oral arguments were heard in April 2019. The conservative justices made particular note that such a question had precedent, both historically in the United States and internationally. This was only partly true.

A question about citizenship (or an equivalent concept) was asked in most US censuses between 1820 and 1950. But after 1950, it only ever appeared on the long form, the sample survey sent to a fraction of households. To use the era before 1950 as precedent in 2020 was to ignore six decades of intentional policy on the part of the Census Bureau to keep the short-form questions—sent to all households—as brief and unobjectionable as possible, in order to maximize response rates.[66]

Internationally, it is true that many countries ask about citizenship— 72 percent, in one survey of the 2010 census round—but largely irrelevant. Each country's census takes place in its own historical, political, and cultural context. Fifty-two percent of countries asked about religion, yet in France that question would be anathema. And while UN recommendations list citizenship as a "core topic" of population censuses, they also list twenty-five other core topics, including "Household deaths in the past 12 months" and "Participation in own-use production of goods." They are recommendations, not rules, designed to be broadly applicable to many countries. Questions should only be included, the same document states, after "a balanced consideration of . . . [the] sensitivity of the topics [and] availability of relevant information held in alternative data sources." These are the exact arguments the Census Bureau itself made against the proposed citizenship question.[67]

In the end neither historical nor international comparisons carried much weight with the Supreme Court. The final, rather complex decision upheld the trial judge's verdict. The court found no reason, in principle, that the citizenship question could not be asked but agreed with Judge Furman's conclusion that the secretary of commerce had lied about his rationale for requesting it. This didn't decisively rule out a citizenship question, and for a moment it looked as if the administration might find a way to try again. But with a printing deadline already passed and time against it, the government eventually backed down. There will be no citizenship question on the 2020 census of the United States.[68]

The courts left one issue unresolved: What was the administration's true motivation in seeking to ask this question? Initially, the leading theory among opponents was that the impact on response rates, far from being an unfortunate side effect of the question, was its purpose. By depressing census participation among people who traditionally lean Democratic and who live in states that do the same, the question could have had an impact on the apportionment of Congress.

But an alternative explanation soon emerged: that the question was part of a campaign to have redistricting decisions based on the population of citizens only, rather than the entire population, as has usually been the case. While the constitution and legal precedent makes it clear that everyone—citizen and noncitizen alike—must be counted in apportioning congressional seats to states, this is not the case for drawing district boundaries within each state. That remains a legal gray area.[69]

Redistricting is surely why the question was initially proposed, but as the case headed to the Supreme Court and the controversy built, the proposed question seemed to serve a new purpose: political symbolism. For many on the right, it was self-evident that a government should be able to number its citizens. For some on the left, the very notion of citizenship seemed suspicious, in conflict with American ideals.

Elizabeth Warren, a leading candidate in the 2020 presidential race, proposed banning "the use of citizenship questions in government surveys" altogether.[70]

For my part, I think that in demanding to ask about the citizenship of every person, the administration was making a statement about who it saw as truly American. Perhaps this occurs to me because I myself am only a permanent resident in the United States and not a citizen. I would have answered no to the proposed question. And that's perfectly accurate. But an answer to a question can be accurate yet still incomplete. There are shades of gray to belonging in America today, as there always have been. The citizenship question, with its yes/no binary, sought to erase those shades. Sometimes the questions we ask say just as much as the answers we give.

• • •

Even without the citizenship question, the 2020 US census will face unprecedented challenges in achieving an accurate count. It was consistently underfunded during crucial preparatory years. It will be delivered into an unprecedentedly challenging field, with people increasingly difficult to reach and unlikely to respond to surveys of all kinds.

Only 60.5 percent of households are currently expected to self-respond in 2020, down from the 64 percent achieved in 2010. In an attempt to maximize this rate, the bureau plans to send up to five mailings to a household before an enumerator visits in person. As I glance, guiltily, at the pile of unopened, unexamined mail in my apartment, I wonder how much this strategy can really help, especially with younger people who have learned to ignore the barrage of junk-everything with which we are now bombarded. Similarly, landline telephones are heading for extinction, in homes at least, and many people ignore cell phone calls unless they recognize the caller. Life for survey takers is becoming increasingly challenging.[71]

The option of responding online should help reach some of these people, but an online census has its own risks. In 2016 Australia attempted its first primarily online census. I was visiting my parents in

Brisbane at the time, and on August 9, census night, we sat, frustrated, in their kitchen trying and failing to connect to the census website. So did millions of others, and by the time we finally succeeded several days later, the hashtag #censusfail was circulating on social media. No doubt the US Census Bureau has carefully studied this episode, but four years later the online environment has become more, not less, challenging, with social media misinformation campaigns and state-sponsored hackers now a very real threat.

Many experts worry that the controversy around the citizenship question has done irreparable damage to trust in the census among Latinos and immigrants. Even with the question gone, there is an understandable reserve of suspicion in the community. In May 2019, neo-Nazi website the *Daily Stormer* published a Swastika-adorned post urging its readers to apply for enumerator jobs, so they could attempt to discover and report undocumented people to immigration enforcement authorities. Such an action would be illegal, with a penalty to the enumerator of up to five years in prison and a $250,000 fine. Yet despite attempts by the Census Bureau and civil society groups to counter such statements, the climate surrounding Census 2020 is as fraught as any in decades. Undocumented people could be forgiven for wanting nothing to do with it.[72]

When will we know if the bureau's efforts to "count everyone once, only once and in the right place" have paid off? The populations of each state, used for reapportionment, will be delivered to the president by December 31, 2020 (they are typically released to the public immediately thereafter). Demographic analysis will provide an immediate check of whether the result matches expectations: as of its most recent public projections, the bureau expects the population for April 2020 to be around 331 million. But those projections are broken down only by age and a simplified racial categorization: black or nonblack—and not the more elaborate racial and ethnic classification of the census itself (which includes Hispanic/Latino). A second, more detailed test of the 2020 results will come when the postenumeration survey results are announced, a year or two later.[73]

Imagine the scene. It's 2022, and the Census Bureau has just finished analyzing the postenumeration survey returns. The secretary of commerce has summoned the director of the bureau, to explain the results. The bulk of operations are now complete, the director explains, and the final bill is firming up. At $16 billion, the 2020 US census has been the most expensive counting exercise undertaken by any country ever. But even with that budget, officials have been forced to make trade-offs that affect coverage and accuracy: no budget, no matter how large, can ensure everyone is counted.

Suppose now that the director must also report that the net undercount has been unusually high: over 2 percent, say, a rate not seen since 1970. Among those with Hispanic, Latino, or Spanish ethnicity it is even higher, triple the 2010 net undercount of 1.5 percent. Many in the bureau think even that is an underestimate: interviewers returning from the postenumeration survey share anecdotes of doors slammed shut and curtains drawn. More than a million people have been missed in California alone. The state stands to lose tens of millions of dollars in federal funding and its solicitor general is rumored to be already preparing a court challenge.[74]

The secretary's reaction to this news depends, one assumes, on who holds that office, which in turn depends on the presidential elections that will intervene in November 2020. So too does what happens next. The director might observe that the Supreme Court has left open the possibility of adjusting the population figures based on this undercount—not for the apportionment of representatives to states, that's true, but for everything else: the drawing of districts within states for congressional, state, and local elections and the allocation of the nearly $1 trillion in federal grants annually that are said to depend on the census.

This has never been done before in the United States. But perhaps the time has come. Suppose this happens, and a new population figure is announced: adjusted, improved, and—according to bureau experts—more scientifically sound. How would we, the public, react?

The late twentieth-century focus on the census undercount coincided with a broader questioning of authority and a challenge to the very idea of statistical objectivity. In the academy, postmodernists like Michel Foucault developed a novel, critical approach to understanding government. This spurred a new interest in the history and anthropology of probability and statistics, a fresh perspective that viewed these fields not as given bodies of knowledge and practice but as products of their social and historical contexts.[75]

As these postmodern ideas escaped the ivory tower, the governmental monopoly on statistical truth diminished. Today, official statisticians must continually earn their credibility: by examining and reporting on their own failures, by being up front about sources of error and uncertainty, and by adapting their methods accordingly. Some governments have tried to fight back: in 2018, Tanzania introduced a law that made it illegal to contradict official statistics. But that approach—quite apart from the free speech concerns it raises—only hurts statisticians in government, who benefit greatly from an open dialogue with academia and civil society. The Tanzanian law was reversed in 2019.[76]

We now know that seemingly straightforward censuses, even honestly and fairly conceived, interact with social and political conditions to systematically exclude or miscount individuals. This understanding has been especially important in empowering those who have been historically oppressed and were undercounted by flawed enumeration techniques even after more formal discrimination ended. It has improved the art of census taking, bringing us closer than ever to the goal of counting everyone, while at the same time showing just how ambitious—and possibly unachievable—that goal is.

But in the era of "fake news," with trust in authority seemingly in a constant state of near-collapse, there is a risk of taking critical reflection too far. The present political moment is notably unkind to the type of narrow expertise found in census bureaus. As a candidate, President Trump repeatedly questioned economic statistics, in particular the unemployment rate. And while it is true that some statistical concepts are complex, subjective, and debatable, others—the number of people in a country or in a crowd—are not. All estimates are imperfect, but some are better than others.[77]

Censuses have never been taken at face value and have always been somewhat politicized, but the risk of controversy in the United States in 2020 seems especially high. Criticism could easily become cynicism, eroding faith in the census and, with it, the institutions of democracy that depend on it.

It doesn't help that accurate census taking really is getting more difficult. In 1998, when Nelson Mandela received the results of his country's first truly inclusive census, he struck an optimistic tone: "No doubt the next census will be still more accurate." It wasn't. Despite the best efforts of South Africa's statisticians, the undercount jumped to nearly 18 percent in 2001. As the euphoria of national rebirth gave way to the hard reality of nation building, the eagerness to count and be counted, it seems, diminished. So far, 1996 has been the high point of accuracy—and of enthusiasm—in South Africa's postapartheid censuses.[78]

Perhaps the United States will look back on 2010, with its zero net undercount, in the same way. Political controversy and public misgivings are one thing; the census has survived those for decades. But with enumeration becoming increasingly difficult and expensive, many statisticians are themselves beginning to question whether a decennial headcount is the best way of estimating a country's population. The long age of the traditional census may be coming to a close.

CHAPTER 7

THE TRANSPARENT CITIZEN

CHINA WILL HOLD its next census toward the end of 2020. India will follow a few months later, in February and March 2021. These will show the two countries all but tied in population, at around 1.4 billion people each. But neither will be the largest enumeration of people in history. That distinction almost certainly goes to Facebook, which had 2.4 billion active users as of June 2019.[1]

Facebook's user data does not, of course, constitute a census in the traditional sense. Facebook is not a state, or a part of a state, and does not meet the fundamental requirement for census taking: universal enumeration over some defined territory. Indeed, it has no territory—although it counts among its users at least seven out of every ten people in countries like the United States, Britain, and Australia. (It is, however, in the process of creating its own currency, a step the French finance minister labeled a threat to the "monetary sovereignty of states.")[2]

What makes Facebook like a census is the information it collects. To first register, the site requests name, birthday, and gender. (No doubt some people lie—as some do on the census—but one of Facebook's key innovations was its controversial policy requiring users to list their real names, which allowed it to reflect real-life social networks.) After the user logs in, the site prompts for additional details like cities of residence and origin, high school and college attended, employer and relationship status. These fields are straight out of the UN census handbook, all designated "core topics." Facebook's stated mission is to connect everyone, and people everywhere freely provide this information in order to be connected. Connecting everyone, it turns out, is necessarily preceded by a kind of enumeration.[3]

While social networks are not states, they are communities or, perhaps, societies. Indeed one definition of society is "the fact or condition of being connected." The way we use them reflects that. If a modern-day Mary and Joseph were, for some reason, called to journey from Nazareth to Bethlehem, the birth of their child would as likely be noted first by Facebook or Instagram as by any government authority. The Star of Bethlehem would be an approving gesture on a social app, and instead of wise men bringing gifts, the newborn would be greeted with Likes (and, almost immediately, targeted advertisements for disposable diapers).

Of course, the Facebook community, such as it is, probably won't last the centuries that many actual states have existed. Perhaps Facebook will simply fade into irrelevance, its database deleted, its ubiquitous blue logo a strange artifact of our early twenty-first-century fad for oversharing online. Perhaps it will be replaced by something even more all-encompassing, as Facebook itself once supplanted MySpace. Regardless, right now Facebook may be the truest incarnation of Josef Körösi's nineteenth-century mission to build "a general knowledge that embraces all humanity."

That acknowledgment challenges a narrow understanding of the historical place of the census. This book has so far traced only one line of the descendants of Confucius, Quetelet, Hollerith, and Körösi: those who laid formal claim to the word "census." The complete family tree is much broader, including not only official statisticians in Washington and Beijing but also their siblings in other government agencies and even their distant cousins, software engineers working in California and Shenzhen.

Enumeration, understood broadly, is now a widespread practice, and for twenty-first-century census takers, the official heirs to the legacy of enumeration, the result is an unexpected tension. We live in the world the census created, a world in which we allow ourselves to be counted, registered, and documented for all manner of purposes. And yet in that world, the traditional decennial census is an anachronism, stripped of its position as the singular source of knowledge about a given population.

• • •

It is ironic that the information society may be what ultimately kills the traditional census. The census has survived attacks in the past. But counting people the old-fashioned way, in the twenty-first century, has the appearance of an increasingly expensive luxury. The census is vulnerable to the complaint that much of the information it collects—the number of people, certainly, but also their characteristics like sex, age, marital status, and educational attainment—is already recorded in other files and databases (albeit often incompletely and inaccurately). Politicians naturally ask why this special, costly exercise is necessary when other government agencies—not to mention Facebook—already hold this data.

The cost concern is real. The 2020 census is expected to cost the US government a total of $16 billion, or $48 for each one of the 330 million heads it will attempt to count. That number grew from $8 per head in 1970, to $24 per head in 2000, to $49 per head in 2010 (all in 2019 dollars)—a sixfold increase. Enumeration is expensive because it is labor-intensive, which is why countries like China and India spend far less; each counted over one billion people in 2010–2011 for under $1 per person. Still, even countries similar to the United States—Canada and Australia, for example—spend less than half what it does on a per head basis. The American census is uniquely expensive because the political stakes are so high—the result of a highly partisan redistricting process—and because sampling and adjustment are legally prohibited.[4]

Of course even in the American case, expensive need not mean wasteful. Annualized over a decade, the census cost of $1.6 billion a year represents less than one-twentieth of 1 percent of federal government spending. Viewed as an information service, the census is comparable to the National Weather Service, which has a budget of over $1 billion each year. As a scientific enterprise, the census is on a similar financial scale to the Large Hadron Collider, Europe's powerful particle accelerator ($1 billion a year to keep running). Viewed as a kind of customer research for government, the census costs less, as a proportion of revenue, than American businesses, on average, spend on market research. Gathering high-quality information is simply expensive.[5]

Still, like many government programs, the benefits can seem elusive and are difficult to quantify. Some countries have tried, identifying end uses of census data, such as efficient allocation of funding and capital investment by government, and assigning them dollar values. Recent studies in the United Kingdom, New Zealand, and Australia found that the benefits of their censuses far exceeded the costs. A rigorous South African evaluation, however, concluded that a mid-decade census in 2016 was uneconomic. As a result, the country has, for now, reverted to a decennial schedule, spending some of the roughly $200 billion saved in 2016 on improving sample surveys instead.[6]

Whether their work is justifiable on a narrow economic basis or not, pressure continues to build on census takers to innovate and cut costs. In 2010, the newly elected government of the United Kingdom announced that the following year's census would be the country's last. For 2021, argued the minister responsible, there were "ways of doing this which will provide better, quicker information, more frequently and cheaper." After a public outcry and parliamentary inquiry, the 2021 census was reinstated. But it looks like a temporary reprieve: the UK's Office of National Statistics is working hard on future alternatives to a traditional census.[7]

• • •

Globally, of course, the traditional census is far from obsolete. Much of the world is not yet awash in information, as Britain or the United States is. In-person enumeration remains the only viable way to reach most people in places like Bangladesh or Sudan. In the roughly eighty countries with literacy rates below 90 percent, even self-enumeration would be difficult. Many countries have poor communications infrastructure or limited government capacity, and while a traditional enumeration is logistically complex, it has a well-understood, robust methodology that can work nearly anywhere. That doesn't mean no innovation is possible: new technologies like satellite imagery for address mapping and handheld tablets for recording data have the potential to lower the cost of even a traditional field survey.

Technology can also drive down census costs in wealthier countries. Statistical offices have been slow to embrace the internet for surveys, especially censuses, but they are rapidly doing so now. As with any technological change, it brings risks. Australia's 2016 census suffered from a serious failure of its website. A low response rate in New Zealand's 2018 count was blamed on "too much focus placed on the digital-first approach," leading to the resignation of the country's national statistician. The 2020 census of the United States will be its first to rely heavily on internet enumeration—a major test.[8]

But even when successful, internet self-response is not as revolutionary as one might expect. It makes the cheapest part of modern census taking—self-response—even cheaper. It may do little to reduce the costs of the most expensive part, the in-person follow-up visits to households that fail to self-respond. Census planners hope for an indirect effect: if people see internet response as easier than filling out a form, self-response rates may increase, reducing the need for costly follow-up visits. But the reverse is also possible: if people see responding online as less secure, for example, then self-response rates could fall.

In countries that still use a long questionnaire—Australia and Britain, for example—savings could come from cutting the number of census questions, relying more heavily on sample surveys. The United States pioneered this approach with its two-part long-form / short-form census in 1970. Canada and China are among countries that now follow the same approach. Aside from lower cost, it has the advantage of pleasing privacy advocates, since less data overall is collected.

But this approach also comes with risks. A sample survey that is not seen by the public as an integral part of the census may suffer from low response rates. In 2010, Canada's conservative government made the 2011 long-form questions voluntary, overruling the warnings of experts, including the chief statistician, who resigned in protest. ("Voluntary surveys," he said, "are simply a waste of money.") As predicted, the response rate for the long form plummeted from 93.5 percent in 2006 to 68.6 percent in 2011. Some users declared the results so biased as to be worthless. Reversing this decision was one of the first acts of the center-left Trudeau administration upon taking office in 2015.[9]

The United States left behind its own long-form decennial census after 2000, replacing it, in 2005, with the ongoing American Community Survey (ACS). Whereas in 2000, 17 million households received the long-form survey all at once, the ACS is administered continuously throughout each decade. Around 3.5 million households are selected each year, so that over ten years around one-quarter of all American households are included. This more complex methodology, trading off precision in any year against more timely data, has generally been seen as a success. But critically, the ACS is treated as a core part of the decennial census program and advertised as such, with the same requirement of mandatory participation.[10]

With census response rates continuing to fall, some American experts see a future of even greater reliance on the ACS. At the extreme, the decennial census might record only the number of persons in each household—the constitutionally mandated minimum—and nothing else. This approach would be a return, of sorts, to the 1790 origins of the United States census.[11]

• • •

Many countries are betting on a different approach to reduce the burden of census taking: greater use of so-called administrative data. This term refers to data already collected in the course of government processes—for example, postal records, tax returns, immigration files, and pension or social security accounts. The proponents of such an approach argue that it is easier and cheaper—and much less likely to arouse complaint—to simply reuse data in existing systems than it is to present each person with a blank form every ten years.

Census takers have been studying this kind of data for decades, using it, for example, to estimate undercount error in the census. But there are hurdles to using it as a wholesale replacement for survey data. In the past it has been difficult to reliably link records for the same person in disparate sources—for example, tax returns and school records. Many countries, too, have had legal restrictions on this kind of matching. But modern computers allow more powerful matching, while better statistical techniques have been developed to minimize the impact of mismatches. Legal exemptions are increasingly being crafted to allow matching for statistical purposes.

Administrative data matching became a central point in the legal battle over the proposed 2020 citizenship question in the United States. Even before the issue came to court, the Census Bureau recommended that citizenship information should be sourced from existing government records rather than by adding a question to the census. The dispute provided a rare public insight into what, exactly, the US government did and did not know: the bureau's chief scientist estimated that citizenship could be determined for around 90 percent of people based on Social Security data and predicted that data for most of the remaining 10 percent could be obtained by matching immigration records. The executive order President Trump eventually issued as part of his administration's back-down on the question instructed the Census Bureau to further pursue this option.[12]

This was not a one-off event. In the United States, the Census Bureau is hoping to use administrative data more generally to reduce the need for nonresponse follow-up on the 2020 census. In Britain, the Office of National Statistics program of post-2021 research focuses on constructing an "administrative census," ideally to replace the traditional method entirely. But administrative data still has limits. There are questions, for example, that people may answer on a census but that they may not share with government authorities otherwise (including race and religion, where these are collected). Whether existing administrative data can really replace a survey-based census remains an open question.

• • •

Arguably, the difficulties of using administrative data for population statistics was solved a century ago, with the rise of the dedicated population register. An "administrative census" such as Britain is contemplating is really the poor relative of a population register, lacking only a few key features of the latter, including universal enrollment and mandatory reporting requirements.

The Nazi misuse of population registries slowed their development in some places. The comprehensive file that René Carmille envisaged for France was abandoned (though the country still has a national identity number based on his work). The Netherlands returned to a system of municipal registries, rather than holding data at a central, easily abused point, as Jacobus Lentz had done. But in the Nordic countries, where the legacy of Nazi occupation lay less heavily, registers developed rapidly over the late twentieth century to support the administration of generous, expanding welfare states.[13]

Other countries are now joining them. In the 2010 round, nineteen European countries used a population register to replace some aspects of a traditional enumeration (up from nine countries using this approach ten years earlier). Many still coupled register data with some form of limited enumeration or sample survey, but six countries—the Nordics plus Austria—used only data in existing registers to perform their decennial count. Several countries outside Europe, including India and Turkey, have also begun to establish population registers.[14]

What distinguishes a population register from other administrative databases and makes it a suitable basis for population statistics is that it

THE SUM OF THE PEOPLE

includes everyone resident in a country, it is accurate, and it can be linked to other government databases and surveys. These attributes mean that a "census" can be generated from the register at essentially any time. Sweden, for example, publishes census-like population totals every month. Each person is identified by a unique *personnummer*, which allows statisticians to link core demographics with other data on employment and education or even follow individuals over time (something that is difficult or impossible with decennial data).[15]

Building a register complete and accurate enough to replace the census is not easy. Although most countries have many separate databases of residents, it is often the case that none contains every resident (not everyone pays income taxes or registers to vote, for example). Once built, such a list must be actively maintained. Many core census attributes are relatively stable from birth, but people's locations change quite frequently (around 10 percent of people move house every year in the United States, nearly half to a different county or state). In countries like the United States, Australia, Canada, and the United Kingdom, there is no general obligation to register address changes with authorities, as there is in many European countries. Without that, a population register could be used to count how many people lived in a country overall, but state or county level results would become increasingly inaccurate over time, as people moved about.[16]

Similarly missing in these countries is a single, universal resident identifier, akin to Sweden's *personnummer*. While Australia and Britain have numbers for identifying individuals to tax and benefits authorities, laws prevent theses numbers—the Tax File Number and National Insurance Number, respectively—from being used for other purposes. The US equivalent, the Social Security number (SSN), is close to becoming a de facto person number, issued at birth to Americans and at entry for migrants. Private companies routinely use the SSN for identification purposes far beyond its original function, despite half-hearted attempts by the Social Security Administration and state governments to restrict this. Canada's Social Insurance Number has a similar role, although more serious national attempts have been made there to rein in widespread private use.[17]

In these common-law Anglosphere countries, there is a deep reserve of resistance to mandatory, unavoidable registration mechanisms—a resistance that the traditional census, with its more limited aims, is often spared. Opponents see a slippery slope leading from mandatory registration, to national identity cards, to laws requiring such cards to be carried at all times, to police checkpoints on street corners. Australians rejected an "Australia Card" scheme in the mid-1980s, citing just such worries. In 2009 India introduced *Aadhaar* (from the Hindi word meaning foundation), a personal identifier linked to a national population register and to biometrics such as fingerprints and facial appearance. The program has been subject to multiple challenges in India's Supreme Court, which have reduced its scope.[18]

It's possible that this cultural aversion to registration is weakening. A poll taken in the wake of the September 11 attacks found a slight majority of Americans in favor of "a law requiring all adults in this country to carry a government-issued national identification card." No such card was introduced, but federal involvement in driver licensing has partially nationalized what was previously a state responsibility. Following the 2005 London bombings, the United Kingdom began rolling out a national identity card, but the initiative was canceled following the change of government in 2010. In a world where terrorism and illegal immigration remain issues of serious public concern, it's not hard to imagine public opinion shifting further in favor of numbers, cards, and registers.[19]

Convenience, too, will continue to push countries toward comprehensive central population registries. Government-citizen interactions have the potential to be much smoother when linked together with a single identifier. The New York state application for Medicaid—medical insurance for low-income people—is six pages, with a further three pages describing necessary supporting documents to prove identity and eligibility. In Sweden, you simply turn up at a medical facility with your *personnummer*.[20]

Many professional statisticians I spoke to felt that population registries are the inevitable future of census taking, at least in middle- and high-income countries. Not all celebrated this anticipated future. Daily contact with intimate personal data can lead to the dreams of omniscience that afflicted Jacobus Lentz, but it can also build a deep respect for privacy and a cautiousness about anything that threatens it.

Since I started writing this book, I have experienced a similar conflict, revolving around this question: Did the census lay the foundation of the Panopticon? Or is it benign, even benevolent, a fundamentally positive idea that has built communities, coincided with the beginning of rational, technocratic government, given impetus to the welfare state, and helped create a world that, for most people, is immeasurably better than two thousand or even two hundred years ago?

Such questions have dogged the census since its birth. From its first biblical description, the idea of counting people has been associated with danger, plague, and calamity. In Jewish theology, to be counted was to risk being seen by the malevolent "evil eye." The evil eye is a primal belief, shared by many cultures. It's an almost animal instinct: to be seen is to be exposed to predators and to be endangered. Exodus offered the Israelites a solution. Instead of being counted directly, each would be counted by the half-shekel coin they gave: counting without counting.[21]

The supernatural superstition was eventually replaced by fear of an all-seeing eye more intrinsic to society: Hobbes's Leviathan, the state itself. Parliamentarian William Thornton invoked that fear in 1753, arguing that a census would be "totally subversive of the last remains of English liberty." Yet the last remains of liberty were not subverted, not in England, nor in the United States, nor in most other countries that were taking censuses by 1850. The limited statistics gathered, often just age, sex, and occupation, proved more or less inert.

Still, a little self-knowledge eventually led to demands for a lot. Questionnaires became more comprehensive and intrusive. People once again grew wary, expressing their aversion to being seen not as a fear but now as a defense of the right to privacy: the right to keep secrets, to be opaque, to be unknown. Census takers answered this concern with a solution no less creative than the indirect counting of Exodus. Under the principle of statistical confidentiality, a state might, by statistical summaries, have a general knowledge of its citizens without having an individual knowledge of any one of them: seeing without seeing.

But even as that solution was popularized, it proved inadequate for the growing needs of general government. While government statisticians were constructing a fortress of confidentiality around their work, other bureaucrats were building the centralized information systems of twentieth-century welfare states. Population registers were one manifestation, but so too were social security files, national health records, school enrollment databases.

By the mid-twentieth century, the relationship between the individual and state had fundamentally changed. A century earlier, few if any countries had a complete, centralized list of citizens or noncitizen residents. By 1948, the state of Israel was declared by claiming both a precise territory and a precise population, the latter registered by means of a census. Even in countries without a central list of citizens, a growing array of benefits and obligations—taxations, pensions, health care—individualized the relationship between the citizen (or resident) and the state. The resulting files were never, perhaps, quite as comprehensive as a census, but they came close.

By the 1960s, nobody could be sure which government agencies held their data or for what purpose. A backlash developed. After Vietnam and Watergate, Americans stopped trusting their government to use their data wisely. A similar swell of concern emerged worldwide, followed by a wave of lawmaking. In 1974, the United States Privacy Act came into effect; by 1980 one-third of Organization for Economic Co-operation and Development (OECD) countries had such a law. Whether the privacy regimes of the 1970s ever really worked as intended is an open question, but in many places they remain in force.[22]

Meanwhile, the frontier of personal data collection has moved on. The most valuable and interesting data today is not who a person is—or who they say they are—but what they do. The data that makes Facebook a $500 billion company is not, in fact, the self-reported demographic answers that users fill out when they join, but the pattern of website visits and product likes that emerges once Facebook's radar locks onto them. This sort of data is just as intimate, and sometimes much more revealing, than the broad categories by which we define ourselves in population censuses.

Behavioral data is increasingly available to governments too. For example, government transport planners have for decades used census items on home address and place of work to identify commuting patterns. Today, this explicit data collection is obsolete. In cooperation with private companies, governments can simply observe where individuals' smartphones usually spend weekdays (work) and nights (home). That's a relatively innocuous case, but it's not difficult to imagine more sinister examples. Whether a census contains a religion question is irrelevant if closed-circuit cameras, equipped with face recognition, record who goes in and out of a mosque every Friday.

. . .

Of course, repressive governments have long tracked behavior in order to identify and persecute dissidents. In East Germany the Stasi (secret police) famously kept files on one-quarter of the population, recording movements, meetings, and overheard conversations. But such an extensive operation required the active collaboration of a significant number of people. At the time the Berlin Wall fell in 1989, around one in every hundred East Germans was a Stasi informant.[23]

Thirty years later, that wouldn't be necessary. That's not a theoretical proposition: the world today offers at least one disturbing laboratory for what a state of total surveillance, updated with twenty-first-century technology, might look like: Xinjiang province in the far west of China, described by the *Economist* in 2018 as "a police state like no other." The province is home to the Uyghurs, people who natively speak a language in the Turkic family and practice Islam. Culturally as well as geographically, these nine million people are closer to their Central Asian neighbors than to the bulk of the Chinese population. Their position in modern China has always been fraught, punctuated by occasional surges of separatist sentiment, followed by government crackdowns.[24]

Since around 2008, however, the Chinese government has responded with increasingly sophisticated surveillance technology. Recent visitors and Uyghur émigrés describe biometric identity cards linked to fingerprints and DNA, mandatory spyware installed on cell phones, blanket CCTV cameras equipped with face recognition, frequent physical checkpoints, and so-called convenience police stations every few hundred meters. Supporting this physical infrastructure, according to Human Rights Watch, is an information system that combines surveillance data from CCTV cameras, Wi-Fi "sniffers," license plate scanners, and identity card scans at checkpoints with more conventional records like "vehicle ownership, health, family planning, banking, and legal records." Jacobus Lentz could only have dreamed of such a system. In Xinjiang, the citizen is not just seen but completely transparent.[25]

All of this, though theoretically applying to everyone, is plainly targeted at the Uyghur population. Surveillance is coupled with repression: around a million Uyghurs are believed to have been sent to reeducation camps, in some cases never to return. Darren Byler, an anthropologist at the University of Washington, uses the Uyghur term *kimeytti*—subtracted—to describe these disappearances. In his doctoral dissertation, Byler tells many such stories, including one of an Uyghur man he calls Hasan.

Hasan was originally from the village of Yarkand, but when Byler interviewed him in 2014–2015, he was living in the provincial capital, Ürümqi. In moving to this city of over two million people, Hasan had discovered a freedom increasingly absent from his smaller hometown. But it didn't last long. In 2014, the provincial government instituted an internal passport, called the People's Convenient Card, which required those living away from their home district to return in order to register. In January 2015, Hasan received such a summons, along with his wife and one-year-old daughter. With little alternative, the family of three boarded an overnight bus bound for Yarkand. They never made it.

THE SUM OF THE PEOPLE

Halfway there, the bus was involved in a traffic accident, which killed Hasan's wife and injured his daughter. Hasan himself was uninjured, but shortly afterward Byler lost contact with him. Byler believes Hasan was sent to a reeducation camp—subtracted from the community.[26]

• • •

Xinjiang-style surveillance is not the inevitable endpoint of today's technology, any more than Nazi card files were the inevitable result of nineteenth-century population statistics. But current technological advances do favor the central accumulation of power, be it in governments or large corporations, not unlike the way that the card file and the punch card did a century ago. As the story of Japanese internment shows, even relatively liberal governments may be tempted to misuse population data if the circumstances seem to demand it.

The census itself has undoubtedly been such a centralizing technology, a key administrative tool of the Roman, Inca, and British Empires, and others besides. And, censuses, especially in antiquity, often were to the detriment of those they counted, imposing taxation or conscription. It was the great achievement of eighteenth- and nineteenth-century census takers to break that nexus and persuade people—the public on one side and their colleagues in government on the other—that states could collect data on their citizens without using it against them.

This version of the census—still used in most countries today—was a compromise. It acknowledged an unavoidable trade-off between privacy and the state's need to see in order to function. The traditional census, at its best, has been able to find a delicate balance between these opposed aims. It has succeeded in this because enumeration, by its very nature, requires mass participation, and so the census is owned neither by the state nor by the people but exists as a continuous negotiation between the two. The resulting institution has a set of valuable characteristics—some inherent and others hard-won—that we would do well to consider as we build the information systems of twenty-first-century societies.

First, a traditional census is honest and transparent about the data it collects. Especially when self-enumeration is used, a government cannot conduct a census discreetly or slip in questions without public knowledge. (The forceful opposition that met the US government's attempt to add a citizenship question is evidence enough of that.) At the other end of the process, most of what the census collects is released back to the public in summary form. Some privacy advocates argue that government surveillance should be met by "sousveillance," the enlistment of ordinary citizens to voluntarily "watch the watchers." That accountability is built into the census.

Second, census takers have, over time, developed strong legal, institutional, and ethical restraints on how and with whom they will share data. For 2020, the US Census Bureau is planning to apply a technology called "differential privacy," a method of reasoning that allows it to prove, mathematically, that publishing certain summaries will not reveal individual facts. That's an important advance, but these technical restraints on the leaking of data are far less important than the human restraints that already exist.

Third—and statisticians don't like to admit this—a census is relatively easy to avoid for anyone who feels sufficiently threatened by it. Though in most places participation is mandatory, penalties for failing to do so are light and rarely prosecuted (at least, relative to the number of people missed). It's as if we have decided that being counted is important enough to make it law, while at the same time acknowledging, at least symbolically, that membership in society, through the act of being counted, remains a choice. When it's working well, people respond to the census out of civic duty and peer pressure rather than legal coercion.

Fourth, and finally, in a time when so much information collection is covert and passive, the census is the opposite: it demands our active attention. There's nothing subtle about millions of enumerators knocking on doors. Once a decade, for a few weeks, people are briefly reminded of the informational compromise we have made as members of a society. The census becomes, fairly or unfairly, a symbol of our lost privacy, both real and imagined.

For a democracy, that attention-grabbing ability is a rare, powerful thing. Perhaps we should take better advantage of it. Since 2007, there has, in theory, been a Data Privacy Day, celebrated annually in a handful of countries on January 28. But an annual event is probably too frequent to observe the gradual shifting of lines that once seemed inviolable. Like the proverbial boiling frog, it's hard to notice our changing notions of privacy in real time. Perhaps we should instead designate census day as a festival of privacy, taking a moment once every decade to turn the mirror back on our governments, reminding ourselves of what they know about us.

• • •

The traditional, decennial census is now almost certainly in the early stages of decline. In most countries, this nineteenth-century invention, which has somehow survived into the twenty-first, will probably, eventually, be replaced by the alternatives described in this chapter. Change may be gradual. Statisticians are by nature fairly conservative, and whatever financial or political pressures they face, today's census takers are keenly aware that they are the custodians of a centuries-old tradition. In some countries, the United States most prominently, the glacial pace of legislative or constitutional reform will ensure the continuation of some sort of traditional census for some time.[27]

But even with gradual change, it is possible that the number of countries taking a traditional census will peak in 2020 and fall in future rounds. It's hard not to be sentimental about that. There is something noble about this exercise in which we line up for enumeration, not because we will individually benefit or, really, suffer if we don't, but because we—most of us, still—believe in government on the basis of fact rather than prejudice or guesswork. There is something admirable, if a little quixotic, in the attempt to reach every person, knock on their (increasingly virtual) doors, and say to each, "You, too, count." There is genius in this system that can absorb our intimate details and return aggregated statistics about our neighborhoods, cities, states, and nations without breaking any individual confidence. Tolstoy's is a kind of trick mirror, in which we see a reflection not of our own selves but of the whole society in which we live.

Of course, even as this particular version of the census fades away, the broader tradition, humanity's millennia-old habit of counting and categorizing ourselves, will not. Even if we could map every star in the sky, it does not follow that we would pack up our telescopes. Having once glimpsed the heavens, we do not then look away. Neither will we stop counting people. With each new birth, the human journey continues, new terms added to the never-ending sum of the people.

ACKNOWLEDGMENTS

THE ENUMERATION that follows is almost certainly incomplete.
The idea for this book came when I was studying at Balliol College, Oxford, sometime around 2009, in advance of the 2010 round of censuses. It moved a step closer to reality in 2013, when I wrote a short piece for *The Conversation* arguing against the cancellation of Britain's 2021 census. It took me another five years to find an opportunity to make it a book. Once that opportunity arose, Umar Serajuddin, Tariq Khokhar, and Haishan Fu encouraged me to take a leave of absence from the World Bank to seize it.

One of the joys of this topic is that it intersects so many time periods and places; I was lucky enough to visit some of the latter. In Israel and Palestine I was graciously received by Susanne Roth of Imbach Travel, as well as guides Mohammad Atari, Nedal Sawalmeh, and Anwar Dawabsha, and the Siraj Center. Staff at the Palestinian Central Bureau of Statistics, as well as Daniel Estrin, Jenny Levy, and Dan Meisler, gave generously of their time and hospitality. In South Africa, Mark Orkin, Pali Lehohla, and Hennie Loots were kind enough to talk with me, and Juliette Alenda shared her work with me.

Travel to earlier time periods is only possibly though libraries, archives, and museums, and I relied extensively on the New York Public Library and Brooklyn Public Library, as well as the Library of

Congress, the Bodleian Libraries, the Hagley Museum and Library, the Metropolitan Museum of Art, and the Apartheid Museum. I received helpful advice from Dag Spicer at the Computer History Museum and Karie Diethorn at Independence National Historical Park.

Patrick Gerland, Meryem Demirci, and Sabrina Juran helped me understand how the various parts of the international statistical system fit together. Robert Groves, Kenneth Prewitt, and Roeland Beerten shared their thoughts on the future of the census. Neema Singh Guliani and Darren Byler helped me understand its risks. Kate Morgan, Clarissa Belloni, and Ed Lewis answered questions for me in their own areas of expertise.

I am a quantitative researcher by training, which makes this book, full of words rather than equations, numbers, or even (with one exception) charts, slightly surreal. Stian Westlake, Olivia Beattie, James Meader, and John Butman helped me find my way into the world of publishing. Many friends, including Jacobus Cilliers, Erica Fox, Ashley Nord, Simon Thwaite, and Ariana Tobin, listened patiently, sometimes at length, to historical census trivia. In addition to some of those already named, my parents, Noela Whitby and Michael Whitby, my sister, Catherine Whitby, and my friend Sara Nawaz provided feedback on early drafts. My agent, Lisa Adams, believed in the project and persuaded others to do so. My editor at Basic Books, Brian Distelberg, challenged me to dig deeper and think harder, while my copyeditor, Beth Wright, shaped my writing into something more closely resembling the ideas in my head.

I am enormously grateful to all of them for helping make this book a reality.

None of it, however, would exist without my wife, Anna Alekseyeva, who listened, read, and otherwise supported me in this journey.

Any errors that remain are my own. Like the seventeenth-century astronomer and proto-demographer Riccioli, I hope only to have "toyed with numbers, and not deceived the world."

NOTES

Prologue

1. "The next great national 'stock-taking'" is how Tasmania's registrar general described the 1891 census of that colony; see Tasmania General Register Office, *Census of the Colony of Tasmania, 1891: Parts 1–8* (Hobart, Tasmania: William Grahame, 1893), x. Before stocktaking was a simile, it was an analogy. William Farr, a famous English census taker, wrote in 1861 that "the householder takes some note of the members of his family; the merchant takes stock; and governments count the numbers of their people." See "The Forthcoming Census," *Illustrated London News,* April 6, 1861.

2. "Census Archive," Burning Man, burningman.org/culture/history/brc -history/census-data/.

3. United Nations Special Committee on Palestine, *Report to the General Assembly (Volume 1),* Official Records of the Second Session of the General Assembly (Lake Success, NY, September 3, 1947), chap. 2, sec. A, and chap. 6, part 1, sec. G.

4. Anat Leibler and Daniel Breslau, "The Uncounted: Citizenship and Exclusion in the Israeli Census of 1948," *Ethnic and Racial Studies* 28, no. 5 (September 2005): 880–902. Quote from UN Statistics Division, *Principles and Recommendations for Population and Housing Censuses, Revision 3* (New York: United Nations, 2017), 103.

5. Leibler and Breslau, "The Uncounted," 891; *Palestine Post* quoted in "Israel Applies a Curfew to Detail All for Census," *New York Times,* November 9, 1948.

6. Central Bureau of Statistics (Israel), "Israel in Statistics 1948–2007," Statistilite, Jerusalem, May 2009.

7. UN Statistics Division, *Principles and Recommendations for Population and Housing Censuses,* 2.

8. "Diplomatic Relations," Permanent Observer Missions of the State of Palestine to the United Nations, New York, October 14, 2019, palestineun.org /about-palestine/diplomatic-relations.

9. "Statistics on Settlements and Settler Population," B'Tselem: The Israeli Information Center for Human Rights in the Occupied Territories, January 16, 2019, btselem.org/settlements/statistics. On legal status, see Security Council Resolution 2334, December 23, 2016, undocs.org/S/RES/2334(2016).

10. Josephus, a historian of the first century CE, writes that "it was the custom of the Galileans, when they came to the holy city at the festivals, to take their journeys through the country of the Samaritans." See Josephus, *Antiquities,* Book 20, chap. 6.

11. This section is based on two interviews, one at the Palestinian Central Bureau of Statistics (PCBS), March 19, 2019, and another initial conversation on January 29, 2019. The officials I spoke to asked not to be named.

12. Joel Greenberg, "Palestinian Census Ignites Controversy over Jerusalem," *New York Times,* National edition, sec. A, December 11, 1997.

13. Quotes from Ibrahim Husseini, "Israel Arrests Palestinians over Population Count," *Al Jazeera News,* November 22, 2017, aljazeera.com/news/2017/11/israel -arrests-palestinians-population-count-171122151547713.html; PCBS, "Population, Housing and Establishments Census 2017: Census Final Results—Summary (Updated Version)," Ramallah, July 2018, [24] and Table 29. PCBS divides the Jerusalem governorate (a Palestinian administrative district that extends beyond urban Jerusalem) into two areas: J1, the land annexed by Israel in 1967, and J2, more outlying suburbs, villages, and camps. By "East Jerusalem" people usually mean only the Israeli area, J1, although the two areas form a continuous urban sprawl, distinguishable only by the barrier and checkpoints.

14. PCBS, "Population, Housing and Establishments Census 2017," Table 29.

15. Ibid., [13], [33].

16. Ibid., [39].

17. Edward Said, "The Morning After," *London Review of Books* 15, no. 20 (October 21, 1993): 3–5. On the population of the Palestinian diaspora, see Ola Awad, "Dr. Awad Presents a Brief on Palestinians at the End of 2018," PCBS, December 31, 2018, pcbs.gov.ps/post.aspx?lang=en&ItemID=3356.

18. Ornan v. Ministry of the Interior, No. CA 8573/08 (Supreme Court of Israel October 2, 2013).

19. Bill Chappell and Daniel Estrin, "Netanyahu Says Israel Is 'Nation-State of the Jewish People and Them Alone,'" NPR, March 11, 2019, npr.org/2019

/03/11/702264118/netanyahu-says-israel-is-nation-state-of-the-jewish-people
-and-them-alone.

20. As in Israel, the census also played a role in enrolling citizens in the independent state. It has been suggested that methodological choices were made in the conduct of the census to buttress the Christian majority. See Rania Maktabi, "The Lebanese Census of 1932 Revisited: Who Are the Lebanese?," *British Journal of Middle Eastern Studies* 26, no. 2 (November 1999): 219–241.

21. Muhammad A. Faour, "Religion, Demography, and Politics in Lebanon," *Middle Eastern Studies* 43, no. 6 (November 2007): 909–921.

22. The Editorial Board, "Will the Census Count All of Us?," *New York Times,* April 21, 2019.

23. For a digestible interpretation of Foucault's views in this area, see Bruce Curtis, "Foucault on Governmentality and Population: The Impossible Discovery," *Canadian Journal of Sociology / Cahiers Canadiens de Sociologie* 27, no. 4 (2002): 505; Bruce Curtis, *The Politics of Population: State Formation, Statistics, and the Census of Canada, 1840–1875* (Toronto: University of Toronto Press, 2001); James C. Scott, *Seeing like a State: How Certain Schemes to Improve the Human Condition Have Failed,* Yale Agrarian Studies (New Haven, CT: Yale University Press, 2008); Benedict Anderson, *Imagined Communities: Reflections on the Origin and Spread of Nationalism,* rev. ed. (London: Verso, 2016), chap. 10. A detailed overview of academic theories of the census is given in Rebecca Jean Emigh, Dylan J. Riley, and Patricia Ahmed, *Antecedents of Censuses from Medieval to Nation States: How Societies and States Count* (New York: Palgrave Macmillan, 2016), chap. 1.

24. This perspective is argued by, for example, Kathrin Levitan, *A Cultural History of the British Census: Envisioning the Multitude in the Nineteenth Century,* Palgrave Studies in Cultural and Intellectual History (New York: Palgrave Macmillan, 2011).

25. In the terminology of Sarah Elizabeth Igo, *The Known Citizen: A History of Privacy in Modern America* (Cambridge, MA: Harvard University Press, 2018).

26. Quote from Emigh, Riley, and Ahmed, *Antecedents of Censuses from Medieval to Nation States,* 3.

27. Leo Tolstoy, *What Then Must We Do?* (1886) excerpted in "Leo Tolstoy on Thoughts Evoked by the Census of Moscow," *Population and Development Review* 37, no. 3 (September 2011): 579–584.

28. John Clark Ridpath, *The Life and Work of James A. Garfield, Twentieth President of the United States* (Cincinnati: Jones Brothers and Company, 1881), 217.

29. James Manyika, "Hal Varian on how the Web challenges managers," *McKinsey Quarterly* (January 2009).

NOTES TO CHAPTER 1

Chapter 1. The Book of Numbers

1. On the sparseness of early humans, see Yuval N. Harari, *Sapiens: A Brief History of Humankind* (New York: Harper, 2015), 47. On Dunbar's number, see R. I. M. Dunbar, "Coevolution of Neocortical Size, Group Size and Language in Humans," *Behavioral and Brain Sciences* 16, no. 4 (December 1993): 681.

2. Nick Murphy, "The Story of 1," BBC, September 28, 2005.

3. Organisation for Economic Co-operation and Development, *Redefining "Urban": A New Way to Measure Metropolitan Areas* (Paris: OECD, 2012).

4. Giovanni Anobile, Guido Marco Cicchini, and David C. Burr, "Number as a Primary Perceptual Attribute: A Review," *Perception* 45, nos. 1–2 (January 2016): 5–31. Specialized brain areas have been discovered that respond specifically to human faces and bodies, and these may even have an intrinsic evolutionary basis, although this is controversial. See P. E. Downing, "A Cortical Area Selective for Visual Processing of the Human Body," *Science* 293, no. 5539 (September 28, 2001): 2470–2473.

5. Herodotus, *The Histories,* ed. Paul Cartledge, trans. Tom Holland (New York: Penguin, 2015), Book 4, para 81. Claudia Zaslavsky, *Africa Counts: Number and Pattern in African Cultures,* 3rd ed. (Chicago: Lawrence Hill Books, 1999), 52–53.

6. On census khipu generally, see Gary Urton, *Inka History in Knots: Reading Khipus as Primary Sources,* Joe R. and Teresa Lozano Long Series in Latin American and Latino Art and Culture (Austin: University of Texas Press, 2017), 4, 189. For possibly the first confirmation of a census khipu, see Manuel Medrano and Gary Urton, "Toward the Decipherment of a Set of Mid-Colonial Khipus from the Santa Valley, Coastal Peru," *Ethnohistory* 65, no. 1 (January 1, 2018): 1–23; Daniel Cossins, "How to Read Inca," *New Scientist,* September 29, 2018, newscientist.com/article/mg23931972-600-we-thought-the-incas-couldnt-write-these-knots-change-everything.

7. Quoted in Urton, *Inka History in Knots,* 179–180.

8. The earliest mention I can find of this 3800 BCE claim is by George Knibbs, Australia's well-regarded first national statistician. He seems to have misinterpreted a statement of the wonderfully named William St. Chad Boscawen. The claim was debunked by A. B. Wolfe in 1932, and yet it persists, especially on the websites of national statistical bureaus keen, as Knibbs was, to establish their heritage. The similar claim of a census of Egypt around 2500 BCE also appears to come from Knibbs. See G. H. Knibbs, *Census of the Commonwealth of Australia: Volume I. Statisticians Report* (Melbourne, 1911), 2; W. St. Chad Boscawen, *The First of Empire: "Babylon of the Bible" in the Light of Latest Research,* 2nd ed.

(London: Harper & Brothers, 1906), 147–148; A. B. Wolfe, "Population Censuses Before 1790," *Journal of the American Statistical Association* 27, no. 180 (December 1932): 357.

9. For the census total of legend, see James Legge, *The Chinese Classics: With a Translation, Critical and Exegetical Notes, Prolegomena and Copious Indexes,* vol. 3, part I (Hong Kong: London Missionary Society, 1865), 76–80. Other sources cite 13,553,935; see, for example, Hans Bielenstein, "The Census of China During the Period 2–742 A.D.," *Bulletin of the Museum of Far Eastern Antiquities (Stockholm),* no. 19 (1947): 126. For modern estimates, see Colin McEvedy and Richard Jones, *Atlas of World Population History,* Penguin Reference Books (Harmondsworth: Penguin, 1978), 170–172.

10. Analysis of Rites of Zhou in Huan-Chang Chen, "The Economic Principles of Confucius and His School" (Columbia University, 1911), 297–299, archive.org/details/economicprincipl00huan; H. George Frederickson, "Confucius and the Moral Basis of Bureaucracy," *Administration & Society* 33, no. 6 (January 2002): 610–628.

11. *Analects of Confucius* (Internet Classics Archive, 2009), section 2, part 10, classics.mit.edu/Confucius/analects.html; Chen, "The Economic Principles of Confucius and His School," 311.

12. Gan Xu, *Balanced Discourses,* trans. John Makeham, A Bilingual Ed., The Classical Library of Chinese Literature and Thought (New Haven, CT: Yale University Press; Beijing: Foreign Languages Press, 2002), chap. 20. For a modern comparison, see "Why We Conduct the Decennial Census," US Census Bureau, October 19, 2017, census.gov/programs-surveys/decennial-census/about/why.html.

13. Chen, "The Economic Principles of Confucius and His School," 298.

14. Confusion between people (literally "mouths") and households (literally "doors") may account for some of this; see ibid., 332; Wolfe, "Population Censuses Before 1790," 359.

15. Exodus 1:5 and 12:37–42. The latter gives a population of six hundred thousand, but that is only adult men.

16. Shira Golani, "Is There a Consensus That a Census Causes a Plague?," TheTorah.Com—A Historical and Contextual Approach (blog), February 21, 2016, thetorah.com/is-there-a-consensus-that-a-census-causes-a-plague.

17. Modern translations usually render the Hebrew word *rōš* as "census" instead of "sum." While clearer for today's audience, it is somewhat anachronistic, as "census" is based on a Latin word, coming some centuries later. For this reason I prefer the simpler translation of the King James Version here. This book takes its title from Numbers 26:4 in the same translation.

18. The grand total is given in Numbers 1:46.

19. On the early Jewish population, see McEvedy and Jones, *Atlas of World Population History*, 141.

20. Colin J. Humphreys, "The Number of People in the Exodus from Egypt: Decoding Mathematically the Very Large Numbers in Numbers I and XXVI," *Vetus Testamentum* 48, no. 2 (1998): 196–213; W. M. Flinders Petrie, *Researches in Sinai* (London: John Murray, 1906), 207.

21. M. McEntire, "A Response to Colin J. Humphreys's 'The Number of People in the Exodus from Egypt: Decoding Mathematically the Very Large Numbers in Numbers I and XXVI,'" *Vetus Testamentum* 49, no. 2 (1999): 262–264.

22. Numbers 26.

23. 2 Samuel 24; 1 Chronicles 21. Intermediate censuses that occur without incident include Joshua 8:10; 1 Samuel 11:8; 1 Samuel 13:15; 1 Samuel 15:4; and 2 Samuel 18:1.

24. Hosea 1:10 is sometimes cited as a scriptural basis for the census prohibition. Although the latter subclause seems to be a straightforward descriptive simile, with some interpretive effort it can be read as a proscription. Genesis 32:12 contains a similar statement.

25. Though Cartledge disputes (in note 87, p. 660) that Athens ever had such a law. Herodotus, *The Histories*, Book 2, para 177.

26. Plato, Book V, *Laws*, trans. Benjamin Jowett, n.d., classics.mit.edu /Plato/laws.html. United Nations, Department of Social Affairs, Population Division, *The Determinants and Consequences of Population Trends*, Population Studies (New York: United Nations, 1953), 22.

27. Tenney Frank, "Roman Census Statistics from 508 to 225 B.C.," *American Journal of Philology* 51, no. 4 (1930): 313–324; Lorne H. Ward, "Roman Population, Territory, Tribe, City, and Army Size from the Republic's Founding to the Veientane War, 509 B.C.–400 B.C.," *American Journal of Philology* 111, no. 1 (1990): 5; Mary Beard, *SPQR: A History of Ancient Rome* (New York: Liveright, 2015), 97–98.

28. William Smith, "Censor," in *A Dictionary of Greek and Roman Antiquities* (London: John Murray, 1875), 260–266, penelope.uchicago.edu/Thayer/E /Roman/Texts/secondary/SMIGRA*/Censor.html; Luuk de Ligt, "Census Procedures and the Meaning of the Republican and Early-Imperial Census Figures," in *Peasants, Citizens and Soldiers: Studies in the Demographic History of Roman Italy 225 BC–AD 100* (Cambridge, UK: Cambridge University Press, 2012), 79–134.

29. A. Cornelius Gellius, *Noctus Atticae (Attic Nights),* Book 4, Loeb Classical Library, vol. 1 (1927), 20:1, penelope.uchicago.edu/Thayer/E/Roman/Texts/Gellius/4*.html#20.

30. For one such press release, see "Census of Population and Housing—The 2001 Census, Religion and the Jedi," Australian Bureau of Statistics, May 2, 2001, abs.gov.au/websitedbs/D3110124.NSF/0/86429d11c45d4e73ca256a400006af80?OpenDocument.

31. P. A. Brunt, "The Revenues of Rome," *Journal of Roman Studies* 71 (November 1981): 163–165; W. Graham Claytor and Roger S. Bagnall, "The Beginnings of the Roman Provincial Census: A New Declaration from 3 BCE," *Greek, Roman, and Byzantine Studies,* no. 55 (2015): 637–653.

32. *Res Gestae,* chap. 8. For interpretation, see Tenney Frank, "Roman Census Statistics from 225 to 28 B.C.," *Classical Philology* 19, no. 4 (1924): 329–341; Elio lo Cascio, "The Size of the Roman Population: Beloch and the Meaning of the Augustan Census Figures," *Journal of Roman Studies* 84 (November 1994): 23–40.

33. For the original census counts and reanalysis, see John D. Durand, "The Population Statistics of China, A.D. 2–1953," *Population Studies* 13, no. 3 (March 1960): 216, 221. A lower estimate of around fifty million is given by McEvedy and Jones, *Atlas of World Population History,* 170–172.

34. J. Reiling and J. L. Swellengrebel, *A Translator's Handbook on the Gospel of Luke* (Leiden: E. J. Brill, 1971), 104.

35. The prophecy is in Micah 5:2. For arguments against the account in Luke, see Lutz Neesen, *Untersuchungen Zu Den Direkten Staatsabgaben Der Römischen Kaiserzeit: (27 v. Chr.–284 n. Chr.)* (Bonn: Habelt, 1980), 39; quoted in Brunt, "The Revenues of Rome," 163.

36. Claytor and Bagnall, "The Beginnings of the Roman Provincial Census," 639.

37. Josephus, *Antiquities,* Book 18, chap. 1.

38. Thorvaldsen pointedly titles a section of his book "Domesday Book—Not a Census." And while it was not a census by modern standards, if we adopt a definition broad enough to include the Roman census, then Domesday undoubtedly is too. See Gunnar Thorvaldsen, *Censuses and Census Takers: A Global History,* Routledge Studies in Modern History (London: Routledge/Taylor & Francis Group, 2018), 12. On the uniqueness of the Domesday record, see V. H. Galbraith, *The Making of Domesday Book* (Oxford, UK: Clarendon, 1961), 2–3; David Roffe, *Domesday: The Inquest and the Book* (New York: Oxford University Press, 2000), 2.

39. David Roffe, "Introduction," in *Domesday Now: New Approaches to the Inquest and the Book,* ed. David Roffe and K. S. B. Keats-Rohan (Boydell and Brewer, 2016), 1.

40. Though there are other possible explanations for these entries; see D. M. Palliser, "Domesday Book and the 'Harrying of the North,'" *Northern History* 29, no. 1 (June 1993): 1–23.

41. These various theories are summarized in Roffe, *Domesday,* 12–16.

42. Given the sometime rejection of Domesday as a census, it is interesting that this single sentence places equal emphasis on people and land. Translation from *The Anglo-Saxon Chronicle,* trans. James Henry Ingram (London, 1823), gutenberg.org/ebooks/657. On the Roman origins of Gloucester, see N. M. Herbert, ed., "Anglo-Saxon Gloucester: C. 680–1066," in *A History of the County of Gloucester: Volume 4, the City of Gloucester,* British History Online, 1988, british -history.ac.uk/vch/glos/vol4/pp5-12.

43. The quote from Luke 2:1 is from the Vulgate. Bates suggests the nativity inspiration theory in "The Domesday Book," *In Our Time,* BBC, April 17, 2014, bbc.co.uk/programmes/b040llvb. See also David Bates, *William the Conqueror* (New Haven, CT: Yale University Press, 2016), 468. On the disadvantages faced by William (or their lack), see 16–24 in the same volume.

44. "Survey and Making of Domesday," The National Archives, nationalarchives .gov.uk/domesday/discover-domesday/making-of-domesday.htm, accessed October 24, 2018.

45. Galbraith, *The Making of Domesday Book,* 37; Ingram, *The Anglo-Saxon Chronicle.*

46. Richard Girling, "The Yellowed Pages," *Sunday Times Magazine,* December 8, 2002.

47. On numerical detail, see Roffe, *Domesday,* 2; "Interpreting Domesday," The National Archives, nationalarchives.gov.uk/domesday/discover-domesday /interpreting-domesday.htm, accessed October 24, 2018. For the unnamed Breton, see Ann Williams, ed., *Domesday Book: A Complete Translation,* Penguin Classics (London: Penguin Books, 2003), 1147, folio 232r; Bates, *William the Conqueror,* 470.

48. The explanation is due to Richard fitz Neal's Dialogue of the Exchequer (1179 CE) quoted in Roffe, *Domesday,* 5. In general, see pages 5–7.

49. Robin McKie and Vanessa Thorpe, "Digital Domesday Book Lasts 15 Years Not 1000," *Observer* (London), March 3, 2002, UK news, theguardian .com/uk/2002/mar/03/research.elearning; "Digital Domesday Book Unlocked," BBC News, December 2, 2002, news.bbc.co.uk/2/hi/technology/2534391.stm.

50. Roffe, *Domesday*, 7.

51. "Granite Mountain Records Vault," The Church of Jesus Christ of Latter-day Saints, 2019, newsroom.churchofjesuschrist.org/article/granite-mountain-records-vault.

52. Domesday was not completely alone. Between the eleventh and eighteenth centuries there was some census-like activity linked to taxation, though less so in Britain than other parts of Europe; see Rebecca Jean Emigh, Dylan J. Riley, and Patricia Ahmed, *Antecedents of Censuses from Medieval to Nation States: How Societies and States Count* (New York: Palgrave Macmillan, 2016).

53. Austin Ramzy, "Q. and A.: Kung Tsui-Chang on Life as the Heir to Confucius," Sinosphere: Dispatches from China (blog), November 14, 2014, sinosphere.blogs.nytimes.com/2014/11/14/q-a-kung-tsui-chang-on-life-as-the-heir-to-confucius.

54. "Gaia Creates Richest Star Map of Our Galaxy and Beyond," European Space Agency, April 25, 2018, esa.int/Our_Activities/Space_Science/Gaia/Gaia_creates_richest_star_map_of_our_Galaxy_and_beyond.

Chapter 2. Political Arithmetic

1. National Archives of Iceland, "International Memory of the World Register: The 1703 Census of Iceland," nomination submission, UNESCO, 2012, sec. 3.4.

2. Jochumsson was writing in the nineteenth century and is quoted in Richard F. Tomasson, "A Millennium of Misery: The Demography of the Icelanders," *Population Studies* 31, no. 3 (November 1977): 407; Colin McEvedy and Richard Jones, *Atlas of World Population History*, Penguin Reference Books (Harmondsworth: Penguin, 1978), 116.

3. National Archives of Iceland, "International Memory of the World Register: The 1703 Census of Iceland," secs. 3.2, 5.1.

4. For much the same reason, the US census begins in Alaska every January, several months ahead of the main count. National Archives of Iceland, sec. 3.4; "The 1703 Census," Culture House, culturehouse.is/vefleidsogn/ut/salur-i/i-vegg skapur-ferdabaekur-og-maelingar/manntalid-1703, accessed August 3, 2019.

5. Tomasson, "A Millennium of Misery," 418–419; National Archives of Iceland, "International Memory of the World Register: The 1703 Census of Iceland," sec. 3.1.

6. On the census being forgotten and rediscovered, see National Archives of Iceland, "International Memory of the World Register: The 1703 Census of Iceland," 6.

7. These numbers are all fiercely contested; see Charles C. Mann, *1491: New Revelations of the Americas Before Columbus* (New York: Knopf, 2005), 105–109, 150–151; McEvedy and Jones, *Atlas of World Population History,* 275–281.

8. John Smith, "The Generall Historie of Virginia," ed. Lyon Gardiner Tyler, vol. 4 (New York: Charles Scribner's Sons, 1907), 329, americanjourneys.org /aj-082. See also Samuel Purchas, *Hakluytus Posthumus, or Purchas His Pilgrimes,* vol. 19 (Glasgow: J. MacLehose and Sons, 1906), 119, catalog.hathitrust.org /Record/006665849; Helen C. Rountree, "Pocahontas (d. 1617)," *Encyclopedia Virginia,* November 30, 2015, encyclopediavirginia.org/Pocahontas_d_1617.

9. Uttamattomakin's count is depicted in Disney's animated film *Pocahontas II.* For a more serious account of Powhatan counting techniques, see Helen C. Rountree, *The Powhatan Indians of Virginia: Their Traditional Culture,* The Civilization of the American Indian Series, vol. 193 (Norman: University of Oklahoma Press, 1989), 49–50.

10. Gunnar Thorvaldsen, *Censuses and Census Takers: A Global History,* Routledge Studies in Modern History (London: Routledge/Taylor & Francis Group, 2018), 14; Rebecca Jean Emigh, Dylan J. Riley, and Patricia Ahmed, *Antecedents of Censuses from Medieval to Nation States: How Societies and States Count* (New York: Palgrave Macmillan, 2016), 146.

11. Thorvaldsen, *Censuses and Census Takers,* 17–19.

12. Emigh, Riley, and Ahmed, *Antecedents of Censuses from Medieval to Nation States,* 145–151.

13. Charles Davenant (1698), quoted in Ted McCormick, *William Petty and the Ambitions of Political Arithmetic* (New York: Oxford University Press, 2009), 296.

14. Tony Barnard, "Petty, Sir William," in *The Oxford Dictionary of National Biography,* ed. H. C. G. Matthew and B. Harrison (Oxford, UK: Oxford University Press, 2004); McCormick, *William Petty and the Ambitions of Political Arithmetic,* 14–83. Karl Marx was rather less generous to Petty, calling him a "frivolous, rapacious and unprincipled adventurer." Karl Marx, *A Contribution to the Critique of Political Economy,* trans. N. I. Stone, translated from the 2nd German ed. (Chicago: Charles H. Kerr & Company, 1904), n. 20, gutenberg .org/ebooks/46423.

15. McCormick, *William Petty and the Ambitions of Political Arithmetic,* 84–131; Samuel Pepys, *The Diary of Samuel Pepys, M.A., F.R.S.,* ed. Henry B. Wheatley (London: George Bell & Sons, 1893), gutenberg.org/ebooks/4200, entry for 27 January 1663/64.

16. The greatest limitation of the bills was that they were based on burials in the established Church of England; hence, they missed perhaps a third of deaths

in the city. John Graunt, *Natural and Political Observations... upon the Bills of Mortality,* 1662.

17. McCormick, *William Petty and the Ambitions of Political Arithmetic,* 131–135; Graunt, *Natural and Political Observations... upon the Bills of Mortality,* chap. 11.

18. Graunt, *Natural and Political Observations... upon the Bills of Mortality,* chap. 11.

19. Leslie Stephen and Sidney Lee, eds., *Dictionary of National Biography,* vol. 8 (Glover—Harriott) (London: Smith, Elder & Co., 1908), 427–428.

20. For an overview of Petty's own contributions to shop arithmetic, see Harald Westergaard, *Contributions to the History of Statistics* (London: P. S. King & Son, 1932). The darker side of Petty's schemes is outlined in McCormick, *William Petty and the Ambitions of Political Arithmetic,* 186, 193, 214.

21. See, for example, Rousseau in 1762: "What is the end of political association? It is the preservation and prosperity of its members. And what is the surest sign that they are preserving themselves and prospering? It is their number and their population." Jean-Jacques Rousseau, "On the Social Contract," in *The Major Political Writings of Jean-Jacques Rousseau: The Two Discourses and the Social Contract,* ed. John T. Scott (Chicago: University of Chicago Press, 2014), 227; Anthony Pagden, *The Enlightenment: And Why It Still Matters* (Oxford, UK: Oxford University Press, 2013), 253.

22. Petty quoted in McCormick, *William Petty and the Ambitions of Political Arithmetic,* 177. "Thou hast ordered all things in measure and number and weight" (Wisdom of Solomon 11:20). For the evolution of political arithmetic, see McCormick, *William Petty,* 287, 294.

23. Westergaard, *Contributions to the History of Statistics,* 53–55. On the influence of Graunt and Petty, see Peter Sköld, "The Birth of Population Statistics in Sweden," *The History of the Family* 9, no. 1 (January 2004): secs. 5–7.

24. Westergaard, *Contributions to the History of Statistics,* 54–57.

25. Ibid., 58–59.

26. T. C. Hansard, *The Parliamentary History of England from the Earliest Period to the Year 1803,* vol. 14 (London, 1813), cols. 1317–1318, 1321.

27. For Thornton's initial speech in opposition, see ibid., vol. 14, cols. 1318–1322. For Ridley's reflections on his own initial position, see col. 1330. For a brief biography, see "THORNTON, William (?1712–69), of Cattal, Nr. York.," History of Parliament Online, historyofparliamentonline.org/volume/1715-1754/member/thornton-william-1712-69, accessed August 8, 2019.

28. In fact, there were French calls for census taking in the seventeenth century, notably the detailed work of the engineer Vauban, but nothing on a

national scale. Estimates of the total population rested on methods like Graunt's; see Thorvaldsen, *Censuses and Census Takers,* 27–30.

29. For the growing opposition, see note in Hansard, *The Parliamentary History of England from the Earliest Period to the Year 1803,* vol. 14, cols. 1317–1319.

30. Ibid., vol. 14, cols. 1330–1331.

31. On colonial superstition, see, for example, Governor Hunter of New York and New Jersey, writing to the Lords of Trade in 1712: "I have not been able to obtain a complete census, the people being deterred by a simple superstition and observation that the great sickness followed the last numbering of the people," and similar sentiments quoted in George W. Schuyler, *Colonial New York: Philip Schuyler and His Family,* vol. 1 (New York: Charles Scribner's Sons, 1885), 428–429. On the shifting center of the English world, Franklin was proved right: the 1850 US census counted twenty-three million people; three million were black slaves, but the vast majority of the rest were of English descent. By contrast, the 1851 census of the United Kingdom, which by then included Wales, Scotland, and all of Ireland, counted twenty-seven million people, but just fifteen million in England.

32. McEvedy and Jones, *Atlas of World Population History,* 47.

33. Thomas Paine, "Common Sense," in *The Writings of Thomas Paine,* ed. Moncure Daniel Conway (New York: G. P. Putnam's Sons, 1894), gutenberg .org/ebooks/3755. On demography and revolution, see Margo J. Anderson, *The American Census: A Social History,* 2nd ed. (New Haven, CT: Yale University Press, 2015), 10.

34. Jill Lepore, *These Truths: A History of the United States* (New York: W. W. Norton & Co., 2018), 120.

35. First census act, March 1, 1790. The second census act, of February 28, 1800, does finally use "census" as a description. In support of the idea that "census" was obscure: an amendment moved by Colonel Mason on September 14 added "or enumeration" after—and "explanatory of" in Madison's record—"census" in section 9. "Census" does not appear in Samuel Johnson's 1755 dictionary, but then neither does "enumeration" or its variants. Both words are listed in Webster's 1828 *American Dictionary,* which gives precisely two very specific senses for census, in reference to the Roman and American institutions.

36. Christopher Tomlins, "Reconsidering Indentured Servitude: European Migration and the Early American Labor Force, 1600–1775," *Labor History* 42, no. 1 (February 2001): 5–43.

37. Russell Thornton, *American Indian Holocaust and Survival: A Population History Since 1492,* The Civilization of the American Indian Series 186 (Norman:

University of Oklahoma Press, 1990), 90; McEvedy and Jones, *Atlas of World Population History,* 290.

38. James Madison, "Federalist No. 54: The Apportionment of Members Among the States," *New York Packet,* February 12, 1788; Franklin quote from the diary of John Adams: John Adams, "[July 1776]" (1776), Founders Online, National Archives, founders.archives.gov/documents/Adams/01-02-02-0006-0008.

39. Anderson, *The American Census,* 12–13.

40. James Madison, *Notes of Debates in the Federal Convention of 1787* (Athens: Ohio University Press, 1987), Wednesday, July 11. Lepore, *These Truths,* 115; Anderson, *The American Census,* 11–13.

41. Albert Bushnel Hart, "The Realities of Negro Suffrage," *Proceedings of the American Political Science Association* 2 (1905): 149–165; Frederick Douglass, *Frederick Douglass: Selected Speeches and Writings,* ed. Philip Sheldon Foner and Yuval Taylor (Chicago: Lawrence Hill Books, 1999), 384. Antislavery sentiments were occasionally expressed in discussing the counting issue; see, for example, Madison's report of Gouverneur Morris's statement on July 11 that he "could never agree to give such encouragement to the slave trade as would be given by allowing them a representation for their negroes."

42. Lepore, *These Truths,* 127; Madison, *Notes of Debates in the Federal Convention of 1787.*

43. Madison, "Federalist No. 54: The Apportionment of Members Among the States." For statements of support by Hamilton and Morris, see Kenneth Prewitt, *What Is "Your" Race?: The Census and Our Flawed Efforts to Classify Americans* (Princeton, NJ: Princeton University Press, 2013), 41. For an example of contemporary debate, see "The Constitution's Immoral Compromise," *New York Times,* February 26, 2013, sec. Opinion: Room for Debate, nytimes.com/roomfordebate /2013/02/26/the-constitutions-immoral-compromise.

44. Madison's justification quoted in Prewitt, *What Is "Your" Race?,* 42; his description of the outcome quoted in Anderson, *The American Census,* 15.

45. Anderson, *The American Census,* 14–15; Carroll D. Wright and William C. Hunt, "The History and Growth of the United States Census," 56th Congress, 1st Session (Washington: Senate Committee on the Census, 1900), 12–17; Frederick S. Calhoun, *The Lawmen: United States Marshals and Their Deputies, 1789–1989* (Washington, DC: Smithsonian Institution Press, 1990), 15–19.

46. Madison, "Federalist No. 54: The Apportionment of Members Among the States."

47. On opinions about the undercount, see Wright and Hunt, "The History and Growth of the United States Census," 14–17; Anderson, *The American Census,*

15. Regarding the missing Franklin grandchildren: A temporary absence would not explain the omission, as the rules set by Congress were that each person should be counted in his or her usual residence, so-called de jure enumeration. It's probably no coincidence that women rather than men were missed in the Franklin Bache household. Interestingly, young children have also been undercounted in recent US censuses.

48. Michel L. Balinski and H. Peyton Young, *Fair Representation: Meeting the Ideal of One Man, One Vote,* 2nd ed. (Washington, DC: Brookings Institution, 2001), chap. 3.

49. Ibid.

50. Anderson, *The American Census,* 15–17; Wright and Hunt, "The History and Growth of the United States Census," 17.

51. Quoted in Ken Alder, *The Measure of All Things: The Seven-Year Odyssey and Hidden Error That Transformed the World* (New York: Free Press, 2003), 1.

52. Alain Desrosières, *The Politics of Large Numbers: A History of Statistical Reasoning,* trans. Camille Naish (Cambridge, MA: Harvard University Press, 1998), 37.

53. Robert J. Mayhew, *Malthus: The Life and Legacies of an Untimely Prophet* (Cambridge, MA: Belknap of Harvard University Press, 2014), 38.

54. Keith Michael Baker, *Condorcet, from Natural Philosophy to Social Mathematics* (Chicago: University of Chicago Press, 1975), 343–373; M. de Lamartine, *Heroic Characters of the Revolution* (London: H. G. Clarke & Co., 1848), 81–88.

55. Baker, *Condorcet, from Natural Philosophy to Social Mathematics,* 348; Marie-Jean-Antoine-Nicolas Caritat, Marquis de Condorcet, *Outlines of an Historical View of the Progress of the Human Mind,* trans. M. Carey (Philadelphia, 1796), oll.libertyfund.org/titles/1669.

56. Mayhew, *Malthus,* 54–65; T. R. Malthus, *An Essay on the Principle of Population,* ed. Geoffrey Gilbert, Oxford World's Classics (1798; repr., New York: Oxford University Press, 2008), chap. 8.

57. Malthus Sr. quoted in Mayhew, *Malthus,* 58–59; Malthus's core argument is described in Malthus, *An Essay on the Principle of Population,* chap. 1.

58. Malthus, *An Essay on the Principle of Population* chap. 1 and 10.

59. Mayhew, *Malthus,* 62.

60. Malthus, *An Essay on the Principle of Population,* chap. 6.

61. Thorvaldsen, *Censuses and Census Takers,* 34–39; Desrosières, *The Politics of Large Numbers,* 24; Frederick Hendricks, "On the Vital Statistics of Sweden, from 1749 to 1855," *Journal of the Statistical Society of London* 25, no. 2 (June 1862): 112.

62. An excellent survey by Thirsk quickly dispels the myth that England entirely lacked census-like activity between 1086 and 1801, but it remained decentralized, uncoordinated, and incomplete. The best counts may actually have approached the thoroughness of the Domesday survey—which was, recall, not thorough by modern standards—and are less well known only for being far less old, and in many cases worse preserved. See Joan Thirsk, *The Rural Economy of England: Collected Essays*, History Series 25 (London: Hambledon, 1984), chap. II. For an example of the effort involved, even for a twentieth-century demographic historian, in reconstructing the population series for just one village over this period, see W. G. Hoskins, "The Population of an English Village 1086–1801: A Study of Wigston Magna," in *Provincial England* (London: Palgrave Macmillan UK, 1963), 181–208.

63. For the direct influence of the US census on the British census, see Roger Hutchinson, *The Butcher, the Baker, the Candlestick Maker: The Story of Britain Through Its Census, Since 1801* (London: Little, Brown, 2017), 25. On the example of King David: within another fifty years, scientists such as William Farr, adopting methods borrowed from Graunt's *Observations,* would finally start to gain an understanding of epidemics as the consequence not of heavenly wrath but of the earthiest of matters—sewage disposal and clean water.

64. By the 1861 census this concept of census as part of citizenship was broadly accepted; see Kathrin Levitan, *A Cultural History of the British Census: Envisioning the Multitude in the Nineteenth Century,* Palgrave Studies in Cultural and Intellectual History (New York: Palgrave Macmillan, 2011), 16–17, 38–46; Emigh, Riley, and Ahmed, *Antecedents of Censuses from Medieval to Nation States,* 129–130; Peter Buck, "People Who Counted: Political Arithmetic in the Eighteenth Century," *Isis* 73, no. 1 (March 1982): 28–45.

65. In fact, catastrophizing was something of a misinterpretation of Malthus's *Essay,* which was more about a present continuous state of misery, rather than a future time of disaster. But it was often, somewhat inevitably, understood as the latter, despite his protests.

66. John Rickman, "Thoughts on the Utility and Facility of Ascertaining the Population of England," *Commercial and Agricultural Magazine* 2 (June 1800): 399.

67. William Cobbett and T. C. Hansard, eds., *Cobbett's Parliamentary History of England,* vol. 35 (1800–1801) (London, 1819), col. 598.

68. John Rickman, *Abstract of the Answers and Returns Made Pursuant to an Act, Passed in the Forty-First Year of His Majesty King George III,* 1802.

69. Levitan, *A Cultural History of the British Census,* 19. For surviving individual and household records, see Richard Wall, Matthew Wollard, and Beatrice

Moring, "Census Schedules and Listings, 1801–1831: An Introduction and Guide," Research Tools, Department of History, University of Essex, 2012.

70. Cobbett and Hansard, *Cobbett's Parliamentary History of England,* vol. 35 (1800–1801), col. 599; Rickman, "Thoughts on the Utility and Facility of Ascertaining the Population of England." Ireland had formally united with Great Britain that same year, but it was not included. It lacked the convenient local administrative infrastructure of the Poor Laws. While an attempt was made in 1813, no really complete enumeration was done until 1821; see Ian White, "A Brief History of the Census in Ireland/Northern Ireland," in *Registrar General Northern Ireland Annual Report 2011* (Northern Ireland Statistics and Research Agency, 2012), 35–68, www.nisra.gov.uk/sites/nisra.gov.uk/files/publications /RG2011%5B1%5D.pdf.

71. Thorvaldsen, *Censuses and Census Takers,* 39–48.

72. Alexander Moreau de Jonnès, *Éléments de Statistique* (Paris: Guillaumin, 1847), 191–192.

73. The first national constitution, following that of the US, to actually use the word "census" or equivalent (*censo* in Spanish) may have been the original Constitución de la Nación Argentina 1853, at article 35. Canada's *Constitution Act 1867* imposed a similar requirement at section 8. For the word "census" in constitutions currently in force, see the Constitute Project, constituteproject.org /search?lang=en&q=census&status=in_force.

74. Mayhew, *Malthus,* 116; Paul Krugman, "Malthus Was Right!," The Conscience of a Liberal (blog), March 25, 2008, krugman.blogs.nytimes.com/2008 /03/25/malthus-was-right.

75. The Oxford English Dictionary dates demography in English to 1834, although it may be an isolated usage. Guillard is traditionally credited with bringing the term into standard use somewhat later, in 1855. Condorcet wrote: "It was not amidst the convulsions of expiring liberty that social science could refine and perfect itself." I'm taking a small liberty here, since the original and standard translation gives "*science sociale*" as "moral science," the direct translation being unfamiliar to the translator. See Baker, *Condorcet,* 372–373, 391–392.

Chapter 3. A Punch Photograph

1. For the competition see Leon E. Truesdell, *The Development of Punch Card Tabulation in the Bureau of the Census, 1890–1940: With Outlines of Actual Tabulation Programs* (Washington: Government Printing Office, 1965), 40–43; Geoffrey Austrian, *Herman Hollerith, Forgotten Giant of Information Processing* (New York: Columbia University Press, 1982), chap. 5. For Hollerith's office, see page

50 of the same book. On the Atlantic Building in general, see Historic American Buildings Survey (Library of Congress), "Atlantic Building, 930 F Street, Northwest, Washington, District of Columbia, DC," Library of Congress, Prints & Photographs Online Catalog, loc.gov/pictures/item/dc0636, accessed April 15, 2019. On the old Patent Office building, which today houses the National Portrait Gallery, see Lawrence M. Small, "A Pantheon After All," *Smithsonian Magazine,* July 2002, smithsonianmag.com/history/a-pantheon-after-all-65879145.

2. A good account of the machine and its operation is given in Truesdell, *The Development of Punch Card Tabulation,* chap. 3.

3. For details of the census cards, see ibid., 39. This list of characteristics is drawn from the 1880 census, records from which were used for the contest.

4. Frederick H. Wines quoted in Robert P. Porter, "The Eleventh Census" (October 16, 1891), 20.

5. Staffing was increased, dramatically; see Margo J. Anderson, *The American Census: A Social History,* 2nd ed. (New Haven, CT: Yale University Press, 2015), 87, 100, 274–275.

6. For the establishment of statistical societies, see Walter F. Willcox, "Note on the Chronology of Statistical Societies," *Journal of the American Statistical Association* 29, no. 188 (December 1934): 418–420. For the establishment of government statistical offices, see Alain Desrosières, *The Politics of Large Numbers: A History of Statistical Reasoning,* trans. Camille Naish (Cambridge, MA: Harvard University Press, 1998), chaps. 5–6. All this took place within a society in which popular numeracy was growing; see Patricia Cline Cohen, *A Calculating People: The Spread of Numeracy in Early America* (New York: Routledge, 2016), Kindle edition.

7. On the involvement of the ASA in the census, see R. L. Mason, J. D. McKenzie, and S. J. Ruberg, "A Brief History of the American Statistical Association, 1839-1989," *American Statistician* 44, no. 2 (May 1990): 69. Over the nineteenth century, the term "census" was increasingly applied to other comprehensive surveys of manufacturing, agriculture, and more. This broader usage of "census" persists today, with some statistical agencies fielding a "census of (business) establishments" or "census of agriculture." In this book I am focused squarely on counting people and will give these others no further attention.

8. The census schedules discussed here are reproduced in Frederick G. Bohme, *200 Years of Census Taking: Population and Housing Questions, 1790–1990* (Washington, DC: US Department of Commerce, Bureau of the Census, 1989), 16–38, census.gov/history/pdf/200years.pdf.

9. Cohen concludes that the South-North pattern arose because the aging northeastern populations had higher numbers of senile white people; a small

percentage of accidental white-to-black transpositions, combined with a lower base population of black people in the North, gave the appearance of a systematic variation in black insanity. See Cohen, *A Calculating People,* chap. 6.

10. The term "nominative" is a little misleading: the system didn't strictly require that names themselves be recorded—although they often were—only that each person had their own independent row. This structure of schedule had scattered use earlier—for example, in Iceland's 1703 census. See Gunnar Thorvaldsen, *Censuses and Census Takers: A Global History,* Routledge Studies in Modern History (London: Routledge/Taylor & Francis Group, 2018), chap. 4.

11. In fact, the switch to nominative census taking seems to have confused some of the enumerators of slaves, who simply wrote 1 in every space in the "Number of Slaves" column, as if they were instead performing a kind of numerical census.

12. Based on a 1790 population of around four million divided by an average household size of six and an 1880 population of around fifty million.

13. Anderson, *The American Census,* 100–102. The final volume of 1880 census results was published in 1888; see Carroll D. Wright and William C. Hunt, *The History and Growth of the United States Census,* 56th Congress, 1st Session (Washington: Senate Committee on the Census, 1900), 68. The quote is from T. C. Martin, "Counting a Nation by Electricity," *Electrical Engineer* 12, no. 184 (November 11, 1891): 523.

14. The instructions to enumerators read: "Be particularly careful to distinguish between blacks, mulattoes, quadroons, and octoroons. The word 'black' should he used to describe those persons who have three-fourths or more black blood; 'mulatto,' those persons who have from three-eighths to five-eighths black blood; 'quadroon,' those persons who have one-fourth black blood; and 'octoroon,' those persons who have one-eighth or any trace of black blood." In fact these fine-grained pseudoscientific categories proved useless for any purpose and were never tabulated. See Kenneth Prewitt, *What Is "Your" Race?: The Census and Our Flawed Efforts to Classify Americans* (Princeton, NJ: Princeton University Press, 2013), 57.

15. For the commission's establishment see Austrian, *Herman Hollerith,* 50. For an overview of the competing systems, see Truesdell, *The Development of Punch Card Tabulation,* 24–25. As further evidence that the contest was real: Pidgin continued to compete, albeit unsuccessfully, with Hollerith after 1890. Hollerith took this threat seriously and even hired a private detective to spy on Pidgin's work. See Lars Heide, *Punched-Card Systems and the Early Information Explosion: 1880–1945,* Studies in Industry and Society (Baltimore: Johns Hopkins University Press, 2009), 51–52.

16. Between 1880 and 1890, the census schedule was rotated 90 degrees, so that questions appeared as rows and persons as columns. Nonetheless, the principle of nominative enumeration remained the same.

17. John S. Billings, Henry Gannett, and L. M. E. Cooke, *Report of a Commission Appointed by the Honorable Superintendent of Census on Different Methods of Tabulating Census Data* (Washington, DC: US Census Office, 1889), 8–9.

18. On the travel plans of Billings's commission, see "Tabulating Census Returns," *Boston Post,* August 14, 1889. On the methods and their results, see Truesdell, *The Development of Punch Card Tabulation.* It's not clear exactly when Hollerith added the bell. It's not present in his patent application filed June 8, 1887, nor a description published April 1889, but it was certainly part of the system by early 1890. See L. D'Auria et al., "Hollerith Electric Tabulating System," *Journal of the Franklin Institute* 99 (April 1890): 301–306; H. Hollerith, "An Electric Tabulating System," *School of Mines Quarterly, Columbia College* 10, no. 3 (April 1889): 238–255; "The Census of the United States," *Scientific American,* August 30, 1890, 132.

19. Karl Marx, *Capital: A Critique of Political Economy,* trans. Ben Fowkes, vol. 1 (London: Penguin, 1981), 557, chap. 15, sec. 5.

20. Scott Reynolds Nelson, *Steel Drivin' Man John Henry: The Untold Story of an American Legend* (New York: Oxford University Press, 2008).

21. Doreen Chaky, "John Henry v. Charles Burleigh's Drill," *Mining History Journal* 1 (1994): 104. There are countless variations on the ballad. This one comes from Anonymous, "John Henry," Poetry Foundation, poetryfoundation .org/poems/42897/john-henry, accessed April 16, 2019.

22. "Hollerith Electric Tabulating System (Replica) (Catalog Number XD231.81)," Computer History Museum, n.d., www.computerhistory.org/col lections/catalog/XD231.81. Regarding Wines: this is in fact unlikely. Hallucinations and delirium are indeed a symptom of acute mercury poisoning: exposure to the heavy metal in the manufacture of wool felts is believed to be the source of the expression "mad as a hatter." But the elemental mercury in Hollerith's machine was fairly well-contained, and modern occupational safety standards notwithstanding, I have encountered no reports of ill effects.

23. See, generally, Austrian, *Herman Hollerith,* chap. 1; Vaclav Smil, *Creating the Twentieth Century: Technical Innovations of 1867–1914 and Their Lasting Impact* (Oxford, UK: Oxford University Press, 2005), 59.

24. For observations of the Exposition, see "Events of Note in Paris: Stage Affairs and the Electrical Exhibition," *New York Times,* September 17, 1881; "Themes of Parisian Talk: Electric Lights for the City and an Odd Will Case,"

New York Times, December 25, 1881. Though invisible, electricity was still potentially as deadly as steam: the first known death from intentionally manipulating electricity was that of the Russian Georg Wilhelm Richmann in 1753, while attempting to replicate Benjamin Franklin's kite-key experiment.

25. "Limelight" as a metaphor comes itself from an early type of stage lighting that harnessed the incandescence of quicklime under a flame. The flame was fed by the rather unstable mix of hydrogen and oxygen. Accidents were common, including an 1876 fire at the Brooklyn Theatre, in which 278 people died. Limelight was on the cusp of obsolescence by 1881, replaced by the electric arc light, a superior technology that nonetheless had the distinction, in 1879, of causing the first death by artificially generated electricity, that of a French stage carpenter. Early incandescent bulbs were dimmer but safer and more practical than arc lights.

26. Hollerith's much later (1919) recollection; see Austrian, *Herman Hollerith,* 5–6.

27. "1880 Census: Instructions to Enumerators," IPUMS USA, May 1, 1880, usa.ipums.org/usa/voliii/inst1880.shtml; Bohme, *200 Years of Census Taking,* 30. The roller-based device was the Seaton machine; see Truesdell, *The Development of Punch Card Tabulation,* 17–24.

28. Austrian, *Herman Hollerith,* 1, 8–9.

29. US Census Office, *Statistics of the Population of the United States at the Tenth Census (June 1, 1880),* vol. 1 (Washington, DC: Government Printing Office, 1883), 426, Table 7. In tabulation, no distinction was made between different parts of Africa; see Table 16, page 538 of the same volume. The slave trade to the United States, outlawed in 1807, had continued illegally on a small scale until the Civil War. The last known African-born ex-slave was long believed to be a man named Cudjoe Lewis, who died in 1935. He had been enumerated in Mobile, Alabama, in 1880, his place of birth recorded correctly, though nonspecifically, as "Africa." See Zora Neale Hurston, Alice Walker, and Deborah G. Plant, *Barracoon: The Story of the Last Slave* (London: HQ, 2018); Recently, another claim has emerged, a woman known as Redoshi, who was brought on the same ship as Lewis; see Hannah Durkin, "Finding Last Middle Passage Survivor Sally 'Redoshi' Smith on the Page and Screen," *Slavery & Abolition,* March 26, 2019, 1–28.

30. *Return of the Whole Number of Persons Within the Several Districts of the United States* (Philadelphia: Childs and Swaine, 1791), 37, archive.org/details/returnofwholenum00unitrich. For Beijing and other large cities, see Tertius Chandler, *Four Thousand Years of Urban Growth: An Historical Census* (Lewiston, NY: St. David's University Press, 1987), 484–485, 523–526.

31. Thomas Jefferson, "Calculation of Population Increase" (October 1801), Founders Online, National Archives, founders.archives.gov/documents/Jefferson /01-35-02-0444. Comments on Malthus contained in Thomas Jefferson, "To Jean Baptiste Say," February 1, 1804, Founders Online, National Archives, founders.archives.gov/documents/Jefferson/01-42-02-0335.

32. US Census Office, *Report on Population of the United States at the Eleventh Census: 1890 (Part I)* (Washington, DC: Government Printing Office, 1895), xviii.

33. US Census Office, *Statistics of the Population of the United States at the Tenth Census (June 1, 1880),* 1:xii–xx. The earlier maps had originally been published in US Census Office, *Statistical Atlas of the United States Based on the Results of the Ninth Census 1870* (New York: Julius Bien, Lith., 1874).

34. Austrian, *Herman Hollerith,* chap. 2; "Charter of the Massachusetts Institute of Technology," MIT, corporation.mit.edu/about-corporation/charter, accessed April 16, 2019.

35. Ernst Martin, Peggy Aldrich Kidwell, and Michael R. Williams, *The Calculating Machines (Die Rechenmaschinen): Their History and Development,* The Charles Babbage Institute Reprint Series for the History of Computing, vol. 16 (Cambridge, MA: MIT Press; Los Angeles: Tomash Publishers, 1992), 54; Stephen Johnston, "Making the Arithmometer Count," *Bulletin of the Scientific Instrument Society,* no. 52 (1997): 12–21. For Hollerith's encounter with an adding machine, see Austrian, *Herman Hollerith,* 10.

36. Michelle P. Brown, "The Role of the Wax Tablet in Medieval Literacy: A Reconsideration in Light of a Recent Find from York," *British Library Journal* 20, no. 1 (1994): 1–16.

37. Lothar Müller and Jessica Sprengler, *White Magic: The Age of Paper* (Cambridge, UK: Polity, 2014), part I, section 2.3.

38. Isabelle Charmantier and Staffan Müller-Wille, "Carl Linnaeus's Botanical Paper Slips (1767–1773)," *Intellectual History Review* 24, no. 2 (April 3, 2014): 215–238.

39. JoAnne Yates, *Control Through Communication: The Rise of System in American Management,* Studies in Industry and Society 6 (Baltimore: Johns Hopkins University Press, 1993), chap. 2.

40. "A Word About T.S.," *Chamber's Journal of Popular Literature, Science and Arts,* no. 549 (July 4, 1874), 424.

41. H. Hollerith. Art of Compiling Statistics. US Patent 395,782, filed September 23, 1884, and issued January 8, 1889.

42. Austrian, *Herman Hollerith,* 14.

43. Ibid., 15.

44. For the invention of the punch card loom, see James Essinger, *Jacquard's Web: How a Hand-Loom Led to the Birth of the Information Age* (Oxford, UK: Oxford University Press, 2004), chap. 4. For Hollerith's family connection to weaving, see Austrian, *Herman Hollerith,* 17.

45. This design was for Difference Engine No. 1, the middle in a sequence of three Babbage designed; see Doron Swade, *The Difference Engine: Charles Babbage and the Quest to Build the First Computer* (New York: Viking, 2001), 45–48.

46. On the Analytical Engine, see Swade, chaps. 5–11. For discussion in a statistics text contemporary with Hollerith's work—indeed authored by one of his census contest competitors—see Charles F. Pidgin, *Practical Statistics: A Handbook* (Boston: William E. Smythe, 1888), 148.

47. H. Hollerith. Art of Compiling Statistics. US Patent 395,781, filed June 8, 1887, and issued January 8, 1889.

48. As with so many American inventions, there is a competing claim of prior art from a Russian, Semen Korsakov, who experimented with using punched holes to store and search for information as early as the 1830s. The early state of electrical engineering meant that Korsokov's invention was purely mechanical, and it's difficult to see how it could have worked efficiently. He appears to have been dissuaded from further work by his invention's lukewarm reception at the Imperial Academy of Sciences in St. Petersburg and so becomes a footnote in this story.

49. Austrian, *Herman Hollerith,* chap. 7.

50. Quoted in Marion Diamond and Mervyn Stone, "Nightingale on Quetelet," *Journal of the Royal Statistical Society. Series A (General)* 144, no. 1 (1981): 73.

51. The Higgs discovery: G. Aad et al., "Observation of a New Particle in the Search for the Standard Model Higgs Boson with the ATLAS Detector at the LHC," *Physics Letters B* 716, no. 1 (September 2012): 1–29. (The "et al." is doing rather a lot of work here.)

52. Kevin Donnelly, *Adolphe Quetelet, Social Physics and the Average Men of Science 1796–1874* (Pittsburgh: University of Pittsburgh Press, 2015), 105–109.

53. Ibid., 115.

54. M. A. Quetelet, *A Treatise on Man and the Development of His Faculties* (Edinburgh: W. & B. Chambers, 1842), 99.

55. For the British society, see Kathrin Levitan, *A Cultural History of the British Census: Envisioning the Multitude in the Nineteenth Century,* Palgrave Studies in Cultural and Intellectual History (New York: Palgrave Macmillan, 2011), 22–23. For the American society, see John Koren, ed., *The History of Statistics: Their Development and Progress in Many Countries* (New York: Macmillan,

1918), 4. For correspondence with Babbage in particular, see Swade, *The Difference Engine,* 117–118.

56. For the history, see J. W. Nixon, *A History of the International Statistical Institute: 1885–1960* (The Hague: The Hague International Institute, 1960), 5–6. For the address, see Adolphe Quetelet, "Opening Address," in *Compte Rendu Des Travaux de Congrès Général de Statistique* (Congrès Général de Statistique, Brussels: Commission Centrale de Statistique, 1853), 20–23. A complete English translation can be found in Edward Young, William Barnes, and Edwin Snow, *Report of the Delegates to the International Statistical Congress Held at St. Petersburg in August, 1872,* 43rd Congress, House of Representatives, 1st Session (Washington, DC: Government Printing Office, 1875), 70–72.

57. Nico Randeraad, "The International Statistical Congress (1853–1876): Knowledge Transfers and Their Limits," *European History Quarterly* 41, no. 1 (January 2011): 54; Garfield quoted in John Clark Ridpath, *The Life and Work of James A. Garfield, Twentieth President of the United States* (Cincinnati: Jones Brothers and Company, 1881), 214–226.

58. Young, Barnes, and Snow, *Report of the Delegates to the International Statistical Congress,* 34, 36–38.

59. Ibid., 39.

60. Billings, Gannett, and Cooke, "Report of a Commission," 9–10.

61. Ibid., 10–11; Robert P. Porter, *Report of the Superintendent of Census to the Secretary of the Interior* (Washington, DC: Government Printing Office, 1889), 8.

62. The processing is described well by Austrian, *Herman Hollerith,* chap. 6. Precise budgetary and operational details are given in George W. Evans and A. C. Tonner, "Report of Examination and Review of the Census Office," 52nd Congress, 1st Session (Washington, DC, March 5, 1892), 11. For enumerator numbers in context, see Anderson, *The American Census,* 274–275.

63. Martin, "Counting a Nation by Electricity," 522–524; Truesdell, *The Development of Punch Card Tabulation,* 61–62.

64. "Counting by Machine," *Evening Star,* June 26, 1890.

65. Wright and Hunt, "The History and Growth of the United States Census," 74; Anderson, *The American Census,* 274–275.

66. Martin, "Counting a Nation by Electricity," 525.

67. Porter, "The Eleventh Census," 20.

68. On release of counts and volume of published outputs, see Wright and Hunt, "The History and Growth of the United States Census," 73–75; Martin, "Counting a Nation by Electricity," 522; Savings estimate from Austrian, *Herman Hollerith,* 69.

69. "No Malthus Needed," *Times-Democrat* (New Orleans), June 20, 1891; As ever, the failure of the census results to match expectations led some to question it; see Anderson, *The American Census,* 108.

70. Robert P. Porter, "Distribution of Population According to Density: 1890," Extra Census Bulletin no. 2 (Washington, DC: US Census Office, April 20, 1891), 4; reprinted in the main volumes: US Census Office, *Compendium of the Eleventh Census: 1890,* Part 1: Population (Washington, DC: Government Printing Office, 1892), xlviii.

71. Henry Gannett, *Statistical Atlas of the United States, Based upon the Results of the Eleventh Census* (Washington, DC: Government Printing Office, 1898), plates 3–6, loc.gov/item/07019233.

72. Additional support for this hypothesis can be found in the maps themselves. The legend used for the 1890 map is inconsistent with the legend common to all the maps that precede it, creating the appearance of a comparatively more densely populated country. Given the manual effort involved in cartography at that time, this seems unlikely to be an accident. See Andrew Whitby, "How the West Was Really Won: By Manipulative Data Vizualization," February 17, 2019, andrewwhitby.com/2019/02/17/how-the-west-was-really-won.

73. Turner later expanded his argument into a book, of which the essay is the first chapter. Frederick Jackson Turner, *The Frontier in American History* (1921; repr. Tucson: University of Arizona Press, 1986).

74. For biographical details, see Richard A. Pierce, "New Light on Ivan Petroff, Historian of Alaska," *Pacific Northwest Quarterly* 59, no. 1 (1968): 1–10.

75. Ivan Petroff, "The Census of Alaska," Census Bulletin no. 15 (Washington, DC: US Census Office, November 7, 1890).

76. US Census Office, *Report on Population and Resources of Alaska at the Eleventh Census: 1890* (Washington, DC: Government Printing Office, 1893), 3. Alaska was actually the only part of the United States whose population was not tabulated by Hollerith machine, being small and outside the general count; see Truesdell, *The Development of Punch Card Tabulation,* 25.

77. Pierce, "New Light on Ivan Petroff," 9.

78. "Indispensable" quote is from ibid., 7. "More lies" quote is from Terrence M. Cole, "Klondike Literature," *Columbia: The Magazine of Northwest History,* Summer 2008, 12.

79. Smil, *Creating the Twentieth Century,* 41.

80. For the company's founding, see Austrian, *Herman Hollerith,* chap. 15. For a theoretical discussion of punch cards as part of a technological system, see Heide, *Punched-Card Systems and the Early Information Explosion,* 5–13.

81. Most of these are available at the census website. Sadly, records from the 1890 census, the first census counted by Hollerith machine, were lost in a fire in 1921. "Famous and Infamous Census Records," US Census Bureau, census.gov /history/www/genealogy/decennial_census_records/famous_and_infamous_census _records.html, accessed April 16, 2009. Robert Porter also capitalized on Hollerith's invention, returning to his country of birth, Britain, to sell the machines there. See Heide, *Punched-Card Systems and the Early Information Explosion,* 138–145.

Chapter 4. Paper People

1. The raid is described in Dutch in "Kleykamp," Andere Tijden, October 23, 2008, anderetijden.nl/aflevering/299/Kleykamp. The most complete English description, including first-person accounts and details of the flight path, is contained in Martin W. Bowman, *Mosquito Menacing the Reich: Combat Action in the Twin-Engine Wooden Wonder of World War II* (South Yorkshire, UK: Pen and Sword Books, 2008), Kindle edition, chap. 8. The squadron was then based at Lasham airfield in Hampshire but that day left from Swanton Morley; see Martin W. Bowman, *De Havilland Mosquito* (Marlborough, UK: Crowood, 1997), chap. 3. For Cohen's perspective including quote, see "Het Bombarderen van Kleykamp," *Dagblat Amigoe Di Curaçao,* May 19, 1944. For "first daylight raid," see "Nederl. Luitenant-Vlieger vertelt over bombardement op Denhaag door geallieerd escadrille" (Radio Oranje, May 6, 1944), nl.wikipedia.org/wiki/Bestand:Radio_Oranje _6-mei-1944_Nederlandse_luitenant-vlieger_vertelt_over_de_aanval_op_Den _Haag.wav.

2. For "last time Cohen had seen this coast," see "Het Bombarderen van Kleykamp." For other *Engelandvaarders* that summer, see "Overzicht van elf pogingen vanaf de kust bij Katwijk," Stichting Monument Engelandvaarders Zeehostunneltje Katwijk, 2016, engelandvaarderskatwijk.nl/11-pogingen-vanuit -katwijk. Some sources are vague on Cohen's Jewishness; however, his grave at the Netherlands Field of Honour in Orry-la-Ville is marked in Hebrew with a common epitaph from 1 Samuel 25:29: "His soul shall be bound in the bundle of life." Cohen was shot down and killed on another mission over France later that summer. For Cohen and de Iongh's crossing, see "Poging 4," Stichting Monument Engelandvaarders Zeehostunneltje Katwijk, 2016, engelandvaarderskatwijk .nl/poging-4. For de Iongh's death, see "Crash No 261: Spitfire BM379: 10-06 -1943, Noordzee," Stichting Wings to Victory (Airwar Museum), n.d., db.wingsto victory.nl/database_detail-du.php?wtv_id=261, accessed June 11, 2018.

3. On the mission plan, see "The Hague-Gestapo Headquarters (Original Briefing Model-Enlarged Detail of MOD 396)," Imperial War Museums, n.d.,

MOD 152, iwm.org.uk/collections/item/object/30018564, accessed June 11, 2018. On Cohen's observations and bombing failure, see "Het Bombarderen van Kleykamp."

4. Cohen quote from "Nederl. Luitenant-Vlieger vertelt." Originally the death toll was reported as fifty-nine; see "Kleykamp." Description of the aftermath from A. Korthals Alter, quoted in Bowman, *Mosquito Menacing the Reich,* chap. 8, location 5095–5110.

5. See generally Lars Heide, *Punched-Card Systems and the Early Information Explosion: 1880–1945,* Studies in Industry and Society (Baltimore: Johns Hopkins University Press, 2009), chap. 6. On the increased capacity of cards, see pp. 57–62, 93; on alphabetic data, see pp. 120–121; on the overall advantages of punch cards compared with written files, see p. 4.

6. For professionalization generally, see Alain Desrosières, *The Politics of Large Numbers: A History of Statistical Reasoning,* trans. Camille Naish (Cambridge, MA: Harvard University Press, 1998), chaps. 5–6. For the establishment dates of offices in European countries, see the long list spanning 1805 to 1873 in J. Adam Tooze, *Statistics and the German State, 1900–1945: The Making of Modern Economic Knowledge,* Cambridge Studies in Modern Economic History 9 (Cambridge, UK: Cambridge University Press, 2001), 1–2.

7. Max Weber, "11. Bureaucracy," in *Economy and Society: An Outline of Interpretive Sociology,* trans. Guenther Roth and Claus Wittich, vol. 2 (Berkeley: University of California Press, 1978); quote on p. 975.

8. Ibid., 988–989.

9. On public display of schedules, see George Gatewood, *A Monograph on Confidentiality and Privacy in the U.S. Census,* US Census Bureau, 2001, 4–5, census.gov/history/pdf/ConfidentialityMonograph.pdf. On the statistical disinterest in the individual, see, for example, the Commissioners for the 1841 Census of Ireland ("in accounts of large numbers, the individual is wholly lost sight of in the average"), quoted in Ian White, "A Brief History of the Census in Ireland/Northern Ireland," in *Registrar General Northern Ireland Annual Report 2011,* Northern Ireland Statistics and Research Agency, 2012, 37, www.nisra .gov.uk/sites/nisra.gov.uk/files/publications/RG2011%5B1%5D.pdf.

10. On the evolution toward confidentiality, see D. Sylvester and S. Lohr, "The Security of Our Secrets: A History of Privacy and Confidentiality in Law and Statistical Practice," *Denver University Law Review* 83, no. 1 (2005): 160–161, 178–179; Gatewood, *A Monograph on Confidentiality and Privacy in the U.S. Census,* 7; and William Seltzer and Margo Anderson, "Using Population Data Systems to Target Vulnerable Population Subgroups and Individuals: Issues

and Incidents," in *Statistical Methods for Human Rights,* ed. Jana Asher, David L. Banks, and Fritz Scheuren (New York: Springer, 2008), 279–281. For an example of reaction to more invasive census questions at the time, see the cartoon "The Great Tribulation," *Saturday Evening Post,* August 18, 1860, reproduced in Frederick G. Bohme, *200 Years of Census Taking: Population and Housing Questions, 1790–1990* (Washington, DC: US Department of Commerce, Bureau of the Census, 1989), 14, census.gov/history/pdf/200years.pdf.

11. On the data quality motivation, see Sylvester and Lohr, "The Security of Our Secrets: A History of Privacy and Confidentiality in Law and Statistical Practice," 160; *New York Sun* quoted in "Those Outrageous Census Questions," *Boston Globe,* May 26, 1890. A similar concern that questions seen as privacy-invading would harm accuracy is noted in Tasmania General Register Office, *Census of the Colony of Tasmania, 1891: Parts 1–8* (Hobart: William Grahame, 1893), xi.

12. On privacy, the 1890 census, "debts and diseases," and arrests, see Sarah Elizabeth Igo, *The Known Citizen: A History of Privacy in Modern America* (Cambridge, MA: Harvard University Press, 2018), 46–47.

13. Farr's memorandum was printed in multiple newspapers; see, for example, "The Forthcoming Census," *Illustrated London News,* April 6, 1861, 524; See also discussion in Kathrin Levitan, *A Cultural History of the British Census: Envisioning the Multitude in the Nineteenth Century,* Palgrave Studies in Cultural and Intellectual History (New York: Palgrave Macmillan, 2011), 45; William H. Taft, "Proclamation for the Thirteenth Decennial Census," March 15, 1910, quoted in Gatewood, *A Monograph on Confidentiality and Privacy in the U.S. Census,* 9.

14. Ivan Fellegi, who was later chief statistician of Canada, characterized it as a "social contract"; see I. P. Fellegi, "On the Question of Statistical Confidentiality," *Journal of the American Statistical Association* 67, no. 337 (March 1972): 7–18. On the role of statistical societies and journals in promoting confidentiality, see Sylvester and Lohr, "The Security of Our Secrets," 174–186. For Germany in particular, Reichardt offers a retrospective on the concept's universal acceptance—from a position of some peril in 1940—in W. Reichardt, "Die Reichsstatistik," in *Die Statistik in Deutschland Nach Ihren Heutigen Stand. Ehrengast Für Friedrich Zahn,* vol. 1 (Berlin, 1940), 77–90.

15. Michel Poulain and Anne Herm, "Le registre de population centralisé, source de statistiques démographiques en Europe," trans. Roger Depledge, *Population (English edition)* 68, no. 2 (2013): 187–188.

16. The administrative uses of a register are summarized in E. Nicolï, "Rapport sur les registres de population," *Bulletin de l'Institut International de Statistique* 15, no. 2 (1906): sec. 6.

17. Poulain and Herm, "Le registre de population centralisé," 188.

18. For instance, the Netherlands had a census, tabulated by Hollerith machines, in 1930. See Centraal Bureau voor de Statistiek, *Statistiek van Nederland: Volkstelling 31 December 1930,* vol. 1–9 ([The Hague]: Algemeene Landsdrukkerij, 1932), volkstellingen.nl/nl/publicaties/publicaties_in_pdf/1930/Volkstelling/index.html. On the family books, see Kees Prins, *Population Register Data, Basis for the Netherlands Population Statistics,* Bevolkingstrends (Netherlands: CBS, September 2017), 3, cbs.nl/-/media/_pdf/2017/38/population-register-data.pdf.

19. The controversial status of index card registers at the beginning of the twentieth century is described in Nicolï, "Rapport sur les registres de population," 343. Some of the Dutch challenges are described in Henri Methorst and J. L. Lentz, "Die Volksregistrierung Und Das Neue in Den Niederlanden Eingeführte Einheitliche System," *Allgemeines Statistisches Archiv* 26 (July 1936): 59–84. A more thorough account is given in J. L. Lentz, *De Bevolkingsboekhouding [Population Accounting]* (Netherlands: VUGA, 1936), chap. 2.

20. Bob Moore, "Nazi Masters and Accommodating Dutch Bureaucrats: Working Towards the Fuehrer in the Occupied Netherlands, 1940–45," in *Working Towards the Führer: Essays in Honour of Sir Ian Kershaw,* ed. Anthony McElligott and Tim Kirk (Manchester, UK: Manchester University Press, 2004), 194, 197–198; L. de Jong, *Het Koninkrijk der Nederlanden in de Tweede Wereldoorlog,* vol. 5 (Den Haag: SDU Uitgeverij Koninginnegracht; Amsterdam: Boom, 1995), 446–451.

21. "Wedded" description by Karel Fredericks, secretary-general of the Interior Ministry, quoted in Moore, "Nazi Masters and Accommodating Dutch Bureaucrats," 198; Methorst and Lentz, "Die Volksregistrierung Und Das Neue," 60.

22. Lentz, *De Bevolkingsboekhouding.*

23. Methorst and Lentz, "Die Volksregistrierung Und Das Neue"; H. W. Methorst, "The New System of Population Accounting in the Netherlands," *Journal of the American Statistical Association* 31, no. 196 (December 1936): 719; H. W. Methorst, "The New System of Population Accounting in the Netherlands," *Journal of the American Statistical Association* 33, no. 204 (December 1938): 713–714.

24. Lentz, *De Bevolkingsboekhouding,* 4, 12. Lentz's list on p. 12 of potential inclusions in the register is worth reproducing in full: "right or denial of right to vote; conscription, military commitment or civilian guard; pensions; social interest; issued passports, nationality certificates or proof of identity; driving licenses and vehicle registrations; special personal permits or powers (carrying firearms, police authority, doctor, pharmacist, obstetrician, etc.); awards; destitution; solvency; guardianship; police or judicial notes; expulsion; financial or other obligations imposed; alimony; thumbprint or fingerprint (dactyloscopy); description;

nicknames, etc., etc." A further list of "more scientific" attributes includes "special abnormalities of the trunk or limbs; inadequacy, harelip, blindness; deafness, insanity, hereditary diseases and occupational diseases; mental development (reading and writing, academic degree); special talent; nomadic tendencies; marital fertility; cause of death." "Total registration" is due to Götz Aly and Karl Heinz Roth, *The Nazi Census: Identification and Control in the Third Reich,* trans. Edwin Black and Assenka Oksiloff, Politics, History, and Social Change (Philadelphia: Temple University Press, 2004), 2; it was originally published in German with the title *Die restlose Erfassung* (*The Total [or Complete] Registration*).

25. Tooze, *Statistics and the German State, 1900–1945,* 27–28.

26. The mechanics of Social Security filing are described in Heide, *Punched-Card Systems and the Early Information Explosion,* 217–221. Figures on its rollout are provided in Herbert R. Tacker, "Social Security Numbers Issued, 1937–71," *Social Security Bulletin,* Notes and Brief Reports, July 1972, 30–32.

27. Dorothy Swaine Thomas, review of *De Bevolkingsboekhouding,* by J. L. Lentz, *American Sociological Review* 2, no. 1 (February 1937): 117. Thomas was a pioneer and proponent of these new administrative data sources. See Dorothy Swaine Thomas, "Utilization of Social Security Data for Sociological Research," *American Sociological Review* 3, no. 5 (October 1938): 718.

28. Timothy Snyder, *Black Earth: The Holocaust as History and Warning* (New York: Tim Duggan Books, 2015), 11–15; Adolf Hitler, "Chapter 14: Germany's Policy in Eastern Europe," in *Mein Kampf,* trans. James Murphy (London: Hutchinson, in association with Hurst & Blackett, 1939). The following were the 1925 population densities (persons per square kilometer), using contemporaneous League of Nations data: Germany, 344; United Kingdom, 479; Netherlands, 565; Belgium, 674. See League of Nations, *International Statistical Year-Book,* 1926, wayback.archive-it.org/6321/20160901163315/http://digital.library.northwestern.edu/league/stat.html, table 1.

29. Quote from Laurence Rees, *The Holocaust: A New History* (New York: Public Affairs, 2017), 318.

30. Galton coins and defines "eugenic" in Francis Galton, *Inquiries into Human Faculty and Its Development* (New York: Macmillan, 1883), 24–25.

31. An entire Wikipedia entry exists on different statistical approaches to this question; see "Checking Whether a Coin Is Fair," Wikipedia, en.wikipedia.org/wiki/Checking_whether_a_coin_is_fair, accessed August 28, 2019.

32. T. R. Malthus, *An Essay on the Principle of Population,* ed. Geoffrey Gilbert, Oxford World's Classics (1798; repr., Oxford, UK: Oxford University Press, 2008), chap. 9.

33. Galton, *Inquiries into Human Faculty and Its Development*, 307–317.

34. Desrosières, *The Politics of Large Numbers*, 13, 18.

35. Raul Hilberg, *The Destruction of the European Jews*, rev. and definitive ed. (New York: Holmes & Meier, 1985), 21–23.

36. US Holocaust Memorial Museum, "Jewish Population of Europe in 1933: Population Data by Country," Holocaust Encyclopedia, encyclopedia.ushmm .org/content/en/article/jewish-population-of-europe-in-1933-population -data-by-country, accessed August 24, 2019.

37. Ibid.; Główny Urząd Statystyczny Rzeczypospolitej Polskiej [Central Statistical Office the Polish Republic], *Drugi Powszechny Spis Ludności z Dn. 9.XII 1931 r. [The Second General Census of 9.XII 1931]*, Seria C, Zeszyt 94a (Warsaw, 1938), tables 10 and 13.

38. On Reichardt and his rise, see Gunnar Thorvaldsen, *Censuses and Census Takers: A Global History*, Routledge Studies in Modern History (London: Routledge/Taylor & Francis Group, 2018), 212–213, 227.

39. "Statistics boom" is Jutta Wietog's description; the period is described in Jutta Wietog, "Bevölkerungsstatistik Im Dritten Reich," *Wirtschaft Und Statistik (Statistisches Bundesamt)*, July 2001, 588–597. This is a summary of a longer work, which unfortunately has not been translated into English: Jutta Wietog and Wolfram Fischer, *Volkszählungen Unter Dem Nationalsozialismus: Eine Dokumentation Zur Bevölkerungsstatistik Im Dritten Reich*, Schriften Zur Wirtschafts- Und Sozialgeschichte, Bd. 66 (Berlin: Duncker & Humblot, 2001). See also the relevant section in Thorvaldsen, which draws heavily on Wietog's book: Thorvaldsen, *Censuses and Census Takers*, 208–231. For the growth in the size of the Reich Statistical Office, see Aly and Roth, *The Nazi Census*, 18.

40. Thorvaldsen, *Censuses and Census Takers*, 214–218; Wietog, "Bevölkerungsstatistik Im Dritten Reich," 588; D. M. Luebke and S. Milton, "Locating the Victim: An Overview of Census-Taking, Tabulation Technology and Persecution in Nazi Germany," *IEEE Annals of the History of Computing* 16, no. 3 (1994): 26.

41. Thorvaldsen, *Censuses and Census Takers*, 215–216. See also p. 223 for Thorvaldsen's own ambivalent assessment of the possibility of individual disclosure of 1933 census records. Heidinger is quoted in translation in Luebke and Milton, "Locating the Victim," 26–27.

42. US Holocaust Memorial Museum, "Germany: Jewish Population in 1933," Holocaust Encyclopedia, encyclopedia.ushmm.org/content/en/article /germany-jewish-population-in-1933, accessed August 24, 2019. On the number of nonpracticing Jews, see a low of 240,000 in Luebke and Milton, "Locating the Victim," 30; a range of under 400,000 to as many as half a million is given in

Deborah Hertz, "The Genealogy Bureaucracy in the Third Reich," *Jewish History* 11, no. 2 (Fall 1997): 53–78. For Goebbels's belief, see Thorvaldsen, *Censuses and Census Takers,* 217.

43. This new definition was no more "scientific" than the previous one, simply pushing the determination back two generations. It was founded on a false belief that, before 1900, intermarriage between Jews and non-Jews was rare, so that grandparental religious practice might align with the Nazi idea of race. See starred footnote in Luebke and Milton, "Locating the Victim," 30.

44. Ibid., 29–30; Robert M. W. Kempner, "The German National Registration System as a Means of Police Control of Population," *Journal of Criminal Law and Criminology* 36, no. 5 (1946): 378–379. Hertz, "The Genealogy Bureaucracy in the Third Reich," 61–63; Luebke and Milton, "Locating the Victim," 32; Aly and Roth, *The Nazi Census,* 73–74.

45. On what files of Jews existed prior to Kristallnacht, see Luebke and Milton, "Locating the Victim," 33. The long-accepted death toll was under a hundred, but new estimates have cast doubt on that, revising it up to account for deaths in concentration camps in the months that followed. See, for example, Alan E. Steinweis, *Kristallnacht 1938* (Cambridge, MA: Belknap of Harvard University Press, 2009).

46. For the *Melderegister,* see Kempner, "The German National Registration System as a Means of Police Control of Population"; Aly and Roth, *The Nazi Census,* 38–43. For the *Volkskartei,* see Luebke and Milton, "Locating the Victim," 32; Aly and Roth, *The Nazi Census,* 43–53. The proliferation of different registers in Nazi Germany can be extremely confusing. In part it was a result of the chaotic nature of the Nazi administration, with responsibilities overlapping between state and party, local and central government. But it is also because of the constraints of what were still largely manual card files. The *Melderegister* was organized alphabetically by last name. It could not simply be reordered by age at will, so an entirely new register was created for that purpose.

47. Aly and Roth, *The Nazi Census,* 81–83; Wietog, "Bevölkerungsstatistik Im Dritten Reich." Interestingly, a very similar supplementary card system was used in some cases to gather sensitive income data in the 1940 US census; see Margo J. Anderson, *The American Census: A Social History,* 2nd ed. (New Haven, CT: Yale University Press, 2015), 182–183.

48. The results are not directly comparable with 1933 both because the question was different and because the census covered a larger territory following the annexation of Austria. The figures are given in Luebke and Milton, "Locating the Victim."

49. On subsequent use of the cards, see ibid.; F. W. Kistermann, "Locating the Victims: The Nonrole of Punched Card Technology and Census Work," *IEEE Annals of the History of Computing* 19, no. 2 (June 1997): 31–45; Wietog, "Bevölkerungsstatistik Im Dritten Reich," sec. 5. On the Jewish markers in the *Volkskartei*, see Luebke and Milton, "Locating the Victim"; Aly and Roth, *The Nazi Census*, 64.

50. On the Reich Office of Genealogical Research, see Hertz, "The Genealogy Bureaucracy in the Third Reich." On the *Volkstumskartei*, see Wietog, "Bevölkerungsstatistik Im Dritten Reich," sec. 3; Aly and Roth, *The Nazi Census*, 83–84.

51. The case that the census was important was first made by Aly and Roth, *The Nazi Census*, 10–22. Thorvaldsen argues, based largely on Wietog's findings, for placing less weight on the censuses; see Thorvaldsen, *Censuses and Census Takers*, 222–226; Wietog and Fischer, *Volkszählungen Unter Dem Nationalsozialismus*.

52. Some scholars have tried to draw a distinction between the main 1939 census schedule and the supplementary card, as is attempted by Kistermann, "Locating the Victims," 39. For a sense of how ordinary people saw things, Aly and Roth quote (source unclear) "Census questionnaires have become something quite familiar…" in relation to the *Volkskartei* registration, which was not officially a census or generally referred to as such. See Aly and Roth, *The Nazi Census*, 46.

53. A brief biographical sketch of Zahn appears in Aly and Roth, *The Nazi Census*, 24–25. His Nazi party membership is noted in Thorvaldsen, *Censuses and Census Takers*, 219. The quote is from Friedrich Zahn, "Die Statistik Im Nationalsozialistischen Grossdeutschland," *Allgemeines Statistisches Archiv* 29 (1940); translation from Aly and Roth, *The Nazi Census*, 2.

54. Reichardt, "Die Reichsstatistik," part 7. The translation is from Tooze, *Statistics and the German State, 1900–1945*, 216–217. However, note that the term "statistical confidentiality" was not yet in use in English in 1940. The term Reichardt uses, *statistische Geheimnis*, translates literally to "statistical secrecy." Today statistical confidentiality is written as the compound noun *Statistikgeheimnis*, paralleling older legal concepts including *Briefgeheimnis* (secrecy of letters), *Bankgeheimnis* (banking secrecy), *Amtsgeheinis* (official secrecy).

55. Reichardt, "Die Reichsstatistik," part 1. For examples of possible resistance by Reichardt, see Wietog, "Bevölkerungsstatistik Im Dritten Reich," 592–593; Kistermann, "Locating the Victims," 39.

56. Das Statistisches Bundesamt, *Kleine Chronik Des Statistichen Bundesamtes*, Festschrift, 1956, 32–33; Thorvaldsen, *Censuses and Census Takers*, 227.

57. Aly and Roth, *The Nazi Census*, 51; Adam Czerniakow, *The Warsaw Diary of Adam Czerniakow: Prelude to Doom*, ed. Raul Hilberg, Stanislaw Staron,

and Joseph Kermish (Chicago: Ivan R. Dee, 1999). On in the initial occupation, see pp. 27–29 of Hilberg and Staron's introduction.

58. Czerniakow, *The Warsaw Diary of Adam Czerniakow,* 78–86.

59. Ibid., 91. For the numbers relocated, see Hilberg, *The Destruction of the European Jews,* 226. For how this worked in other Polish cities, see William Seltzer, "Population Statistics, the Holocaust, and the Nuremberg Trials," *Population and Development Review* 24, no. 3 (September 1998): 519–520.

60. For the elaborate top-down administration of rations, see Raul Hilberg and Stanislaw Staron, "Introduction," in *The Warsaw Diary of Adam Czerniakow,* 55–60.

61. Chaim Aron Kaplan, *Scroll of Agony: The Warsaw Diary of Chaim A. Kaplan,* trans. Abraham Isaac Katsh (Bloomington: Indiana University Press, 1999), 57, 60.

62. Paul Dostert, "La Resistance Luxembourgeoise (1940–1944)," *Ons Stad,* 2002; Gerald Newton, ed., *Luxembourg and Lëtzebuergesch: Language and Communication at the Crossroads of Europe* (Oxford, UK: Clarendon; Oxford University Press, 1996), 16.

63. Paul Weber, *Geschichte Luxemburgs Im Zweiten Weltkrieg* (Luxembourg: Buck, 1948), 56–57.

64. Ibid., 56–57. The slogan is sometimes reported as *dräimol Letzebuerg* or with other spelling variants.

65. Ibid., 58.

66. Ibid., 58; US Holocaust Memorial Museum, "Luxembourg," Holocaust Encyclopedia, encyclopedia.ushmm.org/content/en/article/luxembourg, accessed August 24, 2019.

67. On the order to remain and offer to resign, see Moore, "Nazi Masters and Accommodating Dutch Bureaucrats," 190. On Aryan attestation, see Rees, *The Holocaust,* 184.

68. Moore, "Nazi Masters and Accommodating Dutch Bureaucrats," 195–196.

69. Ibid. The manual is J. L. Lentz, *Persoonsbewijzen: Handleiding Voor de Uitvoering van Het Besluit Persoonsbewijzen* (Arnhem: Van der Wiel, 1941).

70. Rees, *The Holocaust,* 184, 281.

71. For the original purpose of the central register, see Lentz, *De Bevolkingsboekhouding,* 71–73. For the change after 1941, see "Kleykamp"; de Jong, *Het Koninkrijk der Nederlanden in de Tweede Wereldoorlog,* 5:453. The punch card index is described in Edwin Black, *IBM and the Holocaust: The Strategic Alliance Between Nazi Germany and America's Most Powerful Corporation,* expanded ed. (Washington, DC: Dialog, 2012), 308–313.

72. Rees, *The Holocaust,* 282.

73. Later in the entry it is revealed that the notice is not for Anne's father but for Margot herself; see Anne Frank, Otto Frank, and Mirjam Pressler, *The Diary of a Young Girl* (New York: Alfred A. Knopf, 2010), 23.

74. Rees, *The Holocaust,* 184, 283.

75. Weber, "11. Bureaucracy," 987. References to counterfeit German *kennkarten* abound in literature about occupied Poland. For example: Joshua D. Zimmerman, *The Polish Underground and the Jews, 1939–1945* (New York: Cambridge University Press, 2015), 313, 332; Emanuel Ringelblum, Joseph Kermish, and Shmuel Krakowski, *Polish-Jewish Relations During the Second World War* (Evanston, IL: Northwestern University Press, 1992), 102.

76. de Jong, *Het Koninkrijk der Nederlanden in de Tweede Wereldoorlog,* 5:453–455.

77. Moore, "Nazi Masters and Accommodating Dutch Bureaucrats," 197; *Part 5: Public Opinion and Relations to the Jews in Nazi Europe,* in *The Nazi Holocaust: Historical Articles on the Destruction of European Jews,* ed. Michael R. Marrus (Westport, MA: Meckler, 2011), 2:646–648.

78. For the ration card measure, see René van Eunen, "De Geschiednis van Het Persoonsbewijs," Persoonbwijzen.nl (Database Persoonsbewijzen W.O.II), 2019, persoonsbewijzen.nl/passie/sites/index.php?mid=226952&kid=4302&pagina =tekstpagina. For the first bombing request, see "Image of Memorandum Dated 29.11.43, Numbered 3942" (November 29, 1943), Accession number 7.000SPA-ond (inventory number 25024), National Archive of the Netherlands, nationaal archief.nl/onderzoeken/fotocollectie/b2862c13-4364-ddec-9c03-cb9e5682a47a. For the Kleykamp bombing request, see Pieter Schlebaum, "Airraid on Kleykamp," trans. Fred Bolle, Traces of War, December 29, 2011, tracesofwar.com/articles/2441 /Airraid-on-Kleykamp.htm.

79. Bowman, *Mosquito Menacing the Reich,* location 5116.

80. "Kleykamp"; ibid., location 5069.

81. de Jong, *Het Koninkrijk der Nederlanden in de Tweede Wereldoorlog,* 5:456–457.

82. This explanation is put forward by J. C. H. Blom, "The Persecution of the Jews in the Netherlands: A Comparative Western European Perspective," *European History Quarterly* 19, no. 3 (July 1989): 333–351. Croes surveys this and other hypotheses but argues for the importance of more local factors; see M. Croes, "The Holocaust in the Netherlands and the Rate of Jewish Survival," *Holocaust and Genocide Studies* 20, no. 3 (January 1, 2006): 474–499.

83. Heide, *Punched-Card Systems and the Early Information Explosion,* 133–134, 152–160, 192–208, 222–225.

84. Ibid., 225–229; Black, *IBM and the Holocaust,* 321.

85. "Nazis Extend Nuremberg Laws to Occupied France," *Jewish Telegraphic Agency News,* May 12, 1941, vol. 3, no. 128; Black, *IBM and the Holocaust,* 313–318; US Holocaust Memorial Museum, "France," Holocaust Encyclopedia, encyclopedia.ushmm.org/content/en/article/france, accessed August 24, 2019.

86. Black, *IBM and the Holocaust,* 319–322; Heide, *Punched-Card Systems and the Early Information Explosion,* 229.

87. Black, *IBM and the Holocaust,* 322–323.

88. On the worries of traditionalists, see René Rémond, ed., *Le "Fichier Juif"* (Paris: Plon, 1996), 141. On Carmille's letter to Vallat, see Black, *IBM and the Holocaust,* 323–324.

89. Black, *IBM and the Holocaust,* 324–329.

90. Ibid., 328–330. The quote, from Walter Wilde, appears on p. 329.

91. The interview is described in ibid., 432–434.

92. The punch cards used in the census of occupations—not necessarily the only card in use—had two places in which Jewish race might be marked. Column 2 was used for the first digit of an identification number that separated Jews. Columns 40–43 were used for nationality. The card layout is reproduced in Heide, *Punched-Card Systems and the Early Information Explosion,* 228; the structure of the identification number is described in Pierre Piazza, "The Identity Registration System, Identification Number and National ID Card During the Vichy Regime (France, 1940–1944)," *Criminocorpus,* November 15, 2017, journals.openedition.org/criminocorpus/3659. See also the statement on column 11 at p. 329 of Black, *IBM and the Holocaust,* which cites an earlier statement by Robert Carmille that refers to question 11, not column 11: Robert Carmille, "Des Apparences à La Réalité: Le 'Fichier Juif'. Rapport de La Commission Présidée Par René Rémond Au Premier Ministre: Mise Au Point" (1996).

93. US Holocaust Memorial Museum, "Documenting Numbers of Victims of the Holocaust and Nazi Persecution," Holocaust Encyclopedia, February 4, 2019, encyclopedia.ushmm.org/content/en/article/documenting-numbers-of-victims -of-the-holocaust-and-nazi-persecution; US Holocaust Memorial Museum, "France"; US Holocaust Memorial Museum, "The Netherlands," Holocaust Encyclopedia, encyclopedia.ushmm.org/content/en/article/the-netherlands, accessed August 24, 2019.

94. US Holocaust Memorial Museum, "Documenting Numbers of Victims of the Holocaust and Nazi Persecution."

95. Chil Rajchman and Solon Beinfeld, *The Last Jew of Treblinka: A Survivor's Memory, 1942–1943* (New York: Pegasus Books, 2011).

96. Their progressive work on this topic is summarized in William Seltzer and Margo Anderson, "Census Confidentiality Under the Second War Powers Act (1942–1947)," Confidentiality, Privacy, and Ethical Issues in Demographic Data, Population Association of America Annual Meeting, New York, 2007, sec. 1.

97. As with Jews in Nazi Europe, defining who did and did not count as Japanese proved difficult. See Paul R. Spickard, "Injustice Compounded: Amerasians and Non-Japanese Americans in World War II Concentration Camps," *Journal of American Ethnic History* 5, no. 2 (1986): 5–22.

98. A good defense of the ethical acceptability of producing such aggregate, if targeted, statistics is given by a former deputy director of the bureau in Hermann Habermann, "Ethics, Confidentiality, and Data Dissemination," *Journal of Official Statistics* 22, no. 4 (2006): 599–614.

99. Anderson, *The American Census,* 189–190. Capt is quoted from the transcript of the Census Advisory Committee, January 1942, on p. 195.

100. Seltzer and Anderson, "Census Confidentiality Under the Second War Powers Act (1942–1947)," sec. B.1.

101. "Spy Data Sought from 1940 Census," *New York Times*, February 7, 1942; Korematsu v. United States, 323 U.S. 214 (1944). See also Anderson, *The American Census,* 196.

102. "Personal Justice Denied," Report of the Commission on Wartime Relocation and Internment of Civilians, Washington, DC, December 1982, 238; Trump v. Hawaii, 585 U.S. ___ (2018); Ilya Somin, "Justice Scalia on Kelo and Korematsu," The Volokh Conspiracy (blog), February 8, 2014, washingtonpost.com/news/volokh-conspiracy/wp/2014/02/08/justice-scalia-on-kelo-and-korematsu.

103. The definitive prosecution of this case is Black, *IBM and the Holocaust*; IBM's response can be found in IBM, "Addendum to IBM Statement on Nazi-Era Book and Lawsuit," March 29, 2002, www-03.ibm.com/press/us/en/pressrelease/828.wss.

104. For capabilities, see Heide, *Punched-Card Systems and the Early Information Explosion,* 246; Black details an index Lentz created using punch cards, but even here it is not clear that it was used for any purpose other than generating aggregate statistics from the existing card file. See Black, *IBM and the Holocaust,* 308–313. For a list of German installations see Heide, *Punched-Card Systems and the Early Information Explosion,* 180–192.

105. Moore, "Nazi Masters and Accommodating Dutch Bureaucrats," 198.

106. Avinoam Patt, "Jewish Resistance in the Warsaw Ghetto," in *Jewish Resistance Against the Nazis,* ed. Patrick Henry and Berel Lang (Washington, DC: Catholic University of America Press, 2014), 411.

107. Black, *IBM and the Holocaust,* 332.

108. Description of Lentz quoted in de Jong, *Het Koninkrijk der Nederlanden in de Tweede Wereldoorlog,* 5:455.

109. Jonas H. Ellenberg, "Ethical Guidelines for Statistical Practice: A Historical Perspective," *American Statistician* 37, no. 1 (February 1983): 1; Shelley Hurwitz and John S. Gardenier, "Ethical Guidelines for Statistical Practice: The First 60 Years and Beyond," *American Statistician* 66, no. 2 (May 2012): 99–103; UN General Assembly, "Resolution Adopted by the General Assembly on 29 January 2014: 68/261. Fundamental Principles of Official Statistics (A/RES/68/261)," March 3, 2014.

110. Kempner, "The German National Registration System as a Means of Police Control of Population," 374–375.

Chapter 5. A World Census

1. Unless otherwise noted, the sources in this chapter for population totals and related statistics are the following: for estimates from 1950 to 2020 and projections from 2020 onward, UN Population Division, "World Population Prospects 2019," population.un.org/wpp (medium variant projection unless otherwise noted); for estimates prior to 1950, Colin McEvedy and Richard Jones, *Atlas of World Population History,* Penguin Reference Books (Harmondsworth, UK: Penguin, 1978). Unless otherwise noted, the sources in this chapter for estimates of people actually enumerated in each census round are the following: for up to the 1950 round, UN Statistical Office, *Demographic Yearbook 1955* (New York: United Nations, 1955), table 4; for the 1960 round onward, the author's analysis is based primarily on UN Population Division, *Inventory of Censuses, Surveys and Other Primary Sources of Demographic Data by Country or Area* (New York: United Nations, 2019); UN Statistics Division, "Demographic Statistics Database" (updated February 20, 2019), data.un.org/Data .aspx?d=POP&f=tableCode%3a1; UN Statistics Division, *Demographic Yearbook 1997: Historical Supplement* (New York: United Nations, 1999), table 2.

2. For the classic exposition of Malthus in the industrial world, see Arnold Toynbee, "10. Malthus and the Law of Population," in *Lectures on the Industrial Revolution of the 18th Century in England* (1884; repr., Cambridge, UK: Cambridge University Press, 2011). In 1886 Tolstoy called Malthus "a very poor English writer, whose works are all forgotten, and recognized as the most insignificant

of the insignificant," rather undermining his own point. See Robert J. Mayhew, *Malthus: The Life and Legacies of an Untimely Prophet* (Cambridge, MA: Belknap Press of Harvard University Press, 2014), chap. 6, quote at p. 149.

3. For the turn of the century up to the 1960s, see Alison Bashford, *Global Population: History, Geopolitics, and Life on Earth,* Columbia Studies in International and Global History (New York: Columbia University Press, 2014).

4. Matthew James Connelly, *Fatal Misconception: The Struggle to Control World Population* (Cambridge, MA: Belknap Press of Harvard University Press, 2008), 185–187, quote at p. 187.

5. For Nixon, see Phyllis Tilson Piotrow, *World Population Crisis: The United States Response,* Law and Population Series, Special Studies in International Economics and Development 4 (New York: Praeger, 1973), 168–170, quote at p. 169.

6. Paul Ralph Ehrlich, *The Population Bomb* (1968; repr., Cutchogue, NY: Buccaneer Books, 1971), xi.

7. The Carson footage appears lost. See the description in John Tierney, "Betting on the Planet," *New York Times Magazine,* December 2, 1990; also the interview with Ehrlich on Mark Malkoff, "Dr. Paul Ehrlich," *The Carson Podcast,* April 12, 2018; "Playboy Interview: Dr. Paul Ehrlich," *Playboy,* August 1970. For Ehrlich's British visit, see Bernard Dixon, "In Praise of Prophets," *New Scientist and Science Journal,* September 16, 1971. In 1969 Ehrlich lectured at the Institute of Biology. He didn't spare his audience: "I would take even money that England will not exist in the year 2000." For his Australian visit, see George Mc-Gann, "The Road to Extinction," *Australian Women's Weekly,* July 28, 1971.

8. See note 1 for sources of population data used in this chapter.

9. Ehrlich, *The Population Bomb,* 17–19.

10. Ibid., 34.

11. T. R. Malthus, *An Essay on the Principle of Population,* ed. Geoffrey Gilbert, Oxford World's Classics (1798; repr., Oxford, UK: Oxford University Press, 2008), 17. For Ehrlich's explanation of his failure to mention Malthus, see Mayhew, *Malthus,* 197, and note 18, p. 267. Such "ad absurdum scenarios" were written of repeatedly in the years between Malthus and Ehrlich. See Bashford, *Global Population,* 49; Connelly, *Fatal Misconception,* 256. Not even the experts of the UN Population Division were immune to this rhetorical device: see United Nations, Department of Economic and Social Affairs, Population Division, *The Future Growth of World Population,* Population Studies (New York: United Nations, 1958).

12. For a translation of Riccioli's work into English and analysis, see Martin Korenjak, "Humanist Demography: Giovanni Battista Riccioli on the World Population," *Journal of Early Modern Studies* 7, no. 2 (2018): 73–104; William Petty,

Another Essay in Political Arithmetick, Concerning the Growth of the City of London: With the Measures, Periods, Causes, and Consequences Thereof (London, 1682), 464–465, en.wikisource.org/wiki/Another_Essay_(Petty_1683); Gregory King, "Natural and Political Observations and Conclusions upon the State and Condition of England," in *An Estimate of the Comparative Strength of Great-Britain,* by George Chalmers (1696; repr., London: J. Stockdale, 1802), 412–414.

13. See discussion in United Nations, Department of Social Affairs, Population Division, *The Determinants and Consequences of Population Trends,* Population Studies, (New York: United Nations, 1953), 25.

14. Wynnard Hooper, "Population," in *Encyclopaedia Britannica,* 9th ed., vol. 19 (American repr., Philadelphia, 1891), 528.

15. For the "over half" claim, specifically, 44 percent of the world population enumerated by 1880, see "Earth, Area and Population of, The," in *Appleton's Annual Cyclopædia and Register of Important Events of the Year 1891,* vol. 16, new series (New York: D. Appleton and Company, 1892), 262. For Porter's calculation, see Geoffrey Austrian, *Herman Hollerith: Forgotten Giant of Information Processing* (New York: Columbia University Press, 1982), 69.

16. "Project for a census of the world" is the English translation of the title of Joseph Körösi, *Projet d'un Recensement Du Monde* (Paris: Guillaumin, 1881); the longer quote is translated from p. 8. Körösi called for a major effort in 1900; see Josef von Körösy, *Die Seculäre Weltzählung Vom Jahre 1900: Denkschrift an Die St. Petersburger Session Des Internationalen Statistischen Institutes* (Berlin: Putkammer & Mühlbrecht, 1897). Longstaff calls this project "a great object of his [Körösi's] life." See G. B. Longstaff, "Suggestions for the Census of 1891," *Journal of the Royal Statistical Society* 52, no. 3 (September 1889): 436–467.

17. J. W. Nixon, *A History of the International Statistical Institute: 1885–1960* (The Hague: The Hague International Institute, 1960), 148–150.

18. Total ever, see "Earth, Area and Population of The," 262. For the decade to 1900, see note 1, above.

19. A. J. Christopher, "The Quest for a Census of the British Empire c.1840–1940," *Journal of Historical Geography* 34, no. 2 (April 2008): 268–285. On the influence of international recommendations on imperial census taking, see Bruce Curtis, *The Politics of Population: State Formation, Statistics, and the Census of Canada, 1840–1875* (Toronto: University of Toronto Press, 2001), 21.

20. *Census of the British Empire 1901* (London: H. M. Stationery Office, 1906), xxxiv, lxiii, 146.

21. John J. Banninga, "The Indian Census of 1911," *National Geographic,* July 1911, 635.

22. Jill Liddington and Elizabeth Crawford, *Vanishing for the Vote: Suffrage, Citizenship and the Battle for the Census* (Manchester, UK: Manchester University Press, 2014), 125–131, quote at p. 127.

23. Ibid., 231, 296.

24. Christopher, "The Quest for a Census of the British Empire c.1840–1940," 280–281.

25. On the population problem, see Bashford, *Global Population*, 60–67, 133–134, 215. The International Statistical Institute produced its *Annuaire international de statistique* from 1916 to 1921, though only the 1916 and 1919 volumes focus on population totals; while the League of Nations published its *Statistical Year-book* from 1926 until 1942–1944. For a time it looked like the former organization might be endorsed by the latter as an official yet private and independent body, but the proposal was rejected, setting up a couple of decades of uneasy competition. See Nixon, *A History of the International Statistical Institute: 1885–1960*, 22–27 and 27–34.

26. League of Nations Economic Intelligence Service, *Statistical Year-Book of the League of Nations 1931/32* (Geneva, 1932), table 2. For the attempts in China, see Leo A. Orleans, "The 1953 Chinese Census in Perspective," *Journal of Asian Studies* 16, no. 4 (August 1957): 565–573.

27. League of Nations Economic Intelligence Service, *Statistical Year-Book of the League of Nations 1931/32*, 32, table 2. Thirty-two million people left Europe just between 1880 and 1915; see Connelly, *Fatal Misconception*, 27.

28. Margaret Sanger, *Proceedings of the World Population Conference* (London: Edward Arnold & Co., 1927), "Announcement" and pp. 363–368.

29. Malthus refers to "something else unnatural" in *An Essay on the Principle of Population*, chap. 8. He writes of "improper arts to conceal the consequences of irregular connexions" at book 1, chap. 2 of the 1803 edition.

30. Connelly, *Fatal Misconception*, 51. Early editions of Sanger's pamphlet continue the sentence: "and who supply the millions of soldiers and sailors to fight battles for financiers and the ruling classes." This was omitted from later editions. See reproduction in Joan M. Jensen, "The Evolution of Margaret Sanger's 'Family Limitation' Pamphlet, 1914–1921," *Signs* 6, no. 3 (1981): 548–567.

31. Mayhew, *Malthus*, 150–154; Peter C. Engelman, "From Geneva to Cairo: Margaret Sanger and the First World Population Conference," *Margaret Sanger Papers Project Newsletter*, Spring 1994, nyu.edu/projects/sanger/articles/from_geneva_to_cairo.php.

32. The conference description is from the "Announcement" in Sanger, *Proceedings of the World Population Conference*. Also see Bashford, *Global Population*,

84–85, 211–212. The propagandist comment is from the National Catholic Welfare Council, quoted in Connelly, *Fatal Misconception*, 98. Even these changes were not enough to persuade the conservative League of Nations to sponsor the conference, so league staff attended on their own time. See Stanley Johnson, *World Population and the United Nations: Challenge and Response* (Cambridge, UK: Cambridge University Press, 1987), 5; Connelly, *Fatal Misconception*, 69–70.

33. Bashford, *Global Population*, 88–97.

34. Ibid., 241–246. Connelly, *Fatal Misconception*, 65, 105.

35. On the BCIIC see Bashford, *Global Population*, 217–224. Eventually a reorganization of the IUISIPP dropped the word "problems" and changed "scientific investigation" to "scientific study." On the failure of the conference from Sanger's point of view, see Connelly, *Fatal Misconception*, 74.

36. Bashford, *Global Population*, 270; Connelly, *Fatal Misconception*, 106, 124.

37. Frank W. Notestein, "Demographic Work of the United Nations," *Population Index* 16, no. 3 (July 1950): 186.

38. On the formation of the Population Commission, see Johnson, *World Population and the United Nations*, 8. On the family of national income measures that includes GNP, see Diane Coyle, *GDP: A Brief but Affectionate History* (Princeton, NJ: Princeton University Press, 2014), 11–23; Dirk Philipsen, *The Little Big Number: How GDP Came to Rule the World and What to Do About It* (Princeton, NJ: Princeton University Press, 2015), chaps. 5–6.

39. On the year book, see Johnson, *World Population and the United Nations*, 9. For recommendations, see *Population Census Methods (Sales No. 1949.XIII.4)*, 1949. On calls for the 1950 round, see Connelly, *Fatal Misconception*, 142–143. This early history is also covered in Notestein, "Demographic Work of the United Nations."

40. Pierre Martinot-Lagarde, "The Intricacy of Demography and Politics: The Case of Population Projections" (IUSSP General Conference, Salvador, Brazil, 2001). For a stepping stone to global forecasts, produced in the dying days of the League of Nations, see Frank W. Notestein, *The Future Population of Europe and the Soviet Union: Population Projections 1940–1970* (Geneva: League of Nations, 1944); United Nations, Department of Economic and Social Affairs, Population Division, "The Past and Future Growth of World Population—a Long-Range View," *Population Bulletin of the United Nations* (1951): table 5.

41. Johnson, *World Population and the United Nations*, 9–11; Bashford, *Global Population*, 321–322.

42. On the framing as a threat to peace, see Johnson, *World Population and the United Nations*, 28; Connelly, *Fatal Misconception*, 116; Chandrasekhar's comments are quoted in Bashford, *Global Population*, 215, 285.

43. On Soviet opposition to the Population Commission, see Johnson, *World Population and the United Nations*, 8. Marx's dismissal of Malthus appears within a thousand-word footnote; see Karl Marx, *Capital: A Critique of Political Economy (Volume I)*, ed. Frederick Engels, trans. Samuel Moore and Edward Aveling, 1st English ed. (1887), chap. 15, marxists.org/archive/marx/works/1867 -c1, note 6 (within the chapter).

44. Gunnar Thorvaldsen, *Censuses and Census Takers: A Global History*, Routledge Studies in Modern History (London: Routledge/Taylor & Francis Group, 2018), 197–208.

45. George B. Cressey, "The 1953 Census of China," *Far Eastern Quarterly* 14, no. 3 (May 1955): 387. "Nationality" is closer to what would more commonly be called "ethnicity" today. The census reported 93 percent of the population as Han Chinese, with nearly 2.5 percent various Muslim minorities (including Dungan and Uyghur) and 0.5 percent Tibetan. See also Xiaogang Wu, *Census Undertakings in China: 1953–2010*, Population Studies Center Research Report (Ann Arbor: Population Studies Center, University of Michigan Institute for Social Research, 2014), psc.isr.umich.edu/pubs/abs/9011; Orleans, "The 1953 Chinese Census in Perspective."

46. The league was still reporting its 1933 estimate of 450 million in 1945. It seems the league's demographers felt that they had no sensible basis on which to update it. See League of Nations Economic Intelligence Service, *Statistical Year-Book of the League of Nations 1942/44* (Geneva, 1945), table 2. At least one initial reaction to the census was skeptical, stating that the totals "must be regarded with considerable reserve"; see Cressey, "The 1953 Census of China." A later, more thorough evaluation disagreed, concluding that it was the "most current and the best information available on Chinese population"; see Orleans, "The 1953 Chinese Census in Perspective."

47. See note 1, above. Quote from UN Statistical Office, *Demographic Yearbook 1955*, 2.

48. See note 1, above.

49. United Nations, Department of Economic and Social Affairs, Population Division, "The Future Growth of World Population", quote at p. v, detailed projections table 1 (B), p. 70.

50. Nico Keilman, "Data Quality and Accuracy of United Nations Population Projections, 1950–95," *Population Studies* 55, no. 2 (2001): 149–164; ibid., viii.

51. Johnson, *World Population and the United Nations*, 16; Bashford, *Global Population*, 318–322, Huxley quote at p. 319.

52. Connelly, *Fatal Misconception*, 90–91, 113–116; Massimo Livi Bacci, *A Concise History of World Population*, 6th ed. (Hoboken, NJ: John Wiley & Sons, 2017), 172–179.

53. William Paddock and Paul Paddock, *Famine—1975!* (Boston: Little, Brown, 1967), 19–20. For similar sentiments, see "the idea was in the air": Connelly, *Fatal Misconception*, 122; Bashford, *Global Population*, 320. And for prewar statements by eugenicists, see Connelly, *Fatal Misconception*, 55.

54. Quote from Kingsley Davis, "The World Demographic Transition," *Annals of the American Academy of Political and Social Science* 237, no. 1 (January 1945): 1–11. For data, see note 1, above.

55. Bashford, *Global Population*, 310–317.

56. Connelly, *Fatal Misconception*, 175–176, 201–206, 213–231, 251–252.

57. Connelly, 267–269.

58. Connelly, 162; Bashford, *Global Population*, 336–338.

59. For the documentary, see Connelly, *Fatal Misconception*, 187; Georg Borgstrom, *The Hungry Planet: The Modern World at the Edge of Famine* (New York: Macmillan, 1965); Paddock and Paddock, *Famine—1975!*.

60. Rachel Carson, *Silent Spring* (New York: Houghton Mifflin, 1962); Ehrlich, *The Population Bomb*, 60.

61. Johnson, *World Population and the United Nations*, 24–32, 60, 80, Lyndon Johnson quote at p. 26–27. "Washington Report: Birth Control Boom," *Life*, January 29, 1965, 34D.

62. The UN Population Commission itself contained a range of views and was not unanimous in its beliefs about the "explosion." See Johnson, *World Population and the United Nations*, 88–89.

63. Ehrlich, *The Population Bomb*, 15–16.

64. United Nations, Department of Economic and Social Affairs, Population Division, "File 11a: The 30 Largest Urban Agglomerations Ranked by Population Size at Each Point in Time, 1950–2035," in *World Urbanization Prospects: The 2018 Revision*, 2018, population.un.org/wup/Download.

65. Jim Dwyer, "Remembering a City Where the Smog Could Kill," *New York Times*, March 1, 2017, New York edition, sec. A; Eric Monkkonen, "Homicides in New York City, 1797–1999 [And Various Historical Comparison Sites]: Version 1" (Inter-University Consortium for Political and Social Research, November 29, 2001), doi.org/10.3886/ICPSR03226.v1.

66. Harry Harrison, *Make Room! Make Room!* (New York: Orb, 2008), 12, 284.

67. Johnson, *World Population and the United Nations,* 23–24; Ehrlich, *The Population Bomb,* 64.

68. "Growth in United Nations Membership, 1945–Present," United Nations, un.org/en/sections/member-states/growth-united-nations-membership-1945 -present/index.html, accessed September 15, 2019; Neil MacFarquhar, "Renovating the U.N., With Hints of Green," *New York Times,* November 21, 2008.

69. Johnson, *World Population and the United Nations,* 76, 125, quote at p. 125.

70. Johnson, chaps. 6–7; Connelly, *Fatal Misconception,* 304–316; "Chinese Statements on Population at Bucharest, 1974, and Mexico City, 1984," *Population and Development Review* 20, no. 2 (June 1994): 449.

71. Cormac Ó Gráda, *Famine: A Short History* (Princeton, NJ: Princeton University Press, 2010), 23. The exact number is unknown; estimates run as high as forty-five million. See Frank Dikötter, *Mao's Great Famine: The History of China's Most Devastating Catastrophe, 1958–1962* (New York: Walker & Co., 2010).

72. Judith Banister, *China's Changing Population* (Stanford, CA: Stanford University Press, 1991), 12–16; Wu, "Census Undertakings in China: 1953–2010," 81. As late as 1983, the UN Statistical Office was reporting that China's most recent census was in 1953; see UN Statistical Office, *Demographic Yearbook 1981,* 33 (New York: United Nations, 1983), table 1.

73. Connelly, *Fatal Misconception,* 179–180, 339–348; Livi Bacci, *A Concise History of World Population,* 195–197, Zhou quote at p. 195.

74. Connelly, *Fatal Misconception,* 339–348.

75. Ibid., 207–231, 317–326.

76. Christopher S. Wren, "China Counts Its Quarter of the World's Noses," *New York Times,* July 6, 1982, National edition, sec. A.

77. Connelly, *Fatal Misconception,* 341–343.

78. "China, Pop. 1,008,175,288: One-Fourth of the World," *New York Times,* October 28, 1982, National edition, sec. A; Wu, "Census Undertakings in China: 1953–2010," 13. Some official sources still report a different total of 1,031,900,000.

79. On *The Population Bomb*'s success, see Connelly, *Fatal Misconception,* 258–259. For term usage, see "Search for 'Overpopulation, Population Problem, Population Explosion,'" Google Ngram Viewer, books.google.com/ngrams /graph?content=overpopulation%2Cpopulation+problem%2Cpopulation+ explosion&case_insensitive=on&year_start=1800&year_end=2000&corpus =15&smoothing=0, accessed July 6, 2019. For the compete list of Ehrlich's eighteen *Tonight Show* appearances from 1970 to 1981, see "Paul Ehrlich (II) (Writer)," IMDB, imdb.com/name/nm1693584, accessed September 15, 2019.

80. Gallup found that between 1963 and 1992, the proportion of Americans familiar with the population problem declined from 68 to 51 percent. See Mark Gillespie, "Concern Over Population Growth Among Americans Less Prevalent Now Than in Past," Gallup, October 11, 1999, news.gallup.com/poll/3547/concern -over-population-growth-among-americans-less-prevalent-now-than-past.aspx. On the Reagan policy toward UNFPA, see Connelly, *Fatal Misconception*, 351–355. Subsequent Republican administrations have tended to follow suit.

81. Connelly, *Fatal Misconception*, 355–369; Livi Bacci, *A Concise History of World Population*, 186–187; *Programme of Action Adopted at the International Conference on Population and Development, Cairo, 5–13 September 1994* (United Nations Population Fund [UNFPA], 2004). The 2000 and 2015 goals were the Millennium Development Goals and Sustainable Development Goals, respectively.

82. Chris Buckley, "China Approves Two-Child Policy to Help Economy," *New York Times*, October 30, 2015, sec. A.

83. Connelly, *Fatal Misconception*, 87–90, 168–170, 192–193.

84. Connelly, 245–247. For an argument that such measures were impor-tant, see Tiloka de Silva and Silvana Tenreyro, "Population Control Policies and Fertility Convergence," *Journal of Economic Perspectives* 31, no. 4 (November 2017): 205–228.

85. Livi Bacci, *A Concise History of World Population*, 184–191.

86. Connelly, *Fatal Misconception*, 160, 332–333.

87. Liddington and Crawford, *Vanishing for the Vote*, 128–129.

88. For prewar population declines, see Bashford, *Global Population*, 234–238.

89. The countries with a total fertility rate of greater than 5.0 are Angola, Burkina Faso, Burundi, Chad, Democratic Republic of the Congo, Gambia, Mali, Niger, Nigeria, Somalia, and Uganda. All are between 5 and 6, except So-malia (6.12) and Niger (6.95).

90. Sabrina Juran and Arona L. Pistiner, "The 2010 Round of Population and Housing Censuses (2005–2014)," *Statistical Journal of the IAOS* 33, no. 2 (May 12, 2017): 400–401. The African countries that did not conduct censuses were Central African Republic, Comoros, Democratic Republic of the Congo, Equatorial Guinea, Eritrea, Madagascar, Sierra Leone, Somalia, and the disputed territory of Western Sahara; Umar Serajuddin et al., "Data Deprivation: Another Deprivation to End," World Bank Policy Research Working Paper, 2015.

91. UNFPA Evaluation Office, *Evaluation of UNFPA Support to Population and Housing Census Data to Inform Decision-Making and Policy Formulation (2005–2014): Volume 1* (New York: UNFPA, 2016), secs. 3.1, 3.2; World Bank

Independent Evaluation Group, "Data for Development: An Evaluation of World Bank Support for Data and Statistical Capacity" (Washington, DC: World Bank, 2018), 24; US Census Bureau, "International Programs: Capacity Building & Technical Assistance," April 12, 2018, census.gov/programs-surveys/international-programs/about/training-tech-asst.html.

92. Feyi Fawehinmi, "The Story of How Nigeria's Census Figures Became Weaponized," Quartz Africa, March 6, 2018, qz.com/africa/1221472/the-story-of-how-nigerias-census-figures-became-weaponized; Dawit Endeshaw, "Commission Postpones Census," *Reporter* (Ethiopia), March 23, 2019, thereporterethiopia.com/article/commission-postpones-census.

93. For an example of new technologies, see Eric M. Weber et al., "Census-Independent Population Mapping in Northern Nigeria," *Remote Sensing of Environment* 204 (January 2018): 786–798.

94. India and China self-sufficiency indicated in Table 1 of Jennifer Clapp, "Food Self-Sufficiency: Making Sense of It, and When It Makes Sense," *Food Policy* 66 (January 2017): 88–96. Ehrlich quoted in Graham Chedd, "Some Are Paying Heed...," *New Scientist and Science Journal,* September 16, 1971, 635.

95. Amartya Sen, *Poverty and Famines: An Essay on Entitlement and Deprivation* (1981; repr., Oxford, UK: Oxford University Press, 2010).

96. Ehrlich was just the most recent in a long parade of Western visitors to India with the same reaction. See Connelly, *Fatal Misconception,* 89–90. United Nations, Department of Economic and Social Affairs, Population Division, "File 11a: The 30 Largest Urban Agglomerations Ranked by Population Size at Each Point in Time, 1950–2035." US Census Bureau data for 2018 showed New York declining; however, it remains to be seen whether this is a long-term reversal or a one-off event. The UN Population Division's projections show continued slow expansion into the future.

97. "New theory"—the endogenous growth literature associated with Paul Romer. See David Warsh, *Knowledge and the Wealth of Nations: A Story of Economic Discovery* (New York: W. W. Norton, 2006); Committee for the Prize in Economic Sciences in Memory of Alfred Nobel, "Scientific Background on the Sveriges Riksbank Prize in Economic Sciences in Memory of Alfred Nobel 2018," Royal Swedish Academy of Sciences, October 8, 2018.

98. On stalling social mobility, see David H. Autor, "Work of the Past, Work of the Future," *AEA Papers and Proceedings* 109 (May 2019): 1–32.

99. "File 4: Rural Population at Mid-Year by Region, Subregion and Country, 1950–2050 (Thousands)" in United Nations Population Division, "World Urbanization Prospects 2018," 2019, population.un.org/wup.

100. Ehrlich, *The Population Bomb*, 83 (emphasis in original).

101. United Nations Population Division, "World Population Prospects 2019," June 2019, population.un.org/wpp. For an alternative to the UN projections, projecting a peak of 9.4 billion near 2070, see Wolfgang Lutz, William P. Butz, and Samir KC, eds., *World Population and Human Capital in the Twenty-First Century* (Oxford, UK: Oxford University Press, 2014).

102. Robert Frost, "The Census-Taker," in *New Hampshire* (New York: Henry Holt & Company, 1923), 24.

Chapter 6. The Uncounted

1. The account of this meeting is based on Pippa Green, *Choice, Not Fate: The Life and Times of Trevor Manuel* (Johannesburg: Penguin Books, 2012), Kindle edition, location 9104–9121; with additions and minor corrections from Mark Orkin in my interview with him, May 1, 2019; interview with Pali Lehohla, March 23, 2019; "Overview of Key Results," table 2 in Statistics South Africa, *The People of South Africa: Population Census 1996: The Count and How It Was Done* (Pretoria: Statistics South Africa, 1998), https://apps.statssa.gov.za /census01/Census96/HTML/Metadata/Docs/count.html.

2. Green, *Choice, Not Fate,* location 9110–9120.

3. Ibid.

4. "Overview of Key Results," table 2.

5. Green, *Choice, Not Fate,* location 9110–9120; interview with Mark Orkin.

6. M. J. Körösi, "Propositions Pour Arriver a Une Compatibilité Internationale Des Ouvrages de Recensement," *Bulletin de l'Institut International de Statistique* 2 (1887): 215; English translation from G. B. Longstaff, "Suggestions for the Census of 1891," *Journal of the Royal Statistical Society* 52, no. 3 (September 1889): 436. Similarly, William Farr wrote in 1861, that "In Rome, the working classes were not enumerated; in the Domesday-book, and even in some modern states, they are only counted by the head; but in England they are all taken down in the census-books by name, and treated precisely on the same footing as persons of the highest rank." See "The Forthcoming Census," *Illustrated London News*, April 6, 1861, 524.

7. US Census Office, *Compendium of the Eleventh Census: 1890,* Part 1: Population (Washington, DC: Government Printing Office, 1892), xxxv.

8. Margaret M. Jobe, "Native Americans and the U.S. Census: A Brief Historical Survey," *Journal of Government Information* 30, no. 1 (January 2004): 66–80.

9. The exact residence criteria are somewhat more elaborate, but this is the general principle. See those proposed for 2020: US Census Bureau, "Final 2020

Census Residence Criteria and Residence Situations," in *Federal Register,* vol. 83 (Washington, DC, 2018), 5525–5536, federalregister.gov/documents/2018/02 /08/2018-02370/final-2020-census-residence-criteria-and-residence-situations.

10. Australian Bureau of Statistics, "Aboriginal and Torres Strait Islander Population, 2016," 2071.0—Census of Population and Housing: Reflecting Australia—Stories from the Census, 2016, October 31, 2017, 4–5, abs.gov.au /ausstats/abs@.nsf/Lookup/by%20Subject/2071.0~2016~Main%20Features ~Aboriginal%20and%20Torres%20Strait%20islander%20Population%20 Article~12#.

11. Ibid., 8.

12. Boyd H. Hunter and John Carmody, "Estimating the Aboriginal Population in Early Colonial Australia: The Role of Chickenpox Reconsidered," *Australian Economic History Review* 55, no. 2 (July 2015): 112–138; Katherine Ellinghaus, "Absorbing the 'Aboriginal Problem': Controlling Interracial Marriage in Australia in the Late 19th and Early 20th Centuries," *Aboriginal History* 27 (2003): 183–207; Commonwealth Bureau of Census and Statistics, *Census of the Commonwealth of Australia, 30th June, 1961: Statistician's Report,* vol. 8— Australia (Canberra: Australia, 1967), chap. 14, sec. 3.

13. Bain Attwood and Andrew Markus, *The 1967 Referendum: Race, Power and the Australian Constitution,* 2nd ed. (Canberra: Aboriginal Studies Press, 2007), vi–viii.

14. Ibid., chaps. 3–6, especially p. 24 on overseas interest and quote from the *Melbourne Age* at p. 49.

15. Ibid., chaps. 7–8. For one particularly persistent myth, see Sushi Das, "Fact Check: Were Indigenous Australians Classified Under a Flora and Fauna Act Until the 1967 Referendum?," RMIT ABC Fact Check (blog), July 11, 2018, abc.net.au/news/2018-03-20/fact-check-flora-and-fauna-1967-referendum /9550650.

16. Michael Savage, "The Imposition of Pass Laws on the African Population in South Africa 1916–1984," *African Affairs* 85, no. 339 (April 1986): 181–205.

17. South Africa Truth and Reconciliation Commission, *Truth and Reconciliation Commission of South Africa Report,* vol. 3 (Cape Town: Truth and Reconciliation Commission, 1999), 531–537.

18. William Seltzer and Margo Anderson, "Using Population Data Systems to Target Vulnerable Population Subgroups and Individuals: Issues and Incidents," in *Statistical Methods for Human Rights,* ed. Jana Asher, David L. Banks, and Fritz Scheuren (New York: Springer, 2008), 314–316.

19. "Population Registration Act, 1950," secs. 1, 5(1), en.wikisource.org /wiki/Population_Registration_Act,_1950, accessed May 9, 2019.

20. "People's Opposition Halts Nat Race Tests: Attack on Coloureds Has Been Unlawful," *New Age,* August 25, 1955, Northern edition; "Kimberley Begins to Classify Races," *New York Times,* August 21, 1955; "We Must Stop These Nazis!," *New Age,* August 25, 1955, Northern edition.

21. Akil Kokayi Khalfani et al., "Race and Population Statistics in South Africa," in *White Logic, White Methods: Racism and Methodology,* ed. Tukufu Zuberi and Eduardo Bonilla-Silva (Lanham: Rowman & Littlefield, 2008), 73; Donald G. McNeil, "Who Counts in South Africa? Finally, Everyone," *New York Times,* October 30, 1996, National edition. This method of estimating population, sometimes called the "housing unit" method, had a long history in colonial Africa, albeit without the use of aerial photography; see A. J. Christopher, "The Quest for a Census of the British Empire c.1840–1940," *Journal of Historical Geography* 34, no. 2 (April 2008): 277. Done carefully, it can be reasonably accurate. Notably, however, the South African government did not enumerate white South Africans in this way.

22. Khalfani et al., "Race and Population Statistics in South Africa," 77.

23. This section is based on my interview with Lehohla.

24. Pali Lehohla, "Opinion: Lehohla and the Story Behind the Launch of His Yellow Suit," *Business Report,* October 10, 2017, iol.co.za/business-report/opinion -lehohla-and-the-story-behind-the-launch-of-his-yellow-suit-11534892.

25. "ISIbalo: What Is in a Name?," Statistics South Africa, statssa.gov .za/?page_id=7562, accessed September 26, 2019. Lehohla's ox story inspired me to search for humans named Census in the records available on Ancestry.com. Many people ostensibly so named appear to be transcription errors (unless we credit "Census Taken" or "Census Record" as real people). But this elite club seems to include a least a few dozen real people, including Census Peterson, enumerated in South Dakota in 1940, and Census McGee, found in Mississippi in 1920.

26. On the situation in Lesotho in the early 1980s, see, for example, Joseph Lelyveld, "Lesotho Sees Pretoria's Hand in Shadowy Conflict," *New York Times,* September 17, 1981, sec. A.

27. Christopher S. Wren, "South Africa Scraps Law Defining People by Race," *New York Times,* June 18, 1991, Late edition; De Klerk quoted in "South Africa Drops Apartheid Law," *United Press International,* June 18, 1991, upi .com/4982631.

28. Interview with Orkin.

29. F. M. Orkin, P. J. Lehohla, and J. A. Kahimbaara, "Social Transformation and the Relationship Between Users and Producers of Official Statistics: The Case of the 1996 Population Census in South Africa," *Statistical Journal of UN Economic Commission for Europe* 15 (1998): 266; interview with Orkin.

30. Interview with Lehohla.

31. The rough count was 62,480,540; see Robert P. Porter, "Population of the United States by States and Territories: 1890," Census Bulletin no. 12 (Washington, DC: US Census Office, October 30, 1890): 1; The official count was 62,622,250, excluding Indians not taxed. Including the latter, it was 62,979,766; see US Census Office, *Compendium of the Eleventh Census: 1890*, Part 1: Population (Washington, DC: Government Printing Office, 1892), xxxv.

32. Chief Justice Rehnquist of the US Supreme Court noted this apparent paradox in 1996: "One might wonder how the Census Bureau is able to determine whether there is an undercount and its size. Specifically: against what standard are the census results measured? After all, if the actual population of the United States is known, then the conduct of the census would seem wholly redundant." See Wisconsin v. City of New York et al., 517 U.S. 1 (1996).

33. Daniel O. Price, "A Check on Underenumeration in the 1940 Census," *American Sociological Review* 12, no. 1 (February 1947): 44; Margo J. Anderson, *The American Census: A Social History*, 2nd ed. (New Haven, CT: Yale University Press, 2015), 201.

34. Randomization—shuffling or mixing—is the easiest way to guarantee that a sample is representative. Practically all of the intricacies of modern statistical sampling theory come from trying to sample from populations—such as people living in a town—that cannot be so easily, or cheaply, randomized.

35. Anderson, *The American Census*, 176–179; David Card, "Origins of the Unemployment Rate: The Lasting Legacy of Measurement Without Theory," *American Economic Review* 101, no. 3 (2011): 552–557.

36. In fact, Petersen describes several methods of marking the fish and several methods of estimating population and population density. It is the two-sample capture-recapture method that proved most influential. See C. G. J. Petersen, "Report of the Danish Biological Station to the Home Department," 1895, 12–13, archive.org/details/reportofdanishbi06dans.

37. C. Chandra Sekar and W. Edwards Deming, "On a Method of Estimating Birth and Death Rates and the Extent of Registration," *Journal of the American Statistical Association* 44, no. 245 (March 1949): 101–115. There were earlier antecedents to the use of sampling to estimate human populations. Ironically, this line of thinking was killed off by the rise of the census in the nineteenth century

and the almost-fetishization of complete enumeration that accompanied it. See Alain Desrosières, *The Politics of Large Numbers: A History of Statistical Reasoning*, trans. Camille Naish (Cambridge, MA: Harvard University Press, 1998), 25. A good step-by-step example of dual-system estimation—which quickly becomes far more complicated than the description here—is given in Margo J. Anderson and Stephen E. Fienberg, *Who Counts? The Politics of Census-Taking in Contemporary America* (New York: Russell Sage Foundation, 1999), 61–69.

38. Eli S. Marks, W. Parker Mauldin, and Harold Nisselson, "The Post-Enumeration Survey of the 1950 Census: A Case History in Survey Design," *Journal of the American Statistical Association* 48, no. 262 (June 1953): 220, quote at p. 234.

39. From a survey of 138 countries; see Yacob Zewoldi et al., "Report on the Results of a Survey on Census Methods Used by Countries in the 2010 Census Round," Working Paper, United Nations Statistics Division, 2011, 21–22. See also UN Statistics Division, *Principles and Recommendations for Population and Housing Censuses, Revision 3* (New York: United Nations, 2017), 118–123; UN Department of Economic and Social Affairs Statistics Division, "Post Enumeration Surveys: Operational Guidelines," April 2010.

40. C. Y. Choi, D. G. Steel, and T. J. Skinner, "Adjusting the 1986 Australian Census Count for Under-Enumeration," *Survey Methodology* 14, no. 2 (December 1988): 173–189; see also commentary in Anderson and Fienberg, *Who Counts?*, 68. There were several earlier postenumeration surveys on the African continent, but they do not seem to have been used for adjustment. See David C. Whitford and Jeremiah P. Banda, "Post-Enumeration Surveys (PES's): Are They Worth It?," Symposium on Global Review of 2000 Round of Population and Housing Censuses: Mid-Decade Assessment and Future Prospects, New York, 2001, unstats.un.org /unsd/demographic/meetings/egm/symposium2001/docs/symposium_10.htm.

41. Anderson, *The American Census*, 155, 213–214; Anderson and Fienberg, *Who Counts?*, 32–34.

42. Anderson, *The American Census*, 218; For details on differential undercounts today, see William P. O'Hare, *Differential Undercounts in the U.S. Census* (New York: Springer, 2019), chaps. 4–12.

43. O'Hare, *Differential Undercounts in the U.S. Census*, sec. 13.5. For an overview of difficult-to-enumerate groups, see UN Statistics Division, *Principles and Recommendations for Population and Housing Censuses*, 180–182.

44. O'Hare, *Differential Undercounts in the U.S. Census*, secs. 13.7–13.9.

45. Ibid., sec. 13.10.

46. See questionnaires from each decade in the Census Bureau collection: census.gov/history/www/through_the_decades/questionnaires.

47. US Bureau of the Census, *1960 Censuses of Population and Housing: Procedural History* (Washington, DC: Government Printing Office, 1966), 183.

48. Australian Bureau of Statistics, *Informing a Nation: The Evolution of the Australian Bureau of Statistics 1905–2005* (Canberra: Australian Bureau of Statistics, 2005), 98; Australian Bureau of Statistics, "Aboriginal and Torres Strait Islander Peoples and the Census after the 1967 Referendum," Reflecting a Nation: Stories from the Census, 2011, 5; John Taylor, "Census Enumeration in Remote Australia: Issues for Aboriginal Data Analysis," *Journal of the Australian Population Association* 10, no. 1 (1993): 53–67.

49. Australian Bureau of Statistics, "Aboriginal and Torres Strait Islander Population, 2016"; David Martin et al., eds., *Making Sense of the Census: Observations of the 2001 Enumeration in Remote Aboriginal Australia* (Canberra: ANU Press, 2004), 1, 13.

50. Statistics South Africa, "National Population Census—Final Results Announced," October 20, 1998, web.archive.org/web/19990420070932/http://www.statssa.gov.za/censuspr/Announcement%20of%20Census%20'96%20Results.htm.

51. On hostels, see McNeil, "Who Counts in South Africa? Finally, Everyone." On counting the homeless, see Statistics South Africa, *The People of South Africa*, chap. 2; Brenda Goldblatt, *The Great Counting: The Making of Census '96* (South Africa: Mail & Guardian Television, 1997), youtube.com/watch?v=edkhHe-QOCg. On additional forms, see Marius Cronje and Debbie Budlender, "Comparing Census 1996 with Census 2001: An Operational Perspective," *Southern African Journal of Demography* 9, no. 1 (2004): 69–70.

52. Statistics South Africa, "The People of South Africa: Population Census 1996: Calculating the Undercount in Census '96," 1996.

53. Ibid., 17–18.

54. The other error was a failure of randomization in a sampling process. Statisticians in Pretoria, running behind in their work, made some preliminary estimates using a sample of returns rather than a full count. In principle this should have worked, but because not every province had organized their boxes of forms in the same way, the sample turned out not to be random. Statistics South Africa, "The People of South Africa," 11; interview with Lehohla.

55. Interview with Lehohla.

56. Statistics South Africa, "National Population Census—Final Results Announced"; Statistics South Africa, "Census 1998 Results Release Part 01," 1998, youtube.com/watch?v=ARmP3IUicwI.

57. *Preproduction/Location (Census 2010)* (DraftFCB, 2010), adage.com /videos/us-census-bureau-preproduction-location/436; US Census Bureau, "U.S. Census Bureau Announces 2010 Census Population Counts; Apportionment Counts Delivered to President," December 21, 2010, census.gov/newsroom /releases/archives/2010_census/cb10-cn93.html. For a detailed account of census outreach in 2000, see D. Sunshine Hillygus, Norman H. Nie, Kenneth Prewitt, and Heili Pals, *The Hard Count: The Political and Social Challenges of Census Mobilization.* (New York: Russell Sage, 2010).

58. Groves quoted in US Census Bureau, "U.S. Census Bureau Announces 2010 Census Population Counts." Another measure, the gross error rate, provides insight into this. It adds together all those who were missed and all those who were erroneously counted (rather than netting out the two numbers). For 2010, it was around 10 percent. See Anderson, *The American Census,* 265.

59. Anderson and Fienberg, *Who Counts?,* chaps. 3–7.

60. For international comparisons, see Zewoldi et al., "Report on the Results of a Survey on Census Methods Used by Countries in the 2010 Census Round," Table 5.1. For a well-argued critique of adjustment by a statistician, see Leo Breiman, "The 1991 Census Adjustment: Undercount or Bad Data?," *Statistical Science* 9, no. 4 (November 1994): 458–475. For a list of respected statisticians aligned on each side of this issue at the 2000 census, see Anderson and Fienberg, *Who Counts?,* 218.

61. US Census Bureau, "U.S. Census Bureau Announces 2010 Census Population." The error range is my own judgment. The Census Bureau's own undercount estimates imply a range of around a million, based on sampling error in the PES; see Peter P. Davis and James Mulligan, *Census Coverage Measurement Estimation Report: Net Coverage for the Household Population in the United States* (Washington DC: US Census Bureau, 2012). These are the "known unknowns," but the "unknown unknowns" may be even greater. The true US population depends heavily on assumptions made about the undocumented population, which is estimated to be between ten and thirteen million. Just a 10 percent variation in the estimate of this population—whom we might reasonably assume is undercounted by census takers, postenumeration surveyors, and other statistical agents—translates to a million people.

62. Timothy Kennel, "2020 Post-Enumeration Survey: Program Overview," October 19, 2018, census.gov/programs-surveys/decennial-census/2020-census /planning-management/program-briefings/2018-10-19-pmr.html.

63. For an excellent overview of the complicated timelines of this affair, see Hansi Lo Wang and Renee Klahr, "Timeline: The Census Citizenship Question's

Unusual Journey to the Supreme Court," National Public Radio, April 23, 2019, npr.org/2019/04/23/710220622/timeline-the-census-citizenship-questions -unusual-journey-to-the-supreme-court. Quote from Arturo Vargas, executive director of NALEO Educational Fund, in Justin Elliot, "Trump Justice Department Pushes for Citizenship Question on Census, Alarming Experts," Pro- Publica, December 29, 2017, propublica.org/article/trump-justice-department -pushes-for-citizenship-question-on-census-alarming-experts. On the method- ology for estimating the number of unauthorized immigrants, see Jeffrey S. Pas- sel, "Measuring Illegal Immigration: How Pew Research Center Counts Unauthorized Immigrants in the U.S.," Pew Research Center, July 12, 2019, pewresearch.org/fact-tank/2019/07/12/how-pew-research-center-counts -unauthorized-immigrants-in-us.

64. State of New York v. United States Department of Commerce, No. 18- CV- 2921 (JMF) (United States District Court, Southern District of New York January 15, 2019), quotes at p. 245 and p. 98 (paragraph 174).

65. The options suggested by the Census Bureau are summarized in John M. Abowd, "Technical Review of the Department of Justice Request to Add Citizenship Question to the 2020 Census [Memorandum to Wilbur L. Ross, Jr.]," January 19, 2018, documentcloud.org/documents/4500011-1-18-Cv-02921 -Administrative-Record.html#document/p1289. The initial Census Bureau esti- mate is given in J. David Brown et al., *Understanding the Quality of Alternative Citizenship Data Sources for the 2020 Census,* CES 18-38, Center for Economic Studies (Washington, DC: US Census Bureau, 2018), sec. 7. The revised Census Bureau estimate is given in J. David Brown et al., "Predicting the Effect of Add- ing a Citizenship Question to the 2020 Census," *Demography* 56, no. 4 (August 2019): 1173–1194; cost impact based on $55 million per percentage point in- crease in nonresponse follow-up. One widely reported study predicted that the question would reduce the number of Hispanics reported in the census by six million. However, this number, an extrapolation from an online panel survey, reflected respondents who chose not to share their Hispanic ethnicity rather than omissions. Overall the research design was too different from the census to be very informative; see Matthew A. Baum et al., "Estimating the Effect of Asking About Citizenship on the U.S. Census," Shorenstein Center Discussion Paper, Harvard Kennedy School, April 2019. On the whole, none of the various inde- pendent studies were particularly compelling. The real test was expected to be a census test performed by the Census Bureau in the summer of 2019. An initial report from that test suggested—quite unexpectedly—that the question had no overall impact on self-response. At the time of writing, the full report has yet to

be released. See Victoria A. Velkoff, "2019 Census Test Preliminary Results," Random Samplings (blog), US Census Bureau, October 31, 2019, census.gov /newsroom/blogs/random-samplings/2019/10/2019_census_testpre.html.

66. A very helpful summary of citizenship questions is provided by Hansi Lo Wang and Renee Klahr, "See 200 Years of Twists and Turns of Census Citizenship Questions," National Public Radio, April 23, 2019, npr.org/2019/04/23/63056 2915/see-200-years-of-twists-and-turns-of-census-citizenship-questions. Opponents of the history argument also overstated the claim, arguing—somewhat disingenuously—that no citizenship question had ever been asked of every person. Technically that is true, but only because in many years citizenship was a follow-up question to one about foreign birth. This "skip logic" could be used because the United States has birthright citizenship, so only foreign-born people could be noncitizens. The information was still collected on every person.

67. UN Statistical Division, "Recommended Core Topics ('Principles and Recommendations for Population and Housing Censuses') and Their Implementation in the 2010 Census Round," November 2, 2010, unstats.un.org/unsd /demographic/sources/census/wphc/Census_Clock/CountriesPerTopic.pdf; UN Statistics Division, *Principles and Recommendations for Population and Housing Censuses,* 191.

68. Department of Commerce v. New York, 588 US ___ (2019).

69. On the legal status of redistricting, see Wendy R. Weiser and Thomas Wolf, "Why the Census Asking About Citizenship Is Such a Problem," Brennan Center for Justice (blog), March 27, 2018, brennancenter.org/blog/why-census -asking-about-citizenship-such-problem. A new twist was added to this already convoluted story in May 2019, when a woman named Stephanie Hofeller, estranged daughter of a recently deceased Republican strategist, discovered, among his effects, hard drives containing emails that seemed to confirm this theory. Some observers speculate that this news, which broke after the Supreme Court's oral argument but before its decision, may have swung the case. See Charles Bethea, "A Father, a Daughter, and the Attempt to Change the Census," *New Yorker,* July 12, 2019, newyorker.com/news/news-desk/a-father-a-daughter-and -the-attempt-to-change-the-census; on the possible impact on the Supreme Court decision, see Joan Biskupic, "Exclusive: How John Roberts Killed the Census Citizenship Question," CNN Politics, September 12, 2019, cnn.com/2019/09 /12/politics/john-roberts-census-citizenship-supreme-court/index.html.

70. Elizabeth Warren, Twitter, June 27, 2019, twitter.com/ewarren/status /1144292363587719168. A poll in July 2019 found that 87 percent of people identifying as Republican supported asking the question, while only 31 percent

of Democrats did. See YouGov, "The Economist/YouGov Poll: June 30–July 2, 2019," 2019, table 21.

71. For expected 2020 self-response rates, see US Census Bureau, "2020 Census Life-Cycle Cost Estimate: Executive Summary (Version 1.0)," December 21, 2017, 15, census.gov/programs-surveys/decennial-census/2020-census/planning -management/planning-docs/cost-estimate.html. For 2010 self-response rates, see Earl Letourneau, "Mail Response/Return Rates Assessment," US Census Bureau, May 30, 2012, 14. On reaching younger people, see Tim Henderson and Alayna Alvarez, "How the Census Will Reach the New Urban Millennials," Stateline (blog), February 13, 2019, pewtrusts.org/en/research-and-analysis/blogs/stateline /2019/02/13/how-the-census-will-reach-the-new-urban-millennials.

72. Andrew Anglin, "Stormers: It's Time to Get a Job at the Census Bureau and Report Illegals to ICE!," Daily Stormer (blog), May 30, 2019; see also re-porting in Chris Hamby, "Census at Risk from Glitches and Attackers," *New York Times,* July 5, 2019, New York edition, sec. A.

73. Long-range forecasts including 2020 are included in US Census Bureau, Population Division, "Projected Population Size and Births, Deaths, and Migra-tion: Main Projections Series for the United States, 2017–2060," September 2018, census.gov/programs-surveys/popproj.html. Shorter-range forecasts up to but not including 2020 are provided in US Census Bureau, Population Division, "Table 1. Monthly Population Estimates for the United States: April 1, 2010 to December 1, 2019 (NA-EST2018-01)," December 2018, census.gov/newsroom/press-kits /2018/pop-estimates-national-state.html. Based on past experience, updated pro-jections will likely be published in December 2019.

74. This scenario is based loosely on Jackie Barocio, Ann Hollingshead, and Nick Schroeder, *The 2020 Census: Potential Impacts on California* (Sacramento: California Legislative Analyst's Office, 2018).

75. On probability, see Ian Hacking, *The Emergence of Probability: A Philo-sophical Study of Early Ideas about Probability, Induction and Statistical Inference,* 2nd ed. (Cambridge, UK: Cambridge University Press, 2006); also Ian Hacking, *The Taming of Chance,* Ideas in Context (Cambridge, UK: Cambridge University Press, 1990). On statistics, see Desrosières, *The Politics of Large Numbers.*

76. Oryem Nyeko, "Tanzania Drops Threat of Prison Over Publishing Inde-pendent Statistics," Human Rights Watch, July 3, 2019, hrw.org/news/2019/07 /03/tanzania-drops-threat-prison-over-publishing-independent-statistics.

77. For examples across the US government, see Michael Lewis, *The Fifth Risk* (New York: W. W. Norton, 2018).

78. Statistics South Africa, ed., *Census 2001: Post-Enumeration Survey: Results and Methodology,* Report / Statistics South Africa, no. 03-03-17 (2001) (Pretoria: Statistics South Africa, 2004).

Chapter 7. The Transparent Citizen

1. Department of Economic and Social Affairs Statistics Division, "2020 World Population and Housing Census Programme: Census Dates for All Countries," United Nations Statistics Division, May 27, 2016, unstats.un.org/unsd /demographic/sources/census/censusdates.htm. For 2.41 billion monthly active users (that is, users who log in at least monthly) statistic, see "Company Info," Facebook.com, newsroom.fb.com/company-info, accessed September 17, 2019.

2. "Facebook on Top but Instagram and Pinterest Growing Fastest," Roy Morgan Research, May 17, 2019, roymorgan.com/findings/7979-social-media -trends-march-2019-201905170731; Andrew Perrin and Monica Anderson, "Share of U.S. Adults Using Social Media, Including Facebook, Is Mostly Unchanged Since 2018," Pew Research Center, April 10, 2019, pewresearch.org /fact-tank/2019/04/10/share-of-u-s-adults-using-social-media-including -facebook-is-mostly-unchanged-since-2018/. On the currency, see Harriet Agnew, "France Says It Will Not Support Libra's Development in Europe," *Financial Times,* September 12, 2019, ft.com/content/6d414606-d549-11e9-a0bd -ab8ec6435630.

3. UN Statistics Division, *Principles and Recommendations for Population and Housing Censuses, Revision 3* (New York: United Nations, 2017), 175–176.

4. This does not include significant expenditure by states, cities, and civil society groups seeking to encourage participation. The 2020 estimate is from US Government Accountability Office, "High-Risk Series: Substantial Efforts Needed to Achieve Greater Progress on High-Risk Areas," March 2019, 134. Historical US estimates from Margo J. Anderson, *The American Census: A Social History,* 2nd ed. (New Haven, CT: Yale University Press, 2015), 274–275 (inflated using BLS CPI). Other estimates from Morten Jerven, "Benefits and Costs of the Data for Development Targets for the Post-2015 Development Agenda," Post-2015 Consensus, Copenhagen Consensus Center, September 16, 2014, 34–36.

5. Of course, some people would defund the National Weather Service; see Michael Lewis, *The Fifth Risk* (New York: W. W. Norton, 2018). For the Large Hadron Collider, see Alex Knapp, "How Much Does It Cost to Find a Higgs Boson?," *Forbes,* July 5, 2012, forbes.com/sites/alexknapp/2012/07/05/how-much

-does-it-cost-to-find-a-higgs-boson. For more on the science analogy, see Kenneth Prewitt, "Science Starts Not After Measurement, but with Measurement," *Annals of the American Academy of Political and Social Science* 631, no. 1 (September 2010): 7–16. US market research spending calculated as 44 percent of global market research spending of $46 billion, or around 0.1 percent of roughly $20 trillion in GDP for 2017. See American Marketing Association, "Market Research Is up in the U.S. but Down in the EU," AMA Marketing News (blog), October 16, 2018, medium.com/ama-marketing-news/market-research-is -up-in-the-u-s-but-down-in-the-eu-e857c9a6eef4.

6. Office of National Statistics (UK), "2011 Census Benefits Evaluation Report," ons.gov.uk/census/2011census/2011censusbenefits/2011censusbenefits evaluationreport, accessed June 30, 2019; Northern Ireland Statistics and Research Agency, "Northern Ireland Census 2011 Benefits Realisation Report," January 2018; Carl Bakker, "Valuing the Census," Statistics New Zealand, July 2014, stats.govt.nz/assets/Research/Valuing-the-Census/valuing-the-census.pdf; Bruce D. Spencer et al., "Cost-Benefit Analysis for a Quinquennial Census: The 2016 Population Census of South Africa," *Journal of Official Statistics* 33, no. 1 (March 1, 2017): 249–274; Lateral Economics, "Valuing the Australian Census," August 27, 2019, lateraleconomics.com.au/wp-content/uploads/LE-Census-Report -ABS-Full-Final.pdf.

7. Christopher Hope, "National Census to Be Axed After 200 Years," *Daily Telegraph* (London), July 10, 2010.

8. Murray Jack and Connie Graziadei, "Report of the Independent Review of New Zealand's 2018 Census," New Zealand Government, July 2019, quote at p. 10.

9. Quote and figures from Aarian Marshall, "The Tragedy of Canada's Census," Citylab (blog), February 26, 2015, citylab.com/equity/2015/02 /the-tragedy-of-canadas-census/385846/; "Prime Minister Trudeau Brings Back the Long Form," Census, CBC News, November 5, 2015, cbc.ca/news/prime -minister-trudeau-brings-back-the-long-form-census-1.3305924.

10. US Census Bureau, "American Community Survey: Design and Methodology Report (Version 2.0)," January 30, 2014; US Census Bureau, "American Community Survey: Information Guide," October 2017.

11. Interview with Kenneth Prewitt, July 26, 2019. France has gone even further in this direction, eliminating its periodic census entirely and relying on only a rolling survey to collect population data. It is, however, quite difficult to guarantee the accuracy of such a purely sample-based approach, and as yet cost savings have not matched expectations.

12. John M. Abowd, "Technical Review of the Department of Justice Request to Add Citizenship Question to the 2020 Census [Memorandum to Wilbur L. Ross, Jr.]," January 19, 2018, sec. C.2, documentcloud.org/documents/4500011 -1-18-Cv-02921-Administrative-Record.html#document/p1289.

13. Michel Poulain and Anne Herm, "Le registre de population centralisé, source de statistiques démographiques en Europe," trans. Roger Depledge, *Population (English edition)* 68, no. 2 (2013): 183–221; Kees Prins, *Population Register Data, Basis for the Netherlands Population Statistics,* Bevolkingstrends (The Hague: Statistics Netherlands, 2017), cbs.nl/-/media/_pdf/2017/38/population-register -data.pdf.

14. Poulain and Herm, "Le registre de population centralisé," table 2; Ian White, "Overview of the 2010 Round of Population and Housing Censuses: Regional Perspectives—UNECE Region (ESA/STAT/AC.277/P2)," October 29, 2013, unstats.un.org/unsd/demographic/meetings/egm/NewYork/2013/list _of_docs.htm, slide 6; Enver Tasti and Meryem Demirci, "Changing the System from Traditional Census to Register Base Census in Turkey," 57th Session of the International Statistical Institute, Durban, 2009, unstats.un.org/unsd/censuskb20 /KnowledgebaseArticle10647.aspx; C. Chandramouli, "National Population Register (NPR) in India—A Step Towards Register Based Census," 57th Session of the International Statistical Institute, Durban, 2009, unstats.un.org/unsd/censuskb20 /KnowledgebaseArticle10646.aspx.

15. Anders Wallgren and Britt Wallgren, *Register-Based Statistics: Administrative Data for Statistical Purposes,* Wiley Series in Survey Methodology (Hoboken, NJ: John Wiley & Sons, 2007); "Publishing Calendar," Statistics Sweden, scb. se/en/finding-statistics/publishing-calendar/?prodKod=BE0101, accessed September 24, 2019. Within certain circles of enthusiastic policy wonks, "Swedish administrative data" has taken on a kind of talismanic status. See, for example, Jeff Stein, "The Weeds: Examining Some Exciting Swedish Administrative Data," *Vox,* May 27, 2016, vox.com/2016/5/27/11795960/the-weeds-swedish-data-paper.

16. US Census Bureau, "Geographical Mobility: 2017 to 2018," November 2018, census.gov/data/tables/2018/demo/geographic-mobility/cps-2018.html, table 1. In the United States, certain groups face mandatory address registration requirements—for example, immigrants, licensed drivers, and military-age men subject to Selective Service. Even personal attributes that are usually stable can change: people changing gender and racial identification have challenged Sweden's system.

17. On expansion in the use of the SSN, see *Report to Congress on Options for Enhancing the Social Security Card* (Washington, DC: Social Security

Administration, 1997), chap. 2. On SSN automatic enrollment, see Patricia P. Martin, "Why Researchers Now Rely on Surveys for Race Data on OASDI and SSI Programs: A Comparison of Four Major Surveys," *Research and Statistics Note,* Social Security Administration, January 2016, ssa.gov/policy/docs/rsnotes /rsn2016-01.html. On the Canadian SIN, see "Protecting Your Social Insurance Number," Office of the Privacy Commissioner of Canada, July 2017, priv.gc.ca /en/privacy-topics/sins-and-drivers-licences/social-insurance-numbers /protecting-your-social-insurance-number.

18. Roger Clarke, "Just Another Piece of Plastic for Your Wallet: The 'Australia Card' Scheme," *Prometheus* 5, no. 1 (June 1987): 29–45; Alan Gelb, Anit Mukherjee, and Kyle Navis, "What India's Supreme Court Ruling on Aadhaar Means for the Future," Center for Global Development (blog), September 26, 2018, cgdev.org/blog/what-india-supreme-court-ruling-aadhaar-means-future.

19. Helen Mason Kiefer, "Do Americans Want National ID Cards?," Gallup (blog), July 9, 2002, news.gallup.com/poll/6364/americans-want-national-cards .aspx; Alan Travis, "ID Cards Scheme to Be Scrapped Within 100 Days," *Guardian* (London), May 27, 2010, theguardian.com/politics/2010/may/27/theresa -may-scrapping-id-cards.

20. New York State Department of Health, "Health Insurance Application for Children, Adults and Families (DOH-4220-I 3/15)," health.ny.gov/forms/doh -4220.pdf, accessed July 16, 2019.

21. "Rashi's Commentary on Exodus 30:12," translated by M. Rosenbaum and A. Silbermann, Sefaria, September 17, 2019, sefaria.org/Rashi_on_Exodus.30.12.

22. For the US privacy regime, see Sarah Elizabeth Igo, *The Known Citizen: A History of Privacy in Modern America* (Cambridge, MA: Harvard University Press, 2018), chap. 6. For international parallels, see Organisation for Economic Co-operation and Development, *Thirty Years after the OECD Privacy Guidelines* (Paris: OECD, 2011), 15–17. For the inadequacies of the US system, see US General Accounting Office, "Privacy Act: OMB Leadership Needed to Improve Agency Compliance," June 2003. For a personal account of trying to "watch the watchers," see Julia Angwin, *Dragnet Nation: A Quest for Privacy, Security, and Freedom in a World of Relentless Surveillance* (New York: Times Books, Henry Holt, 2015), chap. 6.

23. Deutsche Welle staff, "East German Stasi Had 189,000 Informers, Study Says," Deutsche Welle (blog), March 11, 2008, p.dw.com/p/DMQg.

24. "Apartheid with Chinese Characteristics," *Economist,* May 31, 2018, economist.com/briefing/2018/05/31/china-has-turned-xinjiang-into-a-police -state-like-no-other.

25. Ibid.; "China's Vanishing Muslims: Undercover in the Most Dystopian Place in the World," Vice News, 2019, youtube.com/watch?v=v7AYyUqrMuQ; Darren Byler, "China's Hi-Tech War on Its Muslim Minority," *Guardian* (London), April 11, 2019, theguardian.com/news/2019/apr/11/china-hi-tech-war-on-muslim-minority-xinjiang-uighurs-surveillance-face-recognition; "China: Big Data Fuels Crackdown in Minority Region," Human Rights Watch, February 26, 2018, hrw.org/news/2018/02/26/china-big-data-fuels-crackdown-minority-region.

26. Darren T. Byler, "Spirit Breaking: Uyghur Dispossession, Culture Work and Terror Capitalism in a Chinese Global City" (PhD dissertation, University of Washington, 2018), 260–272; "The Race Card," *Economist,* September 3, 2016, economist.com/china/2016/09/03/the-race-card.

27. As Robert Groves, the former US director of the census, put it to me, "If you're involved in decennial censuses and you have trouble with deferred gratification, find another source of employment."

INDEX

Abbot, Charles, 89–90
Aboriginal and Torres Strait Islander
people, Australia's exclusion of,
221–223, 239–240.
abortion, 185, 196. *See also* birth
control; contraception
accuracy of the census, 18, 32
administrative data sources,
261–262
cultural and political exclusion of
specific groups, 219–220
Hollerith tabulating machine, 105
reconciling the numbers,
230–231
US census challenge, 249–250
actual enumeration, 244
adjusting census totals, 190,
235–236, 243–245,
251, 256
administrative data, 246–247,
259–262
aerial data collection, 226–227
Africa
census taking in, 28, 202

fertility rates and population
growth, 209–210
See also specific countries
African Americans, 102–103,
144–145, 232, 236–237
African National Congress (ANC),
226, 228
Alaska territory, 127–128
Aly, Goetz, 152
Amasis census (Egypt), 37
American Community Survey (ACS),
246, 259
American Revolution, 72, 83
Analects (Confucius), 30–31
Analytical Engine, Babbage's,
116, 119
Ancestry.com, 51–52
Anderson, Benedict, 19
Anderson, Margo, 168
Anglo-Saxon Chronicle, 47, 48
Antarctica, 23
anti-Semitism, 141–142, 146,
157–158. *See also* Jews; Nazi
Germany

337

INDEX

INDEX

poll tax, 32

Poor Laws (England), 89

Population Accounting (Lentz), 139–141

The Population Bomb (Ehrlich), 176–178, 205–206, 211–212

The Population Bomb (pamphlet), 197

Population Commission (UN), 188–190

population control, 86–87, 149, 175–178, 185–190, 197–199, 206

population decline, 208–211

population explosion, 197–198

population growth

accounting for the slowdown, 207–208

Africa, 209–210

cities, 199–201

demographic studies, 201–203

effective government and, 56, 58

international research and initiatives to control, 197–199

Malthusian view of, 85–87, 175–178

mathematical reasoning, 94

mercantilism, 58–61

stability of, 214–215

UN projections, 189

urbanization and, 213–214

US census, 103–104, 124–126, 250–251

US westward expansion, 110–111

population registers

accuracy of the census, 232

complementary function of, 137–138

increasing reliance on, 261–263

Jewish World War II fatality rate, 163

Nazi occupied Netherlands, 156–159

Nazi Volkskartei, 149

privacy and confidentiality concerns, 264

RAF bombing of Nazi data storage, 160–163

replacing decennial census, 20

as updated census, 136–139

Population Registration Act (South Africa), 225, 229

population, global estimates through time, 177–180, 184, 192–196, 214–216

Porter, Robert, 121, 123, 126, 180

positive eugenics, 143–145

postenumeration surveys, 234–235, 240–241, 243–245

prehistoric man, 23–25

premodern societies

early Chinese census, 31

Greek interest in population, 37

purposes of the census, 52–53

Roman Republic and Empire, 2–4, 10, 16, 22, 38–45, 46, 48

social hierarchy, 25–27

Principia Mathematica (Newton), 66

Principles and Recommendations for Population and Housing Censuses, 8

privacy of census data

concerns over population registers, 264–265

differential privacy, 269–270

intrusive technology, 265–266

long form/short form census, 258–259

population registers, 139–140

US census, 135–136

See also misuse of data, statistical confidentiality

ANDREW WHITBY is an economist and data scientist with a PhD in econometrics from the University of Oxford. Most recently, he worked in the development data group of the World Bank, where he was coeditor of the *Atlas of Sustainable Development Goals*. He lives in Brooklyn.